RENTIER ISLAMISM

Rentier Islamism

THE INFLUENCE OF THE MUSLIM BROTHERHOOD IN GULF MONARCHIES

Courtney Freer

OXFORD
UNIVERSITY PRESS

OXFORD
UNIVERSITY PRESS

Oxford University Press is a department of the University of Oxford. It furthers the University's objective of excellence in research, scholarship, and education by publishing worldwide. Oxford is a registered trade mark of Oxford University Press in the UK and certain other countries.

Published in the United States of America by Oxford University Press
198 Madison Avenue, New York, NY 10016, United States of America.

CIP data is on file at the Library of Congress
ISBN 978-0-19-086199-5

9 8 7 6 5 4 3 2 1

Printed by Sheridan Books, Inc., United States of America

Contents

Acknowledgments

I FIRST DECIDED to write about Muslim Brotherhood groups in the Gulf at a dinner party in Doha in 2011. Since that time, I have spoken at length about this topic with scholars, policymakers, and friends, all of whom have helped me refine my ideas. I am indebted to many, many people who allowed me to interview them over the course of my fieldwork in Kuwait, Qatar, and the UAE between 2013 and 2014; without their candor and generosity of time, this project would have been impossible. I also owe particular thanks to the Kuwaiti Ministry of Information, which aided me greatly in the arrangement of field interviews, and to the Brookings Doha Center team, which has been supportive of me in this endeavor since my PhD application process in 2011.

This book represents a reorganization and reworking of my doctoral thesis at the University of Oxford. I am indebted to my supervisor, Philip Robins, for his indispensable guidance and patience throughout my time there, during which he read several (quite long and messy) drafts of the original version. In addition to having a very knowledgeable supervisor, I have been fortunate to have had extremely supportive employers during the period this idea first germinated when I was at Brooking Doha Center, until today, when my colleagues at LSE's Middle East Centre have celebrated my successes as their own and have challenged me to make my work better.

Without the help and encouragement of Shadi Hamid, my former supervisor at Brookings Doha, I may never have pursued my PhD and, accordingly, would never have written this book; he has been a generous mentor and wonderful friend who has challenged me to develop these ideas, has influenced my work with his extensive knowledge of Islamism and excellent research, and has shared his wide-ranging network of contacts with me. Salman Shaikh and Ibrahim Fraihat were also wonderful colleagues at Brookings

Doha, and I became a better researcher and scholar by working with them. In addition, they encouraged me to pursue doctoral studies. At LSE, Toby Dodge has given me invaluable feedback and advice over the past two years and continues to inspire me with his work. Steffen Hertog, who shared his always sharp insights as a reviewer of my thesis at Oxford, has remained a mentor during my time at LSE, encouraging and advising me to move forward with this project. If my work has a fraction of the impact that any of these scholars' work has had, I will consider myself a great success. I am proud to have worked with them and even prouder to call them friends.

I have also been fortunate to have had the constant encouragement of LSE's Middle East Centre, where I wrote nearly all of this book. My position at the Kuwait Programme, with the generous support of the Kuwait Foundation for the Advancement of Sciences, has given me the freedom to pursue this research and the opportunity to connect with many inspiring Kuwaiti academics who have influenced this and other research. My colleagues at LSE have also made the past two years fantastic—Madawi al-Rasheed, Aula Hariri, Zeynep Kaya, Robert Lowe, Jack Mcginn, Chelsea Milsom, Stella Peisch, Sandra Sfeir, Ian Sinclair, and Ribale Sleiman-Haidar have made my workplace not only the site of great intellectual exchange but also plenty of laughter. All of my colleagues have pushed me to improve my work and have been very patient and helpful sounding boards throughout the drafting and editing process.

I have also had the privilege to speak to experts on the Gulf and Islamism outside of LSE about this project. Their time and insights are deeply appreciated. In particular, I am indebted to Ali al-Kandari, Farah al-Nakib, Alanoud Alsharekh, Abdullah Baabood, Nathan Brown, Kristin Smith Diwan, Justin Gengler, Ambassador Edward Gnehm, Adel Hamaizia, Michael Herb, Mehran Kamrava, Jessie Moritz, Gerd Nonneman, David Roberts, Michael Stephens, Steven Wright, and Karen Young.

I would also like to thank the many friends who have influenced my research and writing, and have eased the process of doing the research that led up to this book and of writing the book itself. I am particularly indebted to Daniel Fedorowycz for proofreading nearly everything I have written since 2013, including various versions of this book, and to Andrew Leber for his edits and adding the keen eye of an American-trained political scientist. Jaclyn Lyman, Meredith Morrison, Hussein Omar, Sam Plumbly, Sophie Sportiche, Anna Della Subin, Nouri Verghese, and Thomas Wood made my time at Oxford, during which these ideas first arose, both pleasant and the site of many fascinating late-night conversations. Steffen Hertog and Michael Willis, as reviewers of my thesis, provided me with wonderful feedback and encouraged me to publish this book; their belief in this project pushed it forward.

I am fortunate to have an incredible network of friends and family who have put up with my talking about my dissertation and this book for years. In particular, my brother Collin has encouraged me with his enthusiasm for my work, and my aunt Leslie has provided me with unyielding support. I am also grateful to Alex for responding to my occasional panics about this project with patience, good humor, and buffalo wings.

My parents have been the most important in always supporting my academic endeavors, even when I insisted that I wanted to major in biology for a brief period in 2005. My dad, the first academic I ever met, has provided a model for how to enter the profession with passion, integrity, and an obsessive attention to grammar. My mom has been the sounding board for nearly every idea I have ever had and has handled my many, many phone calls with remarkable patience. This book is dedicated to them.

The fantastic team at OUP has made this process surprisingly painless. I am particularly indebted to Alexcee Bechthold, Angela Chnapko, and Anne Dellinger, as well as many others who have seen this project through to the end.

Note on Transliteration

IN TRANSLITERATING THE titles of Arabic sources and names of organizations, I have used the guidelines of the *International Journal of Middle Eastern Studies*. For Arabic terms found in the New Oxford American Dictionary, I have used the spellings in that dictionary (e.g., sharia rather than shariʿa). For place names, I have used the transliterations most commonly seen in English language sources and translations. And for personal names, I have used the standards of the *International Journal of Middle Eastern Studies* with two exceptions: when a different transliteration is favored by the individual, as seen on his/her website, business card, social media presence, and so forth; and when a different spelling is more commonly used (e.g., Gamal ʿAbdel Nasser rather than Jamal ʿAbd al-Nasir).

RENTIER ISLAMISM

1

Uncharted Territory

POLITICAL ISLAM AND RENTIER STATES

SCHOLARS HAVE STRUGGLED for decades to understand the role of political Islam[1] in the Middle East, and a large body of literature has emerged on this topic. The study of political Islam, however, has primarily been confined to an examination of the region's more democratic states—those in which Islamist[2] groups like the Muslim Brotherhood (also referred to as Ikhwan, the Arabic word for brothers) can participate in parliamentary elections—or those states in which such organizations either provide much-needed social welfare or more broadly constitute powerful social movements. Existing literature on political Islam in such environments does not apply to the wealthy monarchical states of the Arabian Peninsula.

The body of scholarship on political life in the Gulf has similarly overlooked the role of Islamist movements in that region. Since Hussein Mahdavy introduced the theory of the rentier state in 1970,[3] many scholars have deferred to this framework to explain the domestic politics of states accruing substantial oil profit, or rents, in the region. Numerous studies, both qualitative and quantitative, have demonstrated the reality of a "rentier effect," distinguishing these states from those without large external windfalls. In describing the government systems of such states, taxation is emphasized as spurring citizens' demands for representation. According to leading scholar of rentier state theory Hazem Beblawi, "with virtually no taxes, citizens are far less demanding in terms of political participation."[4] The simple formula "no taxation, no representation" is thus often considered to describe the extent of political life within rentier states. The reality, as this work demonstrates, is far more complicated.

This book will examine the role of political Islam in the Gulf through the study of Muslim Brotherhood[5] affiliates in three of the least-examined rentier states of the Arabian Peninsula: Kuwait, Qatar, and the United Arab Emirates (UAE). We will trace how Muslim Brotherhood movements, the most powerful independent voices in the Middle East, originated in and currently influence government policies in states that allow few institutionalized means of political participation, at least outside of Kuwait. Muslim Brotherhood movements in the super-rentiers[6] are able to influence government policy decisions, yet function differently from Ikhwan affiliates elsewhere in the region due to their context within oil-wealthy states. Significantly, there exists variation even among the cases examined here, as political participation is institutionalized in Kuwait through parliamentary elections yet remains far more personalistic in Qatar and the UAE. By examining the unique properties of Muslim Brotherhood activities in super-rentiers, this book will thus fill a gap in the existing literature on political Islam. Neither the body of scholarship on political Islam nor the academic work on rentier states adequately explains the political role of Islamist groups in the oil monarchies of the Arabian Peninsula.

EXPLAINING THE POLITICAL ROLE OF ISLAMIST MOVEMENTS IN RENTIER STATES

Rentier state theory, the primary theoretical framework used in discussions of Gulf politics, allows solely for the presence of economically based political movements in such wealthy states. Indeed, Giacomo Luciani claims, "it is only in the case that an allocation state fails, or is widely believed to fail, to take full advantage of the possibility of receiving income from the rest of the world that substantial political opposition may develop."[7] Examination of the political histories and contemporary political currents in the Gulf, however, disproves this claim; opposition in the Gulf is not dependent on economic largesse or lack thereof. While rulers in the Gulf may consider their duties to citizens to be primarily pecuniary, as they have often answered calls for democratic reforms with economic benefits, continued protest in the face of government disbursements demonstrates that citizens disagree with this simplistic perception of government responsibility.

Ideologically driven Islamist movements are even less likely to be placated by government payouts, making it more probable that they become powerful voices of political opposition in rentier states. Hootan Shambayati's 1994 article about rentierism in Turkey and Iran is one of the few existing pieces of scholarship that addresses the unique ability of Islamist movements to function in rentier states. As he explains, in such countries, "no conflict arises over the ownership of the means of production. Instead, strictly moral and cultural considerations become the legitimizing ideology of groups opposing rentier states."[8] Nonetheless, Islamist movements in such states remain underexamined, and little is known about how exactly they operate.

In his 2011 book on Saudi Arabia, Stéphane Lacroix explains the rise of independent Islamism inside the Kingdom, marking an important development of the literature on rentier Islamists. He traces Muslim Brotherhood infiltration of the education system, outlining the transformation of Islamists into independent actors in the form of the broader-based Sahwa movement (al-Sahwa al-Islamiyya, or Islamic Awakening) and analyzing the ultimate failure of this group. While Islamist complaint initially constituted "politically neutered opposition [that] gradually became primarily a cultural opposition," dynamics changed with the advent of the Sahwa movement of the 1990s.[9] The new group united sectors of society that had previously been separated, namely the ulama[10] and intellectuals, behind an Islamist agenda. During this period of Sahwa activity, in Lacroix's words, "it was precisely the collapse of sectoral barriers and the transformation of the social arena into a unified space that momentarily gave life to what Islamist discourse had long proclaimed: the utopia of a fusion of politics and religion. But the crisis was short lived and inevitably ended with a return to the logic of sectorization."[11] By granting that Islamists in the rentier context came to hold political appeal, Lacroix makes an important contribution.

He also adds the notion "state Islamism" to the discussion of Islamism in the rentier context: "In almost all countries in the Muslim world, Islamism arose and developed outside the state. The converse was true of Saudi Arabia: from the beginning, Islamism was integrated into the official institutions."[12] Because the state dominates so much of life in rentier societies even outside of Saudi Arabia, it has historically played a large role in the Islamic sector. As a result, the trajectory of Islamist organizations is different in Gulf states than elsewhere in the Middle East: they have gained political capital[13] *through* the prevailing system before coming to challenge it. This pattern is confirmed through examination of how Brotherhood affiliates in Kuwait, Qatar, and the UAE came to gain influence through their positions in state apparatuses beginning in the 1950s.

Gwenn Okruhlik also notes the ability of Saudi Islamists to instigate a series of reforms in the Kingdom in the 1990s, specifically the creation of the Consultative Council in 1992, citing the politicization of Wahhabi Islam after Iraq's invasion of Kuwait.[14] She posits that Islamists, more difficult for an avowedly Muslim state to regulate, have "capture[d] the discourse in Saudi Arabia" and thus have "initiated a renegotiation of the social contract in Saudi Arabia and an alternative telling of history."[15] Although non-Wahhabi Saudi Islamists have not secured an institutionalized place in politics, they have had remarkable success in beginning political negotiation and compromise in arguably the most autocratic state of the Gulf. Okruhlik charges that, in the absence of Islamists, such changes would not have taken place.[16] Islamist organizations have managed to gain a political say by "provid[ing] people with common scripts and symbols to utilize when confronting the overwhelming power of state institutions."[17] Islamist movements in the Saudi context also benefit from the fact that the ruling family "cannot easily quash or oppose Islamist arguments, since they stake their right to rule on largely Islamic grounds."[18] The same is true elsewhere in the Gulf to a large extent, though it is logically more amplified in the country that houses the two holy mosques of Islam. Okruhlik's study goes a long way toward demonstrating that Islamist actors in the Gulf do, in fact, hold political influence, yet, like Lacroix's research, it remains focused on such actors in the unique Saudi case wherein religious influence is more institutionalized than anywhere else in the region due to a centuries-old alliance between al-Saʿud ruling family and the Wahhabi ulama. In such a system, a threat to Wahhabism constitutes a threat to the regime.

Eric Rouleau makes the important point that Wahhabi Islam[19] of the Arabian Peninsula, and particularly Saudi Arabia, became politicized with the arrival of members of the Egyptian Muslim Brotherhood escaping persecution under the rule of Gamal ʿAbdel Nasser (r. 1956–1970).[20] This period, he claims, marks when the Saudi ulama "under the impact of the new arrivals . . . began, for the first time, to challenge the House of Saud's temporal power."[21] Still, there has been no comprehensive account of *how* exactly Muslim Brothers came to the broader Gulf or in what ways they affected the domestic political scenes of Gulf countries.

This book will demonstrate that political Islam serves as a prominent voice critiquing social policies, as well as promoting more strictly political, and often populist or reformist, views supported by a great many Gulf citizens. The way that Islamist organizations operate in the unique environment of the super-rentiers is distinct. The smallest and wealthiest states of the Arabian Peninsula—Kuwait, Qatar, and the UAE—are monarchies that, with the exception of Kuwait, do not allow for political participation through parliamentary elections. In the monarchical systems of Qatar and the UAE, Islamist groups do not have the opportunity to compete for institutionalized political power and therefore cannot use the ballot box to gain popularity or influence political life, as they do elsewhere in the Middle East. When the dynamic of electoral politics is removed, the nature of the Brotherhood's function changes. In fact, one interviewee went so far as to state that "the Muslim Brotherhood needs parliamentary democracy as oxygen to function . . . . The Muslim Brotherhood doesn't come to power without democracy."[22] Though the Brotherhood can gain political capital even in the absence of democratic institutions, it does so in different ways, as political opportunity structures are altered.

Further distinguishing these countries from others in the region, rentier states benefit from oil wealth, which allows them to grant generous social welfare benefits to all nationals, obviating the need for Islamist groups to provide such services. The smaller states of the Gulf also differ from the rest of the region in the prevailing importance of tribal social structures. Because these emirates have only existed as independent states for the past four to five decades, they have retained their tribal substructures: kinship ties remain of critical importance in social and political life. The presence of such a strong social network in small and tightly knit states reduces the need for an organization like the Muslim Brotherhood to provide a sense of belonging and an arena for social gathering. Further constricting the space for the Muslim Brotherhood is government co-optation of the Islamic sphere through Ministries of Endowments (or Awqaf)[23] and Islamic Affairs, which monitor mosques, imams,[24] and sermons.

Thus, though Brotherhood movements elsewhere in the region originated in opposition to the existing order, Islamists in the Gulf gained political capital by working *through* the prevailing system before coming to challenge it. As Herbert P. Kitschelt puts it in the context of antinuclear movements in Europe and the United States, "political opportunity structures functioned as 'filters' between the mobilization of the movement and its choice of strategies and its capacity to change the social environment."[25] Like other actors in rentier states, then, Islamists compete for state support because challenging the state outright is irrational, as it holds the monopoly of power and wealth. Since Islamist movements cannot afford to and realistically cannot exist outside of the system, they work gradually from *within* it to promote their ideology. As a result, writing the history of the Muslim Brotherhood in rentier states, especially in the super-rentiers, involves tracing their influence through various ministries, particularly education, Islamic affairs, *awqāf*, and justice. In closed political systems, Sidney Tarrow points out, "elites chose their allies and attacked their enemies, and the state provided opportunities to some groups and not to others."[26] At their inception, Muslim Brotherhood groups in the Gulf were closely allied with their governments; as they became increasingly powerful through state support, however, this relationship changed, in turn altering political opportunity structures.

Despite the unique political conditions inside rentier states, Muslim Brotherhood branches have existed in the Gulf for decades, dating back to the Nasser era in Egypt, when many Islamists moved to the Gulf to escape persecution in Egypt and to take jobs in the understaffed region. Large numbers of Egyptian immigrants worked in the Gulf states' newly established educational and judicial systems, beginning in the 1950s. Gulf governments, under British protection at that time, initially welcomed Islamism as a counterbalance to the rising tide of Arab nationalism, even granting Brotherhood groups funds for social activities.

Today, however, the Gulf states have taken a very different tack toward the Brotherhood, with Saudi Arabia and the UAE, alongside Bahrain and Egypt, leading the charge against the organization as a terrorist group and a major political threat to their governments. Qatar has adopted a relatively sympathetic stance toward the Brotherhood, supporting its cause abroad to a limited extent and providing refuge for influential Brotherhood figures within the country. Even Qatar, however, expelled seven leading Egyptian Brotherhood members in September 2014, pursuant to an article in the Riyadh Agreement signed with the Gulf Cooperation Council (GCC) in November 2013.[27] Bahrain, Saudi Arabia, and the UAE went so far as to withdraw their ambassadors from the state in March 2014 over what they considered Qatar's failure to implement the agreement, which demanded that it withdraw support from "anyone threatening the security and stability of the GCC whether as groups or individuals—via direct security work or through political influence, and not to support hostile media."[28] This veiled reference to the Muslim Brotherhood reveals the degree to which the organization has become politically relevant and polarizing in the region. Meanwhile, Kuwait has remained a mediator as political Islam has divided the other Gulf states, pitting the Emirati and Saudi response against the Qatari approach. These tensions have recently become reignited, with Bahrain, Saudi Arabia, and the UAE once again breaking ties with Qatar in June 2017 while also blocking access to the state through air, land, and sea. The official Saudi news agency explained these actions as a means to "protect national security from the dangers of terrorism and extremism," accusing Qatar of adopting Islamist groups like the Muslim Brotherhood, while the UAE claimed that Qatar engages in "funding and hosting" the Brotherhood.[29] These events, triggering an unprecedented diplomatic crisis in the GCC, have made clear that the large extent to which the organization still holds considerable political capital in the Gulf and deserves greater scholarly attention.

SOURCES

Given the lack of secondary literature on the topic of the Muslim Brotherhood in the Gulf, data have been collected through primary sources (in Arabic and English), namely government documents, such as constitutions and relevant laws—particularly those that regulate civil society[30] and the religious sphere. These sources helped clarify the extent to which independent political and religious associations are permitted in the countries under study. Official documents, such as platforms, petitions, and publications from the national Muslim Brotherhood organizations, were also examined to determine the nature of these groups' goals and their success in achieving them. In addition, secondary sources, such as other studies that critique rentierism and those that concern domestic politics of the Gulf as well as relevant news items, were examined. Analysis of the existing body of literature has made clear where this study adds unique insight.

Extensive fieldwork was conducted from September 2013 to April 2014, divided into roughly two months in each country. During this period, some one hundred open-ended interviews (over thirty in each country under study) were conducted, in English and Arabic, about Islamist movements, and particularly Muslim Brotherhood organizations, in Kuwait, Qatar, and the UAE. Interviewees came from a variety of backgrounds and ideological leanings. They included academics, politicians, activists, and journalists. While in the field, primary source material was also gathered through visits to archives, including the National Library of Kuwait and the UAE Federation Library. Local university libraries,[31] think tanks,[32] the office of Jamʿiat al-Islah al-Ijtimaʿi (the Social Reform Association, hereafter Islah) in Kuwait, the Kuwaiti Ministry of Information, and American and British embassies in Kuwait and Qatar provided useful resources as well. Further meetings with figures in exile were arranged in London, where the National Archives provided a crucial source of information about the history of the Brotherhood inside Kuwait, Qatar, and the UAE when they were British-protected states.

CASE SELECTION: KUWAIT, QATAR, AND THE UAE AS SUPER-RENTIERS

Though the GCC countries are often considered as a single unit, Michael Herb makes an important distinction between the wealthier rentier states of the GCC (Kuwait, Qatar, and the UAE) and their less affluent neighbors (Bahrain, Oman, and Saudi Arabia), explaining that the former group has managed to use petroleum windfalls to perpetuate the strongest support system for their citizens.[33] In addition to providing extensive social welfare benefits, Kuwait, Qatar, and the UAE have "fail[ed] to wean citizens from dependence on public sector jobs,"[34] making employment part of the rentier package.[35] These wealthy states can also afford to import large numbers of expatriates to fill private sector positions, as well as jobs in service industries that nationals consider undesirable, leading the state to employ some nine out of every ten citizens.[36] Further reinforcing the privileged position of nationals, governments of the wealthiest Gulf states have constructed systems of disbursements to citizens so extensive that Kuwait, Qatar, and the UAE provide the best examples of rentierism in the Gulf. We thus have distinguished them as super-rentiers. Rentier state theory would lead us to believe that these states are the least likely to house independent political actors of any type. Table 1.1 illustrates the extent to which these states are economically distinct from other rentiers of the Arabian Peninsula.

TABLE 1.1

Economic Comparison of GCC States

Country	Gross National Income (GNI) per Capita, Atlas Method, 2013 (US Dollar)[37]	Purchasing Power Parity per Capita, 2013 (International Dollar)[38]	Percentage of Nonnational Population (2008)[39]	Percentage of Nonnationals in Labor Force (2008)[40]
Bahrain	19,700	36,290	51	76.70
Kuwait	45,130	84,800	68	83.20
Oman	25,150	52,780	31	74.60
Qatar	86,790	128,530	87	94.30
Saudi Arabia	26,260	53,640	27	50.60
UAE	38,360	59,890	81	85

Aside from economic differences, significant political variations complicate comparisons with other GCC states. Bahrain seems an obvious outlier as the only GCC state with a majority Shiʿi population. Consequently, Bahrain's most powerful opposition Islamist movements (al-Wefaq and the Haq Movement) are Shiʿi and therefore not linked to the Muslim Brotherhood ideologically, as the Ikhwan is Sunni. Interestingly, that country's Muslim Brotherhood branch is often aligned with the government, suggesting the primacy of loyalty to religious sect over political ideology in Bahrain.

Oman, while also having a highly centralized and personalized government under Sultan Qaboos, is influenced by ideologies that differ greatly from those found in the rest of the GCC. A unique strand of Ibāḍī Islam dominates the religious scene,[41] where Sunni Muslims number only 15–20 percent of the population.[42] The state's most prominent independent Islamist movement, Jamaʿat al-Tabligh, has roots in India,[43] reflecting Oman's outward-looking orientation, which has long differentiated it from its Gulf neighbors. Furthermore, the Omani branch of the Brotherhood was effectively shut down in the early 2000s after a preliminary crackdown in the mid-1990s.[44]

Saudi Arabia's opposition movements, specifically Islamist groups, have been the subject of a number of studies, particularly since the 1979 takeover of the Grand Mosque by radical Islamists under the leadership of Juhayman al-ʿUtaybi. Many studies have focused on violent strands of Islamism in the Kingdom,[45] while several others have treated the topic of Islamism in Saudi Arabia more broadly.[46] Aside from hoping to uncover new knowledge about under-studied countries, concerns about access to information and entry into states were taken into consideration in the selection of cases.

Unlike the other GCC states, Kuwait, Qatar, and the UAE are Sunni majority emirates. They are also the wealthiest states of the region, were influenced by British rule, and enjoy relatively placid internal political environments. Nonetheless, these cases demonstrate a spectrum of political activity among the Gulf rentiers. The study of Kuwait, Qatar, and the UAE will be used to build an independent theory of Islamist political action in the Gulf. Nonetheless, each case is distinctive. Indeed, one reason for the case selection is the variety these states provide.

Kuwait, under leadership of the al-Sabah family since the eighteenth century, is the only super-rentier country with an active parliament. Further, the country's Muslim Brotherhood organization has successfully fielded candidates for this body as a bloc since the 1980s. In 1991, the Brotherhood created a specialized political branch, al-Harakat al-Dusturiyya al-Islamiyya (the Islamic Constitutional Movement, also known by its Arabic acronym Hadas and hereafter the ICM), which functions as a political party in all but name (political parties are formally banned in all super-rentiers). It works alongside Islah, the organization's social branch, which was established in 1951. The Kuwaiti Brotherhood is highly organized, well funded, and benefits from a broad support base. Although the Brotherhood boycotted parliamentary elections held between December 2012 and November 2016, it is represented in the current legislature with four seats effectively under its control. Muslim Brotherhood influence also continues to be felt through its social outreach, which is done through its participation in charity organizations, sporting clubs, and educational institutions. Politics in the super-rentiers is often displaced into other groups and institutions, considering the lack of formal political parties and meaningful institutionalized political participation.

Qatar lies on the other end of the spectrum in terms of political freedom. The emirate has one elected political institution, the Central Municipal Council (CMC), yet the body itself plays little more than an advisory role on primarily nonpolitical matters. Policy decisions thus remain in the hands of a relatively small number of people, namely members of the ruling al-Thani family. Current Amir Shaykh Tamim bin Hamad al-Thani (r. 2013–present), who has held this position since his father Shaykh Hamad bin Khalifa al-Thani (r. 1995–2013) transferred power in June 2013, is often portrayed as a pragmatist rather than an ideologue, who is likely to continue his father's policies toward Islamists only to the extent that they are politically useful for his reign at home and his country's relationships abroad. Though Qatar does not have a branch of the Muslim Brotherhood, as it formally disbanded in 2003, Islamist influence remains palpable, if not structurally salient. As mentioned above, charges of Qatari support for Islamist movements worldwide have become more prominent in recent years. Qatar has, since 1961, provided rentier Brotherhood figure Shaykh Yusuf al-Qaradawi a platform from which to spread his ideas; it has also been charged with aiding Islamists in Libya, Syria, and Tunisia, and publicly supported the Mohamed Morsi government in Egypt in 2012 and 2013.

The UAE is composed of seven emirates, with six ruling families. Still, the country is dominated by the ruling families of Abu Dhabi (the president is Abu Dhabian ruler Shaykh Khalifa bin Zayed al-Nahyan, in office since 2004) and Dubai (the vice president is Dubai ruler Shaykh Mohammed bin Rashid al-Maktoum, in office since 2006). The UAE has one partially elected body, the Federal National Council (FNC), yet it is chosen by a small percentage of Emirati nationals and holds only nonbinding advisory power in a variety of federal government matters. Decision-making in the UAE, similar to Qatar, remains personalized and concentrated in the hands of relatively few people, though political and cultural variation exists across the emirates. As the UAE has experienced a meteoric economic rise and resultant social changes, a degree of Islamist backlash has been witnessed, along with secular liberal[47] opposition movements advocating for more participatory governance. The government has responded swiftly and harshly, increasing internal security and arresting over one hundred suspected Emirati Islamists since 2012 on charges of attempting to overthrow the regime.[48] Table 1.2 illustrates these countries' political similarities.

GOALS OF THIS BOOK

This book will shed light on why and how Muslim Brotherhood branches have emerged as important social and political actors in the wealthiest oil monarchies of the Arabian Peninsula. By examining the three super-rentiers of the region, we demonstrate the degree to which rentier state theory underestimates the complexity of domestic politics in states that benefit from large amounts of oil wealth. The variation among these cases in and of itself illustrates the inadequacy of a single theory to describe them all. This book also reveals the shortcomings of the prevailing literature on political Islam, as it fails to account for the presence of politically relevant Brotherhood movements in the Gulf monarchies and thus does not describe how their function differs from that of the Ikhwan in other parts of the region.

As will be shown, Muslim Brotherhood organizations in the Gulf are politically influential entities in terms of shaping government policy. It is important to note, however,

TABLE 1.2

Political Comparison of the Super-Rentier States

Country	Amir	Parliament	Consultative Assembly	Political Parties	Council of Ministers
Kuwait	✓	✓			✓
Qatar	✓		✓		✓
UAE	✓		✓		✓

that these groups often shape cultural and social ideas as readily as political[49] notions; they promote the implementation of conservative social policies while also often advocating for major reforms to government apparatuses and changes in domestic and foreign policies. The division between the social and political sectors is often blurred in the atmosphere of socially conservative states of the Gulf, as political actors operate through channels that are not institutionalized, due to the informal and underinstitutionalized nature of such political systems more generally, excepting Kuwait. Simply because politics is underinstitutionalized in such states does not mean that it is underdeveloped; rather, political opportunity structures are altered, and the informal realm holds considerable political capital. In the super-rentiers, social policies form a major part of local Ikhwan discourse, and opinions about appropriate social practices inform citizens' views of the correct role of the government more broadly. As Kitschelt explains, "[P]olitical opportunity structures influence the choice of protest strategies and the impact of social movements on their environments," allowing for the different shape of movements in otherwise similar states.[50]

There is undoubtedly a social element to political trust within the super-rentiers, and Brotherhood movements have managed to use the links between the social (i.e., informal personal networks) and political (i.e., government institutions) to gain influence in policymaking in such states. In the case of Kuwait, the Muslim Brotherhood wields substantial political capital in the domestic arena, as it forms the most organized political bloc in the country. The Qatari case, however, demonstrates that, even when a formal Brotherhood branch does not exist locally, Islamist ideology is influential domestically in social policy and has affected the government's posturing abroad to a limited extent. In the case of the UAE, the local Brotherhood's involvement in domestic politics and criticism of local policies led to the government crackdown in 2012–2013. Today, the Emirati Brotherhood is vilified, yet its ideology remains influential in some circles. Despite the variety of outcomes in these states, they are critically similar in that the Ikhwan is politically significant even in the presence of vast hydrocarbon reserves and with limited institutionalized political openings.

STRUCTURE OF THIS BOOK

This book is divided into three main sections and seven chapters, in addition to this introduction. In Part I, "Origins," chapter 2 offers a review of relevant literature—namely rentier state theory and significant scholarship on political Islam. By assessing the existing literature on these topics, we clarify where this study adds value. We also consider these two bodies of literature together for the first time to assess their efficacy in describing the Muslim Brotherhood in the Gulf countries under study. The third chapter provides relevant comparative historical background on the political landscapes of Kuwait, Qatar, and the UAE. In tracing the rise of the political systems in these three states, we demonstrate how such systems have constrained independent political (though not necessarily social) action. Historical and political background also provides an important regional context that further clarifies the importance of the case studies.

Part II, "Rise and Fall," comprises two chapters. Chapter 4 covers the foundational periods of Brotherhood branches in the Gulf, ranging from the 1951 establishment of the Kuwaiti Muslim Brotherhood to the 1975 creation of the Qatari Ikhwan, examining the agendas of these groups and the degree of popular support they received in their initial years. Chapter 5 focuses on the period of expansion of the Brotherhood after the fall of Arab Nationalism from the 1970s through the 1990s, with a view to how Ikhwan movements used ties with government and social appeal to earn more popular support.

Part III, "Modern Rentier Islamism," takes up analysis from the twenty-first century. In the sixth chapter, we analyze the changing role of Brotherhood affiliates in the first decade of the 2000s, and in chapter 7, we assess the role of Brotherhood affiliates after the so-called Arab Spring, with the aim of understanding how they function in the present day.

Chapter 8 comprises an extended, substantive conclusion to take into account individual country experiences and to compare these countries along common themes. In this final chapter, we elucidate a new model for understanding how Muslim Brotherhood movements influence government policies in the super-rentier states, which we call rentier Islamism.

PART I

Origins

2

No Taxation, No Representation?

POLITICAL OPPOSITION IN RENTIER STATES AND THE ORIGINS OF MUSLIM BROTHERHOOD MOVEMENTS IN THE GULF

INTRODUCTION

The study of oil-wealthy states in the Gulf has long been dominated by rentier state theory, which endeavors to describe the domestic politics of such countries by their primary economic characteristic as recipients of substantial oil rents. In a similar vein, theories of political Islam have largely failed to examine Islamist movements in rentier monarchies of the Gulf, focusing instead on states like Algeria, Egypt, and Jordan, which have historically provided greater space for institutionalized political activity and participation, and which have also displayed a need for nonstate actors to provide services that financially strained governments have failed to deliver. In this chapter, we examine the scholarship concerning rentier state theory and political Islam. By reviewing each strand of the literature, we assess where and how this study adds value to each and use existing scholarship to craft a theory of rentier Islamism unique to the countries under study.

THEORIES OF THE RENTIER STATE

Since it was defined in 1970, the notion of the rentier state has been a greatly discussed categorization. Though it aptly describes the basic economic characteristics of states with substantial external incomes, traditional views of the rentier state are limited in scope. Most early works on rentierism treat the state as a single, homogeneous unit, leaving little space for political actors aside from what is assumed to be a united government, and devoting scant attention to the internal political workings of such a state. Rentier states are portrayed as little more than passive participants in the receipt of oil rents, and their governments are considered to hold uncontested and absolute economic and political control. Modified theories come closer to uncovering the more complicated nature of political life in the Gulf states, yet most studies on rentierism, as Gwenn Okruhlik highlights, "raise the problem of economic determinism. Clearly left out is politics."[1] Also often absent is discussion of the social, cultural, and religious environments of such states.

Hussein Mahdavy first defined rentier states, in the context of Iran, as "those countries that receive on a regular basis substantial amounts of external rents. External rents are in turn defined as rentals paid by foreign individuals, concerns or governments of a given country."[2] This definition is solely economic, referring to a fiscal reality of countries reliant on outside profit. Mahdavy's description of the rentier state makes little mention of the political system likely to accompany the economic model he describes. He does deduce that the government, as the manager of sizable external income, will have a prominent role in the economy, thereby enhancing its ability to embark on large-scale spending without taxation and boosting its ability to bribe dissidents.[3]

Perhaps more so than later theorists of rentierism, Mahdavy laments poor education and technological development among the populations of rentier states, concluding, "Instead of attending to the task of expediting the basic socio-economic transformations, they [rentier governments] devote the greater part of their resources to jealously guarding the *status quo*."[4] Mahdavy here seems to suggest that the government of a rentier state must work to maintain its position as the primary recipient of the country's wealth, yet he does not specify why or in what way state power would be insecure. Further, while Mahdavy claims that "the mass of the population may remain in a backward state," citing low levels of educational and technological advancement in Iran during the 1960s, he does not imply that citizens are aware of or unhappy with low levels of development.[5] Mahdavy, like other early theorists of the rentier state, presumes that, in a state with such an underdeveloped economic system, the political system and even society are similarly stunted by the receipt of considerable oil rents.

Mahdavy presents a fairly straightforward economic equation: external rents, managed by the government and distributed to the population, create a rentier state in which the local economy and society remain underdeveloped. Politics remains peripheral. Mahdavy therefore suggests that the problem of the rentier state is one for economists, not political scientists.

Hazem Beblawi and Giacomo Luciani are best known for expanding the definition of the rentier state, yet, for the political scientist, their formulation remains similarly unsatisfactory. Beblawi describes four main characteristics of a rentier state: its economy is dominated by rent; the economy is reliant on external, rather than internal, rents; a small number of people is involved in the creation of this rent; and the government is the primary recipient of external rent.[6] Again, the defining features of the state are economic. Beblawi goes on to explain that, in these states, citizens tend to receive payments from their wealthy governments. In such an environment, he posits, "income is no longer a reward of serious and hard work."[7] Rather, nationals are recompensed by virtue of their being citizens, making them less likely to form political opposition or to make demands of the state more generally.[8]

In terms of describing government systems of rentier states, taxation is considered to lead to citizens' demands for representation. Luciani, in his description of these "allocation states," presumes that "whenever the state essentially relies on taxation the question of democracy becomes an unavoidable issue, and a strong current in favor of democracy inevitably arises."[9] Because rentier states do not need to tax their citizens, he concludes, "democracy is not a problem."[10] Citizens' engagement in politics, then, is considered contingent upon monetary benefits. Unless the citizens' share of rent money is threatened, Luciani contends, they will not form political opposition.[11] Again, economic conditions are considered the primary determinants of political behavior, denying the pull of ideological politics.

Giacomo Luciani grants that, in the rentier context, Islam provides the "only rallying point" around which rentier citizens can create independent blocs.[12] Nonetheless, he posits that such groups "represent cultural or ideological orientation,"[13] thereby dismissing the potential political capital held by Islam. In his words,

> The fact that protest is voiced in Islamic terms may give the impression that it adds up to a coherent political opposition movement. However, the common Islamic language is not sufficient to transform generic dissatisfaction and revolt into a political movement, all the more so since Islam is a divisive as much as a uniting factor, and the Saudi government itself legitimizes its deeds in Islamic terms. The situation is no different in the other members of the GCC [Gulf Cooperation Council], including Kuwait—notwithstanding the limited electoral exercise that took place there.[14]

This claim—that Islam serves to divide rather than unite people in rentier states—is unsubstantiated, especially in conservative Gulf societies. Further, the fact that Saudi Arabia, which uses "the common Islamic language" to enhance its legitimacy and is one of the oldest states in the Middle East, illustrates the political capital held by Islam in the Gulf and the degree to which it can be used to unite. Perhaps in the Gulf more so than in any other region of the Middle East, Islam carries substantial political weight. Super-rentier governments in particular invest large sums into Islamic causes to appear as pious rulers and thus to enhance their legitimacy, transforming religion into a potent political force. Islam thus has not only proven successful in strengthening government legitimacy, but also has provided a strong basis for political movements.

Indeed, Hootan Shambayati aptly points out that it is in fact the economic dominance of governments in rentier states that makes religious and cultural opposition the most likely to emerge. He contends that, because economic grievances are unlikely to spur political mobilization in states that provide handsomely for their citizens, cultural and religious rallying points become the primary modes of independent political expression.[15] He explains, "When the government is financially autonomous from its citizens, conditions are ripe for challenging the state on noneconomic grounds . . . . In other words, the relation between the ruled and the rulers is defined in moral and ideological, not economic terms. Consequently, organized challenges to the state are based on moral and cultural issues, where rentier states are most vulnerable."[16] Other literature fails to account for the political vulnerabilities of rentier states, focusing instead on the economic and political dominance of the governments of such states.

Later scholarship describes rentier states as necessarily authoritarian and therefore lacking independent political movements. In *The Oil Curse*, Michael Ross uses Luciani's taxation-representation argument to explain the ability of rentier governments to "maintain popular support and avoid democratizing rebellions."[17] He makes the far-reaching assertion, "While autocracies without oil gradually become democratic, autocracies with oil can remain autocratic."[18] The cases of Libya and Algeria in the Middle East call his claim into question. Again, considering oil as the primary variable is a mistake, due to the widely divergent economic and political outcomes in oil-exporting states around the world.

Ultimately, region-focused empirical studies are more valuable to the advancement of scholarship about the Gulf's rentier states. Kiren Aziz Chaudhry, in her analysis of the influence of oil boom-bust cycles in Saudi Arabia and Yemen, demonstrates the shortcomings of wide-ranging studies of the world's rentier states. In her words, "[e]xternal capital inflows are not of a piece. Their effects depend on a host of historically constituted relationships."[19] She further demonstrates that elites in rentier states do not always maintain autonomy from independent social forces and that the influence of capital inflows must be placed within a local context.[20]

Importantly, Michael Herb contests the much-discussed connection between taxation and demands for representation in a seminal 2003 article, in which he traces the history of representative institutions in Europe.[21] Herb concludes that taxation leads to the growth of representative bodies only in instances where those institutions play a role in administering taxation.[22] While parliaments had such responsibilities in premodern Europe, the same tasks tend to be under the auspices of the executive in the modern period, thus delinking taxation from legislative control; assemblies have acquired power not by starving the government of tax money, but rather by gaining authority over bureaucracy.[23] Further, pro-democracy movements employ means like protests, rather than contesting jurisdiction over taxation, to advance their causes.[24] As Herb explains, "[T]axation does not always lead to democracy: there has been much more taxation than representation in history."[25] Breaking the link between taxation and representation damages traditional rentier state theory, which assumes that lack of taxation preserves authoritarianism, allowing the rentier government to act independently of its politically quiescent citizens.

Another mechanism described as perpetuating authoritarianism in oil-wealthy states is that of inhibiting group formation, explained by Michael Ross. In a 2001 article, he asserts that government funds can be used to prevent the emergence of independent social groups in wealthy rentiers. Ross explains, "[A]s governments increase in size (relative to the domestic economy) they are more likely to prevent the formation of civic institutions and social groups that are independent from the government, and . . . the absence of these groups will hinder a transition to democracy."[26] To test for the presence of this effect, Ross examines the state sector gross domestic product (GDP), positing that the larger this is as a proportion of total GDP, the less likely it will be that independent social groups form. What we find, however, is that independent political and social groups can and do emerge from within the rentier framework, regardless of the government's size as a fraction of GDP. Such organizations garner followers, not by providing material provisions or involving themselves in direct confrontation with the government, but by providing ideological guidance.[27] Further, Islamist organizations, some of which formed prior to oil booms in these states, have faced varying levels of government crackdown and have adjusted their structures to ensure their survival, most commonly turning to the informal social sector as the primary space for mobilization.

Further advancing the literature, Okruhlik highlights the shortcomings of rentier state theory in describing the political process, rightfully cautioning scholars against falling into economic determinism.[28] She contends that the distributive nature of rentier states does not exempt them from political opposition, but rather can help create it. In her view, the political decisions of the leadership, not the existence of oil money itself, lead to political outcomes. As she puts it, "The determining variable in the creation and convergence of opposition is the choices of a personal regime in distributing money inequitable for political reasons, not rent."[29] By granting agency to domestic political actors, Okruhlik helps explain outbreaks of political opposition (both Islamist and secular) in the Gulf. Her study also shows that simply possessing rents is not what differentiates Gulf oil states from other, less stable states; rather, it is *how* they spend these funds that distinguishes them. A government's use of this money can either secure its power or threaten it. This wealth can in fact threaten regime power. As Okruhlik explains, "Wealth generated through oil receipts is a catalyst for opposition to the state, rather than a tool to placate dissent, for two reasons. It is distributed inequitably . . . and it provides potential dissenters with the resources necessary for mobilization against the regime. In short, the state engenders its own opposition."[30] Okruhlik makes the important point that rentier states are not exempt from independent opposition movements, yet she still focuses on economic policies as the starting point for political mobilization in such states.

Steffen Hertog's work on Saudi Arabia also draws out some of the critical complexities of the Gulf rentier states by analyzing the Kingdom's inconsistent record in implementing economic reforms. In particular, he challenges the notion that the rentier state is autonomous from society, explaining that it puts limits on its own authority during the state-building period through its creation of clients.[31] Indeed, the rentier government gains allies at the expense of generating new distributive obligations.[32] Rather than maintaining absolute political power independent of society, as rentier state theory predicts, government autonomy is in fact constricted over time, "as the state gets tied down in society as it incurs micro-level distributional obligations that are difficult to reverse."[33]

Hertog's addition of "segmented clientelism" helps explain how formal and informal rent-based clientelistic relationships sustain stability, in addition to determining "where rentier-derived phenomena kick in and where not as well as which concrete power relations underlie them."[34] He concludes that macrolevel structures like trade unions and mesolevel organizations like professional associations have little space to function within the Saudi system, yet he maintains that informal structures influence policy implementation on the microlevel.[35] Though Hertog ultimately concedes that "Saudi Arabia fully confirms the rentier debate hypothesis that states and, more specifically, executives dominate politics in rentier systems," he highlights the significance of the informal sector in political life in the Gulf.[36] This informal sector has proven particularly important for Islamist groups facing government crackdown.

More empirical study is needed on the Gulf, especially considering that describing these states as rentiers indicates surprisingly little about their political systems and particularly about the type of independent political actors likely to emerge in such states. Just as scholarship on rentier state theory has largely neglected the role of Islamist political actors, so too has the literature on Islamism failed to account for independent Islamist movements within rentier states of the Arabian Peninsula.

THEORIES OF POLITICAL ISLAM

What Is Political Islam?

Scholarship on political Islam has become one of the most expansive bodies of literature in political science. Definitional challenges abound. Terms such as Islamist, Islamicist, and fundamentalist have been used interchangeably, and often incorrectly, to describe a variety of actors. Further complicating the definitions of such terms is the fact that "no two Islamists are alike. Political activities undertaken by Islamists are largely determined by the contexts within which they operate."[37] In this study, the term Islamist is defined broadly, as actors who "mobilise and agitate in the political sphere while deploying signs and symbols from Islamic traditions."[38] We focus solely on strands of Sunni Islamism, as Sunnism is the dominant sect in the states under study.

The general notion of political Islam springs from the fact that "the Islamic tradition provided a normative system in which religion was integral to all areas of Muslim life—politics, economics, law, education, and the family."[39] It is because of the comprehensiveness of this system that, in the eyes of Islamists, religion and politics cannot be separated: Islam affects all spheres of an individual's life, ranging from the religious to the mundane. It is, to borrow John Obert Voll's description, "a total way of life."[40]

At the center of the unity of all aspects of life is the notion of *tawḥīd* (oneness)—a key tenet of Islam stressing its monotheistic and unified nature. Society is meant to reflect divine oneness.[41] As Olivier Roy explains, "[A] *tawhidi* society . . . cannot tolerate either intrinsic segmentation (social, ethnic, tribal, or national) or a political authority that is autonomous with respect to the divine order."[42] This concept of unity explains why Islamists use similar language in both the political and religious spheres.

Due to this central unity, the political inevitably becomes religious and vice versa: "the sovereign has a 'religious' function: to defend Islam and the *sharia*. The state, too, has a goal: to enable Muslims to live as good Muslims. The state is an instrument and not an end in itself."[43] Sharia, the body of law derived from the Qurʾan and the Sunna, is central to the state's role as a promoter of acceptable religious behavior. Because it governs the actions of both the ruler and the ruled and has jurisdiction over matters of personal status as well as criminal law, the application of sharia is an important means of maintaining a *tawḥīdī* society.[44]

With the distinction between the secular and religious thus blurred, Islamist political action seems logical. As Roy describes, "The Islamist movement thus conceives of itself explicitly as a sociopolitical movement, founded on an Islam defined as much in terms of a political ideology as in terms of a religion."[45] The tenet of *tawḥīd* makes it impossible to divide the spheres. Despite this ideological grounding, a great deal of literature tries to determine whether Islamist mobilization at the grassroots is motivated by social, economic, or political considerations.

Motivations for Islamist Mobilization

In recent years, scholars like Quintan Wiktorowicz have used social movement theory to explain Islamist political action, charging that "Islamic activism is not *sui generis*."[46] Academics have debated whether Islamist movements constitute, at their core, a sociocultural or psychological reaction to the failures of the modern state and Western encroachments in the Muslim world, a response of the disenfranchised to economic disappointment, or a political movement agitating for a greater say in government. In so doing, most studies have focused on country cases outside the Arabian Peninsula.

Early social movement theory relied on functionalism, which emphasized the importance of "structural and psychological causes of mass mobilization."[47] Psychological isolation is often cited as a reason for the rise of Islamist groups—particularly in the face of rapidly accelerating urbanization and modernization. Such movements are considered "escapist coping mechanisms through which individuals regain a sense of belonging and empowerment."[48] The Gulf has experienced limited Islamist backlash as a result of its rapid modernization since the oil boom, with nationals urging a return to traditional Islamic values as secularism and Westernism become more prevalent with the rise in number of non-Muslim expatriates and tourists. Still, the sense of social isolation experienced in other parts of the region is less likely to emerge in the Gulf, where most citizens rely on an extended network of family and tribal connections for support. Because, as Frauke Heard-Bey points out, "the tribe is the principal building block for the structure of their society,"[49] other social groups are less necessary.[50] Considering Islamic activism as "a response to cultural imperialism" more aptly describes the psychological appeal of Islamist mobilization in the Gulf.[51] Nonetheless, if Western influence were the sole motivation for Islamist movements, they would be less likely to continue agitating for domestic political changes unrelated to Westernization.

Viewing motivations for Islamist mobilization as socioeconomic, political scientist François Burgat portrays Islamist organizations as antielite social movements. Interestingly, he contends that this antielite sentiment is even stronger in a rentier economy:

> when clientelism is a strong trait in a regime, and when, moreover, there is a rentier economy, the further away from power you stand, the less access you have to the benefits it distributes. It is therefore true to say that a difference of social status separates the anti-Islamist elite in power (who are sometimes rashly labeled as secularists) from the (Islamist) opposition who challenge them, and that poverty may radicalize this movement.[52]

Such a description, though apt in the less wealthy rentier states of Algeria, Jordan, and Tunisia, does not describe the super-rentiers. Because their nationals are so few in number and because their rent income is so high, these small states have managed to provide the vast majority of citizens with impressive benefits through well-established and massive welfare state apparati. Political rulers of the super-rentiers have also proactively responded to critiques about secularization and Westernization, using their ample funds to elevate the role of Islam in public life. Still, some discontent remains about the secularization and Westernization of Gulf regimes.

Economic conditions are also cited as a reason for the rise of Islamic activism. Several scholars have backed this view, pointing out that many recruits of Islamist movements have been recent, relatively well-educated migrants unable to find jobs in cities to which they have moved. Nazih Ayubi asserts that the beginning of the modernization process, which included developments in education, urbanization, and industry, failed to deliver employment opportunities or upward mobility for many members of Middle Eastern populations.[53] Ayubi therefore concludes that Islamist movements are somewhat "a manifestation of, and a reaction to, a developmental crisis in the Muslim part of the Third World."[54] Since modernization has failed them, according to this view, Islamists reject it: "Theirs is the proverbial case of 'sour grapes.' "[55]

Further advancing the theory that Islamist mobilization is motivated by economic interests, nearly all Islamist organizations, ranging from Hizbullah to the Muslim Brotherhood, "began with a focus on social-welfare activities—concrete activities to address the needs of their surrounding populations."[56] Aside from responding to material needs, social welfare institutions of independent Islamist organizations, in Janine A. Clark's words, "represent an ideological and practical alternative to the present system."[57] While the notion of economically motivated Islamic activism is applicable in the poorer states of the region, it does not make sense for the super-rentiers. Although income is by no means evenly distributed in Kuwait, Qatar, and the United Arab Emirates (UAE), these states have the financial wherewithal to provide a certain standard level of material support to their citizens. Their governments have also taken over control of, or at least funded, most local charities—even those with a religious bent.

In the restricted political systems of the Middle East, there are few institutionalized means for citizens to voice their political opinions, leading to "societal frustration and a sense of alienation. The feeling of political impotence is exacerbated in the face of security service repression and administrative processes that attempt to depoliticize civil society and prevent oppositional activities."[58] Islamist movements are thus often seen as voicing primarily political dissent. Further, Islamist movements have more freedom to operate in environments where other political movements are restricted, as they occupy a space that is not solely political. Mosques remain an important site for political discussion, as do organizations like student and professional associations; political activity is thus displaced to spaces traditionally considered more social than political.

Regardless of where they act, according to this theory, Islamist movements "are often explicitly focused and directed toward the political arena."[59] They may act in a political capacity through social activities and the provision of welfare, through the formation of political blocs or parties, or alternatively through the informal sector to influence political opinions indirectly. As Quitan Wiktorowicz summarizes, "At least a few scholars have argued that informality, as opposed to formal organizations, is more effective for protest since the organizational survival imperatives of SMOs [social movement organizations] can undermine the purpose of a movement."[60] Particularly in the politically tightly controlled Gulf states, informal networks become primary means of Islamist mobilization. Past studies confirm the power of informal social networks in advancing Islamist goals, yet the role of political Islam within that sphere in the super-rentiers has not been studied.

Ultimately, social movement theory goes wrong by treating Islamists as fundamentally similar to other such movements, rather than a distinctive type of organization. Carrie Rosefky Wickham's seminal study of the Muslim Brotherhood in Egypt most aptly reflects the multifaceted nature of Islamist movements that differentiates them from other social movements. She describes the Ikhwan as gaining followers not only through the provision of material and social benefits, but also by providing an ideology that influences members' spiritual, social, and political outlooks.[61] Indeed, joining the Brotherhood requires serious spiritual commitment. As Voll puts it, the Islamist trend "would not be a serious movement worthy of our attention were it not, above all, an idea and a personal commitment honestly felt."[62] Islamists provide an all-encompassing ideology, as they seek religious reforms of all aspects of life, including social structures, politics, and economics. Wickham explains, when writing about the Egyptian Muslim Brotherhood, that

> Islamist mobilization on the periphery has created nothing less than a "counter-society" detached from the mainstream social and political order. To reduce the spirit of this community to one of opposition would be to understate its creative, experimental, and comprehensive character. What defined the Islamic movement was less its opposition to a given regime or set of policies than its efforts to construct, from the bottom up and over time, a new kind of society inspired by Islamist ideals.[63]

By advocating widespread reconstruction of the social order and by appealing to faith, Islamists attract followers from varying backgrounds and in different environments. Indeed, as Clark explains, Islamist mobilization is "an attempt to create a seemingly seamless web between religion, politics, charity, and all forms of activism."[64] Rentier state theory's attempt to dismiss the political relevance of Islamist actors in such states, while allowing them a social role, is nonsensical, considering the fact that the social, political, and religious are intrinsically intertwined for Islamists. Further, as Kitschelt explains, the structure of political opportunities influences the protest and political strategies of independent movements.[65] As a result, Islamists in super-rentiers use their social capital to gain political influence.

ISLAMIST POLITICS

Because religion carries substantial social and political significance in the Middle East, "Islam continues to be part of the regimes' legitimacy formula in most Muslim countries."[66] While Brotherhood affiliates work at the grassroots level, at the government level, co-optation of the religious sector is critical to the maintenance of legitimacy.[67] State control of mosques and sermons allows governments to monitor religious messages—amplifying the favorable and muting the problematic.[68] The almost unavoidable use of religion in political discourse also makes it "difficult [for opposition movements] to communicate in purely political terms," even when agitating for strictly political changes like the reform of state institutions.[69] In fact, Brotherhood affiliates tend to divide into *ḥizb* (political party) and *ḥaraka* (social movement) in an effort to balance both pragmatic and spiritual concerns. While the *ḥizb* manages electoral campaigns, the *ḥaraka* is responsible for social outreach, thus allowing an Islamist group to maintain a foothold in both (equally important) sectors.

Government crackdowns on political organizations have thus paralyzed secular liberal groups much more than Islamist ones, which can gain popular support through more difficult to regulate religious and social gatherings.[70] In politically restrictive systems of the Gulf, as Salwa Ismail highlights, "Islamists moved into spaces of cooperation and solidarity like the mosque, the sports association and the neighbourhood society."[71] Islamist movements, like other social movements, thus operate differently depending on the opportunities afforded them by structures of the state, which is why they look so dissimilar across varying environments.[72] Certainly, "Islamists have adopted a multitude of strategies, ranging from outright confrontation and violent action to agitation in the public sphere to infiltration of societal spaces."[73] Political Islam is thus constantly evolving.[74] As explained by Ghassan Salamé, even the wealthiest regimes have failed in the eyes of Islamists, whether due to "the regimes' widespread corruption, their squandering of oil revenues, their reliance on the West, their more recent submission to the International Monetary Fund strictures, or their persistent lack of interest in tradition."[75] In the restrictive states of the Middle East, then, political Islam, multifaceted as it is, has become, in Ayubi's words, "on the whole a protest movement."[76]

Some such protest movements have become violent, in radical reaction to Westernization and failed nationalist movements. These groups, however, are "irrelevant to the day-to-day political struggles within Muslim countries."[77] Organizations like al-Qaʿida and the Islamic State of Iraq and Syria (ISIS) privilege transnational aims, namely the restoration of a unified Islamist state, or caliphate, over immediate domestic political concerns. Aside from lacking specific political solutions to immediate challenges, these violent movements have failed to make meaningful progress toward their political goals—leading to further violence, government crackdown, or both.[78] In addition, extremist movements are ideologically linked to Salafi[79] jihadism. Unlike the Brotherhood, they "embrace a strict, literal interpretation of Islam, but combine it with an emphasis on jihad, understood here as holy war rather than a spiritual struggle. To Salafi jihadists such as al-Qaʿida members, jihad becomes the prime instrument through which the 'Salafi' desire to 'return' to the original message of Islam will be turned into reality."[80] The Muslim Brotherhood, while espousing a return to Islamic practices, certainly does not share this theological belief, and it denounced the use of violence as a political strategy as early as 1969.[81]

Although it is difficult to summarize the agendas of Islamist parties, Michael Hudson describes four common aspects of "Islamic ideological complaint": political, national, social, and moral.[82] Politically, Islamists challenge the policies of current rulers and especially how they were chosen; nationally, they cite failures to pursue Arab and Islamic goals; socially, uneven distribution of wealth is emphasized; and morally, Islamists stress corruption and public ethics.[83] Islamists therefore have a multifaceted political platform with wide appeal. As Roy describes it, Islamism aims to deliver on both ideological and practical promises: "Islamism is the sharia plus electricity."[84] The Muslim Brotherhood has been particularly successful in appealing to followers with its wide-ranging platform and political ideology.

ORIGINS AND IDEOLOGY OF THE MUSLIM BROTHERHOOD

Founded in 1928 by Hasan al-Banna, the Society of Muslim Brothers was initially conceived of as a social movement seeking to re-Islamize Egypt. Al-Banna, as a schoolteacher in the Suez Canal zone, "directly experienced Egypt's cultural Westernization, which he equated with atheism and immorality. Like many Muslims, he reacted with alarm to Mustafa Kemal Atatürk's abolition of the caliphate and his programme to secularize Turkey."[85] Largely in response to what he saw in Egypt and abroad after the fall of the Ottoman Empire, al-Banna founded the Society of Muslim Brothers in an effort to restore Islam to the lives of Egyptians. The Society, as Robert S. Leiken and Steven Brooke summarize, "sought to fuse religious revival with anti-imperialism—resistance to foreign domination through the exaltation of Islam."[86]

Al-Banna, who had been a member of other religious organizations, hoped to create a unique movement. The Society of Muslim Brothers, at its start, "differed from earlier reformers by combining a profoundly Islamic ideology with modern grass-roots activism."[87] The organization was also unique in its focus on improving socioeconomic conditions and promoting social justice.[88] Al-Banna's ideology was "thoroughly, and sincerely, populist."[89] Still, the Brotherhood's bylaws prohibited direct political action until 1934,[90] and it was not until its sixth conference, in 1941, that the Society chose to participate in parliamentary elections.[91]

The Muslim Brotherhood's first activities focused on *tarbīa*[92] as a means of re-Islamizing society from the grassroots, since the road to an Islamic society necessarily involved the conversion of individuals. Al-Banna famously described the Muslim Brotherhood as "a Salafi movement, an orthodox way, a Sufi reality, a political body, an athletic group, a scientific and cultural society, an economic company and a social idea."[93] Such a wide-ranging definition reflected al-Banna's holistic view of Islam's role in society and of his organization's mission to maintain and spread this vision of the religion. A 1943 statement captures al-Banna's hope for the movement to be a means of re-instilling Islam in modern society: "My Brothers: you are not a benevolent society, nor a political party, nor a local organization having limited purposes. Rather, you are a new soul in the heart of this nation to give it life by means of the Qur'an; you are a new light which shines to destroy the darkness of materialism through knowing God; and you are the strong voice which rises to recall the message of the Prophet."[94]

Al-Banna's ultimate goal was to create an Islamic society without political parties or socioeconomic classes: he sought a *tawḥīdī* order.[95] The state would be ruled by a just Muslim leader and would instil Islamic values through education in addition to ensuring that such values were obeyed in practice.[96] The state, in al-Banna's conception, was instrumental to the re-Islamization of society. There were three essential principles that al-Banna specified for the Islamic state: (1) the Qur'an is the constitution; (2) the government operates on the basis of consultation (*shūrā*) with society; and (3) the executive, like citizens, is bound by the rules of Islam.[97]

Perhaps unsurprisingly considering its ideological underpinnings, the Brotherhood became politically active as it gained social popularity.[98] The original conception was that the Ikhwan should come to power politically only after society had been Islamized.[99] The notion of "slow Islamization" was compatible with democracy, as members of a truly Islamic society would support Islamic rulers in elections.[100] Al-Banna was clear about the functions a good government should fulfill. These included "providing security, enforcing the law, spreading education, promoting public welfare, strengthening morality, protecting property and wealth, defending the Muslim nation, and disseminating the call to Islam."[101] If a government failed to fulfill these tasks, al-Banna stated, people should challenge its authority and advocate for governments ruling in consultation with their publics.[102]

The Muslim Brotherhood's original support base reveals the degree to which its message held broad appeal, from among the religious rural population, the urban lower classes, and many in the education sector.[103] As today, the Brotherhood was historically "a very strong movement of students, civil servants, teachers, office workers, and professionals."[104] The organization also provided welfare assistance, religious guidance, and a social community to urban newcomers. The Brotherhood thus spread throughout the Middle East, providing an alternative arrangement to the prevailing government-led order that had proved disappointing. Beginning in the 1940s, the mother organization in Egypt also actively dispatched representatives to various countries in the region to spread the Brotherhood's message, in addition to widely disseminating the organization's literature.

Like many influential ideological movements, the Muslim Brotherhood developed splinter organizations. In the face of ongoing arrests and crackdown under the Nasser regime, some Brotherhood figures encouraged a more radical turn toward violence. Many such figures were under the influence of Sayyid Qutb, executed in 1966 for plotting the assassination of Egyptian President Gamal ʿAbdel Nasser, whose government had imprisoned him. While Hasan al-Banna had encouraged gradual steps toward the Islamization of society and the political order, Qutb contended that the only way to imbue society with Islamic values for the creation of an Islamic state was through jihad, which he considered a military struggle.[105] Inspired by his ideology and frustrated by the current political system, a variety of groups dedicated to the violent overthrow of the prevailing order emerged in the 1970s, including al-Takfir wa-l-Hijra, al-Jamaʿat al-Islamiyya, and Egyptian Islamic Jihad. The third General Guide of the Muslim Brotherhood, ʿUmar al-Tilmisani, made clear in 1982 that Qutb did not speak for the movement, though, stating, "Sayyid Qutb represented himself alone and not the Muslim Brethren."[106] The Brotherhood has thus continued its efforts to gradually Islamize society from the bottom-up, using both *ḥizb* and *ḥaraka* to do so.

THE MUSLIM BROTHERHOOD TODAY

Despite the diversity of Islamist political groups, "[t]he Muslim Brotherhood is the world's oldest, largest, and most influential Islamist organization."[107] It has several national affiliates, yet only a weak central organization exists. While all agree on the important role of Islam in politics, Brotherhood affiliates promote different platforms depending on local circumstances. In essence, as Samir S. Shehata puts it, "[t]he Brotherhood is a collection of national groups with differing outlooks, and the various factions disagree about how best to advance its mission. But all reject global jihad while embracing elections and other features of democracy."[108] The various branches of the Muslim Brotherhood are concerned primarily with domestic politics, but they are all informed by the same ideology.[109] Certainly, "Political Islam is . . . effectively nationalized in the contemporary era."[110]

Largely because the Muslim Brotherhood's platform is so wide-ranging, with only broad outlines for proper governance, the organization has become popular in a variety of cultural and political contexts, taking on different structural forms as well.[111] Linked by their commitment to Islamic governance, the various national branches of the Brotherhood remain only vaguely connected. As Leiken and Brooke explain,

> The Brotherhood's dreaded International Organization is in fact a loose and feeble coalition scarcely able to convene its own members. Indeed, the Brotherhood's international debility is a product of its local successes: national autonomy and adjustability to domestic conditions. The ideological affiliations that link Brotherhood organizations internationally are subject to the national priorities that shape each individually.[112]

The fact that the agendas of the various Brotherhood branches differ so widely demonstrates the primacy of domestic political concerns and underlines the importance of regime policies in determining these groups' compositions and activities.[113] And while such groups are often linked through personal relationships, these are rarely institutionalized or structured.

When Brotherhood affiliates came to power for the first time in Egypt and Tunisia following the Arab Spring, the organization found itself in unfamiliar territory. Ultimately failing to cooperate with other political blocs and overpowered by the military, Islamists were stripped of power in Egypt,[114] while they faced electoral losses in Tunisia amid accusations of inexperience and maladministration.[115] Considered by many to have failed in government, the Brotherhood has been outlawed as a terrorist organization in Egypt, Saudi Arabia, and the UAE, while it has been dubbed as such by the Bahraini foreign minister though it continues to operate domestically. Such governments have attempted to eradicate the Brotherhood even as a social organization, believing its members to be loyal to Ikhwan ideology above their state and considering their ultimate aim to be the overthrow of national political orders. Even in Western powers like the United Kingdom and United States, the Muslim Brotherhood remains the subject of suspicion, as it is considered potentially threatening in those environments as well, since it is seen as promoting transnational above national loyalty.

RENTIER ISLAMISM: MUSLIM BROTHERHOOD ORGANIZATIONS IN THE GULF CONTEXT

Because of the lack of widespread economic grievances and overt organized political opposition in the Arabian Peninsula, Islamist organizations there have traditionally been viewed primarily as a reaction to the rapid Westernization and modernization after the discovery of oil. It has often been assumed that wealthy regimes are well equipped to face down complaints, Islamist or otherwise, using generous welfare packages, repression, or patronage.[116] In addition, Gulf rulers' apparent commitment to Islam leaves little space for Islamists to act. Nonetheless, as John L. Esposito underlines, "[o]ne of the ironies of the Gulf is that, despite the use or manipulation of Islam by many governments as a source of identity and legitimacy and as a high-profile means to promote Islam internationally, Islam also represents a challenge to be reckoned with—a political force with the capability to delegitimate or to support protest and opposition."[117] Notwithstanding this, empirical research on independent oppositional political movements in the Gulf, whether Islamist or secular, is greatly lacking.

The scant scholarship about Islamism in the Gulf portrays the Gulf War as a turning point for the rise of independent Islamist movements, primarily in the form of the Sahwa movement in Saudi Arabia. The Kingdom's invitation to Western forces to assist with the liberation of Kuwait not only exposed the vulnerability of the Gulf states to outside aggression, but also demonstrated their willingness to turn to the West for assistance.[118] Esposito explains that

> [t]he Gulf crisis witnessed a shift among many Islamic movements from an initial Islamic ideological rejection of Saddam Hussein, the secular prosecutor of Islamic movements, and his invasion of Kuwait to a more populist Arab nationalist, anti-imperialist support for Saddam (or more precisely those issues he represented or championed) and the condemnation of massive Western (especially U.S.) military buildup

> in the region and its presence near Islam's sacred cities, as well as the threat of military action against an Arab nation and of a permanent Western presence.[119]

Following the Gulf War, Islamism developed into a form of nationalism in the Gulf and became more widely accepted as a means of expressing political discontent.[120] Nonetheless, this growth of Islamism in the Gulf has been studied primarily in Saudi Arabia.

After the attacks of September 11, 2001 (9/11), the notion that "closed societies can also breed new forms of radicalism" led to more in-depth studies of independent Islamist movements in the nondemocratic states of the Gulf.[121] This trend resulted in several studies focused on violent transnational Islamist organizations, rather than national Muslim Brotherhood affiliates that focus on domestic political issues. Because religious radicalism emerged from the Gulf, with Saudi Osama bin Laden having founded al-Qaʿida and with much terrorist funding ostensibly coming from the region, a great deal of writing has concerned the violent strand of Islamism in the region. Local Islamist movements have largely been left unstudied, despite the fact that these groups dominate the limited space for political activity in the Gulf.

The wealthy states of the Arabian Peninsula, or super-rentiers, are unique in two respects as environments for political Islam. First, they have responded to the rise of religious activism primarily by co-opting the religious sphere and by increasing the government's commitment to religiosity in rhetoric and (to a certain extent) deed, in addition to providing more funding for the religious sector. Ayubi points out that these smaller GCC states are distinctive in that

> practically all these countries also have access to means that bring financial resources in sizable or at least significant magnitude directly to the State (oil, phosphates, and foreign aid). Thus these countries are able to support the sources of their religious (or "traditional") legitimization with substantial amounts of financial resources. Several of these regimes have "incorporated" (rather than simply "controlled") the religious establishments within the educational, judiciary and social affairs.[122]

Government attempts at "ideological outbidding" or the promotion of "establishment Islam," using their ample funds, have largely failed, as Islamist platforms are not solely religious or ideological, but also involve social and political demands that many states have failed to address.[123]

Second, due to the general lack of independent professional organizations, student groups, or political parties in Qatar and the UAE, Islamist organizations benefit from their ability to meet in the informal sector. While the Kuwaiti system allows institutionalized means of Islamist complaint, political parties remain outlawed, and informal ties are critical for such groups. Uninstitutionalized meetings of *dīwāniyyāt*[124] and *majālis*[125] remain primary instruments of civil society in the Arabian Peninsula. The majlis remains an important tribal element of political life, with such a meeting convened by the ruler considered "the final court of appeal on all important matters."[126] The informal institution essentially constitutes "the substance of day-to-day government."[127] Lobbying governing elites in such fora in fact is the primary modus operandi of the Brotherhood in super-rentiers, allowing them to advocate for changes in social policies as well as broader political reform. Considering the uninstitutionalized and highly personalized nature of tribal political life in the super-rentiers, it is unsurprising that social trust remains an important component of political allegiance. Commitment to Islam is one means through which leaders can convey their trustworthiness and alignment with traditional values that are considered to be increasingly eroding; religiosity thus becomes a political asset.

Indeed, despite efforts at modernization and institutionalization, F. Gregory Gause III cites Islam and tribalism in the Gulf as "important arms of the state, providing institutional support and ideological legitimation to the regimes."[128] As a result, public space is granted to these sectors.[129] Limiting public assembly as such has led independent political movements, logically, to form along religious or tribal lines, as mosques, religious schools, or tribal meetings are the primary locations (outside of private homes) where people in the region can easily gather. As Gause explains, "Establishing state authority has necessarily meant subordinating Islamic and tribal institutions to state supervision, if not outright control. However, that does not mean that those institutions, and the rhetoric and symbols that accompany them, are politically unimportant."[130] This study focuses on the Islamic sector specifically, as it has been the most vociferous and organized in its contestation of state policies, as well as the subject of most disagreement among the GCC states in recent years.

We find that Muslim Brotherhood organizations have followed similar trajectories inside the Gulf. Members of the Ikhwan successfully took control of some parts of the rapidly growing and well-funded rentier state apparatuses from the 1950s through the 1970s when they faced a shortage in staff, particularly in the education and justice sectors. The Brotherhood's focus on spiritual grassroots work in lieu of service provision allowed them to fill the civil society vacuum in the Gulf context. Further, their strong reaction against Westernization and secularization allowed them to gain a following among national populations frustrated with changes to their local, majority-expatriate environments. In Kuwait, the Brotherhood is able to effect change through parliament, while in Qatar and the UAE, means of Ikhwan mobilization are primarily through the uninstitutionalized social sphere.

CONCLUSIONS

Both rentier state theory and scholarship on political Islam have fallen short of adequately describing the internal political dynamics of the Gulf's super-rentiers. These states provide a unique arena for Islamist actors. Because governments in these states have made efforts to promote Islam, as well as to diminish sources of social, political, and economic strain, the traditional explanations for Islamist mobilization do not apply. In the absence of a need for social welfare or even less formal social organizations and without electoral campaigns to run (aside from in Kuwait), the function of Islamist organizations in the super-rentiers remains unclear and unstudied.

What is indisputable, however, is that Islam is heavily politicized in the region. With super-rentier governments regularly employing religious language to maintain their legitimacy and attempting to co-opt the religious sector, Islam is politically powerful. To understand the role of Islam in the context of the super-rentiers under study, we next examine their political environments to determine the means by which Islamist organizations mobilize support in such states.

3

Systems of Governance and Politics of Opposition in the Super-Rentiers

AN INTRODUCTION TO HEREDITARY MONARCHIES OF THE GULF

The super-rentiers of Kuwait, Qatar, and the United Arab Emirates (UAE) share considerable economic, political, and social similarities. Their common history as British protected states and later independence under local ruling families created a set of powerful monarchies in which nonstate political actors, secular or Islamist, are uncommon. Ruling families, who cemented political power due to ties they developed with the British in the nineteenth century, remain the primary political actors in super-rentiers, having institutionalized their tribal dominance by placing family members in powerful government and commercial positions.[1] Such families are often considered "synonymous with the state," due to their dominance of the political scene and authority over primary state institutions.[2]

Although all of the super-rentiers are controlled by powerful ruling families, each has a distinctive style of rule. In Mehran Kamrava's words, "The al-Sabah of Kuwait, for example, have such a strong corporate identity and interests that they have evolved an intricate set of organizations, epitomized by a Family Council specifically designed to run the affairs of the royal family. In contrast, the al-Thani in Qatar have at times shown disregard for the ruler's authority and have often demonstrated little corporate identity."[3] The six ruling families in the UAE,[4] on the other hand, at times dispute the dominance of the al-Nahyan of Abu Dhabi and the al-Maktoum of Dubai, yet tend to function together through the UAE's central state institutions. In this chapter, we trace the rise of the political systems in these three states with a focus on how such systems constrain independent political action. We also examine their constitutional frameworks and the laws governing civil society to gain a broader understanding of the political landscapes and the potential place for Islamist actors in super-rentier political systems.

A BRIEF POLITICAL HISTORY OF KUWAIT

Kuwait existed as a political entity long before the other Gulf states, dating back to the eighteenth century with the arrival of the central Arabian Banī ʿUtūb tribe. The Banī ʿUtūb, once its members adopted a settled lifestyle in present-day Kuwait City, became a distinct class with control over the commerce, pearling, and fishing that dominated the Kuwaiti economy.[5] Notably, such a class of sedentarized elites did not emerge in Qatar or the UAE until the twentieth century.

It was the wealthy Banī ʿUtūb elites who elected the first al-Sabah shaykh in the 1750s.[6] The al-Sabah family came to power largely due to its good relations with inland nomadic tribes. While many elite merchant families were oriented toward the sea for trade and commerce, the al-Sabah had links primarily within the desert hinterlands.[7] The al-Sabah family therefore provided important political connections, though it was among the poorest of the area's prominent families.[8] Because the ruling family depended on merchants for funds, "from the beginning governance in Kuwait was based on compromise and coalition-building, not extreme authoritarianism or brute force."[9] As a result, Kuwait's system of government allows for more institutionalized political participation than do other systems in the Gulf.

As early as the mid-eighteenth century, under al-Sabah rule and largely due to a lucrative pearl trade, Kuwait prospered.[10] During this period, the al-Sabah became "the uncontested ruling family of Kuwait" and has retained that power uninterruptedly since the eighteenth century.[11] By the early 1860s, present-day Kuwait City housed twenty-thousand people, making it one of the largest settlements on the Arabian Peninsula at that time.[12]

At the end of the nineteenth century, Kuwait came under British protection due to anxieties held by Shaykh Mubarak al-Sabah (r. 1896–1915) about Ottoman and Saudi advances into his territory. Although initially hesitant to take on additional foreign responsibilities, Britain signed a treaty with Shaykh Mubarak in January 1899, which "promised Kuwait British support in exchange for an exclusive relationship with Britain and British control of Kuwait's foreign policy."[13] This protection allowed Shaykh Mubarak to focus on consolidating his power domestically, with British endorsement of his rule a boon.[14]

Kuwait began to suffer economically in the 1920s, as a Saudi embargo of Kuwait following disagreements about transport and import duties harmed commercial interests.[15] Making matters worse, Japan's Mikimoto pearl entered the global market at the end of the decade, harming Kuwait's pearl trade. Shortly thereafter, however, Shaykh Ahmad al-Jaber al-Sabah (r. 1921–1950) received his first payment for oil exports in 1935, marking the beginning of Kuwait's growth as a major petroleum producer.[16] With the arrival of oil revenues came demands to distribute this wealth. As elsewhere in the Gulf, pleas came first from members of the sizable ruling family who received large portions of the newfound wealth, in addition to benefitting from positions in government, thereby making them both dependent upon, and more likely to be loyal to, the developing state authorities.[17]

In the early 1950s, Shaykh ʿAbdullah Salem al-Mubarak al-Sabah (r. 1950–1965) instituted programs to redistribute oil wealth not only to the ruling family and merchant elite, but also to the rest of Kuwaiti society through ambitious development projects.[18] By the end of the decade, Shaykh ʿAbdullah had come to provide healthcare and education, in addition to other welfare support and government positions for much of the population.[19] Despite these disbursements, the pull of nationalist and Nasserist ideology reached Kuwait, with a large number of Iraqi and Egyptian expatriates transmitting the message of Arab nationalism to the local population.[20] By 1960, many in the shaykhdom were pushing to cut ties with Britain.[21]

In January 1962, after the protected state relationship with Britain formally ended in June 1961, Shaykh ʿAbdullah issued an amiri decree to call for the election of a body to draft the new country's constitution.[22] He demanded that the constitution "be based on 'democratic principles taken from the realities and objectives of Kuwait.' "[23] The 1962 Constitution created a hybrid system, fusing hereditary rule with parliamentary government.[24] The constitution, while designating power to a legislature, established Kuwait as "a hereditary Amirate, and limited succession to the descendants of Shaykh Mubarak. The amir was declared immune and his person inviolable."[25]

Kuwait's System of Government

The amir undoubtedly remains the central figure in Kuwaiti government. As head of state, he is considered "not accountable under constitutional law."[26] Furthermore, the amir enjoys the rights to initiate, suspend, and publicize legislation, as well as to rule by decree when parliament is not in session.[27] His approval is also required before the declaration of any law proposed by the legislature, which he or the Constitutional Court can dissolve at will,[28] provided that new parliamentary elections are called within two months of the body's dissolution.[29]

The Cabinet, or Council of Ministers, chosen by the amir, is led by an amir-appointed prime minister and determines government priorities, in addition to organizing the work of state agencies and ministries.[30] It also tends to be dominated by members of the al-Sabah and other prominent allied families.[31] These ministers, even if not elected, automatically become members of parliament (MPs), though their number in the legislature is not to exceed one-third of the total number of members.[32] Still, "the cabinet is an arm of the rulers" in the legislature.[33] Cabinet members of the legislature vote equally with other MPs on most issues, logically excluding votes of no confidence against ministers.[34]

The National Assembly, Kuwait's legislature, consists of fifty members elected every four years (unless dissolved by the amir or the Constitutional Court before that time), in addition to the aforementioned members of the cabinet. This parliament is undoubtedly the most powerful legislature in the Gulf, with significant abilities to check the power of the executive branch. Parliament's authority ranges from the right to vote a minister out of office, express no confidence in ministers including the prime minister, decline laws proposed by the executive, and draft legislation with the approval of the amir to become official law.[35] Notably, the legislature also holds authority to oversee public finances, which has become a significant policy issue, as repeated allegations of government corruption have emerged and have often been highlighted by the Muslim Brotherhood's political bloc.[36]

From its inception, parliament has proven itself willing to confront the government, though the executive branch retains the upper hand.[37] As David Roberts put it, "The most powerful institution in Kuwait remains the al-Sabah ruling family. Having ruled continuously since the mid-eighteenth century, it has been sewn into the fabric of Kuwait's politics and society not so much through dictatorial methods but rather by conciliation and wholesale co-option in the post-oil era."[38] A vibrant political atmosphere has emerged as a result. Though political parties are banned and political blocs have no legal status, they take on largely the same duties as parties, organizing electoral campaigns and community outreach.[39]

The Muslim Brotherhood is one of the most effective of such blocs, having engaged in community outreach since the 1950s and its members having competed in parliamentary elections as individuals since 1963 and as a bloc since 1981.

Civil Society in Kuwait

According to Article 43 of the Kuwaiti Constitution, "freedom to form associations and unions on a national basis and by peaceful means shall be guaranteed in accordance with the conditions and manner specified by law."[40] These conditions, notably, have changed markedly depending on the domestic political climate. Civil society associations have tended to enjoy more freedom when the National Assembly is in session, while the government has traditionally sought to extend its control over these associations, seen as opposition strongholds, when parliament is disbanded.[41]

Despite certain restrictions, the political force of Kuwaiti civil society is evidenced by the fact that each time the National Assembly has been suspended without the announcement of immediate elections, as required by the constitution, Kuwaiti citizens have managed to force the reinstatement of the legislature and of any suspended constitutional rights.[42] In particular, *dīwāniyyāt* have proven successful in effecting political change when parliamentary life has been suspended. Still, just as the al-Sabah have tried to manage opposition in parliament, the ruling family has sought to co-opt civil society. As Neil Hicks and Ghanim al-Najjar explain, "In order to facilitate the articulation of competing political and religio-political trends within Kuwaiti society—the better to control them—the state has fostered the development of a broad range of semi-autonomous associations. These voluntary, professional, and mosque-based groups benefitted from state subsidies, and are regulated by legislation that ensures ultimate governmental control over their affairs."[43] Clubs and professional associations must be approved by the state.[44] In addition, these organizations are to operate solely within their officially permitted mandate.[45] In practice, however, professional associations have expressed political views, with teachers' associations in particular traditionally aligned with the Muslim Brotherhood.

Labor unions remain ineffectual in Kuwait today, in large measure due to the fact that they can only be formed by nationals, 92 percent of whom work in the public sector.[46] Like professional associations, they are also formally constrained by government charters that prohibit political action.[47] The Kuwait Chamber of Commerce and Industry is an active body, however, and serves as an important means through which merchants' traditional political gravitas has been institutionalized. It has, since the 1982 crash of the informal stock market, or Suq al-Manakh, "figured into policy formulation, negotiation, and implementation."[48]

In 1962, the government passed a law limiting the activities of voluntary associations to "social welfare purposes" and prohibiting nonnationals from becoming leaders in such organizations.[49] Under this law, voluntary associations must register with the Ministry of Social Affairs and Labor, which holds the authority to "deny an association a license, to disband an association if it was not providing benefits to society as a whole, or not following its constitution."[50] In reality, this ministry is overstretched and has not generally imposed such restrictions, leading to the emergence of the political blocs that contest parliamentary elections. In addition, public gatherings are legal, yet must be approved by the government.[51]

Kuwait, as of 2007, contained some three hundred registered NGOs, which primarily deal with issues such as education, welfare, environment, and social awareness.[52] Many of the organizations rely on the government for funding or are run by elites with ties to the ruling family.[53] To be sure, as noted by Paul Salem, "[o]nly a small portion of the NGO sector has been a source of sociopolitical dynamism, hosting debates and participating in public movements. The majority of other NGOs have remained focused on narrower sectoral or service functions, preserving a nonantagonistic relationship with the state and other elites."[54] The National Union of Kuwaiti Students (NUKS) at Kuwait University is undoubtedly politically relevant, however, often serving as a proxy for broader political battles, especially when parliament is suspended.[55] The Muslim Brotherhood, notably, has made considerable inroads in that organization, which will be discussed in chapter 5 at length.

As for media, freedom of the press is enshrined in the 1962 Constitution, and the state has five primary newspapers, all of which are "privately owned and fairly opinionated and influential."[56] In times of political turmoil, though, the government has threatened this freedom of both traditional and social media. In fact, over the course of 2013, twenty-five people, including three former MPs, were arrested for "insulting the amir" through speeches or social media platforms.[57] And between 2013 and 2015, ninety cases were reported in the Kuwaiti media of arrests on grounds of insulting the amir, other state officials, and/or their policies or behavior, or criticizing leaders of allied states.[58] The introduction of a new Communications Law in 2014 and Cybercrime Law in 2015 explicitly allowed such arrests; according to Human Rights Watch, their use of vague language in their definition of criminal offenses allows for the restriction of free expression, granting prison sentences for insulting religion, religious figures, or the amir and expanding the government's ability to control content on the Internet.[59]

The Kuwaiti system of allowing limited freedoms to parliament, as well as to civil society, has distinguished the emirate from its neighbors. In short, as Hicks and al-Najjar put it, "[p]erhaps inadvertently, Kuwait's ruling family can be said to have demonstrated that decentralization of power, and the fostering of a competitive political environment, albeit within limits, can greatly enhance the legitimacy of a government."[60] The government has been credited with allowing the participation of a diverse group of actors in politics, including Islamists, yet it has managed to institute policies to ensure al-Sabah dominance of the political system.[61]

A BRIEF POLITICAL HISTORY OF QATAR

In contrast to Kuwait and largely due to the prominence of the pearl trade in Qatar, a settled community did not develop there until the late nineteenth century. At least half of Qatar's population—the highest ratio in the region—was directly involved in the trade.[62] First-hand reports from the nineteenth century reflected a political scene "of terrible insecurity," with no leader able to control the peninsula's roaming settlements—in particular because pearl merchants could easily opt to move, as their trade did not require a territorial base.

By 1862, three settlements that comprise present-day Doha came under the control of Muhammad bin Thani (r. 1847–1876) alongside a Bahraini governor, representing an important step toward the settlement of the population.[63] Until the 1860s, however, Qatari politics was marked by struggles with Bahrain due to its historical claims over Qatari land. In fact, naval attacks between the two motivated Britain to sign an agreement with Muhammad bin Thani in 1868, which amounted to "the first formal recognition of Qatari independent sovereignty [from Bahrain] by the British."[64] Significantly, this document also stated that it was Muhammad bin Thani's responsibility to protect the tribes of Qatar, thereby institutionalizing al-Thani rule.[65] The 1893 Battle of Wajba, in which Shaykh Jassim bin Muhammad al-Thani (r. 1876–1913), along with a number of tribes in Qatar, defeated Ottoman forces, was another milestone in cementing al-Thani authority. Following the Ottomans' formal renunciation of their claims to Qatar in 1913, the Anglo-Qatari Treaty of 1916 solidified the al-Thani's status as the ruling family and decisively distinguished Qatar as a separate entity from Bahrain.[66] The agreement was similar to those signed with the rulers of the emirates composing the present-day UAE, demanding close cooperation with the British in maintaining maritime peace.

When, in the 1920s, Japanese cultured pearls became popular, and global financial slowdown harmed the pearling market, Qatar's economy was devastated. Unlike its neighbors, Qatar had no other significant commercial activities. The decline of the pearl trade therefore had far-reaching consequences, leading to large-scale emigration. In fact, according to Jill Crystal, this economic crisis "almost destroyed Qatar."[67]

The arrival of oil the following decade changed the nation's fortunes dramatically. As in Kuwait, the new revenue "allowed the rulers to deal directly with the population, to implement distributive policies that bypassed pre-existing alliance structures. By hiring nationals directly into the bureaucracy, the rulers deprived the merchants of a politically useful workforce."[68] Such policies helped the al-Thani, like the ruling families of Kuwait and UAE, to strengthen their authority and to create a super-rentier state.[69] Oil also introduced the problem of distribution among family members, which has been particularly controversial among the fractious al-Thani family.[70] In fact, infighting among the al-Thani family members allowed the British to maintain inroads into Qatari internal politics well into the twentieth century.[71]

In 1968, in an attempt to draw down its forces overseas, the British government announced that it would withdraw from all territories east of the Suez Canal by 1971. This pronouncement was received by leaders in the small Gulf states with shock and trepidation.[72] Eager to maintain security from external threats, the small states of Bahrain, Qatar, and constituent emirates of the present-day UAE (Abu Dhabi, Ajman, Dubai, Fujairah, Ras al-Khaimah, Sharjah, and Umm al-Quwain) began discussions about forming a single independent federation.[73] Throughout these talks, the rulers disagreed about the nature of the union and appropriate leadership of it. When Bahrain withdrew from the proposed body in 1970, Qatar set about writing a preliminary constitution, its first step toward independence, which was formally declared in September 1971.

In February 1972, Shaykh Khalifa bin Hamad al-Thani (r. 1972–1995) instituted an amended provisional constitution and created the Advisory Council, whose thirty-five members he appointed and who could "offer suggestions on draft laws issued by the cabinet."[74] Shaykh Khalifa also passed the 1972 Basic Law, which stated that the amir must be an al-Thani .[75] In addition, he developed the state's welfare system by investing heavily in education, health care, and other programs to assist nationals.[76] By decreasing disbursements to family members and nationalizing the state's oil industry in 1976,[77] Shaykh Khalifa was able to provide a 30 percent increase in social aid, a 20 percent pay raise for members of the military and civil service, and a 25 percent increase in old-age pensions.[78]

Despite launching substantial social development in Qatar, however, Shaykh Khalifa retained power largely for himself. Crystal aptly describes this period in Qatar: "There is no meaningful distinction, either political or legal, between the person of the Emir and the institutions of the state. Sovereignty is unlimited."[79] Unimpressed with his father's approach to ruling, Shaykh Hamad bin Khalifa al-Thani (r. 1995–2013) seized power in a nonviolent palace coup in June 1995.

Shaykh Hamad's takeover ushered in an era of unprecedented political and economic development. In 1999, he created a constitutional committee, charged with drafting a document to replace the provisional constitution that had been last amended in 1972.[80] Upon crafting the committee, the amir stated that the constitution "must be based on Gulf, Arab and Islamic reality, as well as on original Arab traditions and the principles of the Islamic religion."[81] Once Shaykh Hamad approved the drafted document, it was referred to the population for approval. In a referendum held in 2003, 96 percent of Qatari voters accepted the new constitution, though only some 71,400 of the eligible 150,000 nationals voted.[82]

Qatar's System of Government

Despite Article 1's assertion that the Qatari government is "democratic," several clauses preserve the primacy of the amir and the ruling family.[83] Article 67 grants the majority of executive powers to the amir, who is able to overrule legislation and rule in absence of the Advisory Council (or legislature), which he can dissolve.[84] The constitution bars the amir solely from "declaring martial law without cause and approval from the Advisory Council (Article 69), from engaging in offensive warfare (Article 71), and from issuing decrees without the eventual approval of the Advisory Council."[85] Notably, this Advisory Council is yet to be elected.

The Ruling Family Council, created and first appointed by Shaykh Hamad in June 2000, sets salaries for family members, in addition to its primary role of selecting a new amir in the case of a death or illness.[86] Further, it provides a means of granting a voice to disparate branches of the al-Thani family. The amir-appointed Council of Ministers, or Cabinet, is also traditionally composed of members of the al-Thani and notable loyalist families, yet it increasingly includes technocrats. This cabinet drafts laws for the amir to review and to which the Advisory Council can suggest amendments.[87]

The current Advisory Council, consisting of thirty-five members, each appointed for four years, has little independent authority and primarily discusses laws and makes nonbinding suggestions.[88] Most members of the Council hail from important politically allied families.[89] Overall, the body is, in Kamrava's words, "used as an institutional means to keep notable Qataris connected to and vested in the political system."[90] Its members are thus primarily distinguished by their family interests rather than by ideological links. Still, Shaykh Hamad assigned the council the task of preparing the state for elections of the legislative Advisory Council.[91] Despite having been granted this serious duty, members meet solely two hours per week between November and June.[92]

Articles 76–116 of the Constitution outline the duties and procedures of the state's legislative authority—the yet-to-be-elected forty-five-member Advisory Council. The body is to include thirty members elected for four-year terms and fifteen members appointed by the amir.

Its responsibilities include drafting legislation, questioning ministers, debating decisions made by the cabinet, and reviewing the government's proposed budgets.[93] Curbing the council's power, the amir can dissolve the legislature yet must call for new elections within six months of its dissolution.[94] Though Qatar's rulers have repeatedly spoken about the importance of the legislative body, elections have been postponed several times. The date for polls was originally set for 2005 and then was scheduled for June 30, 2013. Following the transition of authority from Shaykh Hamad to Shaykh Tamim in June 2013 and a further announcement in 2016, elections will not take place before 2019, as the existing Advisory Council's term was most recently extended by three years in 2016; this extension was described as "in the public's best interest."[95]

Although the Advisory Council has not yet been elected, the first polls for the Central Municipal Council (CMC) were held in 1999. Qatari male and female nationals were eligible to elect the council's twenty-nine members. Due to the nature of the body as an arm of the Ministry of Municipality and Urban Planning, however, campaigns are apolitical and focus on "local issues" like public health, protection of the environment, and construction of roads.[96] The body itself is by no means a legislature; instead, it is "[r]esponsible for municipal affairs, agriculture, buildings and road, food quality, garbage disposal, and public health."[97]

On the whole, the Qatari government system remains personalistic, with power centralized in the ruling family. The form of government differs substantially from the more representative system described by the Qatari Constitution. Certainly, as Crystal puts it, "[t]he constitution may be a fine document, but it remains largely aspirational."[98] Al-Thani supremacy has been carefully protected, with power centralized among a handful of individuals and with the actions of secular and Islamist independent nonstate organizations facing institutional restrictions yet having informal access to government.

Civil Society in Qatar

As in the other super-rentiers, few civil society groups operate beyond the purview of the state or ruling family, and such groups are primarily apolitical. A 2013 study revealed that, of twenty-six registered organizations examined in Qatar, 65 percent function in "culture and development," reflecting their primarily apolitical nature.[99] Before any NGO can operate, it must be licensed by the government, which has refused approval for certain political, human rights, and women's organizations.[100] In addition to restrictions on the formation of organizations, their activities are constrained. As Crystal explains, "Permits are still required for public gatherings and demonstrations, and the government grants them reluctantly."[101]

Although a revised 2004 labor law granted workers the right to form associations, such groups remain largely inactive because only Qataris, 92 percent of whom are publicly employed,[102] are allowed to participate.[103] Further, labor associations are forbidden from participating in "any activity related to religion or politics."[104] The Chamber of Commerce, though it has elected its own leadership since 1998, "lacks the independence of, for example, its Kuwaiti counterpart," perhaps due to the historic absence of a strong, self-sufficient merchant class and because most of the Qatari business elite remains dependent on government contracts.[105] As far as student activism, in December 1998, Minister of Education Shaykha Ahmad al-Mahmoud al-Thani pledged to bring elected student unions to all schools,[106] yet these bodies remain largely politically irrelevant because, unlike in Kuwait, campaigns are launched by individual candidates rather than by political blocs.

In 2005, the Ministry of Civil Service Affairs and Housing issued new regulations for nongovernmental organizations and professional societies, forbidding "affiliation with groups outside Qatar and restrict[ing] membership of organizations to Qatari nationals over 18 years. The societies are not allowed to deal with political issues and all their activities, including fundraising, are monitored by the ministry."[107] Such rules straightforwardly restrict civil society organizations from political involvement, while also clearly banning membership to transnational groups like the Muslim Brotherhood, though the Qatari branch had completed its dissolution at this time.

The media face similar challenges. Although the Qatari government gained international attention for its establishment of Al Jazeera as an independent entity in 1996, the news agency remains financed by the government through Qatar Gas[108] and under the control of an al-Thani chairman since 2011.[109] The country's major radio and television stations, Qatar Radio and Qatar Television, are state-owned as well. Though Qatar's major newspapers are privately owned in principle, their board members and owners often hail from the ruling family or have ties to the government. For example, the chairman of the influential daily *al-Watan*, Hamad bin Suhaim al-Thani, is a member of the ruling family, while the former foreign minister Hamad bin Jassim bin Jabr al-Thani owns half of the newspaper.[110] Another leading Arabic daily *al-Sharq* and the English daily *The Peninsula* are under the leadership of chairman Shaykh Thani bin ʿAbdullah al-Thani.[111]

A 2012 media law also restricts domestic journalism considerably. Article 53 of the legislation prohibits publishing or broadcasting information that would "throw relations between the state and the Arab and friendly states into confusion" or "abuse the regime or offend the ruling family or cause serious harm to the national or higher interests of the state."[112] Violations may lead to fines of as much as $275,000,[113] while public criticism of the amir carries a five-year prison sentence, according to Article 134 of the penal code.[114] A cybercrimes law introduced in 2014 allows for the punishment of anyone who shares or posts online content that "violates social values or principles" or "insults or slanders others," thus harming freedom of expression, according to Amnesty International.[115] Human Rights Watch identified the closure of independent news website *Doha News* in November 2016 to be potentially a reflection of a tightening media environment in Qatar, though its closure was mandated due to improper licensing[116]

The Qatari government's co-optation of the public sphere, though complete, could be characterized as a soft co-optation. The state has used high-level projects such as the establishment of Al Jazeera and rhetoric reiterating the government's commitment to political reform to enhance public opinion of the government. Nonetheless, domestic political debates continue largely through private majlis meetings, which are the site of "political give-and-take and consensus-building" on social, economic, and political issues and manage to include large swaths of the small national population.[117] It is in these uninstitutionalized settings that Islamists exert political influence in Qatar.

A BRIEF POLITICAL HISTORY OF THE UAE

As the Trucial States under British protection in the nineteenth century, the seven emirates of the present-day UAE were under the control of tribal shaykhs. Each such local ruler was "not so much a territorial overlord as one who held the allegiance of several tribes or tribal groups."[118] Power structures and territorial boundaries remained fluid, though the authority of ruling families was solidified when the British made treaties with them. Certainly, as Christopher Davidson explains, "in many ways the centuries-old ebb and flow of tribal power had been frozen in time, as Britain signed treaties with whichever family happened to hold the reins of power at the time."[119] Aside from strengthening certain families, by categorizing the grouping of seven separate emirates into the Trucial States, the British made these previously independent tribal emirates more likely to cooperate with one another after British withdrawal.[120]

Because its interest in the region was primarily commercial, the British government worked to expand trade with and secure the passage of goods through the Trucial States to India. A mercantile culture already existed in the area, with Dubai a commercial center centuries before the discovery of oil and with Sharjah Port particularly important in the pearl trade. Thus, a merchant class and limited commercial infrastructure existed in parts of the UAE before the arrival of the British and the discovery of oil. The Trucial States had only limited interaction with one another, though, until they came together in 1971 as an independent state.

Local rulers began formulating an independent UAE after the announcement of the withdrawal of British protection in 1968, a proclamation that was received, at least by the ruling elite, with "intense disappointment, as many felt that much of the recent development work would stall or be undone without further British support."[121] The creation of the UAE was therefore a reactive measure following British withdrawal rather than a natural step toward consolidating the existing power of local shaykhs.[122] Abu Dhabi and Dubai were the first to join forces in February 1968 and two weeks later invited the Qatari and Bahraini rulers, as well as rulers of the other five emirates of the present-day UAE, to sign on to their federation.

Despite the withdrawal of Bahrain and Qatar, the union's draft constitution remained largely unchanged and was adopted as a provisional document by the UAE in December 1971. Drafters of the Emirati Constitution clearly took into consideration the political sensitivities of potential members hesitant to surrender their local authority.[123] Even today, Frauke Heard-Bey points out, "the constitution of the UAE reflects the political reality of the time . . . that the individual emirates were not yet ready to give up their identity, and their rulers could certainly not imagine relinquishing their authority in the face of such crucial changes."[124] As a measure of such hesitance, Ras al-Khaimah did not join the union until February 1972. Further, the provisional constitution was renewed several times before it was finally made permanent in 1996, thereby solidifying the existing system.[125] The state also integrated its armed forces for the first time that year, some twenty-five years after the union's establishment.[126]

The UAE's Government System

Notwithstanding its unique federal system, the UAE resembles its neighbors in that it remains "essentially tribal and authoritarian."[127] Nonetheless, the Emirati Constitution commits the union to progress " 'towards a complete representative democratic rule,' but precedes that with the observation that federal rule must be established 'in harmony with the emirates' existing conditions and potential,' clearly indicating that traditional social and cultural norms would shape the new state's evolution."[128]

The federal system described by the Emirati Constitution is hierarchical, with the president and vice president holding central authority.[129] While all emirates retain their individual ruling families, the president is universally considered the leader of the federation, and the vice president also holds considerable political power, namely presiding over the Council of Ministers, or Cabinet,[130] and serving as president in his absence.[131] The president and vice president are chosen from the Federal Supreme Council, composed of the leaders of the seven emirates, for five-year re-electable terms. Despite this election process, the ruler of Abu Dhabi has traditionally held the presidency, while the leader of Dubai has been elected as vice president.[132] As head of the Federal Supreme Council, the president gains a great deal of authority when that body is not in session.[133] The president also serves as ceremonial head of state and retains the last word in the selection of Cabinet, while maintaining authority to oversee the implementation of legislation through the Council of Ministers.[134]

Aside from the president and vice president, there are three primary organs of national government. The Federal Supreme Council comprises the leaders of the seven emirates and organizes the national agenda, in addition to electing the president and vice president, preparing the budget, and approving national legislation and international treaties.[135] The dominance of Abu Dhabi and Dubai is felt in this institution. Article 49 of the constitution specifies that, in the Federal Supreme Council, procedural matters can be determined through a majority vote, yet that votes on substantive matters require a majority of five, provided that Abu Dhabi and Dubai are included.[136] Significantly, no list of "substantive matters" is included in the document, leaving it open to interpretation and possible co-optation by the two leading emirates.[137] In addition, only the rulers of Dubai and Abu Dhabi hold veto power in this body.[138]

The Council of Ministers is considered "the real seat of legislative authority."[139] It is selected by the president in consultation with the Federal Supreme Council and includes members of the ruling families and their allies, in addition to a small number of technocrats.[140] The body is responsible for approving presidential decrees, can write legislation after receiving approval from the Federal Supreme Council, and reports to the president and Supreme Council.[141] The cabinet also allows the rulers to grant positions to politically relevant individuals, endeavoring to strike a balance through "an informal quota system" among the emirates (though the most significant posts go to Abu Dhabians and Dubaians),[142] in addition to "an acceptably high ratio of commoners to shaikhs."[143]

The Federal National Council (FNC), the UAE's only elected body, is sometimes described as the legislative branch of government, though it holds little independent authority. The Council of Ministers determines which issues the FNC can debate and is not legally bound to heed the FNC's suggestions, making the council little more than a forum for debate.[144] The FNC in reality, as Malcon C. Peck observes, "resembles more closely a traditional consultative *diwan* [council] or *majlis* than a modern representative body."[145] Further, the FNC is chosen by an electoral college comprising, as of 2015, 224,279 members, or less than half of the Emirati national population.[146]

At the emirate level, ruler-appointed executive councils have been instituted in all emirates, with Umm al-Quwain the last to do so in 2011.[147] In each, according to Heard-Bey, "the mix of personalities would still today not be very different if the members were chosen by the ballot box, because tribal leaders are trusted representatives of their communities, and a local businessman, who has made good, may be entrusted with public affairs."[148] Such councils thus serve as a means of managing emirate-level affairs while also granting a seat at the table, so to speak, to notables; private interests, rather than political or ideological blocs, are represented. Local authority is also preserved through Article 23 of the Emirati Constitution, which states that "the natural resources and wealth in each emirate shall be considered to be the public property of that emirate."[149] In other words, constituent emirates are not required to share their wealth with other members of the union. This proviso has sparked considerable domestic political debate, as the leading emirates could potentially use it as a means of guarding their wealth from the poorer emirates.

Abu Dhabi continues to underwrite the federation with its oil wealth, while Dubai expands non-oil sectors, and the remaining five emirates seek to develop their economies with varying degrees of success. The smaller emirates, however, "often find it difficult to secure the necessary capital" to embark on infrastructure and business projects that would enable them to become more self-sufficient.[150] The central government, mainly through Abu Dhabi, has funded ruling families of the poorer emirates to allow these local rulers to maintain their authority through the provision of welfare in particular.[151] In so doing, emirate-level rulers have garnered more local authority and have become increasingly hesitant to cede power to the central authorities.[152]

This relationship of reluctant dependence of the peripheral emirates on the leading emirates is an important feature of the Emirati political system. As explained by Heard-Bey, "The integrity of every local emirate's autonomy remains an all-important principle in the UAE's political landscape. Throughout the more than three decades of its existence, the political life of the UAE was beholden to a 'push-me-pull-you' relationship of the local versus the central powers."[153] The most prominent state-wide disagreements in the UAE have concerned the issue of federal versus local authority. Attempts to formulate a permanent constitution between 1976 and 1979 pitted the al-Nahyan of Abu Dhabi, who favored greater integration, against the al-Maktoum of Dubai and the al-Qasimi of Ras al-Khaimah, who preferred local autonomy. This led to the system of reconfirming the provisional constitution every five years, which prevailed until 1996.

Considering that the UAE is religiously, ethnically, and socially diverse, it is somewhat remarkable that the union has proven to be such a success.[154] Still, complete integration of all emirates has not taken place—in large measure due to the prevalence of tribalism, intermittent clashes over land, and what Ali Mohammad Khalifa dubs "the paternal and personal nature of political leadership, and immigration."[155] The government has been careful to ensure that the freedom of independent political actors, especially Islamists, is restricted in a divided environment.

Civil Society in the UAE

The Ministry of Social Affairs grants licenses solely for civil society groups that are not considered "interfering in politics or matters harming the security of the State and the governing regime."[156] Further stifling civil society, public assemblies and associations must receive government approval to function.[157] A 2008 law granted the Ministry of Social Affairs the authority to oversee any society's activities to ensure that they remain within the scope of the document approved by the ministry, in addition to giving it the power to oversee finances of the society.[158] Due to such restrictions, there are few independent civil society organizations, as most remain under the purview of a federal ministry, a branch of an emirate-level government, or a prominent member of a ruling family.[159]

As of 2009, the UAE housed some one hundred registered NGOs.[160] The largest number existed in Abu Dhabi (twenty-eight), followed by Dubai (nineteen), Ras al-Khaimah (twelve), and Sharjah (eleven).[161] The political sector of civil society is virtually nonexistent, however. As of 2017, ninety-two NGOs were listed as registered in the UAE, sixty-six of which were related to development, a category that includes organizations ranging from Emirates Arabian Horse Soceity to the Arab Science and Technology Foundation, and only three of which are faith-based;[162] none of the NGOs listed is related to politics. In fact, Article 180 of the penal code criminalizes the establishment of, or participation in, any organization "aiming at overthrowing, seizing, or opposing the basic principles supporting the government regime in the State, or preventing any institution of the state or any public authority from exercising its functions, or attempting at the citizens' personal or other freedom or public rights guaranteed by the constitution or law, or harming the national unity of social peace."[163] Private majlis gatherings allow a limited outlet for political discussion, self censorship is rather common and the vague language of new legislation allows for greater government reach into private life.[164]

Professional associations provide a forum for employees to share work-related concerns but "are essentially limited to making recommendations on behalf of their members" to the Ministry of Labor and Social Affairs.[165] Notably, such bodies can include expatriates, though these members do not have voting rights and cannot serve on leadership boards.[166] While professional associations have in some instances managed to lobby the government, "ministries retain the right to supervise, inspect, and disband all such organizations."[167] Independent professional associations have been closed or co-opted by government dismissal of elected board members.[168] The UAE Jurist Association and UAE Teachers' Association, both traditional Muslim Brotherhood strongholds, were politically neutralized in this way in 2011.[169]

In addition, trade unions, strikes, and collective bargaining have been outlawed, though a labor strike was staged in May 2013 in Dubai; worker demands were not answered, and those involved in the strike against construction giant Arabtec were deported.[170] A workers' sit-in in Dubai in March 2015 concerning overtime rates was broken up by Dubai Police and similarly failed to lead to policy change.[171] The Chambers of Commerce, one from each emirate, have, for the most part, also been co-opted by the government, as their members are appointed by emirate-level rulers, aside from the Abu Dhabi Chamber.[172] While student associations also exist, they are apolitical. The Muslim Brotherhood once held sway in the Union of Emirati Students, founded in 1982 at UAE University (UAEU).[173] Today, elections to a partially appointed student council are held at UAEU, yet, as in Qatar, candidates run as individuals and thus are not linked with any type of political bloc or ideology.

The central government's restriction of the press has been as extensive as its regulations on civil society. In 2006, the Ministry of Information was dissolved, and many of its former employees moved to the newly established National Media Council (NMC). The council is responsible for "the supply of official press releases through its Emirates News Agency (WAM), the blacking out of nudity in media output (still by using black felt tip on newspaper and magazine articles), and the provision of funding for local filmmakers."[174] The NMC also monitors foreign media sources' output about the UAE and bans materials that it deems inappropriate for social and political reasons.[175] Further, the Federal Press and Publications

Law passed in 2009 announced new, harsher penalties for journalists who write pieces considered " 'disparaging senior government officials or the royal family' or 'misleading the public and harming the economy.' "[176] In 2012, the Federal Decree on Combatting Cybercrimes came into effect, which, according to Amnesty International, "contains broad and sweeping provisions that severely constrain free expression," with punishments ranging from large fines to imprisonment for criticism of the Emirati authorities.[177] The 2014 Terrorism Law, due to its "overly broad definition of terrorism," is also said to further limit free speech.[178]

As in Qatar, domestic politics is rarely mentioned in favor of coverage of economic news and international politics.[179] Further squelching free press is the fact that the majority of the country's most popular newspapers is controlled by the government or receives sizable government subsidies. Dubai's Arabic daily, *al-Bayani*, and two other Arabic dailies are owned by emirate governments.[180] The three other Arabic dailies, like Sharjah's *al-Khaleej*, benefit from government subsidies.[181] English daily newspapers like Dubai's *Gulf News* and *Khaleej Times* and Sharjah's *Gulf Today* also are granted state subsidy support.[182] Two newer publications in Dubai, *Emirates Today* and *Seven Days*, appear to operate independently of the state, yet are primarily marketed as tabloids.[183] In large measure due to the financial control that the government holds over the media, it has been possible for members of the regime to pronounce publicly the need for free press while taking few steps to advance it in practice.

Unlike in the other two states under study, there is a sense that the Emirati government's control goes beyond censorship and involves the monitoring of emails, website visits, and telephone calls, especially when it comes to Islamist activity.[184] In fact, several Emiratis interviewed were hesitant to speak until mobile phones had been switched off or batteries removed, and many spoke only on the condition of anonymity. In the words of one, "The UAE became a full-fledged security state, intervening in all aspects of civil life since 2005 . . . . Security services are in all ministries [and] all active NGOs linked to human rights, journalism, and lawyers."[185] The Emirati government has been particularly sensitive to the popular appeal of Islamists and thus has taken care to restrict their ability to express their opinions and to meet by centralizing state power, particularly in the security sector.

UNDERSTANDING SIMILARITIES AND DIFFERENCES AMONG SUPER-RENTIERS

Governed by powerful ruling families, independent institutionalized political life in super-rentiers is hampered, and civil society and politics remain largely informal. More formal is the power of Islam in these states. The constitutions of all of the super-rentiers proclaim Islam the state religion and Islamic law "a main source of legislation."[186] Despite managing secular styles of government, then, rulers remain reliant on Islam both to direct their rule and to solidify their legitimacy. Still, these states provide different environments for political Islam.

Kuwait's experience has demonstrated that monarchy and parliamentary government can coexist in a super-rentier state. Unlike in the other super-rentiers, the character of Kuwaiti politics is to a large degree determined by which political blocs hold power in the National Assembly. Still, the al-Sabah family retains the privileges of the other rulers in the Gulf. In essence, as Shafeeq Ghabra describes, "[t]he complicated interaction between the state's Sabah rulers, formal groups and society, with all of its informal underpinnings, is a dynamic mix of fluid corporatism and restricted pluralism."[187] While the Kuwaiti political system has allowed Islamist actors to come to the fore, the government continues to retain its authority over such actors, leading to something of a tug-of-war between government and Islamist forces and occasional cooperation between the two.

In Qatar, the ruling family undoubtedly dominates the political scene, which is highly personality-driven and uninstitutionalized. The al-Thani family had the advantage of coming to power in a state with few competing powerful families and without a strong merchant class to challenge its rule.[188] Today, Islam is the primary ideological inspiration for Qatar's national population, yet its influence largely remains uninstitutionalized. In Qatar's personalistic political system, it is perhaps unsurprising that Brotherhood influence is not formalized through an institutional structure.

In the UAE, despite divisions among the various emirates, "most government departments and authorities remain opaque and secretive."[189] In an atmosphere where the federal government has sometimes struggled to maintain control, opposition movements, in particular Islamist groups, have been repressed. The segmented nature of the UAE's federal system, however, made it possible for the Brotherhood to survive for decades. The fact that each emirate differs from the others also adds to societal tensions often expressed by Islamist groups.

While we have established that Islamism functions in different ways in each of the super-rentiers, we have yet to discover exactly how Muslim Brotherhood affiliates have adapted to such circumstances and how they operate in such states, depending on political opportunity structures afforded them. To do so, we turn to our case studies, first examining how the Ikhwan emerged in Kuwait and then in Qatar and the UAE as a social group that has become a major social and political actor.

PART II

Rise and Fall

4

Education and Influence

ORIGINS OF RENTIER ISLAMISM

INTRODUCTION

The Kuwaiti, Qatari, and Emirati branches of the Muslim Brotherhood followed similar trajectories in their first decades. Each gained a following, primarily through the education sector, where many Brotherhood sympathizers from outside the Gulf taught and inspired the creation of indigenous Ikhwan movements. Due to the political challenge posed by Arab nationalism at the time of the Brotherhood's rise, rentier governments welcomed the formation of the Islamist groups, considering them to be a helpful bulwark against pan-Arabism, which they regarded as more threatening to their authority. Aided by their ties to ruling elites, then, rentier Islamists managed to boost their popularity, primarily using avenues of social and cultural activities in their first decades and then turning to more overtly political matters later in their development, particularly in Kuwait. In this chapter, we trace the founding years of Brotherhood movements in Kuwait, Qatar, and the United Arab Emirates (UAE), roughly covering the years 1951–1975 and analyzing how they gained a following and political influence in hydrocarbon states not traditionally known for housing independent Islamist movements.

THE KUWAITI BROTHERHOOD

Kuwait houses the oldest and most organized Muslim Brotherhood branch among the super-rentiers, its affiliate, having been founded over a decade before the others under study.[1] The Kuwaiti organization is also the most entrenched in the institutionalized political system of any Brotherhood affiliate in the Gulf, as it has successfully contested parliamentary elections as a bloc since the 1980s. The local branch of the Ikhwan was founded in 1951, with the aim of Islamizing Kuwaiti society in the face of Western encroachment. Today, in its capacity as a political bloc, the Kuwaiti Brotherhood influences major policy decisions and political debate and continues to hold broader influence through its social arm. Despite the existence of a generous welfare package to citizens, Brotherhood activity has persisted, proving that it cannot be bought off, as rentier state theory predicts. Rather, rentier Islamists adapt to political systems where they are afforded limited political opportunities by infiltrating the social sector before turning to institutionalized politics.

One Islamic Constitutional Movement (ICM) parliamentarian describes the history of the Kuwaiti Brotherhood as having passed through five stages.[2] The first lasted from the 1940s until the 1960s, during which time "there was no political work. The Muslim Brotherhood focused on charity, *da'wa*[3], *tarbīa*."[4] The second phase began in the 1970s, when political work started "but in an independent way, not organized."[5] The third stage came in 1981 when Jam'iat al-Islah al-Ijtima'i (Islah) stood for elections in parliament as a bloc, and thus officially took on a political role.[6] The creation of the ICM in 1991 marked the fourth phase, as "we decided the Muslim Brotherhood needed a political role in a separate way."[7] The MP insists that the ICM has now entered a new stage, during which the ICM and Islah are working increasingly as a political party, with an emphasis on reforming the government system.[8]

In this section, we focus on the Kuwaiti Muslim Brotherhood's development through the first of these stages, revealing how the movement's social activities translated into political capital—a common trajectory for rentier Islamists. The organization's maturation also illustrates the superficiality of the division between the social/cultural and the political in the Kuwaiti context, as the Brotherhood's role in the social sphere heralded its rise to political relevance. Throughout the Gulf, because social policy is highly politicized and a means through which governments can strengthen their legitimacy, it is logical that Islamists who began agitating to challenge cultural secularization or Westernization have become politically relevant actors as well. Another unique aspect of Brotherhood activity in super-rentier states is the degree to which governments there have managed to co-opt the religious arena, making the informal social sector an even more likely place for Islamists to gather.

Challenges to "Establishment Islam"

The Islamic sector has long held substantial social and political capital in Kuwait. The government has spent large sums to fund religious education and mosques to help gain the support of ulama who have historically backed the al-Sabah rule.[9] Furthermore, the Education Ministry, along with the Ministry of Awqaf and Islamic Affairs, oversees the curricula of religious schools and the messages of Friday sermons to ensure that radical ideas, and particularly notions that could challenge Kuwaitis' loyalty to their ruler, are not spread.[10] The al-Sabah leaders have also sought to assure Kuwaitis of their own Islamic credentials by participating in religious events and using Islamic references in public rhetoric. Although the state has largely managed to co-opt "establishment Islam," it has failed to undercut support for the ideology of the Muslim Brotherhood, which has long influenced Kuwaiti society.[11]

Islamist thought was prominent in Kuwait even before the founding of the Muslim Brotherhood, and a history compiled by Ali Fahed al-Zumai is instructive in constructing the movement's background. A group of Kuwaitis, inspired by the literature of Islamic reformers Jamal al-Din al-Afghani, Muhammad 'Abduh, and Rashid Rida, began holding meetings in the house of religious scholar Shaykh Yusuf bin 'Isa al-Qina'i at the beginning of the twentieth century to discuss Islamist ideas of reform. Inspired by their ideas to update the education sector, they established the first modern Kuwaiti school, al-Mubarakiyya, in 1912.[12] As al-Mubarakiyya grew, a new generation was exposed to modern education and reformist visions of Islam. In fact, two other schools were founded by the reformers who established al-Mubarakiyya: al-Ahmadiyya in 1920 and al-Saʿada in 1924.[13] The emirate's first charity institution, the Arab Islamic Charitable Society was also established under the leadership of a well-known Islamist, philanthropist Farhan al-Khalid, in 1913.[14] The organization aimed to Islamize Kuwaiti society, promoting awareness of Islam in the face of the influence of Christian missionaries and providing social services to the poor.[15] Despite such initiatives, a local Islamist organization did not exist. Until the mid-1940s, the Kuwaiti Muslim Brotherhood comprised mainly teachers at al-Mubaraikyya or al-Ahmadiyya, and many non-Kuwaitis.[16] The Brotherhood's presence, then, took on "an embryonic form, without structure or organization" at that time.[17]

During the 1940s, as the Egyptian Muslim Brotherhood began to grow, the influence of Islamists in Kuwait's education system and intellectual life expanded. Many teachers who supported the Ikhwan traveled to Kuwait as part of the Egyptian mission of al-Azhar University and "helped to promote a good reputation in favor of the movement inside Kuwait."[18] In addition, during this period, Brotherhood founder Hasan al-Banna sent supporters of his movement to the Gulf to promote Brotherhood ideology by delivering public lectures and distributing the organization's weekly magazine.[19]

Though the Kuwaiti Brotherhood was undoubtedly influenced by the Egyptian mother organization, its development was also aided by the branch in neighboring Iraq.[20] Brotherhood bookstores in Basra, Az Zubayr, and Baghdad, founded in the mid-1940s, carried the books and brochures of the Iraqi and Egyptian organizations and were commonly brought to Kuwait.[21] Certainly, as al-Zumai describes, "the visits made by Kuwaitis to Iraq for trade and tourism and counter-visits of Iraqis to Kuwait created a kind of contact and effect."[22] By the 1950s, the Brotherhood's ideology and rejection of Western domination had spread, and a group of young Kuwaitis came to admire the organization's political aims.[23] In 1941, one such Kuwaiti man, ʿAbd al-ʿAziz ʿAli al-Mutawa, met with Egyptian teacher and Brotherhood supporter Muhammad Ahmad ʿAbd al-Hamid in Baghdad.[24] Following this encounter and al-Mutawa's expression of admiration of the Brotherhood, ʿAbd al-Hamid sent an application form for al-Mutawa's membership to the Brotherhood and an introductory letter to General Guide Hasan al-Banna.[25] Al-Mutawa then spent Ramadan in Egypt among a group of Brotherhood members in 1945, where he met al-Banna.[26] In 1946, along with his brother ʿAbdullah ʿAli, who also supported Brotherhood ideology, ʿAbd al-ʿAziz al-Mutawa met al-Banna once again at hajj,[27] where they discussed opening a branch of the Brotherhood in Kuwait.[28]

Formal Establishment of a Kuwaiti Ikhwan

The Muslim Brotherhood was formally organized in Kuwait under the banner of al-Jamʿiat al-Irshad al-Islami (The Islamic Guidance Association, hereafter Irshad) in 1951. The membership elected ʿAbd al-ʿAziz al-Mutawa as the group's first General Supervisor. The organization was headquartered at al-Mutawa's home near al-Mubarakiyya School and housed a library, a lecture hall, a management department, and a place for prayer.[29] ʿAbdullah al-Mutawa, quoted in Kuwaiti political scientist Sami Awadh's PhD dissertation, explained the birth of the Kuwaiti Muslim Brotherhood as a counterweight to Western influence: "Our Islamic movement started in the early fifties, during the period in which Kuwait was under the fierce assault from Western concepts and values of secularism and nationalism, the most noticeable of which were the Pan-Arab Nationalism, Baʿathism, and Socialism. Such an assault was meant to distract the Kuwaiti Muslims from their faith. That was the main reason for the establishment of political Islamic activities."[30] Irshad was clearly influenced by the central Brotherhood organization in Egypt, which shared this aim.

Irshad's followers comprised two major groups. First, young people influenced by contemporary Islamist ideology, in al-Zumai's estimation, "found, in this society, the symbolism and required representation enabling them to understand Islam in a modern way by presenting it in a comprehensive, up-to-date style suitable for both practical and theoretical application."[31] Second, conservative religious personalities joined Irshad largely because it "was the only [non-state] Islamic organisation present in Kuwait at that time."[32] The group's members, then, did not enroll to influence domestic political life. In fact, most members of Irshad were similar in social profile to members of other associations and clubs in Kuwait at that time: intellectuals and merchants from established Sunni families who lived primarily in the city and had the leisure time and money to devote to a civil society organization.[33] As explained by prominent Brotherhood figure Tareq al-Suwaidan, Irshad "did mostly social work, *daʿwa*, and some relief work because they [its members] came from rich families."[34]

Official Irshad documents confirm the organization's primarily social and cultural nature. Though Irshad's first constitution has been lost, amendments made by the leadership in 1957 shed light on its official aims.[35] The organization espoused seven primary goals, recorded by Kuwaiti Islamist ideologue Mustafa Muhammad al-Tahan: (1) establishing Islamic tradition and pure monotheism; (2) spreading a religious spirit in the country; (3) advancing Islamic culture and education; (4) working to reform the individual Muslim, the Muslim family, and Muslim society; (5) calling on God for wisdom and good council; (6) eliminating unemployment and fighting illiteracy; and (7) cooperating with other charity bodies both inside and outside Kuwait.[36] Toward these ends, Irshad was formally divided into four sections of organizational management: students, workers, merchants, and *daʿwa*.[37] Irshad listed the following means of achieving its goals in 1957:

> Publicity through different publishing and broadcasting methods.... This in addition to organizing delegations and missions inside Kuwait and abroad.
>
> Training the Society's members in these objectives and confirming a practical religious sense in them as individuals and families; making them bodily sound through sports, spiritually sound through worship and intellectually sound through knowledge. This is in addition to stressing the concept of true brotherhood, perfect complementarity and genuine co-operation among them, so that a united Islamic society is created and a new generation is trained that understands the true meaning of Islam, applies its teachings, and directs the renaissance toward it.[38]

These tools of action were aligned with those proposed by Hasan al-Banna, as the Kuwaiti Brotherhood, through Irshad, aimed to Islamize society from the grassroots through the social sphere—much like the Egyptian mother organization in its first decades.

Irshad's Expanding Social Role

Though Kuwait's education sector had already been exposed to Islamist ideology, Irshad contributed to further Islamist infiltration of the sector. The group established al-Irshad School, which aimed to spread Islamic thought and encourage *daʿwa*. The school grew quickly, with four hundred registered students in its second year.[39] Unlike other schools in the emirate, Irshad did not place restrictions on which students could join the school, other than that they be Muslims. Because Muslims of any nationality could enroll, al-Irshad School became a stronghold for expatriates from states that had influential Brotherhood affiliates.[40] To take on the growing number of students, many Egyptian, Syrian, Palestinian, and other Arab teachers sympathetic to Brotherhood ideology were hired in the 1950s.[41] The Teachers' Club was established shortly thereafter, and the Brotherhood earned the majority of seats in the club's management council, giving Irshad its first public and institutionalized role in a professional association.[42] Adding to its influence, the first Brotherhood student committee began in one of Kuwait's largest schools, al-Shuwaikh Secondary School.[43] Further, Kuwaiti Brotherhood members held a number of positions within state educational institutions like the Institute of Religious Studies, founded in 1947, most of whose faculty members were Egyptian graduates from al-Azhar who were sympathetic to or subscribed to Brotherhood thought; their influence was palpable in the 1950s.[44]

The Ikhwan also established the Irshad Library, which was open to the public, as well as the Center for Youth Sports and Culture, which hosted prominent Brotherhood ideologues and preachers for lectures while also organizing sporting events.[45] Further aiding the growth of Brotherhood thought was the dispatch of key leaders from Egypt to Kuwait.[46] Irshad also opened literacy classes to the general public under the umbrella of its Society Committee for Eliminating Illiteracy.[47] The organization's Department for Propagating Islamic Culture also housed a section that sold Islamic books and brochures at subsidized prices.[48] In addition to its monthly magazine *Irshad*, which was founded in 1952,[49] the organization held daily two-hour programs on the Broadcasting Station, which it managed for one and a half years at the beginning of the 1950s.[50] Irshad's takeover of the radio station from state control resulted from the government's lack of interest in the project, Irshad's impressive degree of organizational sophistication, and the nonthreatening nature of Irshad's message to the government.[51] In fact, because of its reputation for positive social and educational work, the group at first enjoyed excellent relations with the al-Sabah family. Furthermore, ʿAbd al-ʿAziz al-Mutawa was among Kuwait's wealthiest merchants and held the trust of many al-Sabah shaykhs.[52] Though it was not spreading an explicitly political message, Irshad gained control of political tools and became adept at using them to disseminate a message that primarily concerned the Islamization of society.

Islah developed other forms of social outreach as well. In the charity sector, Irshad's committees of zakat[53] created a variety of initiatives to aid the poorer segments of Kuwaiti society. Among these was "the program of dress," through which the organization provided winter clothing for people without means to buy it.[54] Irshad also registered a group of scouts with the Department of Education, which became one of Kuwait's largest scout groups.[55] Irshad arranged other activities, particularly for youth, such as acting, sports, and choral singing.[56]

In terms of strictly political activity, Irshad campaigned to spur the Committee of Kuwaiti Clubs to support Egypt during the Tripartite Aggression in 1956.[57] Similarly, Irshad backed the Algerian revolution and directed a note to the Kuwaiti government encouraging it do to the same, while calling for donations to aid the cause.[58] As far as domestic political issues, Irshad's philosophy, like that of the Kuwaiti Muslim Brotherhood today, was one of reform rather than radical change.[59] It was therefore possible for Irshad to develop "a mutual relationship of trust and respect" with the government.[60] Irshad seemed to support popular participation in government, however. When, in 1954, the term of membership of the state's councils, which oversaw state administration, ended, Irshad recommended the holding of new elections and the formal division of authority among the executive, legislature, and judiciary.[61] Nonetheless, the organization's political ideology remained uncoordinated, as the group expended most of its energy on influencing the social and educational spheres. It also faced a serious ideological challenge from the nationalist movement.

The Rising Tide of Arab Nationalism

While Islamism continued to influence Kuwaiti society, it failed to reach the political relevance of the Arab nationalist movement. The nationalists, unlike the Brotherhood, were unabashedly politically active from the start. The takeover of Gamal ʿAbdel Nasser in Egypt in 1952 led to region-wide prominence of his ideology. Nationalists won support of the Kuwaiti street, as Nasser's successes at home and abroad gave his movement increased popular support.[62] The nationalization of the Suez Canal in 1956, Egypt's unification with Syria in 1958, and the ongoing broadcast of Nasser's Voice of the Arabs radio program throughout the Middle East made Arab nationalism increasingly popular as the 1950s progressed.[63] Though Irshad was sympathetic to Nasser's rejection of Western influence, it considered secular nationalism itself to be an import from the West.

The nationalists established the Nationalist Cultural Club in 1953 as an opponent to Irshad. The movement annexed a number of Arab nationalists from Egypt and Palestine, while a substantial proportion of Kuwaiti elite and intellectuals, foremost among them Ahmad al-Khatib, also supported the nationalist movement.[64] Furthermore, nationalists in Kuwait benefitted from their control of the Workers' Club, in addition to their work in establishing the Public Union of Kuwaiti Workers.[65] Although the Brotherhood had initially found support among the merchant class, nationalists co-opted a great many of them through their infiltration of the Merchants' Market, which became a nationalist stronghold in the 1950s.[66] Sports and cultural clubs, in addition to other youth organizations, came under the control of the Arab nationalists, especially after the appearance of the Committee of Kuwaiti Clubs, the Union of Kuwaiti Clubs, and the Kuwaiti Association, all of which became part of the nationalist strategy to gain broader influence in the 1950s and came to form the backbone of the movement.[67]

Internal Division Begins in Irshad

As Arab nationalism became increasingly popular, Irshad faced challenges due to internal dissension. The first split within the Kuwaiti Brotherhood emerged between the older members of Irshad, led by General Supervisor ʿAbd al-ʿAziz al-Mutawa, and the new generation led by ʿAbd al-Rahman al-ʿAtiqi. Al-Mutawa accused the newer members of trying to co-opt the youth and turn them against him and of opposing the participation of older members who were loyal to him.[68] This clash essentially pitted the younger members, who, as al-Zumai puts it, "by virtue of their age, were free from all business interests and social responsibilities," against "the conservative group of older dignitaries who had extensive business interests, commercial concerns and social responsibilities."[69] While younger members were less compromising in their pursuit of Irshad's goals, the older generation was wary of clashing with or alienating portions of Kuwaiti society or the government.[70]

One area of major disagreement between these factions concerned the proper reaction to arrests of Egyptian Brotherhood members under the Nasser regime. The more moderate faction, led by al-Mutawa and supported by the majority of the organization, urged neutrality on the issue. These members were reticent to risk private interests in Egypt and the strong relationship between the Kuwaiti and Egyptian governments by taking a publicly anti-Egyptian stance.[71] Meanwhile, the younger faction, which represented the student organization and was led by ʿAbd al-Rahman al-ʿAtiqi, Muhammad al-ʿAdsani, and Ahmad al-Daʿij, insisted on action.[72] They argued that the Kuwaiti movement should take a stronger position against the Nasser regime, in solidarity with fellow Ikhwan members. In the end, the moderate faction was successful, yet serious divisions remained. Despite attempts to persuade al-Mutawa to remain in authority, he submitted his resignation in the face of such internal disunity, according to al-Zumai, "on the pretext of his preoccupation with the management of his commercial affairs in Egypt and other Arab countries."[73]

The Downfall of Irshad

Following this split, in the late 1950s, Irshad's activities floundered, and the organization grew more insular.[74] Meanwhile, al-Irshad School failed to attract new, particularly Kuwaiti, students, signaling stagnation of the movement among the local population.[75] Due to the appeal of nationalists among the educated classes, where the Brotherhood had traditionally found support, the Ikhwan lost many backers.[76] The remaining group of Irshad members, al-Zumai notes, "could keep alive the Islamic activities, though on a simple basis, through its coordination and co-operation with non-Kuwaiti Ikhwan groups."[77]

The year 1959 perhaps marked the lowest point in Brotherhood power in Kuwait, as the rising tide of nationalism diminished its appeal. Furthermore, Irshad members' disappointing results[78] in the 1958 Administrative Council elections,[79] and the 1959 government prohibition of all social and cultural clubs put a formal end to its organizational power. Though there is disagreement about whether this ban affected Irshad, the group was so weak at this time that a government-mandated closure would have had little effect. Because the restriction of social clubs and publications stemmed from the government's disapproval of a celebration arranged by nationalists on the occasion of the first anniversary of the United Arab Republic,[80] some scholars maintain that Irshad was not banned, as it was considered a counterweight to the nationalist movement.[81] Regardless, Irshad closed either in 1959, as a result of the government injunction,[82] or in 1960, when members left their headquarters and did not look for a new one.[83] Though Irshad closed, Brotherhood ideology remained, and Ikhwan-led and financed study circles, lectures, gatherings, and charity projects continued.[84] It was not until after a new law for clubs and public welfare societies was established in 1962 that the Brotherhood organized itself again.[85] Significantly, this law specified that new groups "must not interfere in politics, religious disputes or provocation of sectarian or racial fanaticism."[86]

Independence and the Founding of Islah

In 1963, deciding to revive the Brotherhood movement in newly independent Kuwait, former members of Irshad gathered in the *dīwāniyya* of Fahad al-Hamad al-Khalid to discuss the founding of a new association.[87] The result was the establishment of Islah in July 1963, a group that remains active today. The organization's initial membership was composed primarily of "[r]emnants of al-Irshad; some religious scholars; judges with an Islamic cultural background, in addition to numbers of citizens from religious conservative groups (especially of Najdi origin)."[88] The aims and activities of Islah closely resembled those of Irshad.[89] The organization's primary goals were listed as (1) antivice and resistance to social pests and harmful habits; (2) guidance to youth; (3) a return to Islamic legislation, especially in areas of education and media; (4) finding solutions for the dilemmas facing Islamic society; (5) engaging in *da'wa* and spreading virtuous morals throughout society; (6) encouraging acts of kindness and charity as well as advocacy for justice according to the Islamic example; (7) freedom of the mind and thought from ignorance; (8) education of youth in the Islamic manner; (9) maintenance of Islamic rules; (10) realizing social justice and ensuring it for all citizens; and (11) supporting Arab and the Islamic unity.[90] Though several of these goals were strictly social and religious, others had become more focused on changing government policy, with explicit mention of the prevailing political authorities and the need for their involvement in Islamizing Kuwaiti legislation.

Importantly, although the Brotherhood had a principal role in the establishment, management, and administration of Islah, it lacked an independent structure.[91] In fact, Brotherhood members failed to distinguish themselves as committed to Ikhwan ideology and members of Islah.[92] This dynamic was aided by the fact that most Islah members, though most were not Ikhwan, acceded to the primacy of Ikhwan ideology.[93] When Yusuf al-Hajji took over leadership of Islah in 1963, the group began to focus on renewing its efforts to spread Islamist thought and combat the rising tide of Arab nationalism, which aligned with Brotherhood aims.

Throughout the 1960s, the international Brotherhood represented "the cultural and organizational artery of the Muslim Brotherhood movement" in Kuwait.[94] In the mid-1960s, the mother group even sent a group of Kuwaiti Brotherhood youth to Syria and Jordan to take a course on organizational and cultural work, in addition to dispatching several Egyptians to Kuwait to spread the Ikhwan message.[95] During this period and throughout the 1980s, the Kuwaiti Brotherhood, as described by Nathan J. Brown, "was often influenced by the parent Egyptian organization. Formal ties existed (until 1991), but the model of the Egyptian organization—with its networking activities and organizational efforts—proved far more influential than formal ties. More important still were the personal contacts."[96]

Similar to Irshad, Islah has focused on intensive training in ideology and scholarship, as well as athletic and cultural activities, in addition to *da'wa*.[97] Beginning in the 1960s, Islah's Cultural Committee sponsored popular events for specific weeks—weeks of Ramadan, hajj, and the Qur'an, among others—which attracted large numbers of Kuwaitis.[98] In 1968, Irshad opened its first center for the memorization of the Qur'an in al-Irshad School.[99] By 1980, the number of Qur'an memorization schools had reached approximately sixty, with more than five thousand students among them.[100] Islah recruited new members through these centers, as the schools essentially "turned into undeclared party headquarters."[101] Its position in learning centers also allowed Islah to hold sway in a number of mosques and religious foundations, thereby influencing the broader social arena.[102]

In all of its endeavors, Islah enjoyed relative freedom from government influence, since the authorities feared the power of Arab nationalists over that of the religious movement, as evidenced by British records during the 1960s on this matter.[103] Furthermore, the group had long proven effective in hosting social programs and improving education. Because of their good relationship with the government due to their largely nonconfrontational stance, Brotherhood members gained positions in the state apparatus, enhancing their ability to spread Ikhwan ideology. Islah leader Yusuf al-Hajji served as minister of *awqāf* during the 1960s[104] and was named justice minister in 1972.[105] Former Brotherhood MP Yusuf al-Rafaʿi was appointed minister of the state for cabinet affairs in 1967; prominent member ʿAbd al-Rahman al-ʿAtiqi became minister of oil and finance in 1971.[106] The Brotherhood used its long-standing relationship with the ruling family to pressure for the implementation of sharia, conceding in the interim to limited political participation.[107] During this period, for example, the Brotherhood began a campaign to amend Article 2 of the Kuwaiti Constitution to proclaim Islamic sharia *the* rather than *a* primary source of legislation.[108]

The Brotherhood also focused on influencing state educational establishments and instruments of the media to win over the next generation of Kuwaitis.[109] Through its relationship with the government, Islah progressed toward its social goals through its political posts, which they had ironically gained through the organization's social capital. Members of Islah managed to use ministerial positions to advance their Islamist social agenda, with the education and information ministries particularly important, as positions in these institutions allowed them to place restrictions on curricula, books, and television.[110] Despite influence in the ministries, however, the Brotherhood's gains in electoral politics remained limited.

Electoral Politics of the 1960s

Kuwait's first National Assembly elections, held in 1963, confirmed the primacy of Arab nationalism: Islah's seven candidates garnered 2,784 votes, compared to the sixteen Arab nationalist candidates who received 10,277 votes.[111] Though it undoubtedly held political and social capital and gained three seats in the 1963 parliament, members of the Brotherhood, as Falah ʿAbdulla al-Mdaires puts it, "did not raise themselves politically in the period of the 1960s in a clear way except they were active in pressuring the first National Assembly in 1963 to amend article 206 of the penal code and prevent the sale of alcohol in Kuwait."[112] Aside from social policies, the Brotherhood was unable to create any coherent political platform.[113]

The 1967 election saw the beginning of the downfall of the nationalist strand in Kuwait, which was by no means due to the rising popularity of Islamists. Kuwaiti nationalists' involvement in election fraud, in addition to Nasser's defeat to Israel in June 1967, the disintegration of the United Arab Republic, and the fall of nationalism in Yemen and Mosul signaled the beginning of the end for the movement and an opening for the Brotherhood.[114] Despite diminishing support for nationalists, however, only one Islah member gained a seat in the National Assembly.[115]

Internal Reform of Islah

The decline of the nationalist movement coincided with a change in Islah's tactics. The organization's unsuccessful entry into policymaking, such as its failure to amend article 2 of the constitution and to implement strict gender segregation, led many members of the Brotherhood to believe they needed a new means of achieving political influence.[116] Still, the organization held a degree of popular support, as demonstrated by the successful declaration of a law to prohibit alcohol in 1965.[117] To secure greater political relevance, Islah embarked on internal reforms.

Until the late 1960s, Brotherhood members within Islah had "continued to merge themselves into the Jamʿiyat al-Islah as a shapeless inner group of individuals without any special organisation."[118] At that time, the Brotherhood's desire to enter political life was hampered by Islah's establishment as a religious organization. Nonetheless, the board of directors was dominated by Ikhwan members and sympathizers.[119] Frustrated by their lack of political success yet heartened by the decline of Arab nationalism, these Brotherhood members, al-Zumai recounts, "adopted new organisational, dynamic and secret methods, whilst at the same time keeping their strong influence in al-Islah, which in turn became a supporter for their movement. This turned al-Islah into an Ikhwan façade in most of its issues and ideological and cultural attitudes, rather than an independent ally with a separate ideological approach."[120]

At that time, the writings of prominently imprisoned Egyptian Brotherhood member Sayyid Qutb had begun to influence the Arab world, and the Brotherhood started positioning itself as "the revolutionary alternative" to secular and Western nationalism.[121] Qutb's notion of the importance of faith in overcoming society's moral deterioration was particularly appealing to a conservative Kuwaiti public unhappy with the increasing importation of foreign ideas and customs. This influence played a large role in changing the Brotherhood's methods, as a new generation of Ikhwan youth became ever more active and eager to win more popular support inside Kuwait.[122] They called for a re-evaluation of Brotherhood strategy, with the aim of injecting new life into the movement.[123]

As part of this reassessment, Islah expanded its activities. The organization moved its headquarters to a larger facility in Al Rawda in 1970. This building, funded by donations from members and a government grant and still in use today, houses a library, a theater, sports facilities, a mosque, and a youth center.[124] Also in 1970, Islah transformed its internal monthly brochure *al-Islah*, which it had produced since 1965, into the weekly and broadly circulated magazine *al-Mujtama* (The Society).[125] This magazine, which remains in distribution, became the principal voice of the international Brotherhood organization, as government repression in Egypt, Syria, and Yemen prevented these branches from releasing publications.[126] Islah also developed youth and social programs. In addition, zakat committees were established and operated from mosque headquarters to collect and distribute donations and alms for the poor.[127] Women's committees were also successful in explaining and spreading Islah's views to females, displacing the liberal movements that had previously held sway among Kuwaiti women.[128] Further, journeys abroad for umrah[129] and to visit the other Gulf states were arranged with Islamist societies in those countries.[130] The expansion of Islah activities led to an increase in its membership during the 1970s. Certainly, by the end of the 1960s, members of the Kuwaiti Brotherhood had, as described by al-Zumai,

> brought an end to the stage of the Ikhwan's activities based on individual enthusiasm and sentiment, and replaced it with a collective work based on a strict organisation and a defined ideology. Hence the Kuwaiti Ikhwan was renewed in form. It is true to say that this group was identical in ideology and activity to the first faction of the

> Ikhwan that existed in Kuwait in the early fifties. On the ideological level it adopted completely the Ikhwan line of the original Egyptian association, with one difference in the political field, namely, that it believed in reformist work and rejected the radical method in dealing with the political regime.[131]

Within decades of its founding, then, the Kuwaiti Muslim Brotherhood managed to make great strides in terms of creating an effective organizational structure as well as attracting different segments of society through its social outreach. During this initial period of Kuwaiti Brotherhood expansion, the Qatari Ikhwan had not yet been officially established, with the Qatari state itself founded two decades after the establishment of the Kuwaiti Ikhwan, in 1971.

ORIGINS OF A QATARI BROTHERHOOD

The Muslim Brotherhood in Qatar has a shorter history, having formed only after the state's independence in 1975. Nonetheless, Egyptian writer Mustafa ʿAshur divides the Brotherhood's history in Qatar into three stages. The first, in the mid-1950s, involved the arrival of Egyptian Brotherhood members in Qatar, eager to escape Nasser's crackdown.[132] Many of them worked in the education sector, where they influenced the curricula and thus a new generation of Qataris. The second phase of the Brotherhood's development in Qatar occurred in the 1970s when Qataris studying in Egyptian universities, among them former Brotherhood General Supervisor Jassim Sultan, became influenced by Ikhwan ideology and brought it back to Qatar after completing their studies, eager to create an indigenous organization.[133] The third stage involved the influx of Syrian Brotherhood members into Qatar at the start of the 1980s following the Asad regime's violent crackdown on the organization.[134] After this final period of organizational expansion, the Brotherhood entered a stage of internal discussion, which ended with a vote in favor of the organization's dissolution in 1999.

In this section, we trace the Brotherhood's history within Qatar through its embryonic stages and official establishment, highlighting the similarities between its trajectory toward institutionalization and that of its Kuwaiti counterpart. We thus also analyze the role of Arab nationalism as a political force and ideological rival to the Ikhwan during the 1950s and 1960s, as well as the unique political and social environment that Qatar provides Islamist actors.

The Education Sector as an Ideological Battleground

During the first phase of Brotherhood expansion in Qatar, in the 1950s and 1960s, Ikhwan ideology was popularly received, due to its perceived purity as a religious movement that rejected modernity and secularism, something appealing to a conservative society rocked by the (sometimes violent) influence of Arab nationalism. The Brotherhood's allure in Qatar thus resembles its spread through the Egyptian countryside during that era.[135] Because the Brotherhood's focus in Qatar, at that time, was on *daʿwa* and education, rather than on political action, the movement received government support. The first organized Brotherhood activities in Qatar involved groups of young men who studied, among others, the works of

Islamic reformers Fathi Yakan and Muhammad al-Ghazali.[136] They also organized *tarbīa* activities such as trips to various deserts and camps.[137]

Throughout this initial period of the Brotherhood's growth, the Qatari government, like others in the Gulf, considered support for the movement to be a means of promoting its own religious legitimacy, while also benefitting its population through the organization's provision of intellectual and social activities.[138] Early Brotherhood achievements, as described by former Kuwaiti Brotherhood member ʿAbdullah al-Nafisi, include the establishment of the Ministry of Education in 1954 as well as the Religious Institute in 1961—accomplishments that were not labeled as politically threatening.[139] Because Brotherhood members in exile feared that they would be hunted by Nasser's security apparatus overseas, they were careful to focus on grassroots and individual, rather than organized, activities, so as not to raise suspicions of being "partisan."[140] In this way, they differed considerably from the reigning Arab nationalists of the day who launched large-scale protests inside Qatar throughout the 1950s.

As in Kuwait and the UAE, the influence of the Muslim Brotherhood in Qatar started in education, as a large number of Brotherhood sympathizers came from abroad to staff Qatari schools. Formal education in Qatar began in 1952, with 250 male pupils taught by six teachers at one school in Doha,[141] while education for females was instituted in 1955, with 50 students taught by a single teacher in one school.[142] The education sector grew at remarkable speed: 42,610 students were in pre-university education in the 1981–1982 academic year.[143] Overseeing the expansion of formal education was the Ministry of Education, which was formed in 1954 and "followed an Egyptian education model for the first decade or so."[144] At the beginning of this period, not only was the Egyptian model used, but also a large number of Egyptian teachers, particularly those sympathetic to the Brotherhood, worked in Qatari schools. Qataris in the education sector held Islamist leanings as well.

Amir Shaykh ʿAli bin ʿAbdullah al-Thani (r. 1949–1960) was inclined to trust the Brotherhood as an organization that promoted traditional morals in the face of expanding Western influence and Arab nationalism. With his blessing, conservative Islam influenced Qatar's education sector. In fact, Shaykh ʿAli appointed Qatari Jassim al-Darwish, a former pupil of Qatari Wahhabi cleric Muhammad ʿAbd al-Aziz al-Mana, to organize the school system in 1952–1953.[145]

Education Director al-Darwish unsuccessfully tried to persuade Muhammad Fathi Osman, an Egyptian Brotherhood writer of increasing fame at the time, to oversee the education department in Qatar, signaling an early Brotherhood tilt to hiring decisions, which had strong political implications.[146] Prominent Qatari educator and former President of Qatar University ʿAbdulla Juma Kobaisi's PhD dissertation is a key resource in reconstructing the history of the Brotherhood in his country and particularly in documenting its impact on the education sector. He explains, "For a period of three years (1953/54 to 1955/56) most of the teachers who were brought in to run the Qatari schools were ideologically in favour of the Muslim Brotherhood Party, and in particular politically against the leadership of President Nasser. They stamped the educational system with their Islamic ideology since the education department of Qatar was under their control."[147] ʿAbd al-Badiʿ Saqr, a known Brotherhood sympathizer who had been imprisoned in Egypt with Brotherhood ideologue Shaykh Yusuf al-Qaradawi for his leadership of Ikhwan activities, was named joint Director of Education in 1954 along with al-Darwish, on the recommendation of Egyptian religious leader Shaykh Muhib al-Din al-Khatib.[148] Saqr, with al-Darwish and Brotherhood intellectuals like Shaykh

Zuhair al-Shawish, David Roberts describes, "oversaw the expansion of official schools and the bureaucracy of the department and personally sought to bring girls' education under the department's auspices."[149]

Despite the fact that a formal Brotherhood organization did not exist during this period in Qatar, then, Islamist-leaning individuals influenced the education sphere, which became a battleground for competing nationalist and Brotherhood ideologies. With Saqr and al-Darwish heading the education department, and with Saqr serving as a cultural advisor to Shaykh ʿAli, Brotherhood sympathizers supported the amir's rule, thereby spurring division within the ruling family, as not all members approved of the Ikhwan.[150] Indeed, as Kobaisi explains, "the education department was brought into the ruling family's internal conflict, as a means of achieving power and various political objectives. The schools [*sic*] expansion and the educational service with the various inducements it offered to children was seen in a small country like Qatar as more than generous and was considered a credit to Shaikh ʿAli's rule."[151] Shaykh Khalifa bin Hamad al-Thani (r. 1972–1995), himself a "progressive reformer" in support of Arab nationalism, carried on in silent disapproval of his uncle's rule, yet was unable to make advances against the group until the Muslim Brotherhood came under broader political attack.[152]

As conflict between the Muslim Brotherhood and Gamal ʿAbdel Nasser intensified in Egypt in 1954, pro-Brotherhood schools in Qatar publicly insulted President Nasser and Arab nationalism, going so far as to criticize the movement as a Western innovation meant to enfeeble the Islamic state.[153] Such strong political criticism "produced an environment full of misunderstanding and hostility between them [Muslim Brotherhood sympathizers] and their students in the schools as well as the elite of Qatar, people who truly believed in Islam and Arabic nationalism and saw that there was no conflict between the two."[154] The popularity of Arab nationalism and of Nasser more generally spurred opposition to the regime and in particular to Shaykh ʿAli, who, as ruler, headed the educational committee.[155]

In an effort to end divisions, Shaykh ʿAli disbanded the existing educational committee and made Shaykh Khalifa Educational Principal. When Shaykh Khalifa took over the education portfolio in 1956, he aimed to mitigate the Brotherhood's growing presence in Qatar's schools and to quell sympathetic teachers' increasingly public political stances, for fear that they would spread to Qatari society more broadly. To do so, he named Syrian pan-Arab nationalist ʿAbdullah ʿAbd al-Daim Director of Education.[156] Shaykh Khalifa also published the following circular in October 1957 calling on teachers not to participate in politics: "With our appreciation of the teachers and their education role we would like to inform them that their career in this country is purely educational. We shall take severe steps against those who interfere in politics and are connected with political parties which operate against our internal policy."[157] The government thus explicitly recognized the political weight of the education sector, demonstrating the degree to which a sector not traditionally considered political allowed for the advancement of Brotherhood ideology in a super-rentier state.

Under the leadership of al-Daim, teachers who tended toward Arab nationalism and extreme anticolonialism were brought into Qatari schools. Kobaisi claims that "[t]he educational atmosphere in Qatari schools rapidly changed from conservative to progressive," citing mandated in-school celebration of Egyptian-Syrian unity in 1958 as one example of institutionalized nationalist influence.[158] This modification in the education sphere was part of a broader political strategy, as Qatar's rulers recognized the political relevance of schooling.

Shaykh Khalifa, as Roberts points out, "had a plan to use education 'to put himself forward as a mild pan-Arabist . . . using his responsibilities for finding foreign teachers to dabble in foreign affairs.' "[159] The British Political Agent, however, urged Shaykh ʿAli to dismiss al-Daim, for fear that his leadership might spur further nationalist activity in the emirate.[160] As a result of British interference, al-Daim resigned after one year, and Shaykh Khalifa's brother, Jassim bin Hamad al-Thani, took over the education portfolio in 1958, retaining it until 1975, during which time schools remained an ideological battleground between nationalists and the Ikhwan.[161]

Despite Shaykh Khalifa's intentions to diminish Islamist influence in education, Brotherhood scholars still traveled to Qatar in the 1960s, and the Islamist strand was by no means underrepresented in broader Qatari society. One notable success for the Brotherhood was the appointment of Egyptian Ikhwan scholar ʿIzz al-Din Ibrahim as Assistant Director of Knowledge, responsible for creating a school syllabus.[162] Furthermore, when Head of Islamic Sciences at the Department of Education, ʿAbdullah bin Turki al-Sbuaʿi, went to Cairo's al-Azhar in 1960 to recruit Islamic scholars, he returned with several Islamist intellectuals. Most notably, al-Sbuaʿi recruited Shaykh Yusuf al-Qaradawi from al-Azhar to head the university's mission in Qatar in 1961.[163]

Once these scholars arrived in Qatar, their influence went beyond the schools, as "these men used their positions to invite a variety of Brotherhood luminaries to Qatar for lecturing stints of varying lengths. Key examples include Mohammed Qutb, Sayyid Qutb's brother; Mohammed al-Ghazzali, a leading member of the Brotherhood; and Abdul-Wafa al-Taftazani."[164] Ahmad al-ʿAssal, a close friend of al-Qaradawi, arrived in 1960 and "taught in schools, lectured in mosques, and helped form Brotherhood groups."[165] Another member of the Egyptian Brotherhood, Kamal Naji, took on a variety of positions in the Ministry of Education, including head of the publications committee and foreign cultural relations advisor.[166] Yusuf al-Qaradawi, for his part, directed and overhauled the newly founded Religious Institute before later establishing and becoming the dean of the College of Shariʿa and Islamic Studies at Qatar University in 1973.[167]

Egyptian Brotherhood members were, notably, not the only influential expatriate Islamists in Qatar. Beginning in the 1950s, "the first wave of Palestinian intelligentsia arrived," bringing into the education sector many individuals who came to lead Fatah and the Palestine Liberation Organization (PLO), imbuing Qataris with sympathy for the Palestinian cause, also incidentally important to the Brotherhood, from that period. ʿAbd al-Muʿaz al-Sattar, Hasan al-Banna's personal emissary to Palestine in 1946, served as a school inspector and director of Islamic Sciences at the Ministry of Education, in addition to coauthoring "numerous textbooks for the nascent Qatari school system in the early 1960s."[168] From the early 1950s, Rafiq Shakir al-Natshah taught and wrote textbooks in Qatar, as well as serving as director of the Office of the Head of Education.[169] Al-Natshah forged a close relationship with Shaykh Jassim bin Hamad al-Thani while working as his advisor in the education department, and he was granted Qatari citizenship in 1979 before he went on to serve as the PLO representative to Saudi Arabia, Palestinian minister of labor, and chairman of the Palestinian Legislative Council.[170] Current Fatah leader Mahmoud Abbas worked in Qatar's education department during 1957–1969 and in fact signed the official paperwork for al-Qaradawi's entry into the country in 1961.[171] Muhammad Yusuf al-Najjar, one of Fatah's founding members and former head of its security apparatus, also recruited teachers for Qatar's education department.[172] Politically active Palestinians, as well as a large number of Egyptian Ikhwan, thus staffed Qatar's education department, leaving their mark on it.

In such a small state, with a limited number of cultural activities and educational institutions, these individuals had a considerable social and intellectual impact through *ḥalaqāt*[173] and public lectures, as well as through their formal roles in the Ministry of Education, formulating curricula and staffing most primary and secondary schools at that time.[174] At this point, however, Brotherhood influence continued to spread through individuals, rather than through any organized institution, and held limited sway outside of educational and cultural activities.

Further influencing the recruitment of teachers sympathetic to the Brotherhood in particular were concerns about nationalist protest, the primary articulation of political demands in Qatar in the 1950s and 1960s. As Roberts explains,

> The sacking of a Brotherhood head of education (Abdul-Badi Saqr), his replacement by a pan-Arabist (Dr. Al Daim), and the latter's subsequent sacking the next year speaks to the primacy of political over ideological preference. Later, Khalifah bin Hamad's intake of Brotherhood members matches the political context of the time. The 1960s in Qatar were turbulent, involving numerous strikes and increasing popular resentment of Al Thani impunity and their entrenched economic advantages. Notable citizens, such as Hamad bin Abdullah Al Attiyah and Abdullah and Nasser Al Misnad, agitated along pan-Arabist lines, criticizing the Al Thanis; they were arrested, jailed and exiled as a result. That Khalifah bin Hamad, the next in line to the throne at that time, had to carefully calibrate his reactions, empathizing with their plight, but preferring to recruit Brothers so as not to give the agitators more potential fodder, was logical.[175]

In such an environment, education policies were meant to promote regime survival above all. Because Arab nationalism was more threatening to the Qatari elite than the Ikhwan, Brotherhood members were intentionally granted influence in the education department. Certainly, "institutionally it was not possible to promote any line but that of the state," which was, at that time, aligned with the Brotherhood for strategic reasons.[176] The fact that religious Qataris like al-Darwish and al-Sbuaʿi were charged with recruiting teachers from the beginning made their selection of religiously oriented individuals unsurprising. Their decisions in recruitment and curriculum development reflected their ideological leanings and influenced the next generation of Qataris.

From the 1950s, the al-Thani family recognized the power of the education sector in shaping public opinion and political protest, and the turbulence of that era in education left its mark on Qatar. As described in Kobaisi's words, "The result of the period of unrest is that the political system now ensures that schools do not encourage again political attitudes which might be directed against the role of the shaikdom; educational development in general has been strictly and narrowly controlled."[177] While Brotherhood gains during this period were restricted primarily to the educational and cultural spheres (indeed, the organization had not been formally established), Arab nationalists agitated openly for political reform.

The Rising Tide of Arab Nationalism

Nationalists, though briefly able to spread their ideology through schools under ʿAbdullah ʿAbd al-Daim's leadership, found their primary base of support among Qatari laborers, as a working class emerged in the 1950s.[178] Throughout the 1950s and early 1960s, the emirate faced a number of large workers' strikes.[179] As Jill Crystal explains, "Trouble began with the first oil shipment . . . . From then on strikes were the norm."[180] The first strike, in 1951, involved Qatari workers demanding the expulsion of Dhofari workers from Oman whom they considered "interlopers."[181] A series of violent confrontations targeting the British government and local merchant families, the al-Darwish and al-ʿUthman, in 1956 led Shaykh ʿAli to establish a regular police force; in Crystal's estimation, "[t]hese events made it clear that public security threats were emerging outside the family that were not contained in the distant oil fields."[182] Fearing escalation, the government sought to win over nationalists by supporting parts of their agenda, particularly the rights of workers, in addition to allowing them influence through the education system under al-Daim's leadership.[183]

Nonetheless, protests continued, with a large demonstration in 1963 following the overthrow of Iraqi Prime Minister ʿAbd al-Karim al-Qasim by the Baʿath Party.[184] A National Unity Front was established among Qatari workers, lesser ranking al-Thani shaykhs, and "disaffected notables."[185] This group circulated a platform that called for reforms to the government system in addition to, in Crystal's words, "the reduction of shaikhly privileges, expansion of social services, reduction of foreign labor in the government and oil company, establishment of a budget, creation of a representative municipal council, recognition of trade unions, better utility rates, a movie house and a broadcasting station."[186] The group also called a general strike, which lasted three weeks.

In response, the government arrested several of the Front's leaders and, in an effort to appease Qatari members of the group, granted preferential hiring treatment to nationals in the oil industry and public sector.[187] Amir Shaykh Ahmad al-Thani (r. 1960–1972) also set elections in April 1963 for a "Doha Council," or municipal body. These elections, however, were held largely to mollify British advisors urging civil peace and had little domestic significance.[188] In fact, as Allen Fromherz describes, "most Qataris were 'unaware that an election was taking place.' "[189] As a result, "[r]ather than being a democratic outlet, the Municipal Council turned into a flop."[190] The body existed for only three or four years.[191]

Until the 1970s, Arab nationalists dominated the political scene in Qatar. This upswing of nationalism was partly due to shifting demographics, traced by Crystal: "Within a short time oil turned unemployed pearl divers and slaves into a politically significant and volatile concentration of workers, then into a working class, and finally into a nationally identified working class," for whom nationalism was appealing.[192] Indeed, Emirati journalist ʿAbdul Ghaffar Hussain further explains the difficult atmosphere for Islamist mobilization: "The path to expansion was not easy for the Brotherhood and other [Islamist] associations in the Gulf that were not in line with the nationalist movement. Consequently, organized Brotherhood gatherings of any significance were not held until the 1970s."[193] Although Brotherhood figures became influential in Qatar's education sphere as individuals, they were unable to gather sufficient popular support for the establishment of a formal affiliate until the mid-1970s.

The Decline of Arab Nationalism and Establishment of a Qatari Brotherhood

Expatriate Brotherhood sympathizers continued to wield influence in the education sector in the 1970s. During that period, primary school educational curriculum was restricted to Arabic, Islamic studies, and limited science and mathematics.[194] In the 1970–1971 academic year, there were 162 Qatari teachers at the primary school level, compared with 590 non-Qatari teachers at the same level.[195] The disparity between Qatari and non-Qatari teachers became even more noticeable at the secondary level, with 10 Qatari teachers compared to 311 expatriates.[196] In terms of curriculum, at least in the 1970s, there was also, perhaps unsurprisingly considering staffing decisions, a heavier emphasis on religion than elsewhere in the Gulf.[197] The prominence of religious education and Arabic language continued at the secondary level.[198]

Outside of the educational sphere, Islamist-linked activities, such as trips and camps for youth, were conducted yet were, for the most part, arranged spontaneously and lacked any overarching organizational structure.[199] In Qatar's tribal culture, where much social activity is informally organized, this type of uninstitutionalized action was a natural fit.[200] Brotherhood preachers also controlled certain mosques, granting them a mouthpiece from which to use their *khuṭub*[201] to spread Ikhwan ideology.[202]

With the takeover of Anwar Sadat in Egypt in 1970 and the relaxation of restrictions on the Brotherhood, large numbers of Qataris moved to Egypt to attend university, becoming familiar with Brotherhood ideology during that time. Jassim Sultan himself received his education in medicine in Egypt beginning in 1973.[203] While studying, he witnessed the growth of the Brotherhood movement in the College of Medicine and Engineering in Cairo University and became acquainted with leaders of the Islamist student movement as well as prominent Brotherhood figures abroad.[204] At home in Qatar, however, the Brotherhood remained, in Sultan's words, "informal until the late 1970s when people decided to organize. They made a simple organization just to teach children and arrange camping trips."[205]

Indeed, as Islamist influence increased, sympathizers, especially the younger cohort, insisted that an official organization was needed to oversee the organization's activities.[206] The Brotherhood affiliate, founded in 1975, was, in Sultan's estimation, "just collaboration, a simple thing. Only one page described the organization, and no one knows where that paper is."[207] The group focused primarily on *daʿwa*, the intense study of sharia, the organization of sporting activities, and integration into the community, attracting young people in particular to Brotherhood-sponsored trips, sports, charity, and public lectures.[208] To this end, the Qatari Brotherhood had a youth organization, Markaz Shabab al-Doha (Doha Youth Center), which hosted a series of educational, cultural, and athletic activities.[209] It "was the Brotherhood's inculcation tool"[210] and "the main source of Ikhwanization until the Brotherhood was dissolved."[211] Still, the Qatari Muslim Brotherhood remained only loosely organized and contained no more than one hundred people in its early stages.[212]

The Qatari Muslim Brotherhood, then, while following a similar trajectory to the Kuwaiti in its initial stages of development in the education sphere, never reached the organizational strength of that group. The Emirati Muslim Brotherhood, which also gained strength through the education sector and its ties to the government, followed a dissimilar organizational pattern due to the federal nature of the Emirati state. It also has in recent years faced a very different fate from the other rentier Islamists under discussion.

THE EMERGENCE OF AN EMIRATI IKHWAN

In the UAE, as in Kuwait and Qatar, during the 1950s and 1960s, large numbers of Muslim Brotherhood members from outside the Gulf were hired for various professional positions. The small population of educated nationals at independence (only some thirty-nine university graduates were in the country in 1971[213]) necessitated the import of experts to fill a variety of posts, especially in the education sector. Brotherhood sympathizers who took on roles in education had substantial influence on the country's cultural development and became prominent members of Emirati society, thereby creating a local group of Ikhwan. As prominent Emirati commentator Sultan al-Qassemi put it, "The Brothers flourished in the UAE: They were educated, professional, and upwardly mobile individuals who gained employment in various public and private posts, including the judicial and education sector."[214] These roles allowed Brotherhood supporters to influence Emirati society and some of its political leaders until the most recent crackdown beginning in 2012.

The Emirati Brotherhood became formally organized only in 1974 under the banner of Jamʿiat al-Islah wa-l-Tawjih al-Ijtimaʿi (Reform and Social Counseling Association, hereafter Islah) in Dubai, Fujairah, and Ras al-Khaimah, with Jamʿiat al-Irshad wa-l-Tawjih al-Ijtimaʿi (Guidance and Social Counseling Association, hereafter Irshad) a less formal representative in Ajman. These groups, like Ikhwan affiliates elsewhere in the Gulf, engaged in a variety of youth, charity, and educational activities. And although Islah strictly speaking is not a Muslim Brotherhood affiliate, it undoubtedly remains guided by Ikhwan ideology and was founded largely by Brotherhood sympathizers who were inspired by branches elsewhere in the Middle East. In fact, prior to Islah's official establishment, the Muslim Brotherhood wielded ideological influence through the informal sphere. In this section, we examine the unique structure of the Emirati government and the effect of its arrangement into seven separate emirates on the development of the Ikhwan, while also tracing the federal government's increasing attempts at centralization and co-optation. We then analyze the emergence of the Brotherhood up until its official establishment in 1974.

Economic Tensions: Relative Deprivation among the Emirates

Each emirate, aside from having a local ruler, experiences a different standard of living and social environment. As Andrea B. Rugh highlights, "The main distinction between the emirates is their varying levels of prosperity, with Abu Dhabi and Dubai the wealthiest at one end of the scale, and the small backwaters of Fujaira, RAK [Ras al-Khaimah], and UAQ [Umm al-Quwain] at the other. In the middle are Ajman and Sharja located close enough to Dubai to benefit from its modern amenities but with few resources of their own."[215] Accordingly, each emirate contributes a different amount to the federal treasury. The disparity has become so extreme that, in 2008, Abu Dhabi underwrote 56 percent of the total national budget, while Dubai gave 32 percent, with the remaining five emirates financing the outstanding 12 percent.[216] This imbalance has led to feelings of relative deprivation, unexpected in a super-rentier. It also affirms the mechanism predicted by Gwenn Okruhlik and referred to in chapter 2 whereby the disbursement of rentier wealth, when done inequitably, can in fact lead to greater political discontent, rather than assuring stability.[217]

To assist the poorer northern emirates, in particular Ajman, Fujairah, Ras al-Khaimah, and Umm al-Quwain, the federal government has enhanced those emirates' rentier packages, announcing in 2011 that it would grant $1.6 billion in additional aid to such areas, following a grant for $4.3 billion in 2008.[218] Further, as Christopher Davidson chronicles, "The federal government also claims that it has a twenty year plan in place that will address some of the 'gaps and other issues such as healthcare, education, housing, roads, and water.' It also promised to build more than 100 kilometres of new rural roads, and doubled the funding for a small business development programme that aims to increase job creation in the region."[219] Although large sums of money have been earmarked for development of these emirates, they remain markedly less advanced than the leading emirates and Sharjah.

Despite assistance from the central government, blackouts are common, with some businesses forced to shut due to lack of air conditioning.[220] Charges of corruption have emerged, making many citizens of the northern emirates skeptical about the efficacy of government aid, while others consider delays in aid to reflect a policy of intentional underdevelopment[221] to keep the peripheral emirates dependent on the central government's largesse.[222] One interviewee in Ras al-Khaimah insisted that the emirate has not received adequate aid, with the central government publicly supporting development yet privately voting down schemes for its advancement, even vetoing a proposal for a new electricity grid to stop blackouts in the emirate.[223] As another interviewee confirmed, "money is not trickling down as much."[224] Umm al-Quwain, Ras al-Khaimah, Ajman, and Fujairah together accounted for less than ten percent of national GDP in 1998.[225] And dynamics have not changed drastically; one 2011 *Financial Times* report aptly described Ras al-Khaimah as feeling like "a different country" from the state's capital.[226] Due to such economic inequities, logically, "there is a greater pool of dissent in the northern emirates."[227] The economic comparison in table 4.1 reveals the level of economic discrepancies among the emirates.

TABLE 4.1

Economic Comparison of Constituent Emirates

Emirate	Total Population	Gross Domestic Product (GDP)	GDP per Capita	Land Area
Abu Dhabi	2.4 million (2013)[228]	$259 billion (2013)[229]	$44,269 (2007)[230]	67,340 square kilometers[231]
Ajman	262,186 (2011)[232]	$990 million (2012)[233]	$11,577 (2007)[234]	259 square kilometers[235]
Dubai	2.1 million (2013)[236]	$88 billion (2013)[237]	$41,726 (2007)[238]	3,885 square kilometers[239]
Fujairah	191,190 (2013)[240]	$3.5 million (2012)[241]	$16,845 (2007)[242]	1,300 square kilometers[243]
Ras al-Khaimah	416,600 (2012)[244]	$8.4 billion (2013)[245]	$16,624 (2007)[246]	1,700 square kilometers[247]
Sharjah	946,000 (2013)[248]	$24 billion (2013)[249]	$21,133 (2007)[250]	2,600 square kilometers[251]
Umm al-Quwain	Approximately 80,000 (2014)[252]	$974 million (2015)[253]	$16,509 (2007)[254]	770 square kilometers[255]

Support for Islamist organizations has often arisen elsewhere in the Middle East due to frustration with socioeconomic and political status in some areas. As Azzedine Layachi and Abdel-Kader Haireche note, "[E]conomic deprivation, social exclusion, and political under-representation [have] encouraged the development of Islamist movements not only in Algeria but also in many other Muslim countries."[256] Such disillusionment, however, is not expected in rentier states. Nonetheless, when problems of underdevelopment are not shared equally by all members of a society, or remedied by a wealthy government, Islamist groups, perceived to be morally upright, often hold particular appeal.[257] In the words of R. Hrair Dekmejian, "Lack of socioeconomic justice combined with official corruption and failure of political elites to mold strong identities through socialization has produced a crisis of legitimacy, where the moral bases of authority are in question."[258] Although such feelings of disillusionment with the government certainly exist in the UAE, they have limited impact on nationwide policymaking. Indeed, the emirates whose citizens are least content are also those with smaller populations in the periphery.[259] The northern emirates, according to one Emirati academic, remain "completely marginalized" and subject to policies formulated in the leading emirates, yet discontent there does not appear widespread enough to constitute a challenge for the federal government.[260] In fact, a 2014 survey among 5,000 Emirati citizens conducted by market research firm TNS Middle East and North Africa found that 97 percent consider themselves to enjoy a good quality of life, with most responding they were "very satisfied" or "fairly satisfied."[261]

Social Tensions among the Emirates

Perhaps part of the reason for overall contentment in the UAE is the variety of social environments available in different emirates, granting nationals the opportunity to live in more liberal or conservative and traditional areas, depending on their preferences. As Michael Herb describes, Abu Dhabi "in its origins, governance, and ethos was very much more an emirate of the tribal desert than that of a seaside city: the *bedu* predominated. Dubai, by contrast, is resolutely centered on the port, with a desert hinterland that received little attention from the rulers. The northern emirates had substantial tribal populations, but these were tribes of the mountains rather than the pastoral nomads of the Arabian deserts."[262] Each emirate also consequently has a distinct political culture. Abu Dhabians, more influenced by tribal traditions, embrace the use of direct petitions to governors to effect change in issues ranging from greater representation in government and the level of federal integration to matters of social reform and public administration.[263] Peterson goes on to observe that "Dubayyans and Sharjans, on the other hand, relatively more cosmopolitan and less tribal, may find such traditional expressions anachronistic or irrelevant," engaging instead with local councils.[264]

Reflecting different cultural environments of each emirate, policies regarding alcohol range considerably. In Sharjah, alcohol consumption is prohibited even in hotels and private residences. The emirate has also imposed a series of decency laws, contrasting greatly with Dubai's social liberalism. These measures "have covered matters such as dress codes, public conduct, gender separation, and promiscuity. At one point Sharjah even attempted to encourage federal immigration officials to deny residence visas to single women under the age of thirty in an effort to curb the influx of prostitutes into the UAE."[265] This is largely because the ruling al-Qasimi family of Sharjah has been "historically more conservative and outspoken," in large measure due to its close financial ties with Saudi Arabia.[266] Still, Sharjah has not housed a branch of the Muslim Brotherhood and remains more closely linked to the Saudi ulama than to the Ikhwan.[267] This is not to say that it has not contained influential Islamist figures, namely Shaykh ʿAbdullah bin ʿAli al-Mahmud, discussed below.

In contrast, Umm al-Quwain and the other poorer emirates of Ajman, Fujairah, and Ras al-Khaimah house large liquor shops open to the public, in an effort to raise funds and encourage intraemirate tourism.[268] While Dubai remains focused primarily on business and Abu Dhabi on the development of its natural resources, Sharjah is known as the UAE's intellectual hub, and the northern emirates are often considered "more backward."[269] Such variations arguably allow Emiratis the freedom to choose which social environment suits them, creating something of a balance between the Western and traditional. Although this variety may help diffuse social tensions to a certain extent, the national economy and federal politics remain centered on the leading emirates.

Ras al-Khaimah has perhaps been the most troubled of the emirates, reliant on few sources of income and rocked by instability due to a fractious ruling family. Such conditions have made it fertile ground for opposition movements, and divisions between members of the ruling families of the UAE have allowed the Brotherhood to have greater space to act in that emirate. At the same time, some violent plots emerged. In fact, one member of the emirate's dominant al-Shiḥūḥ Shehhi tribe piloted one airplane involved in the attacks of September 11, 2001 (9/11) on the United States.[270] The emirate also housed, until 2007, al-Imam Muhammad ibn Saud Islamic University, a Wahhabi institution, whose Saudi branch one of the 9/11 attackers attended.[271] This university was funded through aid money provided by Saudi Arabia, which has recognized the need for assistance in the northern emirates and has provided it "often with religious strings attached."[272] Following 9/11, the Emirati government found additional links between individuals in Ras al-Khaimah and al-Qaʿida, "with claims being made that recent terror plots in the UAE, including a 2009 attempt to blow up Dubai's then incomplete Burj Khalifa skyscraper, had originated in Raʾs al-Khaimah."[273] In response to such threats, the federal government, led by Abu Dhabi, is trying to prevent extremism largely through centralization, particularly of its State Security Directorate. As one interviewee put it, "Now Abu Dhabi is taking a very strong hand, trying to control everything everywhere because security is centralized. The security apparatus is getting stronger and stronger and more centralized."[274] Over the course of 2016, Emirati authorities, according to Human Rights Watch, improved their ability to use electronic surveillance.[275]

Despite such moves toward centralization of political control, each emirate retains a unique local environment. Segments of populations in some emirates undoubtedly favor Brotherhood influence yet struggle to find institutionalized means of changing policy. As one interviewee put it, "It's not a question of whether they exist; it's if they have any political capital—and the answer is no."[276] In the first decades of the Emirati Brotherhood's existence, however, it did have the power to change official policy due to the prominence of the ideology as well as its members' roles in government.

Origins of Brotherhood Support

At the start of the 1970s, when many Emirati students began returning from studying abroad, particularly in Egypt and Kuwait, they brought with them the idea of establishing a group to organize activities similar to those conducted by the Muslim Brotherhood in countries where they had studied.[277] As described by Islah member and human rights lawyer Mohammed al-Roken in a short history compiled by *al-Sharq al-Awsat*, students returning to the UAE, having been exposed to and become sympathetic to Brotherhood ideology, "held out hope of setting up a group to practice its activities and of establishing its institutions and incubators of *tarbīa* in the country, to attract the youth to thoughts of the group and to prepare them to be influential cadres in newborn Emirati society."[278]

A strong relationship between the Emirati and Kuwaiti Brotherhood also aided the establishment of an Emirati Brotherhood. Shaykh ʿAbdullah bin ʿAli al-Mahmud, one of the most prominent icons of Islamic *daʿwa* in the UAE, was instrumental in forging these ties. He had a major presence in Islamist activities, working in the organization of *awqāf* and mosques in Sharjah throughout his career.[279] Al-Mahmud became Sharjah's first Director of Awqaf and Islamic Affairs, with Shaykh ʿAbd al-Wadud Shalabi, an al-Azhar graduate and Brotherhood icon in Egypt, as his deputy.[280] Al-Mahmud visited the Kuwaiti Brotherhood in the early 1970s and met with, among others, leading figures Yusuf al-Hajji and ʿAbdullah ʿAli al-Mutawa.[281] In fact, al-Mutawa and al-Mahmud together helped promote Islamic *daʿwa* and vied for support by participating in Islamic activities and by converting British churches into mosques.[282] During this period, then, according to Saudi researcher Mansour al-Nogaidan, "[t]he newborn [Emirati] group received parental care and symbolic contribution from the Kuwaiti Brotherhood, where the Islah group in Kuwait contributed to the establishment of its headquarters."[283] This interdependence continued through meetings, visits, organized trips, and summer camps.[284]

Growth of the Brotherhood in the UAE was facilitated by two additional external forces: teachers, professors, lawyers, and researchers from the Egyptian Brotherhood to the UAE as seen elsewhere in the Gulf;[285] and envoys such as teachers and administrators, many of Palestinian and Syrian descent, who came from Qatar and helped formulate educational curricula.[286] Shaykh ʿAbd al-Badi Saqr, one of the leaders of the Egyptian Brotherhood residing in Qatar, was involved in the establishment of the mission and recruitment of its teachers.[287] He also founded al-Iman School in the Al Rashidiya neighborhood of Dubai, which continues to operate as a private school with strong emphasis on Islamic studies.[288] Saqr, along with Shaykh Yusuf al-Qaradawi, often traveled to Dubai from Qatar to lecture at the Public Library, founded by the municipality in 1963, spreading Brotherhood ideology in this way.[289] For his part, ʿAbdul Ghaffar Hussein claims that the Qatari educational mission's Dubai headquarters, which was established as an aid contribution to the UAE in 1962, was in fact the root of Brotherhood activity in the Emirates.[290] It has also been posited that the Qatari Brotherhood actively aimed to expand its organization into the UAE, particularly Dubai. While the Muslim Brotherhood benefitted from the backing and sympathy of many Emirati elites, particularly businessmen and members of the ulama, an indigenous movement did not emerge until the mid-1970s.[291]

The Establishment of Islah

Islah was established in Dubai in 1974, three years after the UAE's independence, as only the second civil society organization to receive approval from the Ministry of Labor and Social Affairs.[292] Notable members from throughout the emirates included Sultan bin Kayed al-Qasimi, Muhammad bin ʿAbdullah al-ʿAjlan, ʿAbd al-Rahman al-Bakr,

Hamad Hassan Raqit al-ʿAli, Hassan al-Diqqi, and Saʿid ʿAbdullah Harib al-Muhairi, who together filed the request to Dubai leader and Vice President Shaykh Rashid bin Saʿeed al-Maktoum (r. Dubai 1958–1990) for the founding of the organization.[293] Shaykh Mohammed bin Khalifa al-Maktoum, cousin of Dubai's current ruler Shaykh Mohammed bin Rashid al-Maktoum, assumed the role as first chairman of the organization's management council, while Shaykh Rashid donated money toward the establishment of the group's headquarters in that emirate, signaling the government's willingness to patronize an Islamist group as a bulwark of Arab nationalism.[294] In the words of one Emirati political scientist, "The initial drive of the Muslim Brotherhood was that the UAE is not Islamic enough, not about justice/injustice, or reform."[295] The government thus did not contest the organization's formation.

After the founding of Islah in Dubai, branches were established in Ras al-Khaimah and Fujairah, with Shaykh Rashid donating toward the cost of their establishment.[296] Emirati President and Abu Dhabi ruler Shaykh Zayed bin Sultan al-Nahyan (r. Abu Dhabi 1966–2004) also contributed land for the establishment of a branch of the group in that emirate at the end of the 1970s, yet an affiliate ultimately never gained permission to form there.[297] As mentioned above, a branch also never opened in Sharjah. Former vice-chairman of Islah in Ras al-Khaimah and lawyer Mohammed al-Mansoori considers the Sharjan government's refusal to allow for the opening of a local branch of Islah to be a reflection of the prevalence, at that time, of Arabism and nationalism, rather than Islamism, in that emirate.[298] Its connections to the Saudi Arabian government, with which it has strong financial ties, also may have squelched any potential Brotherhood movement in that emirate, with the Kingdom a more likely source of religious inspiration. In Ajman, though a branch of Islah was not established, according to al-Nogaidan, "the Brotherhood settled for subordination to the Association of Guidance and Social Counseling [Irshad]."[299]

The organizational structure of the Brotherhood in the UAE has been more complicated than in Kuwait and Qatar due to the state's federalist form. The Ikhwan there is, as described by Wanda Krause, "broken down according to emirate with a further hierarchy of sections and subsections, typically classified according to emirate cities and rank of members, each with different *halaqas* having different curricula. Each subsection becomes relatively small."[300] When the government turned against the organization in the 1990s, its decentralized structure, with many loosely coordinated small networks, actually aided its survival for decades after the government became suspicious of the group.

Like Brotherhood affiliates elsewhere in the region, the Emirati Ikhwan was involved in social and cultural activities, namely sporting and charity events.[301] For instance, "Internal activities include those related to Ramadan fasts, such as sponsoring and holding *iftars* (dinners to break the fast), as well as courses in members' houses for their *halaqas*. The women hold *halaqas* in masjids (mosques) as well as in their homes."[302] One Emirati political scientist described the 1970s as a period during which the Brotherhood aimed to influence two areas on a national level: educational institutions and civil society organizations.[303] As another interviewee put it, "The Muslim Brotherhood used that [the education sector] as a sea they could fish in."[304] Outside of that sphere, the Brotherhood operated through charity as well as teacher and student organizations, from which a new generation of Ikhwan leaders was derived.

Further aiding the Brotherhood's growth was the relative lack of widespread Arab nationalist sentiment in the UAE. A nationalist faction had emerged among merchants in Dubai before independence, as early as 1938, urging more representative government and checks on foreign influence.[305] Following the decline of that movement and a similar one in 1953, however, nationalism did not re-emerge as strongly as it did in the other super-rentiers, remaining "firmly in the background of Emirati politics" since its outbreak in 1953 with Dubai's National Front.[306] Schools in Dubai, like those in Qatar, remained sites of ideological contestation into the 1950s, yet by the time the Brotherhood had formed in the UAE, nationalism had comparatively little influence.[307]

The UAE's federal structure may have made nationalism ultimately less relatable, as Emiratis remained primarily loyal to local rulers for the first years of the union. Further, as Neil Partrick explains, "It was said of the UAE thirty years ago that, 'political loyalty to one's tribe has not as yet given way to loyalty to the state as an abstract political concept.' That the state is made even more abstract by being made up of seven emirates in an ambiguous and ill-defined relationship with each other plainly does not help."[308] The Muslim Brotherhood, on the other hand, held ideological appeal as well as social standing in important segments of Emirati society; in the words of one Emirati political scientist, "the Muslim Brotherhood had a good understanding with government and good backing from business. Arab nationalists hadn't had the same support because they were seen as Western, not genuine."[309] This critique in itself shows the conservatism present in Emirati society. Despite such a pool of recruits for the Brotherhood affiliates inside the UAE, the organization lacked a political outlet to effect change on a broader level and, divided across emirates, did not have as coherent a social agenda as did the other Brotherhood branches in the super-rentiers.

CONCLUSIONS

Though they share similar demographic, economic, and political profiles, Kuwait, Qatar, and the UAE house different types of Brotherhood movements. The Kuwaiti Ikhwan managed to use its social standing to become a major political force, while the Qatari Brotherhood never expanded beyond the social sector. Meanwhile, the Emirati Brotherhood remained somewhat segmented, despite initially enjoying a solid relationship with the ruling elite. Rentier Islamists thus came to hold positions of social capital *through* the systems they criticized due to their peaceful and stable ties with governments that hoped to promote Islamism over nationalism and with rulers who wanted to appear appropriately religious. Having established the means in which Brotherhood branches were formed in Kuwait, Qatar, and the UAE, we now trace the development of these movements after the fall of Arab nationalism, the Brotherhood's primary ideological rival, from the 1970s to the 1990s.

5

Politicians or Preachers?

THE DEVELOPMENT OF RENTIER ISLAMIST AGENDAS IN A POST-ARAB NATIONALIST ERA

INTRODUCTION

Having been established under rather similar circumstances in the 1950s and 1970s, rentier Islamists took on very different forms as they evolved, depending on the political opportunities available to them. Because the Kuwaiti branch was formed in a state with a vocal and regularly elected parliament, its Brotherhood affiliate became politically active through that body, while striving to maintain its social outreach by differentiating a social arm from its political branch. The Qatari Brotherhood, lacking a means of institutionalized political action, focused on changing social policy and garnering support from the grassroots through its ideological appeal, much like the Egyptian Muslim Brotherhood in its early years. Jamʿiat al-Islah wa-l-Tawjih al-Ijtimaʿi (Islah) in the UAE, benefitting from government support and ministerial positions through the 1970s and 1980s, decisively lost the ability to influence policy in that way in the mid-1990s and thus became more vocal in the political reform movement.

That such initially similar groups took on such divergent paths demonstrates the adaptability of rentier Islamism. Because its appeal is based on ideology, rather than on organizational structure or the provision of goods or services, the Brotherhood affiliates in the super-rentiers manage to adjust to a variety of political environments. Further, since rentier Islamists do not need to provide material benefits to their followers or organize electoral campaigns outside of Kuwait, they can take on a variety of structural appearances. In this chapter, we recount how Brotherhood movements adapted to their environments in the super-rentiers over the first decades of their development.

THE KUWAITI CASE

Waning Nationalism and the Rise of Islamism in the 1970s

On the heels of decreasing support for Arab nationalism, once *the* major political ideology inside Kuwait, the local branch of the Muslim Brotherhood became increasingly popular. Because the Brotherhood had gained a following during the oil boom of the 1970s when government spending on social welfare exploded, support for the Brotherhood has never been contingent on receiving material benefits, as it sometimes is in other, poorer, parts of the Arab world. As explained by Kuwaiti political scientist Shafeeq Ghabra, "Human beings don't live only on social services. Kuwaiti society, when Islamists became more popular, in the 1970s and 1980s, was not poor, yet felt the need for something larger. Kuwaitis wanted a sense of belonging to the region."[1] This need for security and sense of identity was particularly acute following the failure of Arab nationalism.

The 1971 National Assembly elections appeared to give the government cause for confidence, as support for Arab nationalism declined, with pro-government candidates taking twenty of the fifty seats. In the 1971 and 1975 elections, the Brotherhood expanded its representation by using coalitions and aligning with independent personalities.[2] As ʿAli Fahed al-Zumai explains, "This method exaggerated the political power of the Ikhwan and gave them importance in the eyes of others . . . . It was also instrumental in promoting many laws and issues of an Islamic nature."[3] In a politically charged environment, an increasingly oppositional parliament was an unwelcome nuisance to the ruling family. Parliament sought greater power in decision-making in fields traditionally dominated by the al-Sabah ruling family, such as foreign policy and national security.[4] The early 1970s marked the first time that the Brotherhood found itself willing to ally with non-Islamist political blocs to expand its representation in parliament. Its agenda remained focused on pushing for social change once in the legislature, however.

When the opposition-dominated 1975 parliament, which included members of the secular opposition and a large number of independents,[5] began taking measures to allow the Supreme Judicial Council to examine the constitutionality of any government order, Amir Shaykh Sabah al-Salem al-Sabah (r. 1965–1977) feared the loss of his prerogative as ruler.[6] Though he vetoed the law, parliament, which could overthrow his decision with a two-thirds majority, tried to vote again. Before this could happen, the government dissolved the legislature in August 1976.[7] The parliament's disbandment after less than one year led to protests among members of workers', students', and teachers' associations. In response, the government replaced the elected boards of professional associations with appointed boards sympathetic to the regime.[8] Still, it did not call for new elections, as required by the constitution.

In the face of increased government control, the Brotherhood failed to comment publicly, while members of the secular liberal political opposition filled the streets in protest.[9] Brotherhood members thus continued to enjoy the cabinet positions they had been granted at the beginning of the decade, with the group's former leader ʿAbd al-ʿAziz al-Mutawa appointed minister of *awqāf* and Islamic affairs in 1976.[10] The Brotherhood's relationship with the government remained strong. In a 1977 *al-Mujtama* article recounting a meeting between ʿAbdullah ʿAli al-Mutawa, chairman of Jamʿiat al-Islah al-Ijtimaʿi (Islah), and Minister of Social Affairs and Work Salim Sabah al-Salem al-Sabah, the minister openly voiced the government's support for and encouragement of the Islamic direction.[11]

Beginning in 1977, Islamist parties, led by Islah, came to control a number of associations, labor unions, markets of cooperative societies,[12] and the National Union of Kuwaiti Students (NUKS).[13] This signaled the beginning of another strategy of spreading Brotherhood ideology. As Sami Awadh recounts, "[T]he leadership of the Brotherhood concentrated on forming public welfare societies, trade associations and student unions.... Then evolved the idea of infiltrating these institutions with the aim of totally dominating them."[14] It is impossible to determine, however, whether the Brotherhood aimed to gain supporters in these bodies primarily to advance its political or social capital, signaling the increasing overlap between the two.

During this period, nationalists had little power in popular associations, allowing Islamists to dominate the political scene not only through their relationship with the government but also through student and professional groups.[15] In particular, as shown in the previous chapter, "schooling and curricula emerged as critical sites of contestation between regimes and Islamists, and cut to the heart of the ideological battle for the control of Gulf polities."[16] As a result, student and youth organizations became more politically important than ever. The most prominent of these youth associations, the Muslim Youth League, was founded in 1972 in the United States under the leadership of Tareq al-Suwaidan.[17] Thereafter, Brotherhood power increased through the Kuwaiti student unions in Cairo, Alexandria, and the United Kingdom.[18] Following successes in student union elections in Cairo and Alexandria, the Brotherhood decided to participate in elections of NUKS in Kuwait.[19] Importantly, Kuwait University's student union had become "a front for political work" when the National Assembly was suspended after 1976.[20] In 1977, the Brotherhood and Salafi faction al-I'tilafia (the Coalition) gained control over four of the nine groups in the Student Union and in 1979 won seats in the student council, displacing the nationalist al-Wasat al-Dimoqrati (the Democratic Center).[21] Throughout Kuwait, the Brotherhood transformed student groups at various levels into, in al-Zumai's words, "Islamic societies that represented their political and ideological viewpoints in all the contemporary issues. This was in addition to their benefitting from them as an organisational means through which to attract supporters."[22]

Remarkably, since 1979, the Muslim Brotherhood-dominated Islamist faction has without fail won the leadership of NUKS. As a result, even today, Islah's primary constituency, as described by Joseph Kostiner, is composed of "young people of professional and academic backgrounds who became acquainted with revivalist ideas during their studies in local or Western universities. They seek to cultivate a meaningful and productive life through religion and to abandon Western-style consumer habits. However, typically, they have not called for complete destruction of the present life-style, but rather to complement and reform it."[23] As in Egypt, Brotherhood influence in student groups allowed the organization to gain support in professional associations, with the Brotherhood garnering seats on many of their management councils by the mid-1970s.[24] The Brotherhood worked specifically within groups of engineers, graduates, teachers, oil syndicates, and general workers' unions.[25] The organization also gained seats on the boards of directors of other popular societies, such as trade unions and cooperatives.[26] In addition to activity in professional associations, charity organizations and solidarity committees represented major funding activities for the Brotherhood, which also raised its profile.

Gaining support among Kuwaiti society even in the absence of parliament and influenced by the 1979 Iranian Revolution, Kuwaiti Islamists became "more vocal and aggressive in their attempts to Islamize society and gain a share of power for themselves. Their ability to infiltrate the government bureaucracy increased."[27] Kuwaiti political scientist Falah ʿAbdullah al-Mdaires describes six indicators of the spread of Brotherhood thought in Kuwaiti society in the 1970s and 1980s. First, the organization came to dominate the students' and workers' unions.[28] Second, Kuwaiti mosques essentially were transformed into "party headquarters."[29] Third, cooperative societies became another sector of Brotherhood control, as members became major shareholders and spread their slogans around the markets.[30] Fourth, rhetoric festivals, Islamic shows, and solidarity weeks were held, raising awareness of Brotherhood activity and ideology.[31] Fifth, charities such as the Africa Muslim Committee and the Asia Muslim Committee became popular and led to Brotherhood control of the World Islamic Charity Body, Zakat House, and Islamic Finance House.[32] Sixth, weekly religious studies groups resulted in the establishment of weekly women's meetings and the Brotherhood's consolidation of female support.[33] Because of the instruments at its disposal, the Muslim Brotherhood's success extended to other parts of Kuwait, both geographically and demographically.[34]

Islamism in the Context of the Ḥaḍar-Badū *Divide*

In a largely homogenous ethnic environment, with the majority of the population Sunni, the major social division in Kuwait exists between fully urbanized, long-time citizens (*ḥaḍar*) and more recently naturalized tribal figures (*badū*, or bedouin). Beginning in 1967, a large number of the *badū* was naturalized, bringing this social cleavage to the fore, as the government granted citizenship to a large voting population that it hoped would become politically loyal. Like many new urban dwellers in Cairo in the 1940s and 1950s, however, these bedouin were socially conservative and initially attracted to the ideology of the Muslim Brotherhood. In this context, belonging to a group like the Brotherhood allowed the *badū* to gain "a sense of equality and belonging and transition to urban life."[35] In fact, despite the Brotherhood's popularity among many educated *ḥaḍar* Kuwaitis, David Commins notes, "it is striking that many Kuwaiti Islamists have humble social backgrounds, including former Beduins, suggesting that the rise of this trend signifies a broadening scope of participation in national politics."[36]

Many *ḥaḍar* Kuwaitis complain that the *badū* have failed to assimilate and consider their naturalization an attempt by the state "to 'tribalize' and 'bedouinize' the whole society."[37] In fact, Brotherhood detractors speculate that the organization's sympathy for the challenges facing Kuwait's *bidūn* (stateless) population, many of whom live in outlying areas, can be explained by the fact that many are members of tribes that have traditionally backed the Ikhwan.[38] Although the Brotherhood has historically gained a following from among the *badū*, tribes also exert independent political power, having held their own primary elections to select parliamentary candidates since 1976.[39] In such races, clan or tribal connections often outweigh ideological leanings.

Despite criticism of its role in outlying areas as politically expedient, the Brotherhood has been involved in tribal districts for decades, becoming one of the first political blocs to do so. Beginning in 1973, it took up work in *badū* areas in an effort to win over some of the country's largest tribes.[40] Ultimately, the feebleness of Wahhabism and the spread of education that advanced a more modern Islam enhanced the Ikhwan's appeal.[41] Due to these efforts, particularly in rural communities, Islah's membership grew throughout the 1970s. The organization's branches in poorer areas, such as Al Jahra, Omariya, and the island of Failaka, were especially important, as these places had never before received attention from non-governmental organizations and often received limited government support, making them fertile ground for new members.[42] Further facilitating membership, at the end of the 1970s, Islah changed the age of membership from eighteen to seventeen years old and decreased the membership fee.[43] The consequent "increase in the membership of al-Islah led to a change in its members which made it the most comprehensive society as far as its membership and geographical spread was [*sic*] concerned."[44]

Accomplishments of Islah in Its First Two Decades

By 1980, Islah had made many notable achievements, such as the establishment of the Kuwait Finance House, Zakat House (the first bank operating under sharia), and Sharia College, each under the leadership of an Islah member; and the undertaking of an Encyclopedia of Islamic Fiqh[45] by the General Authority of Islamic Affairs and Endowments.[46] In addition, Islah succeeded in dismantling so-called Masonic clubs like the Rotary and Lyons clubs, spreading its strong antidrug message, hosting Islamic book exhibitions beginning in 1974, and continuing with the uninterrupted publication of its widely circulated magazine *al-Mujtama*.[47] The organization was also instrumental in establishing women's committees beginning in 1968, hosting lectures and events for special weeks, establishing the first Commission for Islamic Youth Education and a number of other charity groups, including the Commission of the Islamic Public in 1982 and the Commission of Islamic Daʿwa in 1982.[48] Such activities allowed the Kuwaiti Brotherhood to gain a popular following that later translated into institutionalized political capital. The organization's trajectory into politics was indirect and gradual—characteristics of rentier Islamists. Due to restrictions on independent political action and attempted government co-optation of the religious sector, creating social networks and providing spiritual welfare are the logical entry points for Islamists in the Gulf and have proven most effective in the Kuwaiti case.

During the 1970s, the Kuwaiti Brotherhood attracted an increasing number of Kuwaiti members. Also during this period, the reinvigorated Islah began working from mosques, in particular through cultural study circles, to which it often invited young men after they attended prayers.[49] As these gatherings, in which Qurʾanic interpretation and recitation were popular, attracted an increasing number of young people, Islah expanded its activities beyond study.[50] Mosques became central for Brotherhood activities, as al-Zumai describes:

> In each mosque where they were active, they established a public library for lending general Islamic books as well as some books that tackled the Ikhwan ideology and history. In many mosques the Ikhwan established a special section for tapes which were available for people to borrow free of charge. They contained recordings from the Qurʾan, Islamic lectures given by well-known scholars, and tackled various creedal, political, social and historical issues presented from the Ikhwan's point of view. This was in addition to various publications in the form of booklets or brochures on Islamic legislation and ideology. These activities continued to develop until the mosques

> became cultural centres, spread throughout the country, disseminating Islamic and Ikhwan thought through their cultural activities.[51]

Other social programs, sporting activities, cultural exchanges, and trips, as well as supervision of zakat committees and charity projects, were also organized through the mosques, thereby increasing Islah's popularity in the broader Muslim community.[52] The expansion of Muslim Brotherhood activities through mosques changed their traditional function: "every mosque became a complete cultural as well as social unit, managed by Ikhwan members who were inhabitants of the area in which the mosque was situated. This established a strong relationship between the Ikhwan and the general public who frequented the mosques."[53] In a climate of increasing popularity, it was not surprising when the Brotherhood took on a formal role in electoral politics in the 1980s.

The 1980s and Formal Entry into Politics

Although members of the Kuwaiti Brotherhood had run for seats in parliament since the 1960s, they had done so as individuals, rather than as members of the organization.[54] In fact, it was argued that the group's entry into electoral political life represented a deviation from the mission of *da'wa* and incremental progress toward the ideal Islamic state, as promoted by Hasan al-Banna.[55] Reservations also remained about the appropriateness of Islamists contesting elections in a non-Islamic political order.[56] Brotherhood leader Jassim Muhalhal al-Yasin explained the movement's entry into politics in the 1980s: "The purpose of the entry of Islamists into legislative and executive power, despite the reservation about the legitimacy of many of the laws of the constitution for violating the law of God Almighty, is demonstrating the presence and the best example in an effort to Islamize the previous laws and prevent any new laws contrary to the Qur'an."[57] Furthermore, in 1980, Islah was the only Islamist bloc contesting elections, making it the sole avenue through which such views could be articulated in government.[58] Many members thus considered it their duty to represent the Sunni Islamist strand as a bloc in parliament. In addition, Islamic alternatives were becoming increasingly relevant in the region as a whole during this period.

The presentation of a new model of Shi'i theocratic government in Iran in 1979 led Kuwaitis, along with many other Arabs, to question the validity and permanence of current governing structures. In an atmosphere of political change, the Kuwaiti government faced opposition from both Islamists and liberals, as it had failed to fully Islamize legislation and to restore parliamentary life. Increasingly unpopular, the government issued a law in autumn 1979 limiting public gatherings to twenty people and allowing police to attend all public and private meetings.[59] The government finally agreed to hold parliamentary elections in February 1981, yet only after issuing a new electoral law that allowed for significant gerrymandering and vote buying.[60] While previous legislation had divided the country into ten electoral districts, each sending five members to the National Assembly, the new law separated Kuwait into twenty-five districts, each selecting two members of parliament (MPs). Critically, most new districts were created in areas dominated by newly naturalized members of tribes, whom the government expected to be loyal after including them in the state's welfare system.[61] Overall, tribal districts came to account for thirty-one seats in parliament, while those allocated to primarily Shi'i districts decreased from ten to four.[62] More remarkably, secular liberal opposition was competitive in only fifteen of the new districts, and, even in those constituencies, it faced powerful political rivals.[63]

Not surprisingly, the election results dealt a blow to liberals and leftists, with Islamist candidates from Sunni and Shiʿi backgrounds, as well as tribal representatives, faring well.[64] As Mary Ann Tétreault observes, "Although the intention behind redistricting was to hobble what at the time was a predominantly secularist political opposition, among the unforeseen outcomes was to privilege urban as well as tribal Islamists as a political force."[65] Islah won three seats through its participation in a coalition, the Islamic Bloc, with Salafi groups.[66] These more conservative Sunni Islamist organizations also entered electoral politics in 1981 and have found considerable common ground with the Brotherhood since that time, though they tend to take a more conservative social stance and are less flexible in forming electoral coalitions with secular and Shiʿi political blocs.[67]

The new parliament sought to Islamize Kuwaiti society. Islamist MPs again pushed to amend article 2 of the constitution and attempted to ban public Christmas celebrations.[68] Further, the Brotherhood succeeded in limiting Kuwaiti nationality to Muslims in 1982 and in banning the consumption or sale of alcohol in embassies in 1983.[69] In the economic sector, three government financial institutions remained under the control of Brotherhood members: Zakat House and the World Islamic Charity Body, both under the leadership of the Minister of Awqaf Yusuf al-Hajji, and Kuwait Finance House, directed by Ahmad Baziʿ al-Yasin.[70]

The 1980s, with the ongoing Iran-Iraq war and a new Islamist-leaning parliament at home, proved tumultuous. In 1982, the crash of Kuwait's unofficial stock market, the Suq al-Manakh, led to a financial crisis and significant backlash against the government, which had failed to regulate the technically illegal market. Although the government tried to bail out those affected, thousands of Kuwaitis were bankrupted in the aftermath of the crash.[71] On top of the domestic financial crisis and drop in oil prices, a series of bombs was set off in Kuwait in December 1983 by sympathizers of the pro-Iranian Shiʿi organization al-Daʿwa al-Islamiyya.[72] Hijackings of commercial airliners in 1984 and 1985, linked to the earlier bombings, added to the tense environment.[73] In May 1985, the amir himself was attacked in a motorcade, and two of his guards were killed in the assault waged by Islamic Jihad.[74] In July of the same year, two bombings at cafés in Kuwait City wounded ninety and killed eight, including an Interior Ministry official.[75] Overall, the attacks between December 1983 and the summer of 1985 resulted in some two-dozen civilian deaths and over one hundred injuries.[76]

As the government failed to stop such violence, criticisms of the regime became more widespread. Members of the Brotherhood were also censured, even facing limited losses in the 1983 NUKS elections.[77] In the words of Lori Plotkin Boghardt, "Although the Islamist deputies publicly disassociated themselves from the attacks, the public perceived both Sunni and Shiite fundamentalists to be ideologically related to the militant extremists perpetuating the bombings. By 1984, some Kuwaiti press articles were calling for a return to Arabism as the basis for Kuwaiti society."[78]

In this chaotic atmosphere, press suspensions and government subsidies to newspapers increased.[79] Several political dissidents, mostly non-Kuwaitis with various ideological leanings, were arrested, and some fifteen thousand foreigners were deported in 1985 and twenty-seven thousand in 1986.[80] Despite the ongoing unrest, elections were held as scheduled in

1985 and, in Peter Mansfield's description, "produced an Assembly which still had a conservative majority but in which an effective *de facto* opposition of radicals and independents increased in size and cohesion."[81] Notably, Islah retained the three seats in the Assembly that it had won in 1981.[82] It was in this parliament that, for the first time, "the cordial relationship between the Muslim Brotherhood Movement's deputies and the regime . . . was transformed into a confrontational one."[83]

Islamist MPs continued their efforts to Islamize Kuwaiti society and in 1985 successfully ousted Education Minister Hassan al-Ibrahim, whom they regarded as too secular,[84] on account of his, and the government's, attempts to decrease religious studies curricula at universities.[85] Disturbingly for the government, Islah, whose electoral record in the 1980s is illustrated in Table 5.1, seemed increasingly willing to work with other, even secular, opposition blocs to achieve its goals: "the Islamic fundamentalist and pan-Arab, leftist MPs often found common ground in blocking government bills and in sponsoring legislation or resolutions against the cabinet."[86] In fact, a number of political blocs, including Islah, banded together to interpellate, or question in parliament, the oil and finance ministers and helped force the resignation of the aforementioned liberal minister of education.[87] Islah was working alongside other members of the opposition toward common goals, perhaps in reaction to criticisms at that time that Islamists privileged social reform over more immediate issues of national concern.[88]

In July 1986, Prime Minister Shaykh Saʿad al-Salem al-Sabah submitted the cabinet's resignation, claiming that parliament's continued attacks on ministers made it impossible for the government to operate. Two days later, Amir Shaykh Jaber al-Ahmad al-Sabah (r. 1977–2006) dissolved the legislature.[89] With this disbandment, he also placed restrictions on the press and outlawed public gatherings of over five people.[90] During the second parliamentary suspension, another series of bombs, eleven in total, was set off in 1987; the Iran-Iraq war raged on; and another commercial airliner was hijacked in 1988.[91] Meanwhile, opposition coalesced among Islamists, merchants, the growing intelligentsia, and former parliamentarians, all calling for the restoration of parliament.[92] With the end in August 1988 of the Iran-Iraq war, a primary justification for the dissolution of parliament and increased press censorship, pressures arose for the elections to be called and for restrictions on the press to be lifted.[93]

In autumn 1988, the opposition, including Islah, started a petition campaign, calling for the restoration of parliament and reinstatement of the 1962 Constitution.[94] Created by thirty-two members of the dissolved parliament from various ideological factions, the so-called Constitutional Movement circulated the petition that eventually, with the help of student and voluntary associations, gathered thirty-thousand signatures.[95] Unable to meet publicly, members of the opposition instead gathered at private homes in a series of Monday

TABLE 5.1

Islah's Performance in Parliamentary Elections in the 1980s

Election	Number of Brotherhood MPs
1981	3
1985	3

Source: Kuwait Politics Database, http://www.kuwaitpolitics.org.

night *dīwāniyyāt* beginning in December 1989. Such gatherings, in the words of Ghabra, "represented the new cooperation between the various forces of society.... It was supported by the associations, their organizing committees, and many sectors of society."[96] As during the other period of parliamentary suspension, Brotherhood-dominated NUKS played a large role, having been active in the wide-ranging campaign to collect signatures for the petition denouncing the legislature's dissolution.[97]

As the Constitutional Movement gathered momentum among both secular and Islamist blocs, its meetings turned into protests and led to confrontations with police and to government attempts to shut down certain *dīwāniyyāt*.[98] Security forces also attempted to stop public meetings, even attacking a mosque with tear gas, and launched a campaign of arrests, which included former Islah MP ʿAbdullah al-Nafisi.[99] This incident led Islah members to adopt a more conciliatory stance toward the regime, and it stopped participating in public gatherings.[100] Finally, in the face of sustained popular pressure from other groups, Shaykh Jaber agreed to receive the opposition's petition for the restoration of parliament in February 1990.[101]

Rather than agreeing to call for new parliamentary elections, however, the amir proposed the formation of a seventy-five-member National Council, fifty of whom would be elected and twenty-five appointed by the amir. The council would be solely consultative, with the task of studying "the advisability and feasibility of a restoration of parliament."[102] It could propose changes to the constitution, yet lacked the National Assembly's power to question ministers about policies or to debate the budget.[103] NUKS issued a strong statement against the establishment of the National Council, yet the government did not acquiesce.[104] In the face of regime obstinacy, Islah's leaders released a memorandum in May 1990 that called on the amir to limit the National Council's term length to one year, rather than the proposed four.[105] Though the Brotherhood had agreed to back the council for one year,[106] it ultimately supported the broader opposition in boycotting the council's elections, which were held in June 1990.[107]

Despite the boycott, the council's election had an official turnout rate of 62 percent of eligible voters.[108] Because only allies of the government had run for election, however, the National Council was composed primarily of tribal leaders sympathetic to the al-Sabah.[109] The council had begun meeting when, on August 2, 1990, Iraqi President Saddam Hussein invaded Kuwait. During the invasion and occupation, which lasted until February 1991, the Brotherhood's role drastically changed from agitating for political participation alongside broader opposition to forming an integral part of the resistance movement inside Kuwait.

Changing Ideology and the Second Internal Division of the Kuwaiti Brotherhood

The spread of revolutionary Islamist ideology in the 1980s, as relations with the government worsened, led to a second internal split in the Kuwaiti Brotherhood. Two trends emerged: the fundamentalist strand, which rejected participation in a non-Islamic government, and the more moderate one, which considered the practice of political work a means of facilitating *daʿwa*.[110] ʿAbdullah al-Nafisi represented the extreme rejectionist, fundamentalist stance. He considered a clash with the government to be inevitable, even stating that "[t]he greatest actual enemy to the Islamic movement is the regimes. It is clear power we see night and day and it is the obstacle before the march of Islamic *daʿwa*."[111]

Editor-in-chief of *al-Mujtama*, Isma'il al-Shatti, on the other hand, advocated a more moderate stance. He referred to himself as a "gradualist reformer" who hoped to effect eventual progress toward the Islamization of society *through* the political system, rather than by opposing it.[112] Furthermore, al-Shatti "explained that parliamentary work endowed the revivalists with societal credibility."[113] In 1987, al-Nafisi resigned from Islah, on grounds that the discipline of the political bloc was too tightly knit and not suited to the all-encompassing nature of Islam.[114] Although al-Nafisi had served as an Islah MP, he came to believe that reform was too slow in changing society and favored radical changes instead.[115] His very public commentary helped create a new generation of Brotherhood members who challenged the gradualist tactics the movement had developed in the 1970s and instead urged confrontation with the government.[116]

Unlike the division in al-Jam'iat al-Irshad al-Islami (Irshad) in the 1950s, this split did not diminish Islah's membership, with the number of officially registered members of the movement reaching 1,170 by 1989.[117] It did, however, contribute to Islah's use of "inconsistent tactics toward the regime."[118] While Islah participated in the Constitutional Movement, it also retreated when the government failed to fulfill the group's demands.[119]

The Kuwaiti Muslim Brotherhood amid Iraqi Invasion and Occupation

The Kuwaiti Muslim Brotherhood filled the political vacuum that emerged during the Iraqi occupation, taking on roles traditionally filled by the state. Following the crisis, the Kuwaiti Brotherhood began advocating, through the ICM, for broad-ranging political reform, often in cooperation with secular opposition blocs. During this period, the ICM began to increasingly balance its ideological aims with a prodemocracy agenda, transforming itself from a group aiming to Islamize society to an influential member of the broader political opposition.

The Iraqi invasion and subsequent occupation, followed by the American-led liberation of Kuwait, displaced the country's citizens and disrupted the existing political system. Within hours of the invasion, Amir Shaykh Jaber and much of the ruling family had fled to Saudi Arabia. On August 8, 1990, six days after the invasion, Iraq formally annexed Kuwait and declared it its nineteenth province on August 28. Though the border between the two countries had been previously contested, Iraqi actions were shocking.

Life in Kuwait changed dramatically, as a brutal Iraqi campaign of torture and looting took hold and as thousands of Kuwaitis fled the country.[120] The horrors of occupation led more than half of the Kuwaiti population to flee and motivated those remaining to forge a resistance movement using preexisting social institutions—namely mosques and cooperative societies.[121] Notably, both of these were essentially under control of the Muslim Brotherhood.[122] Though cooperative societies originally functioned as supermarkets, they took on political significance, "serving as a forum for public debate on issues of general importance and as a bellwether of political trends."[123] Mosques and cooperative societies, protected by their apolitical appearance, helped resistance groups take up arms against the Iraqi army while also aiding in supplying the Kuwaiti population with food, medical care, and other services.

The Brotherhood's Change in Tactics under Occupation

The new circumstances under occupation led the Muslim Brotherhood to focus primarily on Kuwait's liberation and the provision of services ahead of the issues it had previously promoted, specifically the Islamization of society.[124] The Brotherhood worked toward liberation by establishing a Committee of Social Solidarity, which aimed to increase living standards for Kuwaitis by disbursing treasury rations to markets of cooperative societies.[125] The Brotherhood thus became instrumental in "supervis[ing] the provision of basic services to the citizens."[126] In addition, the Brotherhood established the Harakat al-Murabitun (hereafter Murabitun Movement), which worked to publicize the atrocities of Iraqi occupation and to gain experience in armed resistance and the management of people inside Kuwait during occupation.[127] It also published a weekly magazine, under the leadership of Nasir al-Sani', called *al-Murabitun*, which was issued in London.[128]

Outside of the country, the International Commission of Solidarity with Kuwait was considered the sister movement to the Murabitun Movement on the inside.[129] Tareq al-Suwaidan founded this organization in Washington, DC, yet branches also existed in Saudi Arabia, Egypt, the United Arab Emirates (UAE), and Bahrain.[130] The group aimed to garner popular and material support by raising global awareness of the Iraqi occupation. Namely, it circulated information from inside Kuwait to international media outlets for publication. The organization also promoted awareness of the atrocities in Kuwait through actions like making January 21, 1991 Kuwait Solidarity Day and requesting "that everyone fasts and prays for the oppressed Kuwaitis inside Kuwait and we pray that God protects the innocents and oppressed and the valiant fighters fighting for our just cause."[131] The organization's Islamist tilt was clear from such statements. Both inside and outside Kuwait, members of the Brotherhood led fundraising and support efforts, which were crucial in bringing international attention to conditions inside Kuwait.[132] In the words of al-Suwaidan, "The Ikhwan was in the forefront, even before the government. The Ikhwan were in charge of the needs of people inside and on the forefront outside."[133] For the first time in all the super-rentiers of the Gulf, the Kuwaiti Brotherhood took on a role akin to other Ikhwan movements in the region, providing services and filling the vacuum left by an ineffective (and largely absent) government. Considering the dire circumstances during that period, it is unsurprising that it set aside ideological aims in favor of aiding the Kuwaiti population in the immediate term through material provisions.

Negotiating with the Ruling Family in Exile

Iraqi occupation led Kuwaitis of all ideological strands to rally around the amir, Shaykh Jaber. In fact, some analysts judge that Saddam Hussein overestimated political opposition inside Kuwait, believing that discontented political blocs would welcome his invasion and overthrow of the al-Sabah.[134] Though they supported the amir, opposition leaders insisted on concessions from the government before its restoration to power. The ruling family's behavior in exile and the fact that most of its leading members had left the country immediately following the invasion became points of contention. During the occupation, the Constitutional Movement continued to call for reinstitution of the National Assembly.

In response, Shaykh Jaber held a Popular Congress in Jeddah in October 1990, inviting some 1,200 opposition figures. Notably, the Brotherhood was instrumental in uniting Kuwaitis through its efforts to hold the Congress.[135] At the event, Kuwaitis from a variety of political blocs committed their loyalty to the amir and to the constitution in exchange for the amir's pledge that participatory government would be revived following the Iraqi occupation.

Despite its initial unifying role, the Brotherhood began to pressure other attendees of the summit to push for the Islamization of Kuwaiti society after liberation and boost the movement's own power. Islah, for instance, hoped to have its leader, Yusuf al-Hajji, make the opening speech at the Congress, while most others agreed that Ahmed al-Sa'doun of the Popular Action Bloc was the most appropriate speaker, considering that he had served as president of the most recent National Assembly.[136] Ultimately, Islah compromised with the other opposition groups, and 'Abd al-'Aziz al-Saqr, the president of the first-ever National Assembly, took on the role of opening speaker.[137] Over the course of the summit, Brotherhood members continued clashing with other opposition strands, as described by Awadh,

> align[ing] themselves with the ruling family against the demands made by the nationalist groupings during the congress. These demands centred on the necessity of forming a government of national salvation, representing all political groupings, to oversee the progress of all matters concerning extricating Kuwait from the ordeal it was in prior to liberation. The Muslim Brotherhood Movement managed to block this demand. They succeeded after much insistence to incorporate into the Congress's concluding statement a proviso that affirmed that a future Kuwait would be based upon two important premises: Islamic creed and education Islamic [*sic*] and the insertion of the term *shuri* ["consultative"] alongside the term "democracy."[138]

The Brotherhood thereby managed to preserve its valuable ties to the government while pushing its own agenda. Having become a major political force under the Iraqi occupation, the Ikhwan looked to retain political clout in the postliberation era. The amir, crown prince, and opposition ultimately agreed to reinstate the 1962 Constitution and to allow more popular participation in government, in exchange for opposition support of al-Sabah authority during the occupation.[139]

In January 1991, a second meeting with the opposition was arranged in Jeddah. At this point, however, the ruling family had successfully launched an international public relations campaign "equat[ing] liberation with restoration of the status quo ante," thereby allowing the al-Sabah to maintain support from its traditional tribal supporters and making the regime less dependent on members of the opposition for support.[140] In this way, the ruling family managed to plan for political life in postliberation Kuwait without the input of independent blocs.[141] Still, opposition blocs insisted on the restoration of the 1962 Constitution.

Liberation and Domestic Turmoil

Throughout the Iraqi occupation, the Kuwaiti government urged international support for Iraq's unconditional withdrawal. The government funded media campaigns in the United States and Europe and offered financial incentives to allies for assistance.[142] The aforementioned Brotherhood-led International Commission of Solidarity with Kuwait also played a large role in lobbying governments for assistance. Having secured backing from the international community through Security Council Resolution 660, an American-led coalition began its campaign against Iraq in August 1990. On February 26, 1991, after an air battle under Operation Desert Storm, Iraqi forces left Kuwait.[143] In the aftermath of liberation, the amir declared martial law.[144] During this period, various human rights violations took place at the hands of the Kuwaiti government, namely targeting Arab expatriates, especially Palestinians, whose loyalty was questioned after the Palestine Liberation Organzation (PLO) failed to support the US-led liberation.[145] The Kuwaiti government acknowledged such violations and pledged to put on trial those who had participated in the atrocities. The Muslim Brotherhood was particularly vocal in its demands to hold accountable those responsible for the violence and led efforts to do so.[146]

In April 1991, Shaykh Jaber appointed a new government, consisting primarily of members of the old regime and notably excluding those who had remained inside Kuwait during the war.[147] This move led to complaints from the opposition, including members of the Muslim Brotherhood, whose ranks had not been consulted in the cabinet's formation.[148] The highly contested National Council, which had been elected in 1990 amid an opposition boycott, was also reconvened. The opposition, emboldened after having faced the brutalities of the Iraqi occupation, protested.[149]

Unwilling to make substantial political reforms yet facing increasing opposition, the amir tried to win popular support from Islamists and liberals alike by providing economic disbursements. Although the government owed billions of dollars in debts from the war, it announced plans to "pay existing consumer loans, car loans and mortgage loans to Kuwaitis, pay back salaries to government employees for the occupation period, exempt Kuwaitis from utility and other public service charges and rents incurred during the occupation, and increase government entitlements in a variety of categories (marriage grants, child allowances, aid to orphans, widows and the poor)."[150] In March 1992, all Kuwaitis working in the public sector received a 25 percent salary increase, and the government issued a bailout to the financial sector.[151] This tactic, not only economically unsustainable, also failed to satisfy an opposition that felt entitled to a representative government—particularly after having experienced the Iraqi occupation, which the ruling family had largely fled. Furthermore, Kuwaitis were angered by the government's slow postwar rebuilding efforts and the appearance of corruption in efforts at reconstruction.[152] Contrary to rentier state theory's prediction, then, opposition continued in the face of increasingly generous government handouts.

In such an atmosphere, Islamists garnered additional support, demonstrating the appeal of their ideology as a rallying point for political opposition even in the presence of rentier benefits. As explained by Sami Zubaida,

> The Gulf War and its ramifications were crucial in reinforcing political Islam as the most potent form of nationalism . . . . The clear exposure of their [the Kuwaiti rulers'] dependence on American protection widened the deficit of legitimacy with their own people, opposition being most commonly articulated in the very Islamic idioms used by the authorities. The bounty of oil may no longer be sufficient to maintain the distributive "rentier" state.[153]

The Muslim Brotherhood offered the ideological inspiration that the government could not provide, even in the face of government efforts to buy off opposition. Islam became a weapon of Arabism against the West and became politicized as such. The Iraqi invasion and occupation strained relations between the Kuwaiti Brotherhood and its parent organization in Egypt, however, leading to the formal end of their relationship in 1991.

A Kuwaiti Muslim Brotherhood Independent of the International Movement

As mentioned previously, ties between the Kuwaiti Brotherhood and the central organization remained strong into the 1980s, with the Kuwaiti branch heavily influenced by the Egyptian model and linked through personal connections.[154] Perhaps because of this historically strong relationship, the international Muslim Brotherhood was among the first organizations to condemn the Iraqi invasion of Kuwait. The group released a statement from Cairo in which it disparaged Iraq's actions and demanded its immediate and complete withdrawal from Kuwait.[155] This stance changed, however, following the Saudi Arabian government's declaration of its alliance with a coalition of foreign forces, headed by the United States, to liberate Kuwait. Following that announcement, the international Brotherhood issued a statement stressing the importance of expelling Western troops from Muslim territory.[156] This second proclamation represented the "turning point" in the international Brotherhood's position when it came to fear the social and political consequences of thousands of foreign troops entering the Arabian Peninsula.[157]

Significantly, not every branch of the Brotherhood held the same view. Groups in Lebanon and Iraqi Brotherhood sympathizers abroad stood firmly against Hussein regime, "declar[ing] their support for any action leading to the liberation of Kuwait even if it required bringing in foreign forces to the region."[158] Meanwhile, the Jordanian branch staunchly supported both the Iraqi invasion and the confrontation of foreign troops.[159] The majority of Brotherhood affiliates, including those in Algeria, Egypt, Saudi Arabia, Sudan, and Tunisia, though not necessarily supportive of Saddam Hussein's actions, could not back a non-Arab or non-Muslim resolution to the conflict.[160] Members of these branches therefore continued their ties with the Hussein regime, as they supported his government's opposition to the foreign coalition troops.[161]

The contradictory stances among different national Brotherhood affiliates made it difficult for the Kuwaiti Brotherhood to determine its approach. In October 1990, the Kuwaiti movement sent a formal complaint to the Brotherhood's General Guide in Cairo, Hamad ʿAbd al-Nasir, expressing opposition to the international Brotherhood's stance and explaining the necessity of expelling Iraqi troops.[162] This missive seems to have been ignored. In fact, at an international Brotherhood conference during the occupation, Kuwaiti Brotherhood members were pressured to approve the meeting's final statement, in which the Iraqi invasion was not decried.[163]

Relations suffered considerably following a visit by a delegation of Islamists to Saddam Hussein himself in early 1991.[164] This move, as described by Awadh, "was interpreted as an expression of Islamic advocacy for the Iraqi regime's stance toward the foreign liberation forces."[165] Despite the organization's previous calls for a meeting to help resolve the issue, a statement by ʿAbbasi Madani, leader of the Algerian Islamic Salvation Front (an independent Islamist group not affiliated with the Muslim Brotherhood), seemed to support Hussein. Madani said, "The Islamic movement concurred with Saddam Hussein in one point only, and it is confrontation of the American occupation forces present in the Gulf."[166] The international Brotherhood denied supporting this visit,[167] and in fact no high-level representative from the international section attended, with the Egyptian government having prohibited the travel of General Guide Hamad ʿAbd al-Nasir, as well as of prominent members Mustafa Mashhour and Maʿmun al-Hudaybi.[168] Nonetheless, the visit and resulting statement were considered a sign of the international branch's support for the Iraqi position, leading to a bitter exchange between the Kuwaiti and international Brotherhood.

Following the liberation of Kuwait in February 1991, Isma'il al-Shatti published a series of articles in *al-Mujtama* accusing some Brotherhood leaders in Cairo of misconduct and calling on them to step down from their control of the organization, in addition to demanding a freeze of Kuwait's membership in the international Brotherhood.[169] Meanwhile, Ma'mun al-Hudaybi, official spokesperson of the Egyptian-based Brotherhood, affirmed its strong relationship with the Kuwaiti Ikhwan and claimed that al-Shatti's opinion was personal, rather than reflective of the entire organization.[170]

The Kuwaiti Muslim Brotherhood split into two factions. One group favored the severing of ties with the international branch, privileging local work over a focus on the international sphere.[171] Meanwhile, another faction considered cooperation with the international section critical to the Kuwaiti branch, as it "embodies the dimension of thought, ideology and morale."[172] 'Abdullah al-'Ali al-Mutawa in particular worked to resolve the crisis between the Kuwaiti and international Muslim Brotherhood.[173] Despite the existence of varying viewpoints within the organization, the Kuwaiti Brotherhood ultimately froze relations with the international movement "as a moderate solution to satisfy both sides of the debate within the organization."[174]

The divergence over responses to the Iraqi occupation was not the only time when the Kuwaiti Brotherhood disagreed with the international section, perhaps signaling the Kuwaiti branch's desire to follow an independent path even before the Iraqi invasion.[175] First, the branches differed over the entitlement of women to vote and stand in elections. While the international section publicly supported the extension of such rights, the Kuwaiti Brotherhood maintained that a woman must fulfill certain sharia conditions to vote or stand as a candidate. Sami Nasir al-Khalidi summarizes, "It believes, in fact, that the Muslim woman is not socially, culturally, or politically prepared to enable her to participate in parliamentary elections, whether as a voter or as a candidate for election."[176] The Kuwaiti Brotherhood went so far as to help ensure the passage of a sharia-based fatwa[177] from the Ministry of Awqaf and Islamic Affairs' Department of Fatwas, forbidding women's participation as voters or candidates in parliamentary elections.[178]

Second, the Kuwaiti Muslim Brotherhood tacitly supported Iraq in its war with Iran during the 1980s, though the international section "denounced the continuation of the Iran-Iraq war, as they considered that it was simultaneously draining the resources of the Islamic Umma[179] while serving the interests of other countries, most prominently, Israel."[180] As a result, the international branch was critical of both sides in the conflict, whereas Kuwait quietly backed Iraq's interests due to its function as a bulwark against the spread of Iranian (and Shi'i) power in the Gulf.[181] Third, the international movement found no basis in sharia for the legality of hereditary monarchies.[182] In its view, only if people have the option to accept or reject the monarchy of their own volition is it considered legitimate.[183] The Kuwaiti branch, however, considered hereditary regimes, of the type seen in the Gulf, to be part of sharia and Islamic history, as they ruled during the Umayyad, Abbasid, and Ottoman Empires.[184]

Having weathered such conflicts, the international section and Kuwaiti branch formally parted ways in 1991. In the tense environment after liberation, the Kuwaiti Ikhwan began to expand its role in the local political system by creating an independent political bloc. Because this bloc was autonomous from the international section, the Kuwaiti Brotherhood managed "on a tactical level, to persevere with their political approach without their views clashing with the Muslim Brotherhood structure abroad."[185]

Emergence of the ICM

On March 30, 1991, the Kuwaiti Muslim Brotherhood created the Islamic Constitutional Movement (ICM). Over one thousand people are said to have attended the founding meeting of the movement, where members elected Shaykh Jassim Muhalhal al-Yasin as Secretary General of the ICM and ʿIsa Majid al-Shahin as official spokesperson.[186] The organization's membership was considered "an organic extension" of the Murabitun Movement, as well as of Brotherhood-sponsored *dīwāniyyāt* and social organizations.[187] Overall, the ICM's leadership "tended to be younger" than Islah's initial profile, with many principal organizers having joined the Brotherhood in the 1970s and 1980s as students.[188] The ICM's founding statement describes it as "a popular Kuwaiti movement including in its rank a group of Kuwaiti citizens believing in constitutional legitimacy and in the Kuwaiti constitution as the legal framework for the regime and legislation."[189] The new bloc thus, as explained by Nathan J. Brown, "sought to have a comprehensive political agenda and hardly restricted itself to religious and cultural issues."[190]

Although the Brotherhood had gained considerable influence in the social sector during the occupation, it remained "outside the central structure of political power."[191] Importantly, members of the Brotherhood did not consider their new emphasis on politics to be "a switch" from their past social work;[192] rather, it was seen as a maturation, which came about after Kuwaitis had effectively "run the country by themselves" under occupation.[193] Certainly, members, in the words of one former ICM member of parliament (MP), "felt that this [political branch] was an angle we were missing. The social group is helpful, but without politics you may not enjoy the influence political groups enjoy."[194] Because the Brotherhood had already taken on a political role during the occupation, there was little internal debate about the need for a formal political bloc, and so the division between *ḥizb* and *ḥaraka* became official, with Islah continuing its general social role and the ICM managing electoral campaigns.

In the process of creating a political bloc, the Kuwaiti Ikhwan underwent a number of changes. Most significantly, the Brotherhood gradually learned to work with other, even secular movements toward common goals and seemed willing to accept a middle ground, or an interim period in which sharia was not fully applied, to push for other gains.[195] For example, it "became flexible enough to agree to deal with an economic system involving usury . . . until such time as an Islamic system would demonstrate the advantage of a non-usurial system."[196] Such willingness to compromise differed a great deal from the Qutbism of the 1960s; the ICM's "goals became to reform instead of completely change."[197] As explained by Tareq al-Suwaidan, this approach was "not a concession nor a retrogression, but instead indicated maturity and pragmatism in understanding the arena and weighing the new postulates with the aim of achieving the greatest number of gains possible."[198] Another part of the movement's development was its organization of specialized delegations within the body, each with a separate decision-making body, as opposed to the previous model wherein one body dealt with cultural, social, political, and organizational matters.[199]

At the beginning of the 1990s, as signaled by the Brotherhood's stance during the Popular Congress, the ICM benefitted from relatively peaceful relations with the government. It profited from what Awadh describes as "the political authority's reluctance to confront any political tendency which called for basic theological principles, such as the 'Islamic religion,' while being committed to working within the framework of the constitution of the country."[200] In fact, in December 1991, the Brotherhood scored a political gain when the government created a higher consultative committee to ensure that Kuwaiti laws were in line with sharia, though this body was not granted enforcement authority.[201] As the government began challenging Brotherhood attempts at further social reform and Islamization, the ICM became more strategic in reaching its goals, banding together with members of the opposition to maximize electoral gains, as it had done during other suspensions of parliament.[202]

Restoration of Parliamentary Life in the 1990s

In May 1992, opposition figures from across the political spectrum, including the ICM, called a press conference, criticizing the new and largely pro-government cabinet, and reiterating calls for the restoration of the National Assembly.[203] The government had not granted permission for this meeting, and the lights were turned off as reporters attempted to speak with opposition figures.[204] Despite this setback, "the atmosphere was one where political groups wanted to work together for Kuwait."[205] In June, in the face of continued protest, Shaykh Jaber ended martial law and set a parliamentary election date for October.[206]

The 1992 election focused on two primary sets of issues: "laws for more effective government," namely to reduce corruption, and "expansion and protection of political and civil rights."[207] Notably, neither of these was historically important for the Brotherhood, yet the group recognized their particular importance in that period. Various groups from the opposition coalition won thirty-five of the fifty seats—with sixteen from secular (primarily liberal) opposition MPs and nineteen MPs from Islamist (Brotherhood and Salafi) groups. The ICM had entered seven candidates in the elections, five of whom were successful.[208] It publicly supported twenty-five candidates in total, however, including secular leaders who had pressured the al-Sabah family to restore parliamentary life before the Iraqi invasion, as well as candidates in districts that favored the Brotherhood.[209] The success of opposition candidates further "demonstrated that the al-Sabahs could no longer fully rely on patronage and tribal loyalty" to retain a pro-government majority in the Assembly.[210] Perhaps having seen the inefficacy of economic disbursements in quieting opposition, the amir also granted six ministries (oil, justice, commerce and industry, education, Islamic affairs, labor and social affairs) to new MPs, five of whom were ICM members.[211]

Following their success at the ballot box and in gaining cabinet seats, opposition members of the 1992 parliament, who had initially formed a coalition, became divided on religious and cultural issues, as "[t]he parliamentarians from Islamist groups believed that the vote could be interpreted as a mandate for the Islamization of the country's laws and regulations."[212] The Brotherhood had first used the social sector to influence politics, yet later came to see the political arena as the primary tool for Islamizing society—a controversial move for its secular coalition members. Despite the fact that Brotherhood deputies and sympathizers were the largest minority in this Assembly, they failed to implement the movement's traditional goals.[213] Though secular political blocs had worked with the ICM to guarantee the restoration of parliamentary life, they did not support the Islamists' social agenda, which appeared to have been set aside during the electoral campaign. The ICM's campaign of political liberalness, then, decisively did not extend to the social sphere.

The ICM continued to push the government to implement sharia. In 1994, all but six liberal MPs signed a petition demanding that article 2 of the constitution be changed from "shariʿa shall be *a* main source of legislation" to "shariʿa shall be *the* main source of legislation."[214] A bill to that effect was signed by the majority of elected MPs.[215] To pass, however, legislation must receive two-thirds support from elected MPs *and* government-appointed ministers; it failed to garner necessary support from the ministers following a cabinet reshuffle that year that had harmed the Brotherhood's representation.[216] Following this disappointment, five Islamist MPs unsuccessfully suggested the creation of "an authority 'to direct the public to do good and refrain from evil,'" with offices in every district to promote religiously acceptable behavior and report violations of it.[217]

In addition, Brotherhood MPs demanded several changes in the education sector, spending many parliamentary sessions challenging a decision by the dean of the Faculty of Medicine at Kuwait University to prohibit wearing the niqab in laboratories.[218] Though Islamist parliamentarians attempted to overturn the university's decision, leading to backlash from many professors, the dean's ruling was upheld.[219] Members of the ICM also strongly backed the gender segregation of Kuwait University, and a bill mandating such separation was defeated by a narrow margin in 1994.[220] Ultimately, in 1996, the law for segregation passed, though it specified that the university would be coeducational for five years and that there would be no government interference in private coeducational schools.[221] The Brotherhood also unsuccessfully attempted to remove Education Minister Ahmad al-Rubʿi from office after he had "embarked on a series of educational reforms that aimed to diminish religious influence in the educational system."[222]

The Brotherhood's emphasis on its social platform ultimately led to the crumbling of its coalition in parliament. Repeated demands from Islamist MPs for cultural reforms also, notably, delayed the discussion of what secular members of the opposition considered more substantive and urgent domestic and foreign policy issues and forged "something of an alliance between liberals and government."[223] The ICM's political pragmatism in this period seems to have ended once it entered parliament, from which it hoped to impose controversial social policies to Islamize society. Because of the ICM's focus on such cultural issues in the 1990s, "the government was able to play opposition elements off against each other and opposition movements themselves began to focus on some of the issues dividing them."[224]

In 1994, Prime Minister Shaykh Saʿad al-Sabah reshuffled the cabinet, taking away the ICM's posts, as the cabinet had become fractious.[225] Brotherhood members also lost positions in subcommittees of parliament during the 1995 session.[226] Further diminishing the Brotherhood's position was the government's prohibition of zakat committees in mosques in 1996, which had been an important source of funding for the Ikhwan.[227] Such changes granted the group more freedom "to move into fuller opposition."[228] The ICM worked with secular blocs to move forward with anticorruption legislation. In fact, as a measure of its commitment to rooting out corruption, ICM MPs have made public their personal financial assets in the past.[229]

In an atmosphere of increasing suspicion of the government, elections were held on schedule in October 1996. The government and broader Kuwaiti population were happy to see the dissolution of the 1992 parliament, which "was widely regarded as overly contentious."[230]

TABLE 5.2

The ICM's Performance in Parliamentary Elections in the 1990s

Election	Number of ICM MPs
1992	5
1996	5
1999	4

Source: Kuwait Politics Database, http://www.kuwaitpolitics.org.

In fact, many have insisted that the government intervened in the 1996 election to forge a more cooperative Assembly.[231] Of the fifty new MPs, twenty-one were considered cooperative with the government; eighteen Islamists were elected, with more from the Salafi movement and fewer (five in total) from the ICM.[232] Tétreault contends that "[t]hese results were touted as a popular reaction against the opposition, an electorate opting for cooperation over contention. But the 1996 parliament was even more contentious than its predecessor."[233]

In May 1999, Shaykh Jaber dissolved the National Assembly, scheduling a new election for July. This third dissolution was similar to the 1976 and 1986 closures of parliament in that it was spurred by parliamentary investigations into the behavior of the al-Sabah ministers, yet, in this instance, elections were scheduled immediately after dissolution, as required by the constitution.[234] The 1999 elections were a success for liberals, who earned sixteen seats, while the primary losses went to MPs sympathetic to the government; ICM support remained constant, as it earned four seats.[235] A large number of incumbents lost seats in rural districts, suggesting "[t]he weakening hold of traditional political leaders."[236] The resulting parliament was thus considered "an opposition stronghold."[237] Having established itself as a major political force, illustrated by Table 5.2 which records the number of seats won by Islah in the 1990s, the Kuwaiti Muslim Brotherhood began to assert itself even more in the twenty-first century as part of a broader opposition movement.

THE QATARI CASE

Meanwhile in Qatar, shortly after its establishment in 1975, the Muslim Brotherhood experienced a brief period of expansion during the 1980s, followed by a phase of introspection that ultimately led to its dissolution. In the absence of its ideological rival, Arab nationalism, the Muslim Brotherhood did not hold the appeal or support from government that it once enjoyed. In the increasingly comfortable Qatari domestic environment, largely devoid of institutionalized means of political participation, gaining followers became more difficult, and so the Qatari Ikhwan resolved to remain an amorphous group, rather than a structured organization. In this way, however, it still has managed to remain part of the political conversation and landscape inside Qatar.

The 1980s and 1990s: Internal Review

In the 1980s, recent Qatari graduates began joining the local Muslim Brotherhood affiliate, eager to coordinate activities, having studied in countries with active Ikhwan groups.[238] At the same time, an influx of Syrian Brotherhood supporters entered Qatar following the Asad regime's brutal crackdown on the organization, thus integrating into the existing Qatari structure.[239] It was during this period that the magazine *al-Umma al-Qataria* (The Qatari Umma) was published (from 1980 until 1986), under the leadership of Syrian Brotherhood member ʿAmr ʿAbid Husna.[240] The magazine "expressed the intellectual content of the Brotherhood project."[241]

Returning Qatari students, as they sought to expand and formalize the group's activities, clashed with the older generation, however. As Tarek al-Turabi and Amr al-Mubarak explain, "When Jassim Sultan and other operatives returned to Qatar from their studies at the beginning of the 1980s and assimilated into the local Brotherhood, they were shocked by the leadership's narrow perspective. The organization bore no clear plan or vision for reform aside from that found in the general Brotherhood literature."[242] This signaled the first difference in leadership of the Qatari Brotherhood, similar to generational cleavage seen in the first decades of the Kuwaiti Brotherhood. As in Kuwait, older members were reticent to ramp up Brotherhood activities without first considering their impact, while the younger generation saw no reason not to expand the Brotherhood's presence.[243] Without elections to contest and lacking the need to provide social services, the Qatari Brotherhood found itself in a unique position. Younger members began raising questions about the organization, such as the form it would take in the future (whether a political bloc or cultural organization), the impact it could have on Qatari society, and its overarching goals.[244]

Beginning in 1980–1981 and lasting until 1991, in part to resolve differing approaches in the leadership and partially to maximize the organization's impact, the Qatari Brotherhood undertook an extensive two-part study.[245] The first portion, which was published under the title *On Basics of the Islamic Plan for the Renaissance of the Umma: Readings in the Thought of the Martyr Imam Hasan al-Banna*,[246] focused on the ideology of al-Banna.[247] Interestingly, it was published under the name of ʿAbd al-Hamid al-Ghazali, a member of the Egyptian Brotherhood's Shura Council and the leader of its political department for nearly eight years.[248] The use of such authorship may have indicated tensions between the Qatari affiliate and the mother organization, as the volume reflected on the necessity and best means of updating Ikhwan ideology.[249]

The second part of the study remains unpublished and concerns the affiliate of the Brotherhood in Qatar specifically.[250] Members were assigned to answer a variety of questions about the Muslim Brotherhood's appropriate role in Qatar, using al-Banna's writings as a guide and the Egyptian experience as a reference.[251] The study was, in Mustafa ʿAshur's words, essentially "an intellectual and organizational dissection of the Brotherhood" in terms of its structure, communication, leadership, prevailing culture, and goals, as well as feasibility and risks associated with pursuing them.[252] Important questions included: Is there a real plan for the organization? How much has been achieved (in Qatar and elsewhere), and what remains to be achieved?[253] Generally, as al-Turabi and al-Mubarak describe, "it finished with one of the problems that pushed the re-evaluation to begin: that the Muslim Brotherhood's plans generally lacked clarity—what did it want exactly? And how would it get there?"[254]

After years of research and inquiry, the study revealed that many members considered the Qatari Brotherhood to have "been frozen by dogma, lost direction, and failed to adapt."[255] Members questioned the need for a Muslim Brotherhood organization in Qatar, a naturally conservative and religious society with few major economic, social, or political problems or openings.[256] Such questions led to broader discussion about how Islamist movements can survive in Gulf states where governments derive legitimacy from Islam and therefore support a variety of religious endeavors.[257] As Qatari Brotherhood leader Jassim Sultan put it, "By study and research, the pitfalls were obvious. The program doesn't fit Qatar. There is a major defect in the theory."[258]

Also harming the Brotherhood's popularity as a formal movement in Qatar was the rise of the stricter brand of Wahhabi Islam during the same period that the Brotherhood was undergoing internal examination; indeed, Qatar is the only other state in the world aside from Saudi Arabia whose official religion is Wahhabi Islam. The large group of Wahhabis within Qatar, though "never outwardly hostile to the Brotherhood," knew primarily of its work abroad and believed the organization was too political.[259] For them, loyalty belonged to the ruling shaykh, rather than to an ideology.[260] As a result, members of this strand of Islam were granted government positions. During the 1980s, Shaykh Khalifa appointed a number of Wahhabi exiles to the Interior Ministry, while also promoting a Najdi Wahhabi exile as Qatar's most senior cleric.[261] Further, former Interior Minister Shaykh ʿAbdullah bin Khalifa al-Thani was "appointed from the Wahhabi clique within the Qatari establishment." [262] Many of these officials were removed when Shaykh Hamad, beginning in 2003, replaced many government employees with this leaning.[263] Still, it has been charged that "this [Wahhabi] clique remains embedded among mid-level Qatari security officials."[264] With or without institutionalized government positions, however, Islamist ideologies remain influential inside Qatar.

Formal Dissolution of the Qatari Muslim Brotherhood

The Qatari Muslim Brotherhood was officially disbanded in 1999 through a vote among its members.[265] The process of its dissolution, about which very little is known, was completed in 2003. Deputy Guide of the Egyptian Muslim Brotherhood Muhammad Habib addressed the Qatari branch's decision: "The organization defines the direction and principles [of the group] so that its methodology and principles are not lost."[266] Ultimately, the Brotherhood in its traditional form was considered inappropriate for Qatar for a variety of reasons. The Qatari Muslim Brotherhood thus chose to exist as "an Islamic renaissance movement, rather than remain in the organizational hierarchy."[267]

Qatari Brotherhood members have, for the most part, remained silent about reasons for the organization's dissolution, and a great deal of speculation remains as to the motivations for its disbandment.[268] The primary explanation is that the Brotherhood, in places like Qatar, became "an irrelevant matter," as the organization can easily offer the same services without having any defined structure.[269] As former Kuwaiti Brotherhood member ʿAbdullah al-Nafisi posits, "We in the Arabian Peninsula are not in need of cloning the experience of Egypt (or any Muslim Brotherhood experience), as the conditions in Egypt justified the emergence of a tumor and the establishment of the Muslim Brotherhood in its time 1928."[270] In its comfortable surroundings and lacking institutionalized means of political participation, the Qatari branch, unlike other organizations, was not swayed by strong Islamist emotion or the desire for a political utopia.[271] In the words of Jassim Sultan, "Nobody will listen to any radical ideas when their needs are fulfilled."[272] He also posited that the lack of alternative political blocs in Qatar stunted the Brotherhood's growth, asserting that "these ideas grow if [they exist] in competition with others, but vanish without it."[273] According to Sultan, due to the absence of major grievances spurring political action, as well as the lack of ideological competition in Qatar, the Brotherhood's growth remained stunted.[274]

There are more complicated explanations for the Qatari Brotherhood's dissolution, however. One concerns the Qatari branch's relationship with the mother organization in Cairo. In the words of one Qatari interviewee, the Qatari Brotherhood "made an evaluation of its achievements as well as needed reforms and proposed reforms to the Shura Council [in Egypt], but those were rejected. They were rejected likely due to concerns from the international Muslim Brotherhood in Egypt about how the organization was managed—what should be covert and what should be overt, political versus social reform."[275] Certainly, the published segment of Qatar's internal evaluation revealed a number of problems with the central Brotherhood, particularly its lack of long-term strategy and focus.[276] Jassim Sultan admitted that the "connection to the main organization was sympathy rather than a line of authority; there was no command center."[277] The Qatari Brotherhood thus may have disbanded as a result of disagreements with the international leadership, ending its uneasy relationship with the mother organization by dissolving itself.

Another explanation posited for the Brotherhood's dissolution is the generally favorable stance of the Qatari government toward the organization. According to this theory, the Ikhwan realized that it would be, as Sultan put it, "easier for the Muslim Brotherhood to establish affiliates elsewhere through youth centers, websites. The government in Qatar was supportive of Brotherhood members joining existing institutions because the Brotherhood complemented its own agenda."[278] The arrangement of lectures, religious studies, and *ḥalaqāt*, as well as the organization of student and youth activities and social meetings, could hardly be considered threatening to the state. Harboring no ill will against the government and able to function as they wished under its supervision, Brotherhood members simply did not require a separate organizational structure, which itself was weak and informal even at its height.

A contradictory account maintains that government pressure, rather than an internal Brotherhood evaluation, led to its dissolution. Indirect pressure may have been placed on the organization as the movement became more popular throughout the Arab world.[279] Likely, though, fear of a government crackdown (however unlikely it was) was sufficient to prevent overt political action. The experience of the Saudi Brotherhood was instructive, as that government took a decisive turn against the movement when some of its members began pushing a domestic political agenda through the Sahwa movement in the 1990s. Around the same time, crackdowns on the Brotherhood also took place in Oman and the UAE. As for Qatar, one Gulf analyst explains, "the government sees them [members of the Brotherhood] as moderate but wanting to take power, so they can't give them too much leeway."[280] Perhaps anticipating government action, the Qatari branch was eager "to convert [from a more structured organization] to a trend inside Qatari society, away from the pressure of regulatory frameworks."[281] As an ideological movement, rather than an organization, the Brotherhood is able to maintain its followers and popular relevance, which it may have lost as an institutionalized entity; as Sultan put it, "Ideas live longer than any organization."[282]

One Qatari political commentator posits that the local Brotherhood branch in fact strategically *chose* to dismantle its formal organization to have freedom from government surveillance: "someone within the Brotherhood, after crackdown on the UAE, Saudi Arabia, decided we shouldn't use the Muslim Brotherhood name, be formally organized."[283] Al-Nafisi goes so far as to claim that "Qataris saw regulations and laws and formalization as hindering the natural and spontaneous growth of groups."[284] Further, according to al-Nafisi, members of the Qatari Brotherhood even advised the Emirati branch to disband to avoid potential future crackdowns because, in the absence of a distinct organization, repression becomes impossible.[285] Al-Nafisi thus concludes that the Qatari Brotherhood's decision to dissolve itself "showed gumption" and prevented members from facing problems that members of the Brotherhood encountered in other Gulf countries.[286]

Another theory is that the Qatari government pushed for the closure of the Brotherhood due to pressure from the Ministry of Awqaf and Islamic Affairs, which supported the organization abroad, but not domestically.[287] According to this view, the Qatari government demanded the disbandment of the domestic Brotherhood in exchange for backing its cause elsewhere. Yet another explanation is that the dissolution was "an initiative of Jassim Sultan," the Qatari Brotherhood's leader.[288] Sultan today promotes Mashruaʿ al-Nahda (Renaissance Project), an Islamist group that he has created to educate youth in "a new, more modern format of Islamist."[289] Still, some former members of the Qatari Ikhwan, unhappy with the disbandment, continue Brotherhood activities today in defiance of the dissolution, with Shaykh Yusuf al-Qaradawi said to have been particularly disappointed with the group's closure.[290]

For his part, Sultan insists, "I can assure you that the government did not at any time raise the issue . . . . It's simple—people inside decided to disband."[291] Having no institutionalized means of political participation, lacking experience in government, and not needed as a social support system or to provide services to citizens, there was little space for the organization to function. Sultan explains that "[i]n that particular historical moment we decided we were not adding anything or benefiting society, so we removed [ourselves] from public life."[292] Ultimately, the decision to dissolve was likely taken due to a combination of the fear of government crackdown and the ability of the Qatari Brotherhood to function informally under government supervision. In the absence of an organizational structure, as well as lacking a formal meeting place and publication, individual members of the movement have maintained influence over political debate and policymaking within the country without inciting government action against it. During the period of the Brotherhood's introspection, the ability of the informal sector to influence government calculations and policymaking became clear when the government faced limited challenges from some disaffected citizens.

The Turbulent 1990s

In April 1992, when the Qatari Muslim Brotherhood was undergoing internal examination, fifty-four prominent Qataris signed a petition[293] addressed to then Amir Shaykh Khalifa demanding "an elected council with real legislative and investigatory powers and . . . a constitution to guarantee democratic freedoms."[294] In a move not predicted by rentier state theory, the document also called for freedom of speech and the expansion of citizens' political and legal rights.[295] While the petition was not an Islamist one, it did state that the signatories' demands were "in accordance with our Islamic faith, which directs us to adopt consultations and to abide by them."[296] Writers of the petition thus recognized the importance of justifying their call for reform through religion, reflecting the pervasive influence of Islam in Qatar's political discourse.

Because "[t]he petitioners lacked a broad social base,"[297] Shaykh Khalifa ignored their demands, despite the fact that he had promised to establish a legislative assembly.[298] The amir also "ordered the telephones of the signatories to be tapped, confiscated their passports, barred some from leaving the country, and even arrested a few. After that, all the signatories faced government harassment and were strongly pressured to withdraw their signatures from the petition and to personally apologize to the emir."[299] Crown Prince Hamad, dissatisfied with his father's response, seized power through a nonviolent coup while Shaykh Khalifa was out of the country in June 1995.[300] Shortly after Shaykh Hamad took power, a counter-coup attempt by the former amir, Shaykh Khalifa, reportedly with Saudi support, led to the arrest of some one hundred al-Thani members, the expulsion and arrest of many members of the al-Murrah tribe associated with the coup, and "only reinforced Hamad's determination to present himself as a guarantor of Qatar's progress, modernity, and democracy."[301]

Shaykh Hamad's reforms were not universally accepted, however. In 1998, following the announcement of elections to the Central Municipal Council (CMC) under universal suffrage for Qatari citizens, a group of twenty-two Islamist scholars, under the leadership of ʿAbd al-Rahman al-Nuʿaimi, presented a petition to the Advisory Council.[302] This group objected to Shaykh Hamad's reforms—primarily his granting women the right to vote for and run as candidates in the CMC, "where they would have 'public authority' and the potential for 'leadership over men.'"[303] The petition, which was signed by three members of the ruling family, [304] also expressed discontent about the state's relatively lenient policies regarding alcohol.[305] As a result, al-Nuʿaimi was jailed for three years. Most significantly, Shaykh Hamad's reforms were maintained.[306] The al-Thani family, in this instance, insisted on implementing a liberal policy in the face of Islamist ideological resistance. Still, the regime faced nonideological opposition as well.

In June 1999, Qataris again became vocal about their complaints with the existing system, yet not in the form of a petition or even an organized political movement. Instead, grievances were aired on the government-owned radio program *Watani al-Habib Sabah al-Khair* (Good morning, my beloved nation), which allows callers to voice a wide variety of complaints. In one June 1999 episode, discussion centered on what callers considered to be excessive privileges of the royal family and other inequities in Qatari society. ʿAisha al-Muhannadi's comments were particularly cutting, stating that "[t]he ruling family has become a . . . big emotional and financial weight on the nation and its people."[307] Others echoed her opinion, calling for a decrease in allowances paid to al-Thani family members.[308] Further, the local newspaper *al-Raya* published an editorial on the same subject of the radio program, stating, "While Qataris are suffering from unemployment, lack of adequate housing and reduction of government subsidies . . . the ruling family continues to enjoy privileges."[309] The most vocal complaints were thus not ideological, but rather focused on the one thing rentier state theory predicts that citizens would bemoan: the distribution of rent money. The voicing of such grievances did not form the basis of organized or long-term opposition, however.

Although Shaykh Hamad instituted a series of political reforms, including limiting privileges of members of the royal family, Qatar's political and economic life remains dominated by the al-Thani family and their allies.[310] Matthew Gray clarifies that "[t]he family still wields power and gains wealth through state mechanisms, even if many of the processes of this have changed over time."[311] While economic prosperity in Qatar is undeniable and absolute poverty is virtually nonexistent among nationals, inequalities are still present within Qatari society.

Perhaps the sheer size of the al-Thani family, the largest in the Gulf relative to the size of the national population, has allowed it to infiltrate all areas of public life.[312] The al-Thani also had the advantage of coming to power in a state with few competing powerful families and without a strong merchant class to challenge its rule. As for independent opposition movements, the ruling family appears to have successfully co-opted the most influential independent movement in the present day by forging an alliance with the Muslim Brotherhood, which has long exerted influence on Qatari society. I. William Zartman points out, in the contexts of Egypt, Morocco, and Tunisia, that opposition movements can amplify support of the state: "Neither uses the other, but each serves the other's interests in performing its own role. Thus, stability in the contemporary Arab state can be explained not only by the government's handling of opposition but also by the opposition's handling of itself and the government."[313]

This type of symbiotic relationship may best describe the ties between the Qatari government and the Muslim Brotherhood, though the Ikhwan in that state has historically opposed government policy only in the social realm. In super-rentiers, such social policies carry significant political weight. The Qatari government has historically granted an outlet for the Muslim Brotherhood, and the group has in turn praised the government for its Islamist policies, thereby cementing the al-Thani power and domestic political stability—a testament to the system's strength. In sum, as Allen Fromherz puts it, "Qatar's past does not reveal a weak political and social system doomed to failure in a modern, complex environment, but rather a surprisingly robust, durable and socially cohesive tribal society in which Al-Thani, the ruling tribe, were first among equals. Tribal consensus, not simply top-down totalitarianism, characterized and continues to characterize some aspects of decision-making in Qatar."[314] Simply put, the Qatari regime does not place restrictions on the Muslim Brotherhood because it does not need to do so, marking its successful co-optation of political Islam. This co-optation extends to allowing the presence of a number of influential Brotherhood figures inside the state.

Shaykh Yusuf Al-Qaradawi and Other Brotherhood Members in Qatar

The continued public presence of Muslim Brotherhood ideologue Shaykh Yusuf al-Qaradawi in Qatar is often considered proof of the state's pro-Brotherhood stance and the power of the organization there. Al-Qaradawi is undoubtedly the most influential (and most controversial) Muslim Brother in the Gulf. He is by no means, however, the only such Brotherhood member to emigrate there. As mentioned above, ʿAbd al-Muʿaz ʿAbd al-Sattar, Shaykh Ahmad al-ʿAssal, and Kamal Naji also found refuge in Qatar.[315] Al-Qaradawi alone, though, has reached levels of unprecedented fame and international influence. While studying in the late 1940s at al-Azhar University's Faculty of Theology, he established a Muslim Brotherhood branch among students and preached throughout the Egyptian countryside.[316] Though al-Qaradawi was arrested by Egyptian authorities in 1954 after the Brotherhood was officially banned, he was released in 1956 and began work as a teacher and preacher in a private school as well as at al-Azhar's Institute of Islamic Culture.[317] Al-Qaradawi was transferred to the al-Azhar Mission in Qatar in 1961 and has since that time found a safe haven and platform in the emirate.[318] Once he arrived in Doha, al-Qaradawi developed ties to the al-Thani family. Bettina Graf and Jakob Skovogaard-Petersen explain,

> From the start in Doha Qaraḍāwī began to preach and to give religious instruction during Ramadan. This is how in 1961 he met Shaykh Khalīfa b. Hamad Āl Thānī, who reigned as the Emir of Qatar from 1972 until the coup in 1995. According to Qaraḍāwī's memoirs the Shaykh did not want to do without him, so up until 1995 the Emir of the country received religious instruction from Qaraḍāwī in the mosque during 35 months of Ramadan. As early as 1968, he was offered a Qatari passport by the same Shaykh Khalīfa b. Ḥamad Āl Thānī.[319]

This personal connection helped consolidate al-Qaradawi's position as a prominent (and protected) cleric in Qatar. Interestingly, Shaykh Khalifa, as noted in the previous chapter, was sympathetic to Arab nationalism. The fact that he insisted on al-Qaradawi's continued presence in Qatar demonstrates the preacher's appeal to Muslims who do not necessarily support the Ikhwan as an organization or even as an ideology. It also may have reflected Shaykh Khalifa's understanding that naturalizing al-Qaradawi was politically expedient due to the preacher's prominent position in the Muslim world.

Aside from his religious role, al-Qaradawi has aided the development of Qatar's education system and intellectual life more generally. Beginning in 1961, he served as principal of the Religious Institute and "fundamentally shaped the religious education system in Doha."[320] Al-Qaradawi also created Qatar University's Shariʿa and Islamic Studies Faculty, which opened in 1977.[321] He has earned international fame for his role in cofounding and directing the European Council for Fatwa and Research in 1997 and the International Association of Muslim Scholars in 2004,[322] in addition to having published over 120 books on topics ranging from Islamic jurisprudence and theology to education.[323] The prolific al-Qaradawi has thus made Qatar "an important meeting point for scholars and activists, including Muslim Brothers from Egypt."[324]

More controversially, al-Qaradawi has at times used his privileged position to voice political opinions, leading some to suspect that he serves as a mouthpiece for the al-Thani family. In the words of Bernard Haykel, "From his pulpit, al-Qaradawi has promulgated reformist Islamist teachings and has also intervened in the politics of the Arab world, most famously the Palestinian-Israeli conflict. He has, however, never commented on domestic Qatari politics."[325] Throughout the Arab Spring, al-Qaradawi was a public supporter of Brotherhood movements in the region and Qatar's assistance to them.[326] After the overthrow of Egypt's elected Brotherhood-led government under Mohamed Morsi in 2013, Egyptian Attorney General Hisham Barakat issued an arrest warrant for al-Qaradawi on the grounds of "inciting the murder of security forces," as the shaykh had, during one of his Al Jazeera broadcasts, called upon Muslims to fight to restore the Morsi regime.[327] He also famously delivered the first Friday prayer in Cairo's Tahrir Square after Hosni Mubarak's fall from power in February 2011.[328]

Although al-Qaradawi has made political statements on the air, he "has not been involved in any political or juridical activities on a national level in Qatar."[329] Further, al-Qaradawi has not received "official state backing" in the form of an institutionalized government position; his most prestigious official title remains dean of Qatar University's College of Shariʿa and

Islamic Studies.[330] The fact that al-Qaradawi's formal role has been limited to the arenas of education and media indicates the type of position that the Qatari government wishes him to have—not explicitly political but no doubt indirectly influential in that sphere.[331]

No other ideologue in Qatar, or perhaps even the Gulf, has been given as much of a public platform as al-Qaradawi. As a 2005 cable from the US Embassy in Doha confirms, "al-Qaradawi is the one Islamic thinker in Qatar who matters."[332] In the popular sphere, he was best known for his Al Jazeera Arabic show *al-Shariʿa wa-l-Hayat* (Sharia and Life), in which, until mid-2014, al-Qaradawi introduced what Louay Bahry describes as "more daring ideas to the debates that take place each week for two hours with guests who discuss from an Islamic point of view issues relating to the effect of modernization on the lives of Muslims."[333] This program was similar to his *Hadi al-Islam* (Guidance of Islam) on state network Qatar TV, in which he answered letters about religious questions.[334] In addition, al-Qaradawi's *khuṭub* were broadcast on Fridays on Qatar state television. Both his television programs and the broadcast of his sermons were stopped shortly after the March 2014 withdrawal of the Bahraini, Saudi, and Emirati ambassadors from Qatar following controversial statements made by al-Qaradawi about the Emirati leadership,[335] discussed at length in the next chapter.

By hosting al-Qaradawi as well as by founding Al Jazeera and launching the websites IslamOnline and IslamWeb, Qatar has become "the hub of media production for Arabic-speaking Muslims."[336] In introducing broadcasting platforms for Muslims and arranging conferences for them within the country, Qatar has also managed to gain global standing. Al-Qaradawi has publicly acknowledged the freedom Qatar grants him, stating explicitly that no one in the country has restricted his speech.[337] In short, as Graf puts it, "without the basis of the location in Qatar his activities would not be conceivable, neither on an intellectual nor on an organisational and financial level."[338] By creating a space for influential Islamists, Qatar has positioned itself at the forefront of promoting popular Islam, rather than attempting to stem the tide of popular movements that hold appeal among much of Qatar's local population. Just as it has been relatively tolerant with regards to allowing space for Islamism, so too has the Qatari government been accepting of nonnationals holding a variety of views.

Qatar's Policy of Taking in Exiles

Although it has been argued that Qatar's support for Muslim Brotherhood figures is a recent phenomenon, the country, like others in the Gulf, has in fact hosted them since the Nasser era. Qatar has not taken in only Brotherhood exiles, however. As one Qatari put it, the country "hosted people who were oppressed, and this was the right thing to do."[339] Providing refuge to exiles is a part of Qatar's founding vision. In fact, David Roberts explains,

> Qatar's founder, Sheikh Jassim, once wrote a poem referring to Qatar as the "*Kaaba Lil Madiyoum*," the Kaaba of the dispossessed. To those looking for respite from persecution, Qatar is what the Kaaba—the black box in the center of the grand mosque in Mecca—is to Muslims: their direction of focus. This concept grew up in part because of the lawless nature of the peninsula. When someone had cause to flee, he could go to Qatar knowing that there was no meaningful authority there.[340]

The country's recent history provides examples of its purposeful provision of asylum for a variety of figures. Controversial Indian artist M. F. Husain, former Iraqi Minister Naji Sabri al-Hadithi, much of Saddam Hussein's family, former Mauritanian President Maaouya Ould Sid Ahmed Taya and his family, and former Knesset member and influential pan-Arabist ʿAzmi Bishara, none of whom has any ideological or organizational links with the Brotherhood, all found refuge in the country.[341]

In terms of Islamist figures who found a safe haven in Qatar, Hamas leader Khaled Meshaʿal has lived there since 1999; controversial preachers like Canadian Bilal Philips and Egyptian Wagdy Ghoneim, as well as Libyan cleric ʿAli al-Sallabi and former Algerian Islamic Salvation Front (FIS) leader ʿAbbasi Madani have also settled in Qatar.[342] Although these Islamist figures come from varying nationalities and strands of the faith, their presence is construed as evidence of the Qatari government's sympathy toward the Brotherhood. Qatar's attitude toward the Ikhwan and Islamists in general is certainly far more moderate than that of Saudi Arabia or the UAE, yet likely reflects an understanding of the local population's preferences as well as personal relationships of members of the ruling family, rather than ideological or institutional links with political leadership. Significantly, the government has not used the presence of such figures to impose Islamist policies inside Qatar, though they appear to have influenced the domestic political scene from the grassroots, as has been discussed.

Qatar's policy of accepting exiles is ultimately strategic. In the midst of complaints about the loss of Arab and Islamic culture in the Arabian Peninsula, Qatar has essentially imported significant intellectual figures as a means of maintaining authenticity and promoting Arab and Islamic culture. Allowing exiles into the country has also helped the Qatari government appear sympathetic to popular causes across the Arab world and has afforded it the opportunity to promote political discussion largely divorced from local politics. By granting entry to international political figures of various ideological strands, Qatar becomes part of larger debates, while maintaining power to maneuver them. Islam is critical in such discussions, considering its influence among a local population that remains largely conservative and mainly Sunni Muslim (indeed, the state religion is Wahhabi Islam). This strategy has continued through to the present day, keeping the Muslim Brotherhood a part of the political discussion inside Qatar, as discussed in the next chapters.

THE EMIRATI CASE

The UAE's Muslim Brotherhood-linked Jamʿiat al-Islah wa-l-Tawjih al-Ijtimaʿi (Islah) also enjoyed peaceful ties with the central Emirati government for its first decades, having received state support for its establishment. As noted, regime patronage of Islamist groups was common in the Gulf during this period, as governments feared the influence of Arab nationalism and hoped to promote their own religious legitimacy through backing Islamist organizations. Indeed, as Christopher Davidson puts it,

> in the UAE and Kuwait, where Muslim Brotherhood organisations or "reform associations" have existed for many years, there was a tacit understanding in place that these groups would be tolerated and given some influence over the religious and educational establishments. In the UAE this led to the Brotherhood's de facto control over the

> Ministries for Education and Social Affairs, with its members presiding over curriculum committees and—for many years—dominating the UAE's principal university [UAE University, or UAEU].[343]

Appropriately, then, in the formation of the first-ever independent Emirati government in 1971, a founding member of Islah from Ras al-Khaimah, Shaykh Sa'id 'Abdullah Salman, was named minister of housing, and Muhammad 'Abd al-Rahman al-Bakr was appointed minister of justice and Islamic affairs and *awqāf* in 1977, becoming the second member of Islah to take on a post in a government ministry.[344] Both were appointed on the recommendation of Vice President Shaykh Rashid.[345] In 1979, Shaykh Salman became minister of education and chancellor of UAEU.[346] In the same year, Saif al-Jarwan of Ras al-Khaimah took the post of minister of labor and social affairs.[347] From 1977 until 1983, Shaykh Sultan bin Kayed al-Qasimi, head of Islah in Ras al-Khaimah, directed the national curriculum division.[348]

Because Brotherhood members in the UAE, as in Kuwait and Qatar, came largely from among the educated classes, they were strong candidates for such government posts, particularly in a young country with a small population. Further, as Marta Saldaña highlights, "*al-Islah* members with Law studies, who were the best prepared at the time, became influential within the Ministry of Justice. For more than 20 years *al-Islah* worked side by side [with] the Emirati government, cooperating in areas of social and cultural development."[349] Though they enjoyed less representation following the Iranian Revolution in 1979, when it was considered potentially dangerous to employ Islamists, Brotherhood members retained some important public roles. The government used such inclusion as a means of moderating Islamist complaint. Indeed, Neil Partrick asserts that "it was assumed that the public engagement of Islamists by inclusion in the Kuwaiti parliament, and as officials in the *Awqaf* (Islamic affairs), education and justice ministries in the UAE, for example, would incorporate them politically and by extension, aid the state in its projection of a conservative and Islamic image."[350]

By granting Brotherhood members positions in government, the state allowed them a platform through which they could enact policies that remained in place for decades—particularly in the education sector. In its early stages, the Emirati Brotherhood resembled the Ikhwan elsewhere in the super-rentiers with its initial focus on the social and cultural. Once the Brotherhood gained a following mainly through its involvement in education, however, the government understood the degree to which such cultural posts were politically influential.

Brotherhood Influence in the Emirati Education System

Facilitating the spread of Islamist ideology even before independence, the UAE received considerable foreign aid for the promotion of education and became guided by the Kuwaiti system, which, as discussed earlier, had been shaped by many Ikhwan members and sympathizers. Kuwait financed several educational institutes in all emirates except Abu Dhabi,[351] with the Kuwaiti government providing books and teacher training courses.[352] In the first years of Emirati independence, Kuwaiti inspectors supervised primary education in all emirates aside from Abu Dhabi, providing curriculum (consisting of Qur'an, Arabic, arithmetic, geography, history, music, science, art, physical education, and, at the intermediate level, English), school uniforms, stationary, and meals.[353]

In later years, influence from Egypt became more prominent. In 1979, of 5,500 primary school teachers, the majority was Egyptian, with only 361 Emiratis.[354] Most notably, Egyptian religious scholar ʿIzz al-Din Ibrahim, who had previously worked in Qatar, held the post of Vice Chancellor of UAEU from its founding in 1976 until 1985, further influencing higher education.[355] Under his control, as Malcom C. Peck describes, "the university emphasize[d] law and Sharia studies, with more than 10 percent of the student body (including thirty-two women) enrolled in that faculty."[356]

The newly independent UAE government endeavored to limit the influence of foreign ideologies in education, yet the sector remained a battleground for competing ideologies, as elsewhere in the Gulf. The appointment of Arab nationalist-leaning Emirati ʿAbdullah ʿUmran Taryam as minister of education in 1972 was part of this effort, as he oversaw an extensive review of curricula.[357] Taryam's reforms were overhauled, however, when he was replaced in 1979 by founding Ras al-Khaimah Islah member Shaykh Saʿid ʿAbdullah Salman, whose preferences for hiring fellow Brotherhood sympathizers quickly became clear. The new minister created a committee to review existing curricula, under the leadership of Ishaq Farhan, whom the Emirati Arabic daily *al-Khaleej* described as "a well-known religious activist and the leader of a religious party in Jordan."[358] Unsurprisingly, Taryam's curriculum draft was set aside in favor of the versions privileged by Shaykh Salman, who "gave priority to the Islamic element in education."[359] Shaykh Sultan bin Kayed al-Qasimi also came to oversee curricula for the entire UAE from 1977 to 1983. During this period, the Brotherhood managed "to control the curriculum committee, by issuing 120 courses, which the Brotherhood considered one of its biggest achievements."[360] Meanwhile, Shaykh Salman's educational guidelines, as A. Ann Fyfe explains, "were regarded as 'distorted' by the nationalists, who criticized the Minister particularly for abolishing national history and society as subjects and for banning the daily flag-saluting ceremony as 'idolatrous.' "[361]

Under Shaykh Salman's leadership, the Ministry of Education was greatly influenced by Muslim Brotherhood ideology in terms of both culture and curricula.[362] During this period, the ministry banned gender-mixing beginning in the fourth grade, with classes taught by teachers of the same gender.[363] Music was also prohibited, and girls could not participate in sports.[364] In addition, teachers sympathetic to the Brotherhood were hired in large numbers.[365] Indicative of Islah's concerns regarding education during this period is this excerpt from *al-Islah* magazine:

> We should not be satisfied with the academic degree alone as the basis for selection of university lecturers. The behavioral aspect must be given a basic role. No enemy of Islam should join the university even if he only considers Islam a backward concept unfit for the twentieth century. This is not ideological terrorism. This will only protect the nation from corruption and bring up a generation who believes in his religion and is loyal to his country.[366]

The Emirati Brotherhood aimed not only to revise education itself, but hoped to adjust Emirati culture more broadly, reflecting the doctrine of *tawḥīd*.

As one Emirati political scientist described the Brotherhood's influence in the education sector, "Generations were brainwashed because the Islah education minister exploited his position to recruit Muslim Brotherhood [members] as teachers and kick out others. He recruited the whole ministry based on ideology. [There were] no posts if you were not Muslim Brotherhood."[367] Though this statement may be exaggerated, the Brotherhood undoubtedly retained a strong advantage in the Education Ministry. In fact, in May 1980, Shaykh Salman, as education minister, dismissed six popular professors from Al Ain University, two from politics, two from sociology, and two from history.[368] They insisted that their removal was related to their ideological leanings. Fyfe traces the incident:

> All six complained that no routine disciplinary procedures had been followed before their summary dismissal. All believed that their downfall was due to their refusal to toe the fundamentalist line. *Al-Azmena al-Arabia*, the only journal to carry the story, quoted one as saying that at al-ʿAin, "to speak the word 'Arab'. . . was to blaspheme." Another accused the University of wanting preachers, not teachers, and claimed to have been told that al-ʿAin was not an Arab Islamic university but purely an Islamic one. The historians complained that archaeology had been struck out of the history syllabus as "idolatrous." Some students agitated for the professors to be reinstated and petitioned the Chancellor, but to no avail.[369]

Islah's education policies had long-lasting cultural and social implications, as the group hoped to stop the instruction in the English language at elementary levels and opposed music education, urging students and their parents not to attend dance and music events.[370] In addition, Islah organized lectures and seminars in schools about the dangers of Westernization, and youth groups held festivals to gather donations to support the Palestinian intifada and the mujahidin in Afghanistan.[371] By the beginning of the 1980s, the Brotherhood controlled the management of curricula, authoring a great deal of it and working through the Ministry of Education.

The government noted the Brotherhood's dominance of education, and prominent businessman Ahmed Humaid al-Tayer replaced Shaikh Saʿid ʿAbdullah Salman as minister of education in 1983. The Ikhwan took immediate dislike to the new minister, with *al-Islah* magazine campaigning fiercely against his decision to shift twenty-five Ikhwan-linked employees in the National Curriculum Committee to other positions.[372] *Al-Khaleej* newspaper reported that Islah leader Mohammed al-Mansoori in Ras al-Khaimah had even, during a Friday sermon, accused al-Tayer of being a non-Muslim, provoking the education minister to accuse al-Mansoori of misusing his platform.[373] Al-Tayer remained undeterred, however, issuing new educational objectives that highlighted the importance of modern education in promoting national and Islamic loyalties.[374]

These changes provoked backlash from Abu Dhabi's National Consultative Council (NCC), which demanded a meeting with al-Tayer, in March 1987.[375] The NCC, though by no means Brotherhood-linked, often represents interests of the emirate's major tribes that tend toward social conservatism. The body has long, in Fyfe's words, "campaigned against allegedly unIslamic practices in the schools such as the failure of some women teachers to wear full hajab [hijab], visits by male inspectors to girls' schools, insufficient emphasis (in the NCC's eyes) on religious education and, its particular bugbear, the teaching of music and physical education to girls."[376] The group failed to win major concessions, though, and al-Tayer's reforms continued. Efforts to reorganize primary and secondary education faced further resistance during this period in Sharjah, with Shaykh Sultan bin Mohammed al-Qasimi publicly opposing the changes.[377] In fact, then Under Secretary for the Ministry of Education and Youth Khalifa Bakhit al-Falasi said that when he attempted to reassign some three hundred Saudi teachers who were considered "too religiously conservative," a Saudi cleric issued a fatwa against him, and the government had to arrange his safe exit from the country.[378] Outrage thus came not only from Islah, but also from traditional elements of society more broadly, demonstrating that Islah promoted some widely held attitudes, which perhaps led to the government's ultimate crackdown on the organization.

In 1988–1989, Islah began a new campaign, this time against the education minister's decision to institute standardized basic education for all students entering UAEU, which would require instruction in subjects such as sports, English, and Arabic before university enrollment.[379] Members of Islah began distributing leaflets and organizing speeches about the ministry's plans to corrupt students' morals through the basic education curriculum, which they claimed was designed by Westerners seeking to dissolve the country.[380] One of the most popular cassette tapes in 1989, "Tragedies of Islamic Education," distributed by Arabic language teacher Ahmad Saqr al-Suwaidi, expounded upon these issues.[381] Following their campaign against the educational system after the removal of Islah members from the National Curriculum Committee, Islah leaders resolved in mid-1989 to take a more subdued approach to altering the education sector.[382] Having failed to effect change in curricula through direct attacks on government policy, Islah opted for de-escalation: it did not release *al-Islah* for six months, from October 1988 until April 1989, and started to use a more conciliatory tone in its discussions of government policy.[383] Still, by 1988, the Brotherhood had become the most prominent voice in the country's educational institutions and its first institute of higher education, UAEU.[384]

Beyond Education: The Spread of Brotherhood Ideology in the UAE

By the end of the 1980s, the federal government had become concerned about the amount of influence of Islamism even outside of schools. Dubai's Ministry of Awqaf specifically referenced the " 'excessive extremism' among some religious organizations whose conduct needed to be reviewed."[385] Two decrees from that ministry reflected its desire to contain the religious sphere. The first, enacted in 1986, "asked preachers to steer clear of contention."[386] The second, issued in January 1988, demanded that preachers "deposit written, advance copies of their Friday sermons with the Ministry and to avoid all areas of controversy and sectarian sensitivity, limiting their remarks to guidance on Islamic practice."[387]

Islamist leanings, evident in the judicial sector, also worried the government. In January 1978, the Council of Ministers issued a resolution to Islamize UAE legislation.[388] By aligning the state's penal code with sharia, the government sought to unify the criminal system, as well as to reinforce national identity and integration.[389] The decision had serious social consequences, however. Between 1983 and 1984, the Federal Supreme Court was asked thrice "to declare the imposition of non-Shariʿa sentences for drinking alcohol to be unconstitutional, since the Constitution obliges judges to use the Shariʿa as their principle guide."[390] In each case, emirate-level courts (one in Abu Dhabi, one in Al Ain, and one in Sharjah) sentenced Muslims convicted of drinking alcohol to short prison terms.[391] Three public prosecutors challenged such sentences, stating that Abu Dhabi's 1976 law and Sharjah's 1972 law about the consumption of alcohol did not comply with sharia and thus were unconstitutional.

A. Ann Fyfe explains, "In all three cases, the Supreme Court found that the Rulers, in their temporal capacity, had the right to impose temporal punishments for the temporal aspects of drunkenness and that the two laws in question were therefore not unconstitutional, but that the imposition of such a temporal penalty did not preclude a prisoner's subjection to the Shariʿa punishment as well."[392]

Even after such incidents, Brotherhood-leaning immigrants held sway in the judiciary for decades. In fact, in a 1993 case, an Egyptian judge, presiding in Fujairah, sentenced two convicted smugglers to *hudūd* punishment[393] because "he apparently assumed, incorrectly, that he could and should apply Islamic law strictly."[394] Although an appeals court overturned the sentence, Emirati officials noted with increasing alarm the influence of Islamists in the judiciary.[395] Centralization of the UAE-wide security and crackdown on independent Islamist groups like Islah has helped prevent such misunderstandings more recently.

Another integral part of the Emirati Brotherhood's outreach was its aforementioned magazine, *al-Islah*, established in 1978. The publication attacked leftist and nationalist opponents, with writers suggesting on more than one occasion that communists had penetrated state apparatuses.[396] *Al-Islah* thus cultivated the organization's image as a preserver of traditional social values and frontline fighter against the invasion of outside ideologies.[397] While archives of the magazine are not readily available, a study by Al Mezmaah Studies and Research Center published a number of excerpts from the magazine in the 1970s and 1980s. Examination of these documents demonstrates that the most commonly discussed topics concerned developing Islamic education,[398] censoring Western materials such as magazines and television programs,[399] restricting the sale of alcohol,[400] stopping corruption in government spending,[401] and limiting the encroachment of foreign (particularly Western) businesses and culture in Emirati society.[402] First and foremost, in the words of one Gulf correspondent, "Islah tapped into issues of Emiratis drinking, social issues."[403]

In a less institutionalized way, Brotherhood organizations in the UAE influenced youth through student activities like summer camps and scout groups.[404] In 1982, as President of UAEU, Shaykh Saʿid ʿAbdullah Salman established the Union of Emirati Students in the institution in Al Ain.[405] Having done well in the elections of university student committees beginning in 1977, Islah dominated student union elections until 1992.[406] At that time, the government made an effort to depoliticize campuses, eventually replacing the union in 2012 with student council polls contested by individuals, rather than political blocs; even these are only partially elected.[407]

Through its educational and cultural activities, Islah fostered a following among the Emirati population. Wanda Krause describes the unique ability of Brotherhood members to gain young followers:

> The Ikhwan's discursive spaces take root in concrete settings, such as in the organizations in which they participate, the *halaqas* they control, the lectures they hold, or their places of work. Their agenda is pursued by speaking through their jobs and positions of influence. Teachers attempt to sway the youth through advice, giving their opinions, or less subtly, infusing programs with political ideas. Local and other Arab professors in local and Western universities, some Ikhwan, some Salafi, some from other strains, have access to literally thousands of young minds. Their mode of action is to play the father figure, give advice, and teach the implications of globalization in

> classes. The theme of the inescapability of globalization, and how locals, Arabs, and Muslims must shape their own identities, is popular among university classes, lectures, speeches, and conferences, not to mention the media. Ikhwan members hold various media positions . . . . While the curriculum and agendas will be planned for the *halaqas* and lectures among Islamists, their modes of action within spaces of employment is largely dependent upon individual initiatives.[408]

Though the government initially did not consider Islah to be a threat, granting its members ministerial positions into the early 1980s, its attitude decisively changed in the early 1990s, when the organization became powerful enough to pose a political threat. As one Emirati political scientist explained, "The government really trusted Muslim Brotherhood because they never posed as opposition. The government saw them as providing another layer of legitimacy."[409] By the 1990s, though, the government came to consider the Ikhwan too powerful to be trusted and took steps to diminish the Emirati Brotherhood's organizational capacity. Even in the face of rising profits from oil wealth and a growing non-oil sector in Dubai, ideological complaint continued to influence political opposition. In an effort to maintain control of political dialogue, the Emirati government, like others in the region, has endeavored to monitor the religious sector, where the Brotherhood holds sway. Aiming to limit the impact of independent Islamism, the government has sought to enhance central control of religious discourse.

Government Suspicion and Takeover in the 1990s

Originally tolerated due to its nonthreatening stance, the Emirati Muslim Brotherhood, because its members exerted considerable influence on Emirati society through their positions in the educational and judicial systems, provoked government suspicion in the 1990s. At that time, Sultan al-Qassemi describes, "the UAE's judicial and education sector was effectively a state within a state: The Brotherhood would make sure that those who qualified for educational scholarships and grants were either Brotherhood members, affiliates, or sympathizers."[410] As a result, student councils as well as teachers' and judges' professional associations became "outposts dedicated to advancing their [Brotherhood] interests."[411]

The organization also, more problematically, developed a political reform agenda alongside its social program, pressing for more representative government and more equal distribution of wealth.[412] As early as March 1979, Islah's UAE management council wrote a letter to the local rulers ahead of a meeting of the Federal Supreme Council, supporting the government's attempts to diminish corruption and to spend oil money in a "pious" way.[413] Statements like the following, from *al-Islah* magazine as early as 1982, were more explicit about the organization's potential role as political opposition, in the context of government bans on Islamic magazines: "Why are they afraid of Islam? They know that with Islam we are everything. With Islam we liberate lands of Islam, we stop injustice to Islam. Tyrants are afraid of us because of Islam."[414] Further, the UAE's student union voiced disapproval of the UAE's ties with the United States, urging an end to foreign military bases in the Gulf at the beginning of the 1980s.[415] Islah even tried to gain more of a say in government at the local level, as traced by Krause:

> In one of the emirates . . . the Emirati Ikhwan approached their sheikh declaring that while the group held the utmost respect for the ruling sheikh, its members did not seek any power, and that they requested cooperation with him. Thus, despite their marginal position in the power hierarchy, and perhaps their grudging willingness to work within the status quo, they envisioned a possibility for an incremental step toward power-sharing. The ruler responded by allowing the group to do charitable work, teaching of Qur'an, and organizing youth camps, and banning them from practicing politics of any nature or talking as a group in public.[416]

In the absence of organized political action, which is difficult in the Emirati system, the Brotherhood's all-encompassing ideology had the potential to subvert the system and certainly became a basis for questioning it. Just as the Brotherhood expected to have more sway in the political realm, the government also anticipated its turn toward the political. Perhaps fearing that the Emirati Brotherhood could gain a broader following as a political bloc, as in Kuwait, the government resolved to squash it before the Ikhwan became too powerful to influence politics on an institutionalized level. Allegations about Islah's misconduct provided the perfect opportunity for the Emirati government to move against the organization.

In the early 1990s, investigations by Egyptian security services claimed that individuals involved in Egyptian Islamic Jihad had received monetary donations from Islah's Committee for Relief and Outside Activities.[417] The prevailing argument became that the Brotherhood was, at its core, an international organization, "imported by Egyptians," and therefore used outside groups to further its cause, the establishment of a single Islamic state.[418] As a consequence, the group was considered to hold exclusively "international goals—to create a caliphate state."[419] The Emirati government viewed the oath of *bay'a* or loyalty to the Brotherhood's General Guide to be a direct challenge to allegiance to the UAE, and it demanded that members of Islah pledge loyalty to their country alone.[420]

During the same period, the government began investigating the influence of Brotherhood members within the education sector when promising scholarship applications from non-Islamists were rejected, and it found that the Brotherhood members largely controlled the distribution of educational awards.[421] Trying to regain control, the government dissolved the Brotherhood's previously elected boards of directors in 1994,[422] placing them under the supervision of the Ministry of Social Affairs. This body cannot take punitive action, which is the Ministry of Justice's purview.[423] Nonetheless, the Emirati Brotherhood's internal actions were under surveillance, and its external activities were frozen, reflecting additional concerns about its links to other countries, namely Egypt.[424] Furthermore, the government restricted the political activity of the Brotherhood's members, banning them from holding public office.[425] This decision affected the branches of Islah in Dubai and Fujairah, in addition to the more loosely affiliated Jam'iat al-Irshad wa-l-Tawjih al-Ijtima'i (Irshad) in Ajman.

Abu Dhabi was the first emirate to encourage crackdown on the Brotherhood, having already denied permission for the establishment of a branch in that emirate.[426] Aware of the Brotherhood's eagerness to participate in political debate, that emirate's government promoted the emergence of other, more politically quietist Islamic ideologies instead, specifically Sufism, Jama'at al-Tabligh, and purist, or politically inactive, Salafism.[427] The Brotherhood organization was thus stymied, while its members were individually marginalized. One secular human rights activist described this period:

> There was a change in the mid-1990s when Islah individuals were sent to early retirement from the government; their kids had obstacles getting jobs. They were moved from the education sector to service-oriented ministries. This separation in the mid-1990s was instigated by [Egyptian President Hosni] Mubarak after assassination attempts. He started a tour of the GCC [Gulf Cooperation Council] to turn rulers against the Muslim Brotherhood. In Kuwait it didn't work. The Muslim Brotherhood were exorbitantly peaceful in the UAE, didn't even raise their voices against harassment, which led the government to crack down more.[428]

The clampdown coincided with the deportation of prominent Egyptian and Syrian Brotherhood sympathizers, many of whom had worked in the education sector.[429] The most renowned was Iraqi Brotherhood ideologue ʿAbd al Munʿim al-ʿIzzi (also known as Muhammad Ahmad Rashid), who authored a great deal of the Brotherhood literature and had once served as an advisor in Dubai's Ministry of Awqaf.[430]

Notably, the Ras al-Khaimah branch of Islah was exempted from ministerial control, though it was forced to curtail its external activities.[431] Until the most recent crackdown in 2012, it remained independent under the protection of its sympathetic ruler Shaykh Saqr al-Qasimi (r. 1948–2010),[432] who "rejected the dissolution of al-Islah because he felt it played a role in preserving the youth."[433] Further, the head of Islah in Ras al-Khaimah, Shaykh Sultan bin Kayed al-Qasimi (in prison since 2012), was the cousin of the ruler at that time.[434] The al-Qasimi family's relationship with Islah, while granting the Brotherhood protection, led to tension with the central government after its issuance in 1996 of a warrant for the arrest of Islah member Mohammed al-Mansoori. Shaykh Saqr refused to dismiss al-Mansoori from his position in Islah in Ras al-Khaimah.[435] Nonetheless, al-Mansoori was briefly arrested in 2006 without a judicial warrant for "insulting the Public Prosecutor," was placed on a travel ban in 2007, and was stripped of his passport in 2008.[436] He was also dismissed in 2009 from his position as legal advisor to the ruler of Ras al-Khaimah after criticizing the lack of free speech inside the UAE on al-Hiwar television station.[437]

Al-Mansoori was most recently arrested in July 2012 along with other members of Islah, including Shaykh Sultan bin Kayed al-Qasimi, and he received a ten-year prison sentence for his involvement in Islah, in addition to a fifteen-month sentence in January 2014 after standing trial with nine other Emiratis and twenty Egyptians.[438] Ultimately, then, the central government's policy toward the Muslim Brotherhood, which has changed markedly since the 1970s, prevailed, its actions demonstrating the degree to which security has been centralized and the extent to which the Muslim Brotherhood is perceived today as an existential political threat. The strengthening of control over the periphery, particularly in the poorer northern emirates, is considered crucial to maintaining peace and the primacy of government control over social movements like Islah.

CONCLUSIONS

As demonstrated above, the forms adopted by Muslim Brotherhood movements in the super-rentiers, similar to Ikhwan elsewhere in the region, were dictated by the political opportunities available to them. Opportunities became increasingly available to Ikhwan branches in the Gulf with the fall of Arab nationalism, which had been the Brotherhood's primary ideological rival. Remarkably, Brotherhood groups managed to establish themselves even as super-rentier governments were expanding handsome welfare packages to citizens throughout the 1970s. The appeal of their political ideology thus has proven itself able to survive decades of great political change in both informal and institutionalized forms in the super-rentiers. We now move to a discussion of the role of rentier Islamism in the 2000s, when the organization came under greater scrutiny worldwide as a potential source of political opposition.

PART III

Modern Rentier Islamism

6

Rentier Islamism after Pan-Arabism

INTRODUCTION

As the Muslim Brotherhood has developed, it has become increasingly locally focused, with each individual national affiliate progressively defining its agenda based on domestic concerns. Nonetheless, these branches have remained inspired and guided by the common Ikhwan ideology, which has come to be seen as a bulwark against encroaching Westernization that has accompanied modernization of the super-rentiers in the past decades, along with anticorruption that has increasingly formed a part of Islamist political platforms. In this chapter, we examine developments of rentier Islamists through the first decades of the 2000s, analyzing how they have changed, with the Kuwaiti branch gradually more politically active and the Emirati progressively more silenced.

THE KUWAITI BROTHERHOOD IN ITS FIFTH DECADE
Disappointment and Reform

The Islamic Consittutional Movement (ICM), since its establishment in 1991, maintained relatively consistent presence in parliament, winning five seats in 1992 and 1996 and four in 1999; this changed in 2003. Though the 2003 election marked a victory for Sunni and Shiʿi Islamists, who together gained more than one-third of the seats in parliament,[1] the Islamic Constitutional Movement (ICM) earned only two seats, prompting the organization to make substantial internal reform. Electoral success had become the primary measure of the organization's relevance. In Nathan J. Brown's words,

> The lackluster electoral performance and the sense of political change prompted Hadas [or the ICM] to reorganize itself in a significant way. Some of the founders of the party were gracefully shunted out of a public role; instead of relying primarily on its most dynamic and prominent parliamentarians, Hadas brought in new, still younger leaders to run the party itself.... The party leadership embarked on an effort to revive

and professionalize its operations, hiring, for instance, an outside communications and marketing firm to help fine-tune its message to Kuwaiti voters.[2]

As part of this overhaul of its image and message, the ICM's views became increasingly aligned with those of secular liberal blocs on issues of political reform, such as changing electoral and political party laws, enhancing parliament's authority, and combatting corruption.[3] In summary, as Carrie Rosekfsky Wickham observes, "[a]fter 2004, the ICM participated in several cross-partisan initiatives."[4]

Notably, the 2003 election was also a major setback for liberal groups, which had run primarily on the promotion of female suffrage, a contentious issue for the Brotherhood. In November 1999, parliament had voted down a bill to grant women the right to vote and run for parliament, by a margin of forty-one opposed to twenty-one in favor.[5] The ICM, along with Salafi groups, did not change its stance on granting women the right to vote and run as candidates, despite internal dispute and a statement from the Egyptian General Guide of the Muslim Brotherhood publicly supporting women's political rights.[6] With the proposal for women's political rights voted down in 1999, Amir Shaykh Jaber granted these rights by decree in 2005. Realizing how contentious the decision was, the government even went so far as to suspend twenty-six preachers who publicly criticized the amir's decision.[7] Though their political miscalculation embarrassed the Brotherhood in the short term, in the long run, it aided the ICM in several ways.[8]

The amir's granting of political rights to women helped resolve debate within the bloc about granting such rights and demonstrated the ICM's willingness to accept female suffrage, despite its initial opposition to this decision.[9] Perhaps most unexpectedly, as Brown describes, "the addition of women voters may have strengthened the ICM—members recount how one of their leading parliamentarians, Nasir al-Sani', was going down to defeat in the 2006 elections until women's ballots (cast separately in gender-segregated polling) were counted."[10] The Kuwaiti Brotherhood had engaged in outreach to the female population since the 1970s through Jam'iat al-Islah al-Ijtima'i (Islah) and knew firsthand the importance of female votes in student union elections. Recognizing the rising tide of women's movements, like the Sufi group Bayader al-Salam, the ICM created a popular women's committee.[11] Once women were granted the right to vote, the Brotherhood managed to gain their support. In Alessandra L. González's words, "Ironically, Islamists arguably incorporated women more effectively than the Liberals in a practical way that helped them to win parliamentary seats in following elections."[12] Many women, especially those from the middle classes, welcomed involvement in the Islamist movement as a means of preserving Islamic culture, indicating the appeal of the organization's ideology and ability to translate social to political capital, a critical tool of rentier Islamism.[13]

2006 and the Consolidation of Opposition

A 2006 cabinet reshuffle brought Isma'il al-Shatti into the position of minister of communications, yet the ICM broke ties with him when he voted to delay electoral reform.[14] In 2006, then, the bloc wholeheartedly joined the cross-ideological opposition coalition in demanding political reform.[15] In the same year, a group of lawyers questioned the constitutionality of the law that had banned public gatherings since 1979, leading the Constitutional Court to remove it.[16] The National Assembly, under pressure from civil society, also succeeded in passing a new press and publication law in March. This legislation differed from the previous framework in two ways: first, it allowed applicants to appeal if their newspaper licenses were rejected by the Ministry of Information; and second, the government lost its ability to close newspapers as a matter of "a simple administrative procedure."[17] Nonetheless, the press law retained a prohibition on directly insulting God, the prophets, Islam, or the amir, in addition to a vague ban on "disclosing secret or private information and calling for the regime's overthrow."[18]

In the midst of such reforms, opposition and youth organizations renewed their cry for amendments to the electoral law imposed by Shaykh Jaber in 1981, demanding the reduction of electoral constituencies from twenty-five to five.[19] As Mustafa Muhammad al-Tahan explains, "In the opinion of reformers, this matter would transform elections from occasions to buy votes and to launch campaigns to a race on the basis of program and ideology."[20] Due to Kuwait's relatively small population size and comparatively large number of electoral districts, a candidate could win a seat with fewer than one thousand votes.[21] As the country's most organized political bloc, the ICM played a leading role in opposition agitating for reform, which dubbed itself the "We Want Five" Movement and included activists ranging from Salafis to secular liberals.[22] This ideologically broad-based movement's supporters organized large demonstrations throughout May 2006, even entering the National Assembly to place leaflets on the desks of cabinet ministers. Ultimately, as Mary Ann Tétreault explains, "the intensity of the movement forced the emir's hand."[23] The government first offered to reduce the number of districts from twenty-five to ten.[24] This proposal led to additional demonstrations outside parliament, which were monitored by police and became violent, spurring some four thousand people to gather against the government.[25] Following this display, the amir called for the dissolution of parliament and new elections.

These June 2006 polls, though organized under the twenty-five-district voting system, affirmed popular support for the opposition. Among the surprising results were "victories for 35 candidates from across the political spectrum who had been endorsed by the anti-corruption movement in return for pledges to fight corruption if they were elected."[26] This election was also the first in which women could vote and run as candidates. Islamists did particularly well, with the ICM alone gathering its largest share of seats, at six (the group had only run six candidates).[27] Support for Islamists, however, was primarily due to "the decision of the liberal Alliance to back candidates who supported redistricting and the fight against corruption regardless of their other leanings."[28] The ICM ultimately disagreed with its coalition members on a number of other matters, and the alliance fell apart—but, notably, only after working together to pass a law to reduce the number of electoral districts to the desired five.[29] As in the 1990s, the ICM's political pragmatism helped it earn seats in parliament, yet did not last long after the campaign.

Although the opposition coalition crumbled, the government failed to capitalize on divisions in parliament. Brown explains that "[t]he government could not muster a majority for many of its efforts and complained instead that various groups in the parliament seemed to be engaged in a rivalry over which one could criticize more ministers."[30] The legislature attempted to interpellate Prime Minister Shaykh Nasser al-Sabah, the amir's nephew, on suspicion of corruption, and staged interpellations of several other ministers.[31] It also demanded pay increases for state employees to counteract the effects of inflation.[32] When the government refused this request, the cabinet resigned, and Amir Shaykh Sabah dissolved the assembly, setting the date for new elections for May 2008.[33]

The 2008 election, the first held with five electoral districts, did not yield the expected benefits for organized political parties or the anticipated losses for tribal candidates. In each of the five districts, every Kuwaiti citizen had four votes, a system expected to aid minorities at the expense of the larger groups (especially tribes). When tribes held their technically illegal primary elections, police arrested several tribal leaders.[34] Though such primaries had been held since the 1970s and were formally outlawed only in 1998, the law was laxly enforced.[35] In Tétreault's assessment, "It is unclear why the law against tribal primaries was suddenly applied for the first time in the unscheduled 2008 election campaign, but the most likely reason is that the large tribes, whose choices had the best chances of finding themselves in the parliament, had become too strong to ignore."[36] The crackdown led tribe members to attack police stations, provoking a forceful response with tear gas, "a level of violence on both sides unprecedented in Kuwaiti elections."[37] Adding to the political strain, earlier that year, sectarian tensions had flared after Shiʿi politicians attended a ceremony to commemorate the death of Hizbullah militant ʿImad Mughniyya.[38] Also notable in 2008 was the establishment of a self-proclaimed Salafi "party" and the success of a number of Salafis in gaining seats.[39] Salafi candidates had taken the opportunity to publicly decry the ICM as an organization pursuing political rather than religious gains.[40] Ultimately, then, "[t]he 2008 election was held in a tense and divided country," leading to overall decreased voter turnout.[41]

In large measure due to the fact that political blocs had focused on discrediting each other rather than on uniting to face down the government, the 2008 parliament was quite fractious.[42] The ICM, which itself had helped design the new electoral system, lost half of its seats, retaining only three.[43] Though ICM spokesperson Muhammad ʿAbdullah al-ʿUlaim was made minister of oil, the bloc, as Brown observes, "began to feel that its participation in the government allowed it little influence while still forcing it to support official policy. It withdrew from the cabinet and launched an attempt to bring the prime minister in for questioning before parliament."[44] In December 2008, Amir Shaykh Sabah reappointed the unpopular Shaykh Nasser as premier.

The amir's selection of regime loyalists to government discouraged the opposition, which united once again in efforts to interpellate Prime Minister Shaykh Nasser on charges of corruption. A premier had never been subjected to parliamentary questioning, and the amir called for a new election in May 2009.[45] As Mary Ann Tétreault and Mohammed al-Ghanim explain, "The refusal of the Al Sabah to permit the premier to submit to questioning had also precipitated the unplanned election of 2006. Although the reasons for the confrontation between government and Parliament were different on that occasion, they were equally threatening to Al Sabah authority."[46] As in 2008, tribal leaders protested the ban on tribal primaries, leading to a series of arrests yet not the level of violence seen in the previous year.

Ultimately, "all of the 'political groups' that function as Kuwait's substitute for political parties did poorly in May 2009, whether their orientation is center-left or religious;" the ICM won its lowest share yet, at only one seat.[47] As a result, Brown explains that "[t]he movement's leadership resigned—a step that certainly indicated their failure but in an odd sense also showed one sign of organizational health."[48] It also again demonstrated the degree to which electoral opinion, rather than progress toward its ideological goals, had become an indication of success for the ICM.

What was remarkable about the 2009 election was that, as Tétreault and al-Ghanim highlight, "so many candidates, including several who had run as group representatives in previous elections, chose to run as independents."[49] This rise in independent candidates suggested a rejection of the country's political blocs as ineffective. The parliament was the first regime-friendly legislature in almost two decades.[50] Ultimately, Tétreault points out, "[t]he amir's strategy of calling election after election, with the effect of alienating Kuwaiti voters, depressing voter turnout, and delegitimizing the entire electoral enterprise and the parliament it produces, shows how elections become instruments of authoritarianism."[51] Polls held in such a discordant environment encourage social division and thereby strengthen the power of the executive rather than temper it, in something of a divide and rule scenario.[52] The new parliament stripped the political opposition of strong representation.

Prime Minister Shaykh Nasser was finally interpellated, behind closed doors, in December 2009 about his handling of the financial crisis and possible misuse of public funds, marking the first time a premier had been interpellated. Still, he was questioned by a sympathetic National Assembly,[53] thirty of whose voting members had signed a statement pledging support for the prime minister before the interpellation.[54] Predictably, the vote of no confidence failed, and Shaykh Nasser was not removed from office.

The Arab Spring Reaches Kuwait

In the October 2010 parliamentary session, Amir Shaykh Sabah again appointed government allies to key positions, and "[t]he tensions that built throughout 2010 carried over into 2011," with sustained demands for the interpellation of Prime Minister Nasser and new calls for similar questioning of Interior Minister Jaber al-Khaled al-Sabah after police were accused of fatally torturing a prisoner.[55] Although Interior Minister al-Sabah resigned, ongoing protests throughout the Middle East as the Arab Spring gained momentum spurred more unrest in Kuwait. In March, a Shiʿi member of parliament (MP) asked to question the foreign minister about Kuwait's involvement in the crackdown on protesters in Bahrain, leading the cabinet to resign.[56]

A new cabinet was formed in May 2011, featuring six new faces, yet it was still under the leadership of Prime Minister Shaykh Nasser. The issue of corruption was pervasive in the new government, as authorities were increasingly seen as unreliable and ineffective. In fact, the next political crisis emerged in September 2011, when reports surfaced that major Kuwaiti banks had deposited $92 million into the accounts of several pro-government MPs, suggesting the government's purchasing of political support.[57] Earlier that year, the parliament had removed through a vote of no confidence the Deputy Prime Minister and Minister of Development and Housing Affairs Shaykh Ahmad al-Fahad al-Sabah, on charges of corruption.[58] Foreign Minister and Deputy Prime Minister Mohammad Sabah al-Salem al-Sabah resigned amidst these corruption charges, and one of the largest demonstrations in Kuwaiti history, with an estimated one hundred thousand participants, took place in September.

In November 2011, following repeated calls for his resignation amid increasingly large protests, Prime Minister Shaykh Nasser resigned. In Doron Shultziner and Mary Ann Tétreault's assessment, "The Amir's selection of a new premier, which might have appeased protesters had it been made a few years earlier, did not satisfy them by the end of 2011."[59] Kuwaiti youth and MPs from liberal and Islamist groups (including the ICM and some Salafi blocs), outraged at what they considered rampant corruption within the political system, also began demanding that the prime minister be elected rather than appointed by the amir. Continued protests led to the government's resignation and the dissolution of parliament in December.[60]

The February 2012 election "produced a landslide victory for the opposition, mainly Islamist (Brotherhood and Salafi) and tribal candidates, who won 34 of the 50 parliamentary seats."[61] The Brotherhood and main Salafi bloc each won all four seats they contested. The liberal and merchant factions did less well, thereby widening divisions between the urban merchant elite and tribal constituents.[62] This parliament was voided, however, four months later, as the Constitutional Court declared the dissolution of the previous parliament unconstitutional.[63] The Court thus reinstated the pro-regime 2009 National Assembly. Encouraged by this political victory, Shaykh Sabah asked the court to review the legality of the 2006 redistricting law, yet it rejected this request.[64] The secular-Islamist opposition coalition widely protested the reimposition of the 2009 parliament, which ultimately never met because its reinstitution was so controversial.[65] At this point, with the government, both executive and judiciary, showing itself increasingly willing to challenge the movement for political reform to enhance its own power, the ICM privileged the need for political change over its social goals, planting itself firmly with the ideologically broad-based opposition.

In October 2012, Shaykh Sabah, cautioning against "chaotic sedition that could jeopardize our country (and) undermine our national unity," instructed the cabinet to change voting rules ahead of the December elections, "abolishing the country's complicated system that allowed each voter multiple votes. This move disregarded the court's previous ruling on the matter, as well as the opposition's demands of complying with the 2006 electoral law."[66] In this new system, each person has only one vote, a move expected to harm the country's most organized political blocs. As a result, the opposition, including the ICM, boycotted the December 2012 polls, leading to a low 39 percent turnout rate (compared to 60 percent in February) and, predictably, returning a pro-government National Assembly.[67] Sunni Islamist representation was the most drastically affected, decreasing from twenty-three MPs to four, and taking the ICM out of the legislative body for the first time since the bloc's creation.[68] The parliament was dominated by independent MPs, with the historically pro-government Shi'i Islamic National Alliance the largest bloc represented, with five MPs.[69]

In June 2013, the Constitutional Court once again dissolved parliament, after facing down opposition claims that it was voted in under an invalid electoral law. Most opposition groups, including the ICM as well as several tribal leaders and liberal groups, boycotted the July 2013 polls, again in protest of the change in electoral law. As a result, the parliament was dominated by a blend of liberal and tribal blocs, with independents, including "service" or pro-government MPs, holding thirty of the fifty seats. When asked about the logic behind the ICM's two consecutive boycotts, one former ICM MP explained that these were meant to expose the government as the source of political gridlock.[70] He stated, "the more we stay away, the more we show it's the government that cannot perform."[71] Consequently, the ICM continued to operate alongside the ideologically broad-based political opposition and as an active social movement outside of parliament in the aftermath of increased government restrictions spurred by the Arab Spring, coming to resemble more closely a social movement as seen in Qatar than the political force it tends to be in Kuwait. Table 6.1 summarizes the number of parliamentary seats won by the ICM from 2000–2013, as well as its boycott campaign.

TABLE 6.1

The ICM's Performance in Parliamentary Elections in the 2000s

Election	Number of ICM MPs
2003	2
2006	6
2008	3
2009	1
February 2012	4
December 2012	0 (boycott)
July 2013	0 (boycott)

Source: Kuwait Politics Database, http://www.kuwaitpolitics.org.

THE QATARI CASE

Since the rise of Arab nationalism in the 1950s and 1960s, Qatar has enjoyed a rather placid political environment. No group has attempted to make drastic changes to the government system, and the Muslim Brotherhood has remained only informally organized. The Qatari government, particularly since the Arab Spring, has been increasingly responsive to popular demands, especially those regarding social policies, reflecting the ability of the informal sector to articulate Islamist demands and to influence government decision-making. More controversially, Islamist sentiment in Qatar has been perceived as driving the country's foreign policy, specifically during the Arab Spring. Although there is no institutionalized government bias toward the Muslim Brotherhood, Qatari decisions abroad reflect a desire to promote something of Muslim nationalism on the international level.

In this section, we analyze the role of the Qatari Brotherhood since its disbandment, examining how its presence has influenced domestic and foreign policies under Shaykh Hamad (r. 1995–2013) and Shaykh Tamim (r. 2013–present). In so doing, we demonstrate the ability of Islamists and other political actors to act gradually through the informal sector while using links to the political leadership to influence government policies—a mechanism unique to super-rentiers.

Islamism and Qatar's Government System

The fact that Qatar remained largely undeveloped until the al-Thani rule has led many Qataris to link the family's rulership with their country's advancement. In Allen Fromherz's view, "Historically, the lack of distinction between state and ruler has been more pronounced in Qatar than in other Gulf sheikhdoms," resulting in an intense association between the al-Thani family and the state of Qatar itself.[72] Because of the power wielded by the al-Thani family since the mid-nineteenth century, it has a great deal of freedom to enact policies of its choosing.

While it has maintained its control of the state, the al-Thani family itself is notoriously fractious.[73] Reflecting intrafamilial power struggles, three of the last four changes in leadership (1960, 1972, and 1995) resulted from "forced abdications" or palace coups.[74] Only the latest transition in power, in 2013, was voluntary, when Shaykh Hamad, who had ruled since 1995, passed on power to his then thirty-three-year-old son, Shaykh Tamim. Mehran Kamrava posits that historical uncertainty about succession has actually helped consolidate the al-Thani's institutional control in government, with amirs eagerly appointing family members to government positions in an effort to secure their rule.[75] As Fromherz aptly explains, "Al-Thani have actively bureaucratized traditional tribal leadership roles, putting local leaders and representatives on the government payroll and quieting dissent over the distribution of resources through a slow reformation of Qatari identity and tradition."[76] In this way, Qatar under al-Thani rule has maintained a relatively calm political environment.

Nonetheless, rumors of failed coups persist, especially those originating from outside the country. In 2009, Jordan-based newspaper *al-Bawaba* and American intelligence firm Stratfor reported the failure of an attempted overthrow led by current Defense Minister Major-General Hamad bin ʿAli al-Attiyah.[77] In February 2011, *al-Bawaba* reported on another failed coup, which it said resulted in the arrest of thirty members of the military.[78] Yet another coup attempt allegedly took place in April 2012, according to Iran's Fars News Agency and Saudi Arabia's Al Arabiya, "with high-ranking military officers being rounded up and placed under house arrest after clashes between Royal Guard troops and regular military personnel outside one of the ruler's palaces."[79] Although it is difficult to gain reliable information about any such events, especially since they were not mentioned in the local press, it is certain that familial rivalries persist within the al-Thani. Some of these follow ideological lines, as certain branches of the family are more conservative than others. Since Shaykh Tamim's 2013 takeover, however, domestic relations have appeared relatively calm, despite increasingly volatile relations with Gulf Cooperation Council (GCC) neighbors, discussed at length in the next chapter.

While the regime has not faced major challenges in recent years from outside the ruling family, political opposition still exists; in Jill Crystal's words, "Dissent in more recent times has been muted, but not muzzled."[80] Discerning the type of domestic political opposition and its influence in Qatar is difficult, however. In the absence of a legislature, the ruling family and elites hold almost all decision-making power, leading the country's policies to be remarkably personality driven.

The only outlet for institutionalized popular participation is the election of the Central Municipal Council (CMC) every four years. Due to the nature of the body as an arm of the Ministry of Municipality and Urban Planning, its election campaigns are apolitical, as the body deals almost exclusively with matters of public health, maintenance of roads, and other logistical issues. Interestingly, it has, in recent sessions, backed conservative social policies resembling those demanded by Brotherhood groups in other countries, like the reinstitution of so-called family days in Qatari malls that prohibit the entry of single blue-collar males into shopping centers,[81] an increase in the number of female taxi drivers and female-only seats in public buses,[82] and the enforcement of a 2011 directive banning men from selling women's clothing and other products for women.[83] That the Ministry of Municipality and Environment chose in 2016 to implement a ban on unaccompanied men from Al Khor Park twice, rather than once, per week, implies that it is aware of CMC and other Qataris' social preferences.[84] An elected Advisory Council could similarly reflect such conservative attitudes, possibly at the embarrassment of the ruling family. Indeed, though the Qatari Constitution allows for the implementation of an elected Advisory Council, repeated delays in its election have led many to question the leadership's commitment to creating a legislative body, especially since it could change the somewhat liberal social atmosphere that sprang up under Shaykh Hamad.

One explanation for the delay in elections is that the government fears that the Council could be used as "a Trojan Horse" for other branches of the infamously fragmented al-Thani to take power.[85] Additional questions remain about technicalities of voting in such a small state. As seen in Kuwait, the drawing of electoral districts greatly influences the vitality of democratic life. It is likely that, as political scientist Justin Gengler posits, "people would vote in districts where their father was from, and this would cement tribal, familial, geographic differences and would help the government because it knows how to deal with tribes."[86] Another unresolved issue is which citizens would have the right to vote. Questions also remain about the efficacy of a parliament in a country as small as Qatar, which has a tiny national population,[87] of which a large proportion comprises the al-Thani family or people connected to it.[88] As one Qatari interviewee put it, "The families that would be represented in a parliament already have a say through other means, and the Advisory Council is not the only venue for reform. The amir has his own majlis, meets with tribal leaders. This system works now."[89] Notably, concern about Islamist groups coming to power has not stymied democratic reform in Qatar, as it has in the United Arab Emirates (UAE).

The majlis is a crucial element of Qatari civil society, as well as a means for the government to track public opinion. A great deal of consensus building takes place in these informal gatherings, which promote discussion of political and economic topics, while also cementing tribal and social relations.[90] Crucially, as Shadi Hamid points out, "Qatar is still small—and rich enough—to have a largely consensual style of politics."[91] In fact, some Qataris consider majlis meetings important enough to be formalized as part of the political apparatus, with the amir's majlis meeting weekly and with other shaykhs holding regular *majālis* to hear citizens' grievances.[92] Because privately held "*majālis* are composed not along ideological lines but based on social groups," they provide a helpful microcosm of the Qatari political scene.[93] As described by an advisor to Shaykh Tamim,

> The regime is made of various rings of hierarchy, is communitarian. Qataris have their own democracy because people know each other and know they can influence decision-making. People in Western Europe think it's an absolute monarchy; it's not. Qatar is more like feudal Europe, with the amir as *primus inter pares*. In *majālis*, every public issue is discussed . . . . Free discussion in the majlis gets to the amir, and he has to take this into consideration.[94]

Although Qataris seem to have faith that their complaints in *majālis* will be passed on to the leadership, there is no indication of how exactly this happens, as the system remains uninstitutionalized and largely based on personal relationships.

Political life in Qatar is, by its very nature, informal. In fact, the three states under study can be placed along a continuum of formal and informal, with Kuwait the most formalized and Qatar farthest toward the informal end. As such, the fact that the Qatari Brotherhood lacks an institutionalized framework does not mean it is politically irrelevant, as a great deal of politics is displaced into the social sphere in super-rentiers, making political life there look very different from elsewhere in the region. Qatar in particular is, in the words of one long-term resident, "intensely political but not democratically political. The amir deals with loads of politics every day, but tribal politics."[95] The experience of the 1990s, discussed in the previous chapter, demonstrates the political vitality inside Qatar, as the regime faced opposition from both liberal and Islamist segments of the population, yet outside the limited institutionalized means of political participation. The regime's strength was also demonstrated during the Arab Spring in 2011, when the government and ruling family experienced surprisingly little public outcry for expanded political representation, despite similar such movements emerging in neighboring rentier states.

The Arab Spring Reaches Qatar

Barring complaints about disbursements to nationals, the domestic political scene remained stable during the Arab Spring. In fact, some speculated that Qatar supported the uprisings in other countries largely because there was no domestic threat of an uprising. Still, limited internal dissent was expressed. At the beginning of 2011, local newspaper *The Peninsula* reported on Qataris' postings on Internet fora about the need for increased state support, particularly as Kuwait granted its citizens free food for fourteen months in addition to a payout for nationals as protests continued there.[96] Qataris charged that additional government aid was needed, specifically for "low-income families who are living off [a] meagre monthly state dole."[97] Others argued that, despite receiving high salaries, "resources got exhausted by the middle of the month since rents and food prices were skyrocketing."[98] As a result, they cited an increasing need to cross the border to eastern Saudi Arabia to purchase cheaper household goods.[99] The government responded to these grievances, even though they were not lodged through any institutionalized means or even by an organized political bloc.

In September 2011, civil employees gained a 60 percent increase in pay and social allowances, with defense staff receiving raises of 50–120 percent.[100] In addition, civilian retirees gained a 60 percent increase in pensions, with retired military officers receiving a 120 percent raise and other ranks a 50 percent salary increase.[101] As rentier state theory predicts, citizens voice political complaints when their share of rent income is threatened. This does not preclude them, however, from also holding ideological beliefs. Because economic grievances are easily answered in a super-rentier state, they do not form the basis of long-lasting political mobilization. In fact, after the latest disbursements, most domestic political complaint has centered on broader social issues in Qatar.

Though Qatar experienced no public protests and faces no sustained political opposition, some *majālis* gatherings discussed problems in Qatari society and politics. A Facebook page entitled "The Qatar Revolution 2011 against Hamad bin Khalifa," with over five thousand followers, called for demonstrations against the amir, claiming that he had met with Israeli officials.[102] Despite the protest page and a planned "day of rage" in March 2011, no gatherings took place in Doha, as the effort appeared to be primarily supported by non-Qataris or Qataris outside of the state.

Beginning in March 2011, a more organized political grouping emerged, composed of some sixty Qataris, who began holding meetings to discuss political and economic reforms.

These gatherings, "Monday Meetings," led by Qatari academic ʿAli Khalifa al-Kuwari, resulted in the pamphlet *Qataris for Reform*, which, as Lina Khatib summarizes, "highlights key concerns, such as the lack of public consultation on domestic and foreign policy, lack of access to information on public affairs, and the lack of boundaries between the private and public, with policy recommendations for the Qatari state to address these shortcomings."[103] Al-Kuwari and his cohorts later produced a book in 2012, *al-Shaʿab Yurid Islah . . . fi Qatar Aidan* (The People Want Reform in Qatar . . . Too), in which they highlight what they consider necessary reforms for Qatar. Notably, the book focuses on four main issues: the population imbalance between nationals and expatriates, economic underdevelopment stemming from the state's reliance on the export of oil and natural gas, the absence of political participation, and the GCC-wide dependence on foreign powers for security.[104] Al-Kuwari's recommendations thus involve reforming or amending, rather than upending, the existing system. They also clearly extend beyond the economic complaints anticipated by rentier state theory and foresee major problems with the system it describes. Notably, al-Kuwari, though often referred to as a secular figure, promotes enforcement of the government system described in the constitution—"a democratic system of government with Islamic law as the principle source for legislation."[105] Al-Kuwari thus embraces portions of both government and Islamist agendas, demonstrating the prevailing importance of religion in Qatari politics and society.

Al-Kuwari is undoubtedly the best-known Doha-based reformist ideologue, though he is not considered to be, as one Gulf analyst put it, "fundamentally important to Qatari politics. He's no Aung San Suu Kyi, Nelson Mandela."[106] In fact, al-Kuwari refers to himself as "not an activist in political or social issues," but "an academic, a researcher and a writer."[107] On the whole, then, as one Qatari put it, "there is no domestic opposition per se in Qatar but a call to reform. There is no war of ideology in Qatar. Al-Kuwari wants more transparency, more of a role for people in the constitution and in legislation. As for the Advisory Council, Qatar is moving toward it slowly but surely. The executive wing of the country is being reformed."[108] The government is very careful to appear responsive to popular demands by reiterating its commitment to enhancing popular participation.

Perhaps for this reason, most political complaints do not aim to overturn the prevailing political system. The Qatari government, aside from voicing its commitment to representative government, has also distinguished itself by not cracking down on the scant existing dissent, aside from a few notable episodes. Qatari poet Muhammad ibn al-Dhib al-ʿAjami was famously arrested in early 2011 after he posted a video of himself reciting a poem that was considered to incite overthrow of the regime and to insult Shaykh Hamad.[109] Originally sentenced to life in prison, al-ʿAjami's term was reduced to fifteen years, and he was pardoned by Shaykh Tamim in March 2016.[110] Interestingly, Qatari interviewees supported the government's initial decision to punish the poet, with one stating that its "reaction should be severe . . . . It's a strong lesson for him and anyone else who may come behind. He shouldn't have said what he said."[111] Qatari blogger Sultan al-Khulaifi was also arrested in March 2011 and detained for one month, allegedly due to his writings about censorship in Qatar.[112]

Aside from these isolated incidents, evidence of political arrests or repression is lacking, or at least is not publicly available; Islamist groups seem to be safe from crackdown. More common is self-censorship or the state's encouragement of it—in particular for expatriates. For instance, the Doha Center for Media Freedom, established in 2008, became the focus of a scandal when Founding Director Robert Ménard left in May 2009, leading to the Center's temporary closure.[113] Ménard claimed that his work had been "suffocated," as he was discouraged from criticizing Qatar.[114] More recently, in May 2015, members of the BBC who had been invited by the Qatari government to assess living conditions of laborers in newly constructed worker cities were arrested on government claims that the team did not have permission to enter the private property; this incident followed the detainment in March 2015 of a German Broadcasting team also reporting on workers' conditions.[115]

Islamist Complaint and Responsiveness of the Qatari System

On the whole, the population of Qatari nationals seems satisfied with the current system of government. Public opinion polls carried out by Qatar University's Social and Economic Survey Research Institute (SESRI)[116] revealed that, during the period between December 2010 and June 2011, "support for democracy and interest in political participation has dropped markedly among Qatari citizens. The proportion of survey respondents who report being 'interested' or 'very interested' in politics decreased by almost 20 percent over this period, while the proportion of Qataris who say that living in a democratic country is 'very important' to them dropped from 74 percent to 65 percent."[117] During the same period, Qatari citizens' confidence in the governing institutions saw impressive increases of 8 to 18 percent.[118] The Arab Spring thus seemed to reinforce Qataris' contentment with their own government system—particularly as neighboring countries faced violent protests and unsteady transitions to democracy. In Gengler's estimation: "The lesson: don't try to fix what isn't broken, for others will see to it that you wind up with something much worse."[119]

Perhaps adding to general contentment inside Qatar, the government has also become more responsive to Islamist-leaning demands for social reform since the Arab Spring. It has been particularly attuned to complaints about the availability of alcohol. In December 2011, alcohol was banned in restaurants throughout the Pearl-Qatar development. Shortly thereafter, objections from Qatari nationals led to the 2012 closure, in a number of days, of a Pearl-Qatar branch of the Qatar Distribution Company (QDC), which sells pork and alcohol. Additional changes have also been made more recently. In April 2015, Qatar Tourism Authority forbade hotels from serving alcohol in the nine days preceding *ʿĪd al-Aḍḥā*, in observance of *Dhu al-Ḥijjah*, during which hajj is undertaken. Although alcohol is traditionally not sold in hotels during Ramadan or on the birthday of the Prophet Muhammad, 2015 marked the first time it has been banned during the hajj period.[120] Further, the country's only liquor distributor, QDC, announced in 2016 that it will begin charging residents an annual fee to visit the store;[121] the government also announced its intention to implement a "sin tax" in 2017 on items like alcohol and cigarettes,[122] yet its implementation has been delayed to mid-2018, likely due to rising food prices since the advent of the 2017 Gulf crisis.[123] Such restrictions may signal the government's efforts to balance the desires of national and expatriate populations. When asked about the reason behind such changes, one advisor to Shaykh Tamim charged that "alcohol is not essential to modernization."[124]

A group of Qataris also took aim at the national airline, Qatar Airways, launching an online boycott campaign in 2012 due to the company's sale of alcohol and pork products through its QDC subsidiary.[125] As former Justice Minister and human rights activist Najeeb al-Nuʿaimi tweeted, "This is the Qatari spring against Qatar Airways. The people demand employment for Qataris, the people demand a reduction in rates, and the abolishment of the monopoly of Qatar Airways."[126] An earlier online campaign, in July 2011, targeted the national airline for similar reasons. A group of Qataris, using the hashtag #qatarairwaysfail, claimed that the airline favored foreigners, serving alcohol and stopping the on-board *qibla* service to help Muslims face Mecca during prayers.[127] Although the boycott campaign seems to have had no major effect on the airline, the *qibla* service has returned, and Qataris continue in their efforts to change social policy from the ground up, having seen the efficacy of this approach with a government largely willing to accede to such demands.

Other recent examples of the government taking a cue from the public complaints include the removal in 2013, after only three weeks, of a statue of French soccer player Zinedine Zidane head-butting Italian player Marco Materazzi during the 2006 World Cup on the Doha Corniche. It was eliminated following complaints from locals about the inappropriateness of the statue, as the depiction of humans and animals is discouraged in the Hadith and as the act portrayed was considered to be "morally wrong."[128] A series of fourteen Damien Hirst sculptures depicting the fertilization of an egg were also covered (first with plastic coverings and now with walls), less than a year after their unveiling in 2014, supposedly to shield them from sand as landscaping for the new Sidra Medical and Research Center behind them is completed, but, according to residents, due to controversy they spurred.[129] In addition, one former advisor to the Amiri Diwan related that a statue of an oryx marking what was once known as Oryx Roundabout was removed in 2013, having provoked similar complaints about the portrayal of animals since its construction in the 1980s.[130] Though values likely have not changed a great deal since the 1980s, the government has become more proactive in addressing such complaints in recent years, eager to maintain Islamic and Qatari culture in the face of an increasing expatriate population.

The grassroots campaign to foster modest dress, launched in 2012 as "One of Us," and recently rebranded as "Reflect Your Respect," represents another effort by nationals to maintain traditional values, fostering "modesty in all behaviors."[131] Rather than singling out expatriates, this campaign hopes to appeal to them to monitor their behavior, using the slogan "you matter in Qatar."[132]

The above actions demonstrate that a vocal segment of the Qatari population, which favors conservative social policies, can and does influence the government's domestic social policies. Similar efforts elsewhere in the region could easily be led by the Brotherhood yet seem informal and spontaneous in Qatar. As the number of expatriates rises since more workers are needed to prepare for the 2022 World Cup and as the Qatari government attempts to cater to the needs of that population, locals have become increasingly vocal about their grievances, making it more difficult for the government to balance the demands of expatriate and local populations. It is fair to say that, in Qatar, "the amount of say people have depends on the question. If it is a question of how to allocate state budget, people have less of a say. If it is a local matter or something less political, people have more say in government . . . . People are content to leave decisions to others but also to voice displeasure."[133] Most recent complaints bemoan the growth of the expatriate population and the consequent loss of Qatari and Islamic culture; in this prevailing environment, religiosity is often linked to nationalism. The government has attempted to answer citizens' concerns, particularly as the proportion of Qatari nationals diminishes in the face of an upsurge in expatriates.[134] Islamist sentiment has often revolved around the same complaints, and the influx of non-Muslim expatriates has been a lightning rod for Islamist movements.

The *majālis*, particularly of local political and tribal leaders, and the popular radio show *Watani al-Habib Sabah al-Khair* grant Qataris the opportunity to voice their grievances while also allowing the leadership to hear about such complaints.[135] Because Qatar's native population is the smallest of the super-rentiers, at under three hundred thousand people, citizens are assured that their grievances are heard and oftentimes addressed.[136] Ultimately, in the words of Michael Stephens, "Qataris can get access to the channels of power; it is representative in that sense."[137]

In a context wherein politics remain largely informal and uninstitutionalized, it is perhaps unsurprising that the Brotherhood exerts political influence without a formal structure. In such an environment, it is also difficult to discern which political trends are most popular among nationals. While the above social policies suggest a leaning toward social conservatism favored by the Brotherhood, they could also reflect the desires of a conservative Wahhabi population. Either way, Islam clearly has political weight. Further, Qatar's foreign policy decisions seem to mirror such interests as well, while also changing depending to a large extent on which figures are at the top of the political hierarchy.

Qatar's Role in Promoting the Muslim Brotherhood Abroad: Ideologically Driven Foreign Policy?

Claims about Qatar's tilt toward the Muslim Brotherhood often center on the state's foreign policy. The notion that Qatar has managed to squelch Brotherhood activity at home by promoting the organization abroad has become particularly popular. Certainly, the Qatari leadership was public about its willingness to accept Brotherhood movements that came to power during the Arab Spring. Former Prime Minister and Foreign Minister Shaykh Hamad bin Jassim al-Thani, in a December 2011 interview, said that Islamists were likely to win elections in several countries that experienced political upheaval and that "we shouldn't fear them, let's cooperate with them."[138] Promoting a similar standpoint, then Amir Shaykh Hamad said of Islamist groups in 2011: "I believe you will see this extremism transform into civilian life and civil society."[139] While not open endorsements, such statements reveal some degree of trust in Islamist organizations and certainly a much more tolerant stance than that held by the UAE.

To the extent that links exist between the Qatari government and the Muslim Brotherhood, they are at the level of personal relationships, fostered through social relationships and *majālis*, involving high-ranking members of the cabinet and the Brotherhood, rather than any institutionalized strategy. As explained by Steven Wright, "Support for the Muslim Brotherhood is a reflection of the personalized nature of foreign policy; it is case of who can help rather than a grand strategy."[140] Because decisions are made by very few people at the head of the government, according to David Roberts, "it's a question of who has access to the advisor for foreign policy because it is not an institutionalized system. The foreign ministry has a bureaucratic structure, but decision-making is at the top, formulated by five people at most."[141] While such personality-driven policymaking affords Qatar flexibility, it also limits the capacity of the foreign ministry. In fact, one Western diplomat explained that, in a meeting with members of the Ministry of Foreign Affairs, one official admitted that no Qatari expert on the Muslim Brotherhood exists and had only vague answers to questions about how the government distinguishes violent Islamists from nonviolent ones.[142] Such a lack of institutionalized capacity suggests that any tilt toward the Brotherhood in foreign policy is not due to an ideological leaning or structural linkage, but is likely to change depending on the person (or people) making foreign policy decisions.

The Qatari government, particularly under Shaykh Hamad, backed Brotherhood and other Islamist movements overseas, largely to advance the country's power globally. Instead of using its links to Islamists to influence domestic politics, where Islamism has at least some grassroots support, however, Qatar has attempted to increase its standing in the international order more broadly.[143] Pragmatism overrides ideology for the Qatari leadership.[144] In the view of Gerd Nonneman, "The Qatari government has and continues to behave internationally not out of an ideological commitment but out of a pragmatic assessment of how the region functions. Islam is important; the Muslim Brotherhood is the biggest group among Islamists and is considered to be effective, seen as not corrupt."[145]

Related to Qatar's willingness to engage with the Brotherhood to boost its international standing is the leadership's desire to distinguish itself from Saudi Arabia. This was particularly important for Shaykh Hamad, as the Saudis backed a coup attempt against him in 1996.[146] Further, Shaykh Hamad's generation had a "living memory of subservience to Saudi Arabia."[147] Backing the Brotherhood, or at least not cracking down on it, gave Qatar a means of distinguishing itself from the Kingdom, which has been particularly outspoken against the organization. While Qatar has considered the organization an important regional player, as Khatib puts it, "Saudi Arabia has traditionally seen the Muslim Brotherhood, an Islamist group with political ambitions, as a potential political challenger, and thus has been cautious in its dealings with the group."[148]

Under Shaykh Tamim's leadership, the relationship with Saudi Arabia initially appeared to be changing, reflecting how personalistic the government system is. Tellingly, Shaykh Tamim's first trip abroad was to Saudi Arabia, perhaps signaling a desire to reach a rapprochement.[149] He also acceded to conditions of the November 2013 GCC Agreement, which required Qatar to expel seven senior members of the Egyptian Muslim Brotherhood and to "stop attacking Egypt in al-Jazeera broadcasts," largely by removing Shaykh Yusuf al-Qaradawi's platform on the station and on Qatar TV.[150] Since the implementation of the GCC deal, relations were improving immensely between Qatar and Saudi Arabia and the GCC more generally until the most recent June 2017 crisis, described in detail in the next chapter. In fact, following Shaykh Tamim's first visit to Saudi Arabia, and in the face of accusations from the Egyptian government in 2015 that Qatar supported terrorism in Libya, the Secretary General of the GCC, ʿAbdul Latif al-Zayani, defended Qatar. He proclaimed that the accusations are "unfounded, contradict reality, and ignore the sincere efforts by Qatar as well as the Gulf Cooperation Council and Arab states in combatting terrorism and extremism at all levels."[151] The Qatari government also reaffirmed in 2017 that it has not been involved in internal Libyan politics, though the extent of Qatar's involvement abroad was increasingly called into question by fellow GCC members in the summer of 2017.[152]

Willing to set aside its support for the Brotherhood after it became too controversial in an effort to improve regional relations, Qatar's pragmatism has become clear. Ideological links exist only to the extent that the Qatari leadership is religious, as is the Brotherhood.[153] Furthermore, because the organization never openly challenged the government, the regime has no reason to bemoan its existence. In Jassim Sultan's words, "From the start Qatar has had very good relations with the Muslim Brotherhood. They put them in a frame where they are part of the system but cannot disrupt it."[154] Though Qatar's links to the Muslim Brotherhood dates back to the 1950s, there is "no sign that the regime is seeking to mark Qatar out in a religious sense except as a conservatively oriented but appropriately open

Sunni society."[155] Ultimately, Qatar's actions in the international scene have been interest-driven, promoting regime survival above all else.[156] In the words of one Qatari, "Our leadership is secular, nationalist. It has never been and will never be Islamist."[157]

Qatar and the Arab Spring: Policies Abroad

Qatar's policies during the Arab Spring distinguished it from neighboring Gulf states, which some in the region considered to lead a counterrevolution against the region's popular revolts.[158] Taking a proactive stance, Qatar was the first country to grant official recognition to the rebel-led Libyan National Transitional Council; in addition, Qatar hosted a meeting for the Libya Contact Group and sent six fighter jets as part of the North Atlantic Treaty Organization (NATO)-led no-fly zone in March 2011.[159] Qatar also stirred controversy in its backing of Libyan Islamists, as it hosted several key Islamist figures, primarily those from the Libyan Islamic Fighting Group (LIFG), most prominently ʿAli al-Sallabi, who had been jailed in Libya for attempting to assassinate Colonel Muʿammar al-Gaddafi.[160] The link with al-Sallabi, who has lived in Qatar for nearly ten years, and his brother Ismaʿil, who also fought with Qatar-funded militias in Libya, is "probably personal more than ideological."[161] Even if it were ideological, though, this link would not be to the Muslim Brotherhood, as neither al-Sallabi brother was active in the organization at this time. The Brotherhood notably rejected a proposal from ʿAli al-Sallabi to form a coalition with his bloc in 2011.[162]

Qatar's support for Libyan Islamists, however, may have had an impact on the ongoing Syrian crisis, with support going to Syria through former Libyan rebels who took over in the post-al-Gaddafi era.[163] In November 2012, the Syrian opposition's primary source of funding was revealed to be the new Libyan government, of which Qatar was the second largest funder.[164] Because the Syrian Muslim Brotherhood formed a major portion of the primary opposition body at that time, the Syrian National Council (SNC), some suspected that behind Qatari support was the intention to promote the Ikhwan.[165] Now that the SNC is no longer the primary representative of the opposition, the Syrian Brotherhood's role has been somewhat dissipated. Still, the Qatari government is reported to have backed the Islamist militias al-Nusra Front and Ahrar al-Sham in Syria, maintaining, however, that its primary intention has always been advancement of the cause against Bashar al-Asad, rather than the promotion of any one (particularly Islamist) political bloc. In fact, Qatar has been an outspoken and active member of the United States-led coalition against the Islamic State of Iraq and Syria, reiterating its ultimate aim of promoting regime change above all.[166] It has also taken measures to hamper attempts at financing terrorist organizations outside of the state.[167]

Qatar's backing of Mohamed Morsi's Brotherhood-led government in Egypt was considered the clearest evidence of its Islamist leaning. During the year that Morsi was in power (June 2012–July 2013), Qatar gave or lent $7.5 billion to Egypt.[168] Still, Qatar maintained its support not for the Muslim Brotherhood per se, but rather for a popularly elected Egyptian government. Qatar also condoned supporting the Egyptian Brotherhood as a means of expanding its regional power; as Hicham Mourad puts it, this policy "was justified by reasons of realpolitik and not ideology."[169] Since the fall of Morsi, the military regime under ʿAbdel-Fattah al-Sisi has suspended negotiations on the purchase of Qatari natural gas,[170] in addition to returning $2 billion that Qatar had deposited into the state's central bank under Morsi's tenure, following Qatar's postponement in granting the aid and its imposition of new conditions for its receipt.[171]

Qatar's perceived support of Islamists certainly damaged ties with Egypt and marred its reputation regionally. Al-Sisi's government in Egypt very publicly closed Al Jazeera's offices, claiming that the station held an institutional bias because of Qatar's pro-Morsi stance.[172] Three Al Jazeera journalists were also arrested in 2013, as their presence was said to be "damaging to national security," due in large measure to their alleged meetings with members of the outlawed Muslim Brotherhood.[173] These journalists were imprisoned until February 2015.

In the aftermath of such public gaffes and the surrounding controversy, Qatar has been dubbed "a mini Ikhwanistan."[174] Despite international speculation about its ties to the Brotherhood, however, to the extent that it has a vision, according to Muhammad al-Mukhtar al-Shangiti, "Qatar is trying to promote what they call the 'elements of strength' of the Arab nation, that's their vision—meaning Islamists and Arab nationalists.... They think they have a historic responsibility to strengthen these elements in Arab societies. Tactics change, they can be on good or bad terms with this or that leader, but the broad vision is there."[175] For a small country, Qatar's active foreign policy has been a source of pride, as it is considered to defend the Arab and Islamic world. Part of Shaykh Tamim's vision has involved boosting the role of Islam more generally, promoting something of Muslim nationalism. In a February 2015 opinion piece written in *The New York Times* on the eve of his state visit to the United States, Shaykh Tamim explained,

> I know that many in the West look at the terrorist threat and say that the problem is Islam. But as a Muslim, I can tell you that the problem isn't Islam—it's hopelessness. It's the kind of hopelessness that abounds in the Syrian and Palestinian refugee camps, and in war-weary towns and villages in Syria, Iraq, Yemen, Libya and Gaza. It's the hopelessness we see in the poorer neighborhoods of Europe's great cities, and, yes, even in the United States. And it is this hopelessness, which knows no state or religion, that we need to address if we are to stem the tide of terrorism.[176]

Qatar's rulers endeavor to portray themselves as promoters of the Islamic faith by framing the debate around Islam rather than attempting to diminish its presence or importance. Similarly, in a May 2015 speech, Shaykha Moza bint Nasser al-Missned, the most active and public wife of Shaykh Hamad and mother of Shaykh Tamim, spoke about the rise of "Muslim-phobia" and double standards faced by Muslims.[177] By fostering "a prevailing state of tolerance" and embracing some Islamist causes, the Qatari government has allowed for limited expression of Islamism within its borders and through its policies abroad and has, crucially, made itself vital to conversations about the place of religion in the Muslim world.[178]

Balancing: A Signature of Qatari Foreign Policy

Qatar's foreign policy has long been characterized by a willingness to balance the interests of a number of different parties, often with competing agendas, to gain influence globally. Its backing of Islamists of varying types during the Arab Spring is only one example of this policy, and its past actions demonstrate that no single ideology has governed its foreign policy decisions. As one Qatari official explained in the early 2000s, "'The idea is to try to keep everybody happy—or if we can't, to keep everybody reasonably unhappy.'"[179] Qatar's support of Islamist groups, its sometimes-cordial relations with Iran, and its former ties with Israel are often cited as proof of its ideological flexibility, borne out of political pragmatism.

In one assessment, "[b]y balancing Iran against Iraq in the pre-2003 era, Israel against the Arab world, and the US against all other regional actors, the Amir kept Qatar safe from aggression and also ensured that it attracted regional attention. True, this *modus operandi* did not find favor in the eyes of other GCC members, but it was obviously quite satisfying for the Amir."[180] Further, because Qatari foreign policy is formulated by very few people, it can take different turns depending on the country's prevailing interests.

By forging a strong relationship with the United States and by taking stances independent of the GCC, Qatar also managed to escape security dependence on Saudi Arabia—a policy it aimed to advance long before the Arab Spring. Khatib explains,

> Qatar can therefore be seen as creating friends and avoiding enmities by appealing to all sides at once while remaining within the lines of "good neighbour" conventions in the Gulf, namely *vis-à-vis* Saudi Arabia—a classic example of political pragmatism. Its wide and varied network of "guests" and "partners" can also be seen as an example of political aspiration: Qatar seeks to identify emerging trends (and actors) and create a place for itself within those trends in order to maintain political currency.[181]

Further, by involving itself in international dispute resolution in places ranging from Lebanon to Darfur, Qatar in the early 2000s made its security important on a global level.[182] Qatar's image as an impartial arbitrator changed with the advancement of the Arab Spring and its perceived support for Islamists. Nonetheless, similar to its policy of taking in exiles, Qatar's balancing abroad demonstrates that support for certain Islamist groups is not proof of an ideological affinity, but in fact a testament to its flexibility and pragmatism in the formulation of foreign policy made possible because it is so uninstitutionalized and personalistic. Qatar's policy of balancing also mirrors its efforts in the domestic arena to pacify both national and expatriate populations, with a tilt toward Arab and Islamic causes. Al Jazeera, a critical arm of Qatar's soft power, has at times held appeal among both segments of the population, though it has recently been accused of harboring a Brotherhood tilt.

Al Jazeera: An Ideological Outlet?

Among Shaykh Hamad's first reforms was the founding of Al Jazeera Arabic by amiri decree in February 1996. This action, along with the abolition of the Ministry of Information, suggested a commitment to encouraging free speech and was followed by the founding of Al Jazeera English in 2006. Despite its reputation as an independent media outlet, Al Jazeera has been run, since 2011, by an al-Thani chairman, and the station "is fully state owned, controlled by Qatar Media Corporation."[183] Though the channel's slogan, "the opinion and the other opinion," signals a desire to cover stories even-handedly, Al Jazeera's coverage has been largely outwardly focused, with several domestic stories, such as delayed Advisory Council elections, largely ignored by the channel.[184] Certainly, as Matthew Gray asserts, "the reformist nature of Al Jazeera has never been absolute. Domestic political issues, especially controversies involving the royal family, such as [former amir Shaykh] Hamad's legal battles with the deposed father or issues of corruption, remain unaddressed by the channel. Moreover, there remains some censorship and bullying of the media."[185] When asked about the lack of coverage of local news, though, Al Jazeera officials explain that "Qatar is too small a story."[186]

In recent years, particularly in its coverage of the Arab Spring, Al Jazeera has been accused of granting "an open and accessible platform for the Muslim Brotherhood," as well as for other Islamist organizations.[187] In a similar vein, the station's airing of Osama bin Laden's tapes beginning as early as the 1990s led some to speculate about a possible association with al-Qaʿida.[188] Claims that the station used its position to promote the Brotherhood are likewise misguided. The network insists that it merely grants a platform to important parties of the region, which were, during 2011–2012, Islamists; prior to that, during the initial uprisings of 2011, the spotlight had been on secular pro-democracy groups.[189] In giving such organizations a voice, Qatar gains influence over political debate. In fact, as Fromherz explains, "[t]here is perhaps no better way to subtly tune the ideas that will determine the future of the Arab and Islamic world than to own the stage upon which those ideas are expressed."[190]

When the Ikhwan government under Mohamed Morsi was overthrown in Egypt, Al Jazeera was accused of retaining Brotherhood sympathies, almost immediately dubbing al-Sisi's takeover a "coup" and giving the story considerable coverage.[191] Both the Arabic and English arms of Al Jazeera were also accused of releasing overly positive stories about Morsi's rule, as well as failing to ask difficult questions of Brotherhood-affiliated guests.[192] This led some to believe that, as one former advisor to the Amiri Diwan[193] put it, "Al Jazeera is perhaps an institutional bridge between the government and Islamists. It is a semi-structure."[194] While supporting Islamists is by no means an institutionalized policy at Al Jazeera, individuals sympathetic to Islamist causes seem to have influenced its broadcasts.

The resignation of four journalists from Al Jazeera Arabic in August 2013 complaining of bias, along with Al Jazeera English presenter Jane Dutton's removal from her role as a news presenter, raised suspicions.[195] Executive producer Hany el-Konayyesi allegedly pulled Dutton off the air in the midst of an interview that reflected negatively on the Brotherhood.[196] Al Jazeera English staff also complained about institutional bias in two instances in 2013:

- That several presenters were "moved around" the rota [schedule] on short notice on the day of Dutton's removal, to make way for inexperienced presenters who allegedly had more favorable views towards the Muslim Brotherhood; and
- That staff have felt uncomfortable about the number of days that the situation in Egypt has been at the top of the news agenda, even when they felt the story didn't warrant it.[197]

In conversations with Al Jazeera English employees, they confirmed that certain editors would ask them to provide more sources for a story, in particular if it cast the Brotherhood in a damaging light.[198] Such censorship more likely reflects personal, rather than institutional, bias, however, as it is not enforced consistently. Further, at the institutional level, Al Jazeera is, in Marc Lynch's assessment, "driven more by market share than by ideology . . . . Al Jazeera rose to prominence by giving voice to public opinion rather than directly attempting to mobilize or lead it."[199] Although Al Jazeera does not adopt a strictly pro-Brotherhood stance, it, as Jamal Abdullah describes, "has goals, and one is to support Arabic nations and Muslim nations—that's why some think it supports the Brotherhood."[200] Interestingly, since the Arab Spring, in an era of sustained low oil prices, Al Jazeera has experienced major cutbacks, with plans to reduce its staff by about 11 percent.[201]

Aside from its role as a news broadcaster, Al Jazeera Arabic also promoted Shaykh Yusuf al-Qaradawi through his program *al-Shari'a wa-l-Hayat*, which had the distinction of being the network's "only specifically religious programme."[202] Al Jazeera's granting of a platform to Islamists like al-Qaradawi, which ended amid international complaints in 2014, did not necessarily demonstrate an ideological leaning, but rather a desire to engage with Muslim populations. In short, "Not everyone at al-Jazeera might agree with Qaradawi about the role that Islam should play in the world of today; but they do seem to agree that this question is absolutely necessary and crucial for the future of Arab societies. As such they have a common agenda: an agenda which through opinion formation creates what media researchers have called an opinion based community."[203]

Al Jazeera's position, similar to that of Qatar's foreign policy more broadly, seems to be one of advocating for Arab and Muslim, though not necessarily Islamist, ideology. By sponsoring Al Jazeera, a unique means of media sponsorship only available to a super-rentier government, the al-Thani family has helped promote Arab culture and causes in a country greatly changed by modernization and Westernization and with a massive expatriate population. In granting members of the organization access to media outlets, Bernard Haykel notes, "Qatar has done a better job of managing the energies of the Brotherhood and channeling these towards the outside world."[204] Certainly, Al Jazeera and websites like IslamOnline and IslamWeb are important outlets both for Brotherhood sympathizers and for the religiously conservative population in Qatar.[205] By hosting such international platforms, Qatari rulers have managed "to direct its [Brotherhood] activities and energies overseas and to establish the clear understanding that domestic Qatari politics are off limits."[206] While not completely independent media, neither is Al Jazeera an ideological outlet for the Brotherhood.

Balancing Different Expatriate and Qatari Interests in the Domestic Arena

Limited Muslim Brotherhood influence in Qatar's religious and education sectors is perceivable, yet like much else in the country, uninstitutionalized and largely informal. In the words of one Qatari interviewee, "There is influence of Muslim Brotherhood in justice, education, *awqāf*—not in terms of policies but in terms of influencing people who do make policy; this influence is not institutionalized."[207] As a result, studying the Brotherhood as a movement in Qatar is difficult, especially because its ideology shares many common points with conservative Islam of the Gulf, particularly the state religion of Wahhabism, which retains considerable social influence. Although personal ties undoubtedly exist with Brotherhood members, some at high levels of government, Islamist influence is not necessarily nefarious and often rests on personal relationships. As explained by Michael Stephen, "It's not that these ties don't exist but that they are more benign than people realize."[208]

Overall, Qatar's strategy of managing and co-opting the Islamic sector, rather than seeking to eliminate it, has allowed it to maintain a placid environment, even during the Arab Spring. Further, the state has never had a confrontational relationship with the Brotherhood. In the words of Kristian Coates Ulrichsen, "Although Qatar subscribes officially to Wahhabism and adheres to the Hanbali School of Islamic Law, whose emphasis on political obedience of subjects to their ruler differs radically from the populist and activist nature of the Muslim Brotherhood movement, close ties nevertheless built up between them. These had historical depth."[209] By using tools like social policy, media, and foreign policy, the Qatari government maintains religious legitimacy while subtly channeling the debate about Islamist politics outside of the country, something its neighbors, particularly the UAE, have been less successful in doing.[210] We next turn to the Emirati experience, where the government has taken a much harsher stance against the Brotherhood in an effort to stem the tide of Islamism, which it considers an existential political threat, rather than a potential ally.

THE EMIRATI CASE

Although the Emirati affiliates of the Muslim Brotherhood-linked Jamʿiat al-Islah wa-l-Tawjih al-Ijtimaʿi (Islah) benefitted from government support for their first two decades in existence, the tide turned decisively against the Ikhwan in the 1990s, amid fears, discussed in the previous chapter, that the organization held too much power in the educational arena and in the aftermath of accusations from the Egyptian government that Islah's charity organization was involved in terrorist activities in that state.[211] By that time, Islah had become "the most organized nonstate actor in the country," granting it considerable political capital due to its members' prominent positions in the education and judicial sectors.[212] Emiratis associated with Islah also became "key participants in calls for political reform despite the government outlawing political organizations and discouraging political debate."[213] As the group garnered increasing popularity and became progressively more vocal about politics, the government framed it as a danger to national stability—an argument made more palatable by international fear of any strand of Islamism following the attacks of 9/11.

9/11 and Crackdown on Islamists

The already tense relationship between the Emirati government and the Muslim Brotherhood became even more confrontational following the attacks of September 11, 2001 (9/11). The fact that two Emiratis were involved in the incidents made the government eager to prove to the international community that it would not tolerate religious extremism or in fact any independent religious movement. As part of this effort, Emirati authorities increased internal security. The State Security Directorate in 2002 arrested over 250 individuals accused of terrorism, though they mainly solely harbored Islamist sympathies, leading most to have been released by 2004.[214] As one Emirati political scientist explained,

> After 20–25 years of penetration, the security-conscious UAE found out that the Brotherhood have their own organization. That is not fitting with laws. The government began tracking them, but it was too late because they had power. 9/11 was very important, a wakeup call that Islamists could lead the younger generation down a bad path and bring pressure from the US.[215]

The government attempted to persuade Islah to disband following 9/11, but the organization refused, also declining to divulge the names of its members.[216]

Following its failure to convince Islah to dissolve, the central government began, in 2003, hosting talks between Abu Dhabi Crown Prince Shaykh Mohammed bin Zayed and Islah to persuade the group to stop organizational activity inside the UAE and to sever its ties with the international Ikhwan.[217] In exchange, the government would support the organization and allow it to continue its work in Islamic *daʿwa*. Emirati officials requested that Islah follow Qatar's example because, in their view, if it were not a politically subversive group, it would not require independent organizational capacity.[218] After months of talks, Islah rejected the government's invitation to continue engaging in *daʿwa* without an organizational structure.[219] In an effort to calm Emirati concerns about the Ikhwan's loyalty, Islah leader Mohammed al-Mansoori announced in 2003 that the Emirati Brotherhood had stopped pledging allegiance to the General Guide in Cairo, a declaration that ultimately "only confirmed people's doubts of the strength of the relationship."[220] The government's primary objection to the group, according to one Emirati political scientist, was its alleged foreign funding, which made its members loyal not to their country but to the organization and its ideology.[221] In her view, "no country would accept such an organization."[222]

Realizing that it could not force the group's disbandment, the Emirati government tried to mitigate the Ikhwan's influence. It transferred some 170 Brotherhood members, including 83 officers from the Ministry of Education, to other government departments to diminish their impact in that sector.[223] Mansour al-Nogaidan claims that the government, at this time, offered three options to those Islah members holding jobs in the education sector: they could retain their positions in education if they abandoned their oath of loyalty to the General Guide of the Muslim Brotherhood and agreed to contribute to the promotion of so-called moderate Islam; they could continue supporting the ideology of Islah, as long as they left the organization, did not promote it, and did not teach or have direct interaction with students; or the government could provide employment opportunities outside of educational institutions for those who chose to retain their group affiliation.[224] When many Islah members refused to comply, Christopher Davidson recounts that

> the previous concessions granted to the Muslim Brotherhood were soon reversed, with hundreds of teachers, academics, and ministry employees being fired in 2006 from their jobs on the grounds of Islamist affiliations. Some have since been accused of "dual loyalties" or threatening "violent acts in the occupied Arab emirates," and in 2008 a large number of activists were imprisoned and accused of being part of an "underground movement in the UAE trying to promote their own strict view of Islam."[225]

Despite this setback, the Muslim Brotherhood, as represented by the remaining three branches of Islah (Dubai, Fujairah, and Ras al-Khaimah) and Jamʿiat al-Irshad wa-l-Tawjih al-Ijtimaʿi (Irshad) in Ajman, continued hosting discussions, lectures, and Qurʾan recitation competitions, in addition to publishing *al-Islah* magazine.[226] Islah responded to the 2006 crackdown with protest rallies, articles on the Internet, and media appearances.[227] In a November 2008 article, one of the leaders of the group, Hamad al-Raqit, claimed that Islah never had the opportunity to speak to the government about its decision to remove the management board of the Dubai and Fujairah branches and place them under ministerial control in the 1990s, which he said revoked leadership from those entitled to it.[228] By the mid-2000s, it had become clear that "[t]he regime in the UAE is not friendly toward Islamists, and prominent Islamists have been arrested, barred from teaching at university, and otherwise harassed by the government."[229] In such an environment, it has become increasingly difficult for members of Islah to pursue their independent activities. Still, the Brotherhood's brand of conservative Islam has remained attractive, especially for those suffering from unequal economic conditions in the poorer emirates and for those resentful of Western influence more broadly, fueling further government fears of an Islamist takeover.[230]

Islah inspired the creation of other Islamist organizations as well, making it even more dangerous in the government's eyes. The Emirates People's Rights Organization (EPRO) was established in 2004 as an independent human rights group under the leadership of former Islah member and self-proclaimed Sharjan human rights activist Hassan al-Diqqi.[231] One WikiLeaks documents confirms that "[i]t was clear from the website that al-Diqqi had Islamist views and was vociferous in his criticism of the UAEG [UAE government]."[232] In fact, he had left Islah, preferring "more Islamist ideas about development."[233] The federal government refused to recognize the organization, instead establishing the Emirates Human Rights Association (EHRA) in 2005, which primarily included members of government or people closely allied to it.[234] In addition, the government demanded that al-Diqqi shut down his group's website, on which he had "denounced the UAE's lack of civil liberties and alleged political abuses and human rights violations."[235] He also decried the construction of Christian churches and Hindu temples and Western, especially American, universities in the UAE.

Al-Diqqi, though he had left the Brotherhood, became a victim of government intimidation because he harbored Islamist sympathies and created an independent group to support and promote them. Shortly after establishing the organization, al-Diqqi was arrested on charges of raping a housekeeper and went into hiding.[236] He was sentenced to death in absentia, was arrested in Sharjah in July 2006 on the rape charge, and ultimately spent nine months in prison.[237] After his release, in 2012, al-Diqqi tried to launch a political party inspired by Salafism called Hizb al-Umma (the Umma Party),[238] which has since been dubbed a terrorist organization in a list released in November 2014.[239] The group has branches in Saudi Arabia, where it is also outlawed, and Kuwait, where it operates openly.[240] The Ministry of Foreign Affairs considered the development "surprising and regrettable," and al-Diqqi is thought to be living in exile in Turkey today.[241] In the face of such attempts to promote Islamist thought, the federal government has taken the lead on the crackdown against any independent religious thought that could undermine its sovereignty.

Escalating Tensions and a Political Reform Movement

Following its confrontations with the government in the 1990s and 2000s, Islah had far less freedom to exercise political influence yet continued agitating privately for enhanced political participation. The Emirates Discussion Forum, or uaehewar.net, which has since been suspended, was founded in summer 2009 by a diverse group of Emirati students and activists and resurrected a loosely organized reform movement among Islamists and secular Emiratis. This online platform, as Davidson explains, "quickly gained the reputation as being the best place to put forward grievances, challenge the authorities, and discuss the country's future."[242] In early 2010, the government blocked the website within the UAE, yet it remained an active discussion board outside the country. The website, though not explicitly linked to Islah, brought to the fore a number of concerns, shared by the organization, about the non-participatory nature of the Emirati government, as well as corruption within it. Thousands of users had become involved by January 2010 and wrote about the acquittal of a member of the al-Nahyan ruling family of Abu Dhabi, following accusations of torture and sodomy.[243] Discussion over that incident led to broader debate about the ruling families; Davidson found that "[m]ost of the threads touched on the concerns of nationals regarding the application of the rule of law to the ruling families and the broader impact of the verdict on the UAE's international reputation."[244] Attempts to hold the central government accountable for its policies, a complaint that rentier state theory would not predict, largely went unanswered.

Still, the opinions expressed on the website about expanding political participation were not particularly surprising. In fact, a 2010 survey conducted by *al-Emarat al-Youm* showed that 73 percent of respondents wanted to increase the power of the Federal National Council (FNC), the country's only elected body.[245] Further, President Shaykh Khalifa bin Zayed al-Nahyan has repeatedly stated his intention to grant the FNC greater decision-making power, saying that it will have a "bigger role . . . by empowering it to be an authority that will provide great support and guidance of the executive."[246]

Frustrated with its inability to use institutionalized means to voice its grievances, Islah took a more oppositional stance.[247] One Gulf analyst explained the Emirati government's reaction to this change:

> You can be here and believe whatever you want but don't bring your politics here. Brotherhood supporters became politically active during the Arab Spring, and this led to the crackdown. Every few years there were arrests, deportations, and trials because the Brotherhood has been a perennial problem for the UAE since its inception. The Arab Spring and election of Mohamed Morsi brought the Muslim Brotherhood issue to a head, so there were many more public arrests and deportations, as well as subsidizing the Egyptian state under Sisi and driving the Muslim Brotherhood underground.[248]

The reform movement, tacitly supported by Islah for years, became stronger and more active during the Arab Spring, as the government continued to promise (yet failed to deliver on) greater political participation to citizens. As in Qatar, though, Emirati citizens have only been able to use uninstitutionalized means to voice political concerns.

By couching the Brotherhood's goals in terms of a security threat, the government has justified its crackdown against the organization. The super-rentier government was unable to stem the tide of Islamist sentiment with payouts in 2011 and thus inflated the movement's political strength as a means of justifying its actions. As historian and former French diplomat Jean-Pierre Filiu put it, in the broader context of the Arab Spring,

> "rulers became well versed in their routine of no alternative argumentation: towards the West, they posed as the only ones able to deter an Islamist takeover." Moreover, it was argued that there is a now a ". . . sad irony that the powers in place have ended up believing their own fantasies about the Islamist threat; they not only displayed that card for external consumption, but they also fed their own masses with gory stories about the inevitability of . . . ruin."[249]

In an environment of fear and increasing paranoia, after the arrests of over one hundred Brotherhood members and sympathizers since 2012, the movement has been driven underground.[250]

The Petition Movement and First Government Crackdown

A petition, addressed to President Shaykh Khalifa bin Zayed al-Nahyan and the Federal Supreme Council in March 2011 and endorsed by 133 intellectuals, among them Islah members, led to the most significant government crackdown on all strands of opposition, which increasingly became focused on Islah and the Muslim Brotherhood. The immediate catalyst for the petition was the government's failure to introduce legislation to increase the pool of voters for the FNC, which many members of the Council itself had advocated since March 2010.[251] The petition garnered support from citizens representing various ideologies, as it called for universal suffrage in an elected legislature, with expanded constitutional powers to produce legislation and supervise the executive.[252] Notably, four professional organizations (the associations for jurists, teachers, national heritage professionals, and university faculty), all of which were traditionally known for their Brotherhood ties, signed the petition. They also issued a joint statement, announcing that "civil society in the UAE considers that the time has come to ensure the right of political participation of every citizen, with direct elections for a council with full federal oversight and legislative powers, and lamented 'the lack of involvement of citizens to choose their representatives, decades after the establishment of the state.' "[253]

The petition marked the first time that secular liberal and Islamist opposition had come together in such a public political undertaking and "gathered signatures from across the political spectrum, including nationalists, Islamists and others."[254] One secular human rights activist explained that the petition's goal was "to bridge the gap between different factions—to get liberals, Islamists, and nationalists to get together on a national course."[255] Cooperation among various factions led to a number of compromises. He described the process of drafting the document: "We decided to limit the petition to improvement of the FNC to get the maximum number of people to sign. Islamists did not start this petition . . . . We wrote the petition in very soft language, very diplomatic and fatherly language to attract more signatures."[256] Despite signatories' efforts to strike a balance between demanding reform from the government and maintaining ties with it, the petition provoked a crackdown. Still, it did not advocate much reform beyond what had been previously promised by the state regarding increased representation in the FNC.

In early April 2011, five of the one hundred and thirty-three signatories of the petition (the so-called UAE5),[257] said to be its primary backers and including Mansoor, were arrested. They were charged with " 'publicly insulting' the UAE's President, Vice-President and [Abu Dhabi] Crown Prince in comments posted on an online discussion forum [UAEHiwar] . . . . All five were convicted in November 2011 after a trial that failed to satisfy international standards of fair trial, and sentenced to prison terms of up to three years."[258] Shortly after their sentencing, the five (none of whom was an Islah member) were released through a presidential pardon due in large measure to international media attention and a November 2011 report by the United Nations Working Group on Arbitrary Detention condemning the arrests.[259] After their release, they continued voicing their political opinions, primarily through social media.[260]

Nasser bin Ghaith, one of the UAE5 who was rearrested in August 2015,[261] expressed surprise at the initial crackdown: "I am politically neutral and well-connected, so it was surprising what happened to me—people were shocked. It shows the rising power of state security in our country."[262] He was sentenced to ten years in prison in March 2017 for promoting "false information in order to harm the reputation and stature of the state and one of its institutions," through a series of posts on Twitter in which he claimed he had been denied a fair trial in the UAE5 case.[263] After the economist's second arrest, Ahmed Mansoor, another of the UAE5, was detained again in March 2017, on charges of making social media posts that "harm national unity and social harmony and damage the country's reputation."[264] Several international human rights bodies have lamented this arrest, as Mansoor has become a prominent activist, winning the Martin Ennals award in 2016; he has yet to be sentenced yet remains in custody.

In attempts to bolster domestic support for the government despite the crackdown it was undertaking, a widely publicized "statement of allegiance," released in May 2011 and sponsored by a lawyers' association, voiced support for the monarchy; several pro-government rallies were arranged by loyal tribes; and the monarchy successfully persuaded various tribal leaders to release statements denouncing the opposition movement.[265] Hoping to stifle dissent from the civil society sector, the government also disbanded the boards of the independent Jurist Association and Teachers' Association in 2011, both of which had supported the petition movement. The government had become more explicit about denying the civil society sector a political voice. According to Amnesty International, "By summarily dismissing their executive boards and appointing government nominees to replace them, the authorities compromised the independence of the two organizations and effectively sent a warning to other NGOs to toe the line or risk opening themselves to similar government intervention."[266] Further restricting civil society, in 2012, the government closed the local offices of four foreign NGOs, including two whose remit is to promote democracy (National Democratic Institute and Konrad Adenauer Stiftung), as well as the RAND Corporation in Abu Dhabi and Gallup Center, in addition to denying the renewal of the Gulf Research Center's business license,[267] due to "objections by the Dubai government to various aspects of [its] work."[268]

Hoping to deflect attention from incidents like the arrest of the UAE5 and the closure of several NGOs, the government made limited efforts to respond to domestic political opposition, while also boosting financial disbursements, in an effort to buy off dissidents. The government thus expanded the FNC electorate to 12 percent of the national population for the September 2011 elections[269] and announced that universal suffrage could be introduced by 2019.[270] It also granted huge public sector pay increases (in some cases up to 100 percent) and boosted welfare benefits by up to 20 percent, in addition to signing a $2.7 billion agreement to help poorer nationals pay off outstanding loans.[271] Shortly after the petition, in March 2011, the federal government also announced a new investment of $1.6 billion to improve infrastructure in the northern emirates.[272] In addition, several supermarkets across the UAE agreed with the Ministry of Economy to slash prices for food and other essential items by up to 40 percent for one month.[273] The expansion of the FNC electorate was the primary political reform, yet resulted in no substantial change: only half of the FNC is elected; the body itself still lacks legislative power, and a meager 28 percent of the eligible voters took part in the 2011 election.[274] The super-rentier government's largely economic response to political opposition reflects the regime's understanding of politics as primarily pecuniary, considering citizen approval to be determined by the distribution of resources rather than the state's provision of public access to institutionalized political life. In this environment, Islamist complaint remains a viable independent voice in super-rentiers, as its supporters are not swayed by government handouts.

Islah tacitly supported the UAE5 and other imprisoned activists as the crackdown continued into 2012. Although liberal and Islamist activists had worked together on the petition, the government appears to have exaggerated links between them in an effort to dramatize the danger to the system. As one Gulf analyst explained, "The government wanted to conflate the two to show it's a big threat. The government never took liberals very seriously. The government saw Islamists as more dangerous due to links with the Muslim Brotherhood."[275] The government, in turn, charged that Islah exploited the controversy surrounding the UAE5 to increase its own influence, "using the umbrella of reform to reach their goals" of larger government takeover.[276] While the first wave of crackdown focused on the petition, the second was directed at Islah, largely due to the fact that, unlike the secular liberal movement, the Brotherhood, as represented by Islah, had enhanced organizational capacity and a long history inside the country.

Government Crackdown on Islah

In 2012, the government launched a campaign of arrests targeting Islah due to its links to Muslim Brotherhood ideology, which it considered to be the primary political threat inside the country. In the words of one secular human rights activist, the Ikhwan "was more popular and well-known [than the liberal movement] due to its social activities. Many of its members were seen as the cream of society . . . with good reputations and important positions."[277] In April 2012, seven Islah members (the so-called UAE7),[278] who were signatories to the March 2011 petition and whose citizenship had been stripped in December 2011, were sent to prison after they failed to leave the country as the government requested.[279] They contended that they had been "unjustly targeted for their political views" since they had signed the petition on behalf of Islah.[280] These arrests marked only the beginning of the crackdown on Islah.

By the end of July, fifty-four Islamists had been arrested, including academics, activists, and even Shaykh Sultan bin Kayed al-Qasimi from the ruling family of Ras al-Khaimah.[281] Attorney General ʿAli Salim al-Tunaiji announced that "the country's national security was under threat from a group of people with ties to 'foreign organizations and agendas'—a clear reference to Egypt's Muslim Brotherhood organization. Al-Tunaiji accused this group of plotting 'crimes against state security' and of opposing 'the UAE constitution and ruling system,'" yet presented no evidence to that effect.[282] Later that month, he confirmed that Islah members in custody were accused of creating and operating a secret organization whose "undeclared objectives were to seek to succeed in taking over the authority in the country and oppose the fundamental principles on which it is based."[283] Al-Tunaiji went on to say that Islah had aimed to tarnish the government's image and that the trial for these suspects would be held in Abu Dhabi at the State Security Chamber of the Federal Supreme Court.[284]

In September 2012, the government claimed to have received confessions from imprisoned Islah members, admitting that their organization had an armed wing and aimed to overthrow the existing order to re-establish the caliphate, a claim not substantiated by any independent Islah documents, public statements, or discussion with Islah members.[285] Still, one government report claimed that "investigations have revealed that the structure of the organization included committees and local branches in every emirate, as well as consultative and executive councils and a military wing."[286] Other sources added that Islah coordinated its efforts with Brotherhood organizations elsewhere in the region and even received financial assistance from Brotherhood affiliates in other Gulf countries.[287] Because Islah had an organizational structure and some of its members had personal ties to other Brotherhood sympathizers outside the country, the Emirati government considered it to necessarily harbor nefarious political aims. Islah denied all charges, stating that the organization is "pacifist, civilian and moderate and has never, and will never, choose to take up arms."[288] By the end of 2012, ninety-four alleged members of Islah had been arrested. In response to this government crackdown, "the opposition seemed to have broadened, with the government facing further criticism."[289] Still, the government's campaign of arrests continued.

In January 2013, thirteen women were arrested, many of whom were relatives of men previously jailed.[290] The ninety-four detained in 2012 were tried together, eight in absentia, beginning in March 2013. In July 2013, sixty-nine of the defendants, including the eight outside the country, were convicted and received sentences ranging from seven to fifteen years, while twenty-five were acquitted, including the thirteen women.[291] The UAE7 had been added to the UAE94 trial and were convicted of posing a security threat due to their membership in Islah; they were sentenced, aside from twenty-five who were found not guilty, to ten years in prison each, with three years of probation to follow.[292] The UAE94 were denied the right of an appeal, and the prosecution used evidence primarily of confessions that were allegedly obtained through ill treatment or torture.[293] Although seven independent international human rights agencies urged Emirati authorities to make UAE94 trial proceedings open to the public,[294] authorities did not allow entry to international media or independent observers, making it difficult to discern how fair the trial was.[295]

The Crackdown Widens

In addition to the series of arrests, as seen immediately following 9/11 and as described by one Emirati human rights activist, the crackdown involved "a massive media campaign; businesses, bank accounts were suspended, and people were threatened."[296] Using both the trials and the State Security Directorate, "[a]t one stroke, the authorities removed their most prominent critics and the country's leading advocates of reform from the public arena, while signaling to other potential dissenters that they will not tolerate open political debate in the UAE."[297] Since 2011, the UAE has become increasingly insular and restrictive. Aside from the closure of international NGOs mentioned above, the government has become more selective in allowing non-nationals inside the country. In February 2012, the residency permits of approximately sixty Syrian citizens were cancelled after they staged a protest outside their country's embassy, reflecting the Emirati government's intolerance of expatriates participating in politics inside the state.[298] As Michael Hudson highlights, "[T]he action against Syrian protesters, despite strong public sympathy with their plight, points to a broader intolerance for political activism of any kind, including internal dissent. This is particularly so if it is perceived to involve the Muslim Brotherhood."[299] Following the UAE94 trial, another security trial was held in November 2013, wherein ten of the ninety-four, along with twenty Egyptians (six tried in absentia), were charged for creating an international branch of the Muslim Brotherhood and for stealing and circulating classified state documents.[300] They were convicted in January 2014, despite complaints of being forced to make confessions under torture, and were granted sentences of one to five years, with the Egyptians to be deported immediately after serving their sentences.[301]

In February 2013, Qatari doctor Mahmoud al-Jaidah was arrested for transporting monetary support for Islah as he was transiting through Dubai International Airport. The State Security Chamber of the Federal Supreme Court "convicted Mahmoud al-Jaidah under

Article 180 of the Penal Code for allegedly providing financial support to families of the members of al-Islah who were detained following their arrests in 2012. The court sentenced him to seven years of imprisonment."[302] Another public gaffe occurred in February 2013, when the London School of Economics canceled a conference cohosted with the American University of Sharjah on the Arab Spring "in response to restrictions imposed on the intellectual content of the event that threatened academic freedom."[303]

Further cementing the Emirati government's stance against the Brotherhood and in fact any independent organization, an antiterrorism law passed in August 2014 updated the 2004 legislation, allowing for expanded use of the death penalty and other severe punishments.[304] The legislation, though cracking down on violent extremist groups at a time of regional fear about a resurgence of violent jihadist activity in Syria, also, according to Amnesty International, "has the potential to be used against peaceful activists and government critics due to the broad ambit of its provisions, their vague definition, and the range of actions that may be considered under the law to amount to terrorism."[305] As Sarah Leah Whitson of Human Rights Watch put it, "In the UAE it's now a case of 'you're with us or you're a terrorist.' "[306] In November 2014, the UAE released a list of eighty-two organizations that it considers terrorist groups. Although this record includes violent organizations such as al-Qaʿida and Islamic State of Iraq and Syria (ISIS), it also comprises nonviolent groups like Islah and the Egyptian Muslim Brotherhood, in addition to advocacy organizations like the Council on American-Islamic Relations.[307]

Many Emiratis insist that the government's swift crackdown intentionally created "the impression of political dynamism that doesn't exist."[308] Others support this response as the government enforcing laws that restrict the formation of any independent political organization, under the penal code.[309] Still others consider it a means of promoting Emirati national security. Ultimately, within the UAE, "people value stability."[310] Government rhetoric has been instrumental in promoting the authorities' narrative about Islah as a dangerous international organization intent on dismantling the prevailing order.

Creating an Enemy: The Government's Rhetoric about the Muslim Brotherhood

The Emirati government has been surprisingly outspoken in its recent campaign against the Muslim Brotherhood, dismissing the organization and associating Islah's calls for reform as attempts to dismantle the regime. Although the government's actions against the Ikhwan only made headlines during the Arab Spring, members of the government had expressed concerns about the organization in conversations with American officials as early as 2007. At that time, they used " 'quiet marginalization' and support for reintegrating MB [Muslim Brotherhood] members back into mainstream society. Members of the ruling families often got personally involved in this process."[311] Despite their massive wealth, the UAE's ruling families long feared Brotherhood influence, demonstrating the salience of ideological politics in a super-rentier state. Having failed to buy off such movements, the government resolved to quash it.

Some Emiratis claim that the government's new, harsher response is a reaction to a "more radical" younger generation of Islamists "fired up" to take over power after the successes of Islamists in Egypt and Tunisia during the Arab Spring.[312] Even so, the rhetoric used about the organization appears to have greatly exaggerated Islah's popularity and political aspirations.

During the January 2012 GCC National and Regional Security Conference sponsored by the Bahrain Center for Strategic, International and Energy Studies, then Chief of the Dubai Police Force Dhahi Khalfan went so far as to state, "The Muslim Brotherhood is a security threat to the Gulf, and is no less dangerous than Iran."[313] Emirati Foreign Minister Shaykh ʿAbdullah bin Zayed al-Nahyan similarly denounced the Brotherhood as "an organization which encroaches upon the sovereignty and integrity of nations" and called on Gulf governments to work against its expanding influence.[314] Such language illustrates government attempts to use fears about emerging Islamist political parties in the region as an excuse to dismiss such groups' demands for political reform within the UAE. As early as 2009, a WikiLeaks document revealed that "[b]eing labelled a Muslim Brother is about the worst epithet possible in MBZ vocabulary," suggesting that he always intended to wipe out the group.[315] Rather than attempting to quietly co-opt the religious sphere as in Qatar, the Emirati government has embarked on a public offensive against Islamist reformers, raising their profile in the process. The authorities perhaps recognized the power of the Brotherhood's ideology and its ability to garner support from among the Emirati citizenry and thus came to consider a full-scale crackdown its only option.

The UAE's containment of Islah has garnered international attention, in addition to provoking a clash with Qatar, considered to be sympathetic to the Muslim Brotherhood. In February 2014, Shaykh Yusuf al-Qaradawi, on his program *al-Shariʿa wa-l-Hayat*, accused the Emirati leadership of "standing against every Islamic rule, punishing Islamists and sending them to prison."[316] These remarks led to a major rift between the UAE and Qatar. The Emirati Foreign Ministry summoned the Qatari Ambassador to the UAE to lodge a formal complaint, and the UAE, along with Bahrain and Saudi Arabia, withdrew their ambassadors from Qatar shortly thereafter.[317] Dhahi Khalfan even opined that Interpol should issue an arrest warrant for al-Qaradawi.[318] In April, al-Qaradawi took a more conciliatory stance, also making clear that he does not speak for the Qatari government and stating, "I love all the countries of the Gulf, and they all love me: Saudi Arabia, Kuwait and the United Arab Emirates, Oman, and Bahrain. I consider them one country and one house."[319]

As the intra-Gulf conflict continued, *The New York Times* revealed in September 2014 that the UAE hired American consulting firm Camstoll Group to plant stories critical of Qatar, particularly its alleged support for the Muslim Brotherhood.[320] The feud became bitter, pitting two opposite approaches to handling Islamist complaints against one another, yet this rift seemed to be resolved in November 2014 after al-Qaradawi was taken off the air and after seven Egyptian members of the Brotherhood were expelled from Qatar.[321] In the international standoff, the Emirati position seemed to prevail, especially after the fall of Islamist governments in Egypt and Tunisia, which fueled criticism of the group and its ideology more broadly. As one signal of rapprochement, the UAE pardoned Qatari Mahmoud al-Jaidah in May 2015, with the state news agency dubbing this move a means to "strengthen the close fraternal relations between the leaderships and peoples of the two brotherly countries."[322] Nonetheless, five Qataris were fined or sentenced in absentia in May 2015 after an Emirati court convicted them of insulting the Emirati leadership through social media platforms.[323]

In the domestic sphere, the Emirati central government has faced minimal public backlash, despite its crackdown. The government did, in 2015, again expand the size of the FNC's electoral college by 66 percent, though it still represents under half of the total Emirati population.[324] Further, voter turnout remained low, though higher than in 2011, at only

35 percent of eligible voters, or about 79,000 people, indicating the relative irrelevance and unimportance of the body.[325] Among Emiratis, rhetoric about the Muslim Brotherhood within the UAE remains extreme, with interviewees comparing the organization and its members to Nazis,[326] the Ku Klux Klan,[327] and the Taliban.[328] Newspapers throughout the country have run stories about the Brotherhood's plans to take over the state, claiming that it "infiltrated societies, schools, universities, ministries and families under the pretense of doing social work to conceal their actions and 'divert their loyalty to the organization and its leadership after preparing a general climate in society to accept this by turning public opinion against all the authorities of the state.'"[329] Aside from state news agencies, institutions like Al Mezmaah Studies and Research Center, described by one Gulf analyst as "government-centered civil society," are instrumental in spreading negative information about the Brotherhood—in particular on university campuses where the Brotherhood has traditionally found support.[330] Al Mezmaah promotes the notion that the Muslim Brotherhood uses the façade of an Islamic program to shroud its real goal of dismantling the nation state in order to create a caliphate. The founder of Al Mezmaah went so far as to claim that "those who follow the Muslim Brotherhood are not humans but machines."[331] Such extreme remarks, aside from showing the illogical and extreme nature of the fear of the Brotherhood inside the UAE, demonstrate attempts to dehumanize, in an effort to strip the legitimacy and appeal of, Brotherhood organizations. Had such groups not been politically influential, the government would not have embarked on such a public and wide-ranging crackdown. Further, because it could use grassroots social outreach to expand its support base, the Brotherhood was seen as ever more dangerous to the Emirati authorities and to the existing order.

CONCLUSIONS

As has been demonstrated in the preceding analysis, super-rentiers have adapted to their local environments in a variety of ways yet have remained critically similar in their ability to gain followers primarily due to their ideological appeal at the grassroots level. While super-rentier states have successfully provided material well-being to their citizenry, they have failed to provide strong ideological justification for their rule, leaving a vacuum for Islamist opposition. Further, more space has traditionally been allowed to Islamist causes due to the desire of regimes to appear appropriately religious, and so opposition has managed to cluster around that sector. Following the Arab Spring and the rise of Islamist parties to political prominence, each of the small Gulf states under study has taken a very different tack toward the organization, revealing the degree to which they consider the group politically threatening. Kuwait has allowed its Brotherhood branch to continue to contest elections and run its social arm, Islah, while the Qatari government, lacking a domestic Brotherhood to manage, backed Islamist parties that won elections abroad. The UAE, however, came to view the Ikhwan as an existential threat to the state's sovereignty and to their rulers' vision for the country; as such, they embarked on a substantial crackdown on the organization. In the next chapter, we assess state treatment of their Muslim Brotherhood affiliates and the potential future role for rentier Islamism, especially as the Emirates, along with Bahrain, Egypt, and Saudi Arabia, has taken its fight against Islamism regional in a campaign targeting Qatar.

7

Challenges and Opposition in the Twenty-First Century

INTRODUCTION

As noted above, in this chapter we trace the means in which the post-Arab Spring era has influenced political discussion and treatment of rentier Islamists, as well as their own reactions to developments of 2011–2012. While the Kuwaiti and Emirati branches moved increasingly toward pushing political agendas, the Qatari affiliate remained focused on effecting change in social policies inside the state. The Kuwaiti and Emirati authorities reacted differently to this turn to the political—the Kuwaiti government with tolerance and the Emirati with containment. Below we detail where the rentier Islamists stand in the present political spectrum and prospects for their future involvement in government, once again demonstrating the organization's political capital in oil-wealthy states and in a variety of structural forms.

THE KUWAITI MUSLIM BROTHERHOOD'S INCREASING POLITICAL PRAGMATISM

The Kuwaiti Muslim Brotherhood's institutionalized political activities grew out of its presence in the social sphere and positions in government bureaucracy. Through social and educational activities, aided by government backing, the Brotherhood gained popular support in the 1950s and 1960s, despite the pervasive influence of Arab nationalism at that time. The Ikhwan's popularity allowed it to garner political capital in the 1970s and 1980s. Once in institutionalized political roles as government ministers and members of parliament (MPs), Brotherhood members continued pushing their social agenda. Following the invasion and occupation by Iraq in the early 1990s, the Muslim Brotherhood became more pragmatic, focusing on political gains ahead of ideological goals. In such a climate, it even created a separate political wing (the Islamic Constitutional Movement, or ICM), distinguished from its social wing (Jamʿiat al-Islah al-Ijtimaʿi, or Islah), thus officially dividing into *ḥizb* and *ḥaraka*. Today, these organizations work toward largely the same goals but with different supporters and various priorities.

Islah in a Contemporary Perspective

As discussed above, Islah became, after the occupation of Kuwait, the social arm of the Kuwaiti Muslim Brotherhood, with the ICM established to manage the Brotherhood's political projects. Islah continues to host a variety of social programs—particularly among youth. Related activities involve sports organizations, in addition to classes on ethics, morals, and piety. Though Islah is formally apolitical, its activities bring together like-minded people into a single community, which has strong political implications. As one interviewee who attended such programs explained, "It is not at all political, but these people will be loyal."[1] The Brotherhood's charity networks and social programs are similarly seen as means of complementing the ICM's institutionalized political activity.

Many non-Islamist Kuwaitis also consider Brotherhood-sponsored activities and charities means of enticing new members and view the group's educational efforts as tools of indoctrination. As one Kuwaiti political scientist described it, "The Ikhwan bribes kids in the streets with footballs, fixing football fields, then invites them to pray."[2] Still, most charity remains focused outside the country. Due to Kuwait's infamously lax financial laws,[3] which did not criminalize terrorist financing until 2013, many fear that Brotherhood charities fund Islamist organizations abroad, in particular Islamist militias in Syria, despite Kuwaiti government pledges to enhance oversight and has introduced anti-terrorist financing legislation.[4] Rumors about the Brotherhood's financial strength and its misuse of charity funds abound. Still, members of the organization insist that "they have trouble raising the funds necessary."[5] In fact, in 1996, the government took over control of zakat committees that had once been a source of financial and popular support for the Brotherhood, "causing the Movement to lose the funds' life blood necessary to maintain the normal level of activities."[6] The Brotherhood is still able to fund charity activities abroad and domestic social programs, attractive largely to a self-selected group of people drawn to the organization's ideology.

The ICM's Goals and the Separation of the Political and Social

In the current era, most of the ICM's primary goals have become focused on domestic politics and a pro-democracy agenda, as the organization pushes for reforms such as an elected prime minister, a new electoral law that reduces gerrymandering, the legalization of political parties, and, eventually, the creation of a constitutional monarchy. The organization also has more wide-ranging social and economic aims. In a document explaining the platform of the ICM, released in 2007, seven general goals are listed. They include the following:

1. To develop and encourage the political regime towards an active popular interaction, and amend the Kuwaiti Constitution for the application of the optimum, sublime Islamic rules and principles.
2. To consolidate and establish justice in the State of Kuwait, apply equality between its citizens, and maintain principles of democracy and counseling in compliance with the Islamic Sharia principles.
3. To shape the Kuwaiti citizen according to his unique Islamic identity and true Arab loyalty, in a manner that meets the development plans, takes part in the reform of society and assists in the formation of the future of Kuwait in all fields.

4. To underline the sovereignty of Kuwait on all its territories and secure the defensive methods under patronage of the national unity and in accordance with the verse "and all of you shall take refuge of Allah and do not be separated from each other . . . ."
5. To reform the economic system in the State of Kuwait in line with the fair wealth distribution principles, and change it into a more productive system in accordance with the Islamic principles of containment and integration.
6. To impress the social, educational and informative systems into the State of Kuwait in a way that involves quality Islamic thinking and keeps pace with the aspirations of development, progress, and civilization.
7. To establish unity between the GCC [Gulf Cooperation Council] countries in order to be able to achieve a comprehensive economic, political and military integration, and to achieve the Arab and Islamic unity in the future in a way that reflects the principles of Islam calling for unity and condemning disunity.[7]

This list highlights the overwhelmingly domestic agenda of the ICM, as well as the myriad similarities between its goals and those of secular liberal opposition parties.

Despite the fact that they share some common aims, however, secular liberal political blocs and the ICM have clashed in the past over the issue of civil liberties. The ICM, in Nathan J. Brown's estimation, "supports liberalizing political reforms rather faithfully, but it draws the line when liberalization leads in a cultural direction."[8] For example, in the 1990s, the ICM backed a press law that would decrease licensing requirements while also insisting that the publication of material insulting to Islam be a punishable offense.[9] In such an instance, "[t]he party argued that justice had to come before freedom."[10] In other cases, the ICM has promoted measures that place limits on personal freedoms, such as the rejection of female suffrage, the criminalization of religious blasphemy in the press, and the imposition of laws restricting hours when women can work. One Kuwaiti political scientist charged that "the Brotherhood used democracy to establish laws that are unconstitutional and against the law."[11] Indeed, liberal-leaning secular MPs often express their hesitance to ally with the Brotherhood, as they fear it would impose limits on their social freedoms. When asked about such restrictions, one former ICM MP explained, "of course we want Islam to be our social norm and the government to respect Islam."[12] The group is therefore both staunchly liberal (in terms of demanding more representative government) while maintaining its social conservatism.

Notwithstanding its commitment to conservative social mores, Kuwait's Brotherhood is "politically more liberal than those who call themselves liberal."[13] In fact, in Brown's words, the ICM's "leaders are frustrated because they feel that in a sense they have become more democratic than the political system in which they operate—and perhaps more than Kuwaiti society is ready for."[14] The ICM's democratic credentials are proven by its internal structure, which is far more sophisticated than that of any other Kuwaiti political bloc (see figure 7.1). One current ICM MP explained the party's democratic bylaws: "we change the leadership and group inside every four years to give a chance to have new blood."[15] The level of organization within the ICM is impressive. Its general membership, all of whom have passed through a probationary period and pay dues, form a General Assembly.[16] The elected Secretary General, Secretariat, and eight-member Political Bureau handle day-to-day decision-making and running of the bloc, while a Parliamentary Committee oversees the

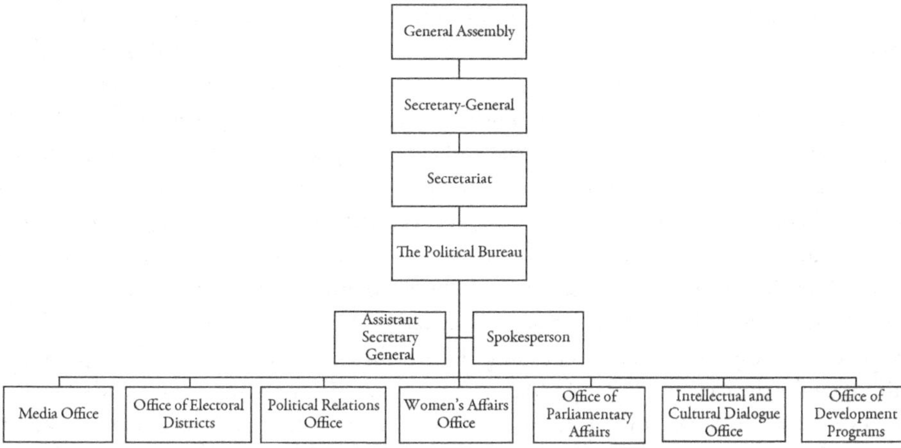

FIGURE 7.1 ICM Organizational Chart
"ICM Vision, Mission and Objectives."

activities of the organization's MPs, who have been selected by party leadership to run.[17] Such structures at the national level, in addition to local bodies, maintain the bloc's discipline, guaranteeing that "the ICM is more than the sum of a few leading personalities."[18]

Perhaps because of its modern democratic structure and focus on political reform, the ICM has been criticized by more conservative Islamists for focusing on political rather than religious matters, allowing for the growth of Kuwait's Salafi movement.[19] Further reflecting its accommodationist and politically pragmatic turn, the ICM has attempted to cooperate with a variety of political blocs, including Shiʿi Islamist groups, yet has been held back, at times, by a coalition with the Salafis: "As a result, Shiite Islamist deputies do not vote with the Islamist bloc but instead with the populist one."[20] When asked about their willingness to form coalitions, members of the ICM responded that they were in favor, as the organization is ultimately flexible.[21] The popular perception is that, in the words of one Kuwaiti academic, "you can speak reason with the Ikhwan. They're part of the system of elites, so they would never dream of overturning [the system]."[22] Ismaʿil al-Shatti, for his part, called for the implementation of all parts of sharia over time, considering that "[t]he Quran came in stages."[23] This more moderate stance prevails today, as issues of government reform appear more urgent than the traditional social reform agenda associated with Islamists.

Regarding its work through social services, the ICM's association with the Brotherhood's social organization, Islah, "may have actually proved a liability when other parties levied the charge (denied by Hadas [or the ICM]) that charitable funds were being used for an expensive political campaign."[24] As for the ICM's relationship with Islah, a current MP explained, "We cooperate with Jamʿiat Islah in general. We need their support in elections, and we support them in parliament if they need it for social issues."[25] Members of Islah can join the ICM, yet cannot serve on elected boards as leaders of both groups, and the ICM is in no way governed by Islah or vice versa.[26] The formal division between the social and political arms (*ḥizb* and *ḥaraka*) of the Brotherhood highlights that each is equally important in maintaining popular support. At the same time, this separation is not always logical, considering how much each branch depends on the other.

The Kuwaiti Brotherhood's agenda, at least on the part of the ICM, remains exclusively domestic. In the view of one Kuwaiti sociologist, "The Kuwaiti Muslim Brotherhood are Kuwaiti first and Muslim Brotherhood second."[27] Furthermore, the organization's agenda is shaped by local realities more than a desire to take over rule. As another current ICM MP explained, "we are 100 percent loyal to [the ruling family]. We want reform, repair, not change."[28] In fact, the amir meets with members of the Brotherhood and attends their *dīwāniyyāt*, demonstrating that the Kuwaiti government, unlike others in the Gulf, "isn't in panic mode."[29] While the Kuwaiti government has never legally recognized the ICM,[30] its approach in dealing with the bloc, and with the Brotherhood in general, is far more moderate than the repressive security-led approach seen in the United Arab Emirates (UAE), in part because the group's status as a primarily local political bloc has been established. A lawsuit called for the closure of Islah in March 2014;[31] one MP tried to persuade parliament to outlaw the Brotherhood as a terrorist organization in July 2014;[32] and rumors swirled about purges of Brotherhood supporters from government in 2013.[33] Nonetheless, large-scale government action has not taken place against the Ikhwan, despite the fact that it holds popular support.

The ICM and Kuwaiti Politics Today

A national malaise prevailed as the ICM and the rest of the opposition sustained its boycott from December 2012 and July 2013. Secular opposition leader and former Popular Action Bloc MP Musallam al-Barrak led the call, beginning in 2014, for a return to protests until a new election was called and cabinet positions became elected.[34] Although the ICM supports al-Barrak's ultimate goal of a constitutional monarchy, its social program may hinder the coalition, as has happened in past ICM alliances with secular blocs. Still, in early 2013, the ICM signed on to a twenty-three-page document on reform drafted by al-Barrak, along with ICM parliamentarian Jamaʿan al-Harbash and Tariq al-Mutairi of the liberal Civil Democratic Movement.[35] Political trends ranging from secular leftists to Salafis, as well as the National Union of Kuwaiti Students (NUKS), have signed the document, which "proposes a full parliamentary system, with a stronger legislature, independent judiciary and revised criminal code."[36]

Significantly, as part of the opposition coalition, the ICM dropped its once primary demand of amending article 2 of the constitution and seems increasingly willing to work alongside other opposition movements to ensure political reform and to stamp out corruption.[37] Impressively, the opposition gathered some six thousand people in protest in June 2014, claiming to expose the corruption of Nasser Mohammed al-Sabah, an influential member of the Amiri Diwan, and Judge Faisal al-Marshad, the head of the Supreme Judicial Council, in addition to other judges.[38]

The government has reacted against such opposition unity since the Arab Spring. It revoked the citizenship of five opposition members in July 2014, a step that Joe Stork, Deputy Director for Middle East and North Africa at Human Rights Watch, dubbed "another downward step in Kuwait's assault on the right to free speech."[39] Although those stripped of citizenship, including thirty-three in 2014 alone,[40] did not include members of the ICM,[41] the organization released a statement dubbing the situation a "regretful example of utilizing the state's capabilities in fighting reformists instead of supporting the process of reform."[42] In January 2015, former ICM MP Mubarak al-Duwailah was arrested on charges of endangering ties with an ally and insulting leaders of that state following his statements, on Kuwait's parliamentary television channel, about Abu Dhabi Crown Prince Shaykh Mohammed bin Zayed al-Nahyan being "against Sunni Islam."[43] Though al-Duwailah was not charged in Kuwait, his case was referred to the UAE's Federal Supreme Court, which sentenced him to five years in absentia.[44]

In the face of greater government restriction, the ICM is likely to continue to privilege political reform over social policies, as opposition groups focus increasingly on pursuing common goals of political reform.[45] In fact, al-Duwailah explicitly called for overcoming traditional differences in a January 2015 statement released shortly after his arrest, and such opposition unification appears to be taking place.[46] The ICM, along with al-Barrak's Popular Action Bloc and the Salafi Umma Party, led the charge in continued protests in 2015 against judicial corruption and the government's policy of stripping citizenship from dissidents,[47] while calling for new parliamentary elections and the release of political prisoners.[48] Al-Barrak's sentencing to two years in prison in February 2015 led to a renewed call to protests.[49] Opposition rallies followed in March, protesting al-Barrak's arrest and were broken up by security forces, resulting in the arrest of dozens of opposition leaders and the alleged assault of participants.[50]

Musallam al-Barrak was released from prison in April 2017, but faces new charges as of November 2017 (discussed below). He has remained outspoken, stating that Kuwait has reached "the lowest point in its modern history" and "is so close to becoming a failed state" after his release in April.[51] While he has become less visible, al-Barrak does continue his calls for government reforms and reconciliation, reasserting that "no one disputes the constitutional legality of the al-Sabah family."[52] The more the government excludes opposition political blocs from instruments of institutionalized political power, the more they are likely to privilege a pro-democracy agenda over ideological differences. In this way, government restrictions on the political opposition have encouraged the moderation of traditional Islamist social aims, as the Brotherhood and some Salafi strands promote broad-ranging political reform, rather than Islamization of Kuwaiti society. This trend seems likely to continue, with an opposition bloc in parliament today eager to challenge the government, since the opposition returned to the polls in 2016.

Facing resistance even from the loyalist parliament as the government attempted to implement highly contested subsidy reforms in an era of low oil prices, Amir Shaykh Sabah al-Ahmed al-Sabah dissolved parliament months ahead of the scheduled June 2017 polls, in October 2016, with elections scheduled for the end of November. The loyalist parliament had, critically, passed a controversial law barring those who had been jailed for insulting the amir from contesting parliamentary elections,[53] in addition to a bill mandating DNA testing for all Kuwaiti citizens,[54] which was struck down by the Constitutional Court in October 2017.[55] Such legislation spurred suspicions of government corruption and centralization of power and galvanized opposition blocs that had boycotted the legislature since the December 2012 polls. The ICM was among the first blocs to announce its intention of contesting elections, hoping to put an end to pro-government legislative control.

Despite the fact that elections were held under the contested electoral law imposed in 2012, the current parliament is the first to include opposition since February 2012's legislature, in which it controlled thirty-four seats. After the November 2016 election, 60 percent of seats changed hands amid 70 percent voter turnout—a major indictment of the previous assembly.[56] The ICM and independent Salafis won three seats each (though a fourth seat is less formally under ICM control), securing a voice for Islamists. Smaller tribes also have a surprisingly large presence in the new parliament. Though tribes in outlying districts have traditionally supported the government, an increasing proportion has joined the opposition, with members lamenting what they perceive as their economic and political marginalization at the hands of the urban elite. While tribal leaders tend to gain popularity primarily among members of their own tribes, opposition figure Musallam al-Barrak of the al-Muṭairī tribe was the first such leader to become influential at the national level, finding a political support base even after boycotting his tribe's primaries. Because al-Barrak was still in prison for insulting the amir when polls were called, the al-Muṭairī tribe was divided about whether to run, and only one member of the tribe won a seat—a major setback for a group that tends to hold about four seats. Two of the other largest tribes in Kuwait—ʿAjman and ʿAwazim—faced losses, winning only seven seats altogether with al-Muṭairī, as opposed to their usual fifteen.[57] Tribal constituencies are still represented, though primarily by members of smaller tribes, who have also voiced their concerns about equal treatment under the law and corruption in the Kuwaiti government system.

If the opposition bloc, a group of twenty-seven MPs, manages to come together to challenge the government, which seems likely after a scheduled interpellation against the minister of information, another early dissolution of parliament could take place. This bloc has already listed some of its major priorities as examining the plight of Kuwait's stateless population, addressing revocations of citizenship for political reasons, safeguarding the welfare package and incomes currently enjoyed by citizens, and changing the electoral law that provides each citizen one vote.[58] The amir reappointed the former prime minister to appoint a cabinet in November 2016, implying his reluctance to accept political change. Wasting little time, in May, the parliament interpellated, in a thirteen-hour session, Prime Minister Shaykh Jaber al-Mubarak al-Sabah and State Minister for Housing Yasser Abul on allegations of corruption in both portfolios and on the revocation of citizenship from Kuwaitis particularly during the Arab Spring.[59] Nonetheless, the legislature did not submit a noncooperation motion against the premier or a vote of no confidence against the minister of state. Allegedly, a deal had been forged in May 2017 between the opposition and government as a means of avoiding the premier's grilling by securing the return of citizenships of six families, including that of former MP ʿAbdullah al-Barghash, owner of al-Yawm satellite television and *al-ʿAlam al-Yawm Ahmad Jabir al-Shammari*, former Popular Action Movement spokesman Saʿad al-ʿAjmi and Islamist preacher Shaykh Nabil al-Awadhi.[60] Such signs of even limited collaboration are significant, considering that an opposition parliament has not been active since 2012; they also indicate that the Kuwaiti Brotherhood has learned from the mistakes of the Ikhwan elsewhere in the region, which has been accused of being majoritarian and failing to foster cross-ideological cooperation once in positions of political power. The government has responded, however, in a way that may unite the opposition further, particularly after the resignation of cabinet in October 2017. The next month, the appeals court granted 67 opposition activists – including three current MPs (one from the ICM) long jail terms for storming parliament in 2011. Musallam al-Barrak was also granted a nine year sentence. A group of opposition MPs, from both Islamist and secular blocs, responded by requesting a meeting with the amir, yet it appears that all will need to await a final ruling from the Court of Cassation.

Popularity of the ICM and the Muslim Brotherhood

The ICM, as Kuwait's most organized political bloc, and as the largest Islamist group in a conservative country, has gathered a considerable following. Support for the ICM comes from many sectors of Kuwaiti society, ranging from segments of the urban merchant class to tribal constituents of the outlying districts. The Brotherhood's political bloc has also been remarkably popular among women, as it is seen to promote conservative social values that many women hope to maintain within their families.[61] One veteran ICM politician, when asked how he served as MP for over seventeen years and six terms, stated that it was "not through providing social, economic benefits to people, but I visited them, opened weekly *dīwāniyya* every Tuesday where they make comments, I say what I've been doing, they give advice . . . . People appreciate this kind of openness."[62] Certainly, in Kuwait, as throughout the super-rentiers, there is a social element to political trust—people tend to support candidates who stress their personal moral uprightness in a country plagued by corruption, and so religiosity becomes politically useful. As this veteran ICM MP explained, "People don't vote for our candidates because they're ICM but because those people have worked hard to go to the grassroots."[63] A critical part of this grassroots outreach is sustained involvement in the social sector, managed by Islah. Largely through such social outreach, the Brotherhood in Kuwait is entrenched and has become, in the words of one Kuwaiti academic, "a fundamental component of the political scene."[64] As such, it will likely remain a strong political force; it has managed to work with liberal secular trends toward political reforms while also maintaining its identity as an Islamist party.

Brotherhood candidates have fostered a sense of community with their constituents, which has made them popular. One ICM parliamentarian explained the group's appeal as its relatability: "we are from the people, and we are with the people. I drive a Ford. I live in an apartment."[65] The Brotherhood, by pushing for transparency, and by opening the finances of its MPs to the public in the past,[66] has managed to appeal to Kuwaitis fed up with what has been ranked as the world's sixty-ninth least corrupt government, ranking well below Qatar and the UAE.[67]

Furthermore, in the Kuwaiti context overall, as one former MP put it, "religious affiliation is stronger than the liberal one because it is ideology-based and uses religion, the heritage of the people."[68] The Brotherhood's popularity, though undoubtedly linked to its political agenda, could not have been achieved without its social programs. Further aiding the spread of Islamism, in Ahmed al-Baghdadi's words, "Kuwait has liberals, but there is no liberalism. There is a big difference between the two. You will find liberal individuals, but liberalism as a concept in society remains weak."[69] In such an environment, the Muslim Brotherhood is poised to remain ideologically and politically dominant, in particular as it adopts a pro-democracy agenda attractive to Kuwaiti liberals. As the oldest and most organized political bloc, also with an associated social group, the Brotherhood additionally benefits from holding a degree of influence in the education sphere, crucially granting it the ability to influence new generations of Kuwaitis.

Islamist Influence in the Education Sector

Although changes have been made to the curricula in recent years, it is almost universally acknowledged that Islamists have had or continue to hold influence in education, particularly through their positions in the Ministry of Education. In his extensive 1988–1989 study of Kuwait's primary school curriculum, Kamal al-Manufi noted that religious texts in Kuwaiti schools "encouraged the idea that religious fundamentalism should be followed as a way of life and thinking to achieve better life for individuals and the whole society."[70] He concluded that the curricula highlighted five general sets of values: obedience and disobedience, division of labor, equality and inequality, religious fundamentalism, and scientific thinking.[71] All of these values are, notably, ones that the government would logically hope to promote. Indeed, some Kuwaitis consider this the "regime [having] tailored the curriculum to their needs."[72]

Educational requirements still involve "heavy emphasis on Islam and Arabic."[73] Even in private schools, Islamic religion is a required course and is taught in a variety of languages.[74] All schools must also adhere to standards for government-issued exams on Arabic and religion.[75] Some Kuwaitis consider state-mandated texts to go beyond fostering Islamic or even Islamist education and in fact to encourage extremism. In fact, one tenth-grade book was cited as an example of such teachings, as it featured a passage stating that one who kills an infidel will not face punishment.[76]

Islamist influence in education goes beyond curriculum, with the major goals of the system highly influenced by religion and politics. Article 3 of the Public Education Act of 1987 explicitly lists the goals of education as "providing opportunities for individuals to achieve full and comprehensive spiritual, moral, intellectual, social, and physical development . . . in light of the principles of Islam, Arab heritage, and contemporary culture, and the nature, customs, and traditions of Kuwaiti society, and instilling in individuals spirits of socialization and loyalty for the Nation and His Highness the Amir."[77] Conservative Islam has also influenced the culture of the education system, with gender segregation mandated at Kuwait University and the Public Authority for Applied Education in 1996.[78] In addition, Law 34 passed in 2000 required that each private university and college, as well as branches of foreign universities, "1. Operate its buildings to ensure gender segregation in all departments, disciplines and student activities. 2. Observe Islamic values and time-honored traditions in relation to students' costumes and activities."[79] The policy of gender segregation has notably been challenged, with the Constitutional Court rejecting a petition in December 2015 challenging the constitutionality of the directive in institutions of higher education.[80]

Brotherhood influence in education is most visible in NUKS, as mentioned in previous chapters. With a student population of some thirty-six thousand students,[81] Kuwait University is a major political force. There are several theories about why the Islamist al-I'tilafia bloc has had such uninterrupted success in NUKS elections since 1979. One is that students vote for Islamist candidates because an increasing number hails from conservative tribal areas, making it difficult for liberal parties to garner conservative *badū* votes.[82] A second theory is that women make up the majority of students at Kuwait University, as men are more likely to attend universities abroad, and have shown great support for Islamist parties in the past, thereby giving the Brotherhood a boost.[83] A third explanation for al-I'tilafia's success is that, because elections are held early in the term, the incumbent gains "the first mover advantage."[84] A fourth theory is that well-connected members of the Brotherhood offer jobs to students who vote for their candidates.[85] A final explanation for the Islamists' popularity is that an official alliance between the Brotherhood and Salafis allows Islamists an advantage over the less organized liberals. Ultimately, al-I'tilafia benefits from better organization and from strong tribal links. It also holds ideological appeal. Taken together, these factors have helped ensure Islamist control of the country's largest organ of civil society.

As a former President of NUKS and member of al-I'tilafia explained, the Union's goal is "to represent young people of Kuwait."[86] The Islamist trend remains dominant among this segment of society because people choose to support it. In fact, students voted under his tenure to ban music at any and all Kuwait University parties.[87] Furthermore, gender segregation, according to the former NUKS president, "is something the students wanted because of academic, social, Islamic reasons. Kuwaiti society is conservative. Men and women don't mix. Islam also mandates this."[88] NUKS, under Brotherhood influence, continues to be a site for proxy fighting among secular and Islamist blocs in parliament, giving the Brotherhood a distinct advantage. It also serves as a training ground for new generations of Kuwaiti politicians, particularly for the ICM.

Social and Ideological Appeal of the Brotherhood

The Muslim Brotherhood no doubt retains ideological appeal, having formed a major part of Kuwaiti intellectual life through institutionalized government positions for decades. One interviewee explained, "The government cannot provide an ideology for the street."[89] Notions of Islam providing solutions and of the necessity of Muslim piety are attractive in a society that remains, by and large, conservative, traditional, and religious. Kuwait, particularly due to its ban on alcohol, feels more conservative than do Qatar and the UAE—a testament to the ability of Kuwait's more participatory governmental system to reflect stances of a large portion of the population, including Islamists, who support conservative social policies. Further distinguishing it from the other cases, unlike Qatar and the UAE, Kuwait pushed for independence from British control a decade before British withdrawal from the other super-rentiers, suggesting a desire for indigenous rule. In addition, while Qatar and the UAE vie to host popular concerts and sporting events, particularly those that appeal to their large expatriate populations, as one employee of the Ministry of Information put it, "there is no real entertainment in Kuwait."[90] The recent opening, in October 2016, of Sheikh Jaber al-Ahmad Cultural Center, or the Kuwait Opera House, could signal a sea change, offering new entertainment options aimed to appeal primarily to the Kuwaiti population. Still, today, although Kuwait is in many ways the most politically open country in the Gulf and has long held a reputation for being liberal, it remains the most socially traditional of the super-rentiers, catering less to expatriates and tourists than its neighbors. It is no coincidence that one of the more socially conservative countries in the Gulf is home to the GCC's oldest and largest branch of the Muslim Brotherhood.

Unlike other Brotherhood affiliates in the Gulf, the Kuwaiti Ikhwan has also benefitted from years of experience in the legislature. Perhaps because of its active involvement in public office, the Kuwaiti Brotherhood has learned to balance its conservative social goals with its pro-democracy agenda into a politically influential platform. The surprising marriage between Islamism and pro-democratic liberalism, and between Islam and politics, may ultimately be part of Kuwaiti political culture. As one interviewee put it, "Kuwaiti Islamists are liberal politically but conservative socially. This is the culture."[91] Such an atmosphere differs greatly from that seen in Qatar, where no institutionalized means of voicing dissent exist.

THE QATARI MUSLIM BROTHERHOOD AFTER FORMAL DISSOLUTION

Government Influence in the Religious Sphere

Unlike the other Wahhabi state in the region, Saudi Arabia, the Qatari government has not co-opted the religious institution through a formal alliance with the ulama. While the al-Saʿud family used Wahhabism to expand its political influence, Qatar's rulers feared that the implementation of religion to legitimize their rule could ultimately confuse their citizens' loyalty, motivating them to follow ulama aligned with the Saudi state rather than becoming devoted to an independent Qatari entity.[92] As a result, as Birol Baskan and Steven Wright highlight, "Qatari religious scholars do not have an institutionalized role in the political decision-making process. There is no religious office, like the office of the Grand Mufti,[93] within the Qatari state system."[94] Further, Wahhabi tenets are not applied in public spaces in Qatar.

Also unlike the Kingdom, Qatar has been forced to rely on outside clerics due to its small indigenous population.[95] As explained by Baskan and Wright, "The actual state-building project of the al-Thani and their desire to maintain relative autonomy in their domestic affairs, dictated limiting the development of an indigenous Ulama class through reliance on controlled non-native Ulama."[96] Because some 73 percent of the state's religious employees was estimated, as of 2012, to be non-Qatari, the amir retains the power to deport any who prove uncooperative.[97] Importantly, "the historical reliance on non-nationals for religious guidance has allowed for a great deal more autonomy on behalf of the government, and ruling tribe in particular, in regard to state-religion relations."[98]

The establishment of the Ministry of Awqaf and Islamic Affairs in 1993, over two decades after independence, as well as the 2008 unification of sharia and secular courts represent substantial, though delayed, gains for Islamists inside the country, highlighting the lack of institutionalized involvement of ulama in government policymaking: "As the Ulama in Qatar have historically been non-nationals, they would have lacked the capacity to press the ruling elite to give them an institutional role within government."[99] To ensure that sermons do not spur antigovernment sentiment, as Mehran Kamrava explains, "the Ministry [of Awqaf and Islamic Affairs] provides a list of topics for preachers to discuss during their sermons—e.g. the plight of Palestinians, or the harmful effects of smoking—but does not dictate the content of what is said by the preacher."[100] These *khuṭub* are published, and many religious programs air on national television, bringing Islam into the public sphere while keeping it largely under state control.

Qatar's Ministry of Awqaf and Islamic Affairs is widely believed to harbor Islamist leanings, yet it lacks substantial institutionalized or political power, and it remains unclear which strand of Islamism it seeks to promote, if in fact any. Though it monitors mosques, the ministry "is not an institutionally meaningful arm of the bureaucracy."[101] Further, the dominant Islamist influence in the Ministry of Awqaf appears to be the stricter Salafi strand, rather than the Brotherhood-related one. As one analyst of the Gulf explained, "There is not much space for the Muslim Brotherhood in Qatar for two reasons. One, Salafis dominate *awqāf* ministry—it's all Salafi, and they don't like the Brotherhood pushing into their territory. Two, every mosque has an informer in it. If you stray, you're finished—either deported or sent to a small mosque."[102] Despite a tendency toward more conservative Islam in some Qatari mosques, relatively unsurprising in a Wahhabi state, it is uncertain whether they are formally affiliated with the Brotherhood. The Ministry of Awqaf and Islamic Affairs has worked to maintain a balance between conservative and more moderate Islam, however. For instance, one Egyptian imam whose sermons favored more radical anti-Western opinions was removed from his mosque in 2012—demonstrating a self-conscious tempering of the anti-Western thought sometimes associated with Salafism.[103]

In such a small and homogenous state, it has been simpler for Qatari authorities to appease (to a certain extent), rather than squelch, Islamist influence. Unlike the UAE, Qatar's government aimed to integrate Islamism, at least to a certain extent, rather than to attempt to eliminate its influence. Hesitant to discourage an ideology that holds popular appeal and eager to keep its Islamic credentials intact, the regime has allowed for its limited expression under supervision. This policy has been used with the traditionally Islamist-dominated charity sector as well.

Qatar's Islamic Charity Sector

As in Kuwait, the Islamist trend has greatly influenced the country's charities. In Qatar, however, the philanthropic sector has largely been co-opted by the government and the ruling family, with major charities like Reach Out to Asia and the Social Development Center under the purview of the Qatar Foundation for Education, Science and Community Development, founded in 1995 by Shaykh Hamad and his wife Shaykha Moza bint Nasser al-Missned al-Thani.[104] Only Qatar Charity is run by a non-al-Thani, ʿAbdullah al-Nameh.[105] Despite its technically independent status, though, Qatar Charity "maintains close 'cooperative' links and 'partnerships' with a host of key government agencies."[106] All charities also come under the umbrella of the Ministry of Civil Service and Housing, which maintains "authority to dissolve an association based on membership of fewer than twenty persons, violation of the provisions of stipulated laws, or involvement in political activities."[107]

Notwithstanding government oversight, charities maintain a religious bent, with the majority holding some type of Islamic leaning. A 2012 survey demonstrated the degree to which the religious sector dominates charities in the country, with almost 80 percent of Qatari participants saying they donated primarily for religious reasons.[108] In addition, some 72 percent of Qataris responded that it is highly important that the recipients of their donations be Muslims.[109] Further, what attracted many young Brotherhood followers to the group was the appeal of helping others. Jassim Sultan went so far as to say that a primary basis for Brotherhood work in the wealthy Gulf states is charitable: "Apart from charitable work and moral guidance, there is not much room for them to occupy. . . . Islamists in the Gulf mostly work in charity."[110]

Due to the lack of absolute poverty in Qatar, most charitable contributions are sent abroad, spurring recent accusations that such funds support Islamist groups overseas.[111] Several Qatari charities are touted as strongholds for Salafis, with a 2014 Carnegie Endowment report calling Qatar's Eid Bin Muhammad Al-Thani Charitable Association "probably the biggest and most influential activist Salafi-controlled relief organizations."[112] In the face of allegations about unregulated funding going abroad, particularly to Islamist groups, the Qatari government in September 2014 issued a new set of regulations for charity organizations, stating that those "indulging in politics, or sending or receiving money to/from other countries without approval from the regulatory authority, will face action, including termination of their activities."[113] As part of this crackdown, in August 2015, the US Treasury Department imposed sanctions on Qataris Saʿad bin Saʿad Mohammed Sharyan al-Kaʿabi and ʿAbd al-Latif bin ʿAbdallah Salih al-Kawari for providing financial support of al-Qaʿida and al-Nusra Front in Syria.[114] With the charity sector largely under the umbrella of government ministries, it seems likely that any bias held by such organizations reflects the leanings of powerful individuals, like al-Kaabi and al-Kawari, rather than an institutionalized partiality. Again, Islamist influence is personalized and informal rather than institutionalized or systemic.

Qatari Society and the Muslim Brotherhood

Government oversight of the Islamic sector is pragmatic considering the political relevance of religion in Qatar. Indeed, in John Duke Anthony's estimation, "[i]n Qatari society, where

Qur'anic learning and adherence to the Islamic faith are values that are still held in high esteem by the ruling family and the majority of the population, the religious leaders are of special political importance. Traditionally, in addition to their theological role, they have had a strong influence on the shaykhdom's educational, legislative and judicial systems."[115] Simply because these religious leaders have influence, however, does not mean that it is formal or structured. Religious elements in Qatar exert pressure on the government to implement conservative social policies, although they lack institutionalized positions in government.[116] For instance, Anthony points out that "[o]nly in 1970 did the government lift its ban on public cinemas . . . . A national television system, in existence since the early 1970s, was established only after considerable procrastination due to pressures from the religious establishment."[117] The Ministry of Culture, Arts and Heritage continues its censorship of foreign magazines and books to ensure that offensive or blasphemous material is removed.[118] Periodic grassroots campaigns also emerge, as described in the previous chapter, primarily concerning social issues such as dress codes, availability of alcohol, and appropriate public behavior. While such campaigns are sponsored by Muslim Brotherhood affiliates in other Gulf states, they have developed more informally and spontaneously in Qatar or have been promoted by the government, making it difficult to determine the Muslim Brotherhood influence and involvement on policymaking in isolation from other Islamist strands or conservative Muslims.

In large measure due to the nature of Qatari society, the Muslim Brotherhood has not gained a foothold as an organized group. Shadi Hamid explains,

> Outside of the issue of government pressure, there is less of a need for Muslim Brotherhood [in Qatar]—even less than in Kuwait. The reasons for this are a small population and societal strength. The Muslim Brotherhood provides an alternative family; its basic unit is even called family, *usra*, something people do not need in a tribal society . . . . There is also the obvious economic reason the Brotherhood is weak in Qatar. To the extent that the Brotherhood provides financial benefits in the sense of helping with marriage, apartments, freer subsidized social services, access to employment; none of this is needed in Qatar.[119]

In an environment in which a social network is provided, the government does not openly oppose or repress Islamists, elections are not held, and material needs are met, there is less motivation for the group to risk a crackdown by organizing itself formally. Although the government jailed Islamist 'Abd al-Rahman al-Nu'aimi for three years following his involvement in a 1998 petition criticizing reforms under Shaykh Hamad, discussed in chapter 5, few other examples exist of Islamists being imprisoned, at least in the public record. As compared to Egypt and elsewhere in the Gulf, as one Gulf analyst put it, "the level of repression isn't as high, so there are fewer grievances against the government."[120]

In terms of having a concrete structure, the Qatari Brotherhood has failed, yet its philosophy remains influential, as reflected in conservative social policies and to a certain extent foreign policy, discussed in the previous chapter. In the words of Hamid, "There is interest ideologically, but the Brotherhood's social structure is not as helpful in Qatar. It is perhaps least helpful there than in any other Gulf state."[121] Aside from providing intellectual and spiritual guidance through *ḥalaqāt* and various charity and youth activities, there is little space for organized Brotherhood activity in Qatar. Nonetheless, Brotherhood ideology continues to appeal to a Qataris seeking to stem the tide of Westernization and secularization in the state with the highest expatriate population in the region. Qatar provides a unique model of informal and unstructured Brotherhood influence that is unique to the Gulf. Because it does not need to run electoral campaigns or provide material welfare benefits, the Qatari Ikhwan can be more flexible in terms of structure and can exist largely as an ideology with the ability to mobilize people in favor of certain policies.

The Influence of the Muslim Brotherhood inside Qatar Today

Determining what exactly it means to be a Muslim Brotherhood member in a state lacking a formal organization, and with a majority of its population religiously conservative, is challenging. Few Qataris identify themselves as members of the Brotherhood even if they agree with its ideology, making it difficult to determine the organization's domestic popularity and strength. A difference in labeling comes into play; as Michael Stephens put it, "It is very complicated because lots of Qataris agree with the Muslim Brotherhood but don't even realize it."[122] The conflation between support for the Brotherhood and allegiance to conservative Islam further complicates the study of the organization in isolation in Qatar. Stephens went on to explain that "lots of Qataris agree with what al-Qaradawi is saying but they see this as being religious, not as being Muslim Brotherhood."[123]

All in all, the group's sympathizers, at least in the organized sense, do not likely constitute a large proportion of Qatari society. One Qatari interviewee said he would "be surprised if there was any substantial number [of Muslim Brotherhood sympathizers]—two thousand to three thousand maximum."[124] Others maintain that the organization is even smaller, "just a few people," and remains highly informal.[125] Furthermore, due to successful government co-optation of the religious sphere, there are few Brotherhood imams, preventing the spread of Ikhwan ideology in this way.[126]

In terms of activities, Qatari Brotherhood sympathizers still gather primarily to recite the Quʾran. Such meetings tend to involve "a couple hundred [people], at most."[127] The organization exists on a structural level only at the simplest unit, the *usra*; "the usra in the Brotherhood is the basic, smallest part of the organization where they attract newcomers, and they read the Qurʾan, [engage in] *tafsīr*,[128] play sports. They know each other, go on trips together."[129] Without a means to disseminate its ideology through an official publication or even a formal meeting place, the Qatari Ikhwan does not appear to harbor ambitions beyond continuing intellectual and spiritual pursuits, which is not to say that these do not have a social agenda or a political influence. Further, simply because official estimates of the number of Brotherhood supporters inside Qatar are small does not mean that the ideology does not hold appeal for a broader segment of the socially conservative national population.

A primary component of the Brotherhood's political ideology is *shūrā*, or consultation, which often involves a call for popular participation in political life. The Qatari Brotherhood, unlike the other affiliates under study, has not voiced demands for such reforms. Possibly because of the lack of a political opening and partly due to general satisfaction with the prevailing system, the Islamic sector in Qatar has not become active in any nascent pro-democracy movement. Further, because the government has been public about the need for democratic reforms, there is less space for Brotherhood agitation in this field. Although the Advisory Council still has not been elected, it is arguable that "publicity for democratization is as important to the amir as the steps themselves."[130]

Having witnessed crackdowns on Brotherhood organizations elsewhere, Islamists in Qatar may also be unwilling to risk losing the peaceful and relatively free environment they enjoy in Qatar. In addition, because many Brotherhood members hail from ruling or prominent families, the organization is "hardly subversive."[131] This nonconfrontational relationship has led the government to be more accepting of the Brotherhood. As a former advisor to the Amiri Diwan put it, "Why should the government put pressure on the Muslim Brotherhood when the Brotherhood doesn't challenge it? The two are interdependent."[132]

In its current form, the Qatari Brotherhood exists as "a tendency," or "a current," conceived of as an ideology or set of beliefs, rather than a political bloc.[133] In such a loosely organized form, members are able to meet without fearing consequences of a crackdown from authorities. Furthermore, their goals *of daʿwa* and Islamic education are achievable without the implementation of a structure that the state may find objectionable.[134] By remaining amorphous, the Brotherhood can continue to enjoy state backing while maintaining its independent activities. One area in which it has lost institutionalized standing, however, is in the education sector.

Brotherhood Influence in the Education Sphere Today

Perhaps because of the immense impact that Brotherhood scholars had during the establishment of the Qatari education system and due to the degree to which education became politicized in the 1950s and 1960s, the government has gone to great lengths to diminish such influence and to modernize education in recent years. In 2002, Shaykh Hamad announced a broad-ranging educational reform initiative to facilitate economic and social progress under the Education for a New Era program, proposed by the US-based RAND Corporation.[135] After being presented with three options for primary school education reform, the Qatari leadership selected a model reliant on the creation of independent schools, with the hope that these would be less dependent on the Ministry of Education while providing a variety of schooling options for parents and teachers.[136] The reforms also involved the use of standardized national testing to ensure that students reach international benchmarks for curriculum criteria.[137] To facilitate these changes, the Supreme Education Council (SEC) was created by amiri decree in 2002. Some considered this restructuring a means of eradicating ministry influence, "being frustrated with the old-fashioned mind-set and traditionalist attitudes and ineffectivenss of much of the ministry."[138] Certain members of the ministry moved to the SEC, which was dismantled in 2013 and replaced by the Ministry of Education.[139] This revamped Ministry of Education seems focused primarily on improving the quality of public education, rather than implementing any type of Islamist agenda.[140]

Because curricula come from the state, which was (until 2013) advised by RAND, any remaining Islamist influence in education is personalized, rather than institutionalized; a SESRI curriculum report affirmed in 2012 that "religious scholars have no input in textbooks, curriculum and administration."[141] The very fact that Qatar outsourced major education reform, at both the primary and secondary levels, to the US-based RAND Corporation indicates the degree to which Qatari leadership hopes to promote an educational system that is aligned with Western standards.[142] As a consequence, though, many Qatari parents today "believe that students are not getting enough instruction in Arabic language and culture and Islamic studies. They also believe that studying the Qur'an is becoming a secondary issue, and not as 'an integral part of education' as they would like."[143] The use of English in mathematics and science instruction, as well as the reduction of time for Arabic and Islamic studies, are lingering issues.[144]

Still, some teachers harbor Islamist sympathies, which the state cannot control. As one interviewee explained, "The teachers are generally women and come from conservative neighborhoods in Egypt, Jordan, Syria. Most have a conservative religious attitude; they sympathize with the Muslim Brotherhood, though they may not be involved in its politics. It is unclear if there is an impact on students."[145] Still, informal guidelines seem to exist for the behavior of teachers, particularly regarding religion. In May 2013, Nepali teacher Dorje Gorung at Qatar Academy, a private school associated with the Qatar Foundation (discussed below), was imprisoned after being fired for allegedly insulting Islam in a discussion with students.[146] Following international outcry, he was released to his home country.[147] While Islamism is no longer promoted in the education sector, the study and respect of Islam remain crucial.

In terms of higher education, several foreign branch campuses operate in Qatar, in addition to the publicly owned Qatar University, established in 1977. Education City, under the umbrella of the Qatar Foundation led by Shaykha Moza, offers education at six American universities (Carnegie Mellon University, Georgetown University School of Foreign Service, Northwestern University, Virginia Commonwealth University, Weill Cornell Medical College, and Texas A&M University), one British university (University College London), one French university (HEC Paris), and the Qatari university Hamad bin Khalifa University (HBKU). Attendees of these universities, where courses are conducted in English, tend not to come from among the local population, reinforcing existing divisions between locals and expatriates and raising concerns about retaining Qatari culture.

A recent debate about the language of instruction in institutions of higher education brought to the fore underlying tensions between Qataris and expatriates, fueled by the new reforms following Western standards. In 2005, Qatar University, on the recommendation of RAND, began instruction in English rather than Arabic. In 2012, the university began using Arabic again.[148] Though it inflamed cultural sensitivities, the change in languages was primarily a "reflection of structural problems in the educational sector."[149] As many as five thousand to ten thousand Qatari students were unable to gain entry to Qatar University because their English skills were inadequate, resulting in "a vitriolic campaign [by Qataris] against the university saying it is for expats."[150] Further fuelling the dispute, a series of editorials in local daily *al-Sharq* decried "a 'devastating war' between Qatari students and 'the favored sons of expats.'"[151] By restoring Arabic instruction at Qatar University, the government showed its commitment to modernizing in line with local preferences. As an advisor to Shaykh Tamim put it, "Switching to Arabic is modernization. You modernize in your own language."[152] The government appears responsive to popular complaint, despite the fact that it is not organized through any institutional structure. The government also seems aware of the fact that cultural symbols like language are in fact a major part of political debate.[153]

Foreign Policy and Qatar's Links to Islamists

While Qatar's ties with its GCC neighbors markedly improved (at least temporarily) following the November 2013 agreement, its relationship with Egypt has remained sour, leading many to believe that Qatar backs the Muslim Brotherhood and eschews ties with the military-led Egyptian government that overthrew Ikhwan leader Mohamed Morsi, as described in the previous chapter. Relations worsened in November 2016 when Al Jazeera released the documentary *The Soldiers*, which featured a negative portrayal of the Egyptian military and was publicly denounced by the Egyptian Ministry of Foreign Affairs on Egyptian television.[154] Nearly a month later, the Egyptian government went so far as to accuse Qatar of having played a role in the December 2016 bombings of a Cairo church by allowing members of the Muslim Brotherhood to live and supposedly train terrorists in Qatar.[155] Six months later, Qatar's GCC neighbors Bahrain, Saudi Arabia, and the UAE, alongside Egypt, publicly proclaimed it a supporter of terrorism in the region's worst diplomatic crisis since the Gulf War.

Qatar came under fire in 2017, as in 2014, due to alleged links to Islamists. The row began on May 24, 2017, when the website of the state-owned Qatar News Agency provided details about a speech given by Amir Shaykh Tamim in which he supposedly dubbed Hamas "the legitimate representative of the Palestinian people" and called Iran an "Islamic power" with which Qatar enjoys a "good" relationship.[156] While the Qatari government denied the veracity of the report (indeed, Shaykh Tamim had reportedly not spoken at the event at which this speech allegedly was made[157]), Bahrain, Egypt, Saudi Arabia, and the UAE responded on June 5 by severing diplomatic ties and even cutting off all land, air, and sea links with Qatar, in addition to granting fourteen days for all Qataris to leave their countries and barring their own citizens from travel to Qatar. [158] Chad, Comoros Islands, Maldives, Mauritania, the exiled Yemeni government, and Libya's eastern-based House of Representatives also severed ties, while Djibouti, Jordan, and Niger downgraded their diplomatic representation in Qatar. Saudi Arabia justified its decision on grounds of "protection of national security from the dangers of terrorism and extremism," while the UAE openly accused Qatar of spreading al-Qaʿida's ideology through the media, especially Al Jazeera, and by harboring militants.[159] The UAE has also used the crisis to further strengthen and centralize its security apparatus, imposing prison sentences for "anyone who shows sympathy or any form of bias towards Qatar, or anyone who objects to the position of the United Arab Emirates, whether it be through the means of social media, or any type of written, visual or verbal form."[160] Qatar meanwhile insists that the decision to break ties "was founded on allegations and have no basis in fact."[161]

This latest diplomatic crisis, while at face value about national security and fighting extremism, is in fact, as in 2014, an attempt to overpower Qatar's independent foreign policy, particularly when it comes to Islamists, demonstrating the degree to which they wield influence even in the wealthiest region of the Middle East wherein they have never seriously threatened government power. The coalition of Bahraini, Egyptian, Emirati, and Saudi governments released a list of fifty-nine individuals and institutions that it claims have financed terrorist groups and have received Qatari support. The list includes Brotherhood ideologue Shaykh Yusuf al-Qaradawi, in addition to several other Bahraini, Egyptian, Jordanian, Kuwaiti, and Libyan individuals, charities, and even a technology firm, though excluding Hamas and indeed any Palestinian individual.[162] Qatari Foreign Minister Shaykh Mohammed bin ʿAbdulrahman al-Thani responded by insisting that Qatar is "a platform of peace not terrorism . . . . We are not ready to surrender, and will never be ready to surrender, the independence of our foreign policy."[163] The battle reflects the extreme dislike of Islamists in the UAE, as documented above, as well as its desire to scapegoat Qatar as a means of bolstering other Gulf countries, namely Saudi Arabia and the UAE.

Emboldened by a visit in May 2017 by American President Donald Trump, whose administration has pondered designating the Muslim Brotherhood a terrorist organization,[164] the Saudi and Emirati governments have doubled down on their anti-Qatar rhetoric. But tensions had certainly been building and date back to the previous amir's reign. In fact, it is likely that the Saudi-backed coup against former Amir Shaykh Hamad bin Khalifa al-Thani in 1996 led him to pursue a policy toward Islamists completely different from the Saudis, choosing to cooperate with them rather than attempting to dismantle their organizations.

Over the course of 2017, tensions had built ahead of the crisis, bringing back old issues to the fore. For instance, in May, Qatar hosted a Hamas meeting wherein it publicly dropped any link to the Muslim Brotherhood and introduced a political program meant to soften its image as a terrorist or extremist organization, since it included acceptance of the Palestinian state along 1967 borders.[165] Such a move highlighted not only the prevailing political influence of Islamists, but also the way in which Qatar has found a foothold in critical regional issues by providing a haven for political exiles. Further reflecting tensions, at the end of May, the Saudi Minister of Islamic Affairs demanded that Qatar change the name of its state mosque, which is dubbed be Imam Muhammad Ibn Wahhab Mosque, amid claims that the al-Thani ruling family is not related to al-Wahhab.[166] Such a public campaign questioning the authenticity of Qatar's status as a Wahhabi state was likely an effort to dissociate Wahhabism from terrorism, important for the Saudis who wanted to designate their Wahhabi neighbor a sponsor of terrorism. Statements from Qatari Foreign Minister Shaykh Muhammad bin ʿAbdulrahman al-Thani in mid-May 2017 supporting negotiations between the GCC and reaffirming that Qatar has not banned the Muslim Brotherhood did not help ease existing tensions. While stating that "we do not, will not, and have not supported the Muslim Brotherhood," Minister al-Thani was also unapologetic about Qatar's policy of "support[ing] any individual that assumes the presidency in Egypt in a clear and transparent manner."[167]

Egypt, Saudi Arabia, and the UAE have designated the Brotherhood a terrorist organization; these are also, critically, the Middle Eastern states upon which President Trump is likely to rely the most for his policies in that region. Abu Dhabi Crown Prince Mohammed bin Zayed seems to hold the strongest opinion about the Muslim Brotherhood, based on his policies at home and statements against the Brotherhood since the early 2000s. Further, while it has been posited that Saudi Arabia's stance toward the Brotherhood initially softened under King Salman, Crown Prince Mohammed bin Salman appears to have changed course since his meteoric rise to power as crown prince in June 2017. The then Deputy Crown Prince spoke in May about Osama bin Laden's alleged ties to the Brotherhood with the American president, reflecting a turn against the group as linked to violent organizations and therefore destabilizing.[168] Further, the Saudi government suffered political setbacks under the previous American administration, during which the Justice Against Sponsors of Terrorism Act (JASTA) was passed with bipartisan support in the US Congress, allowing families of the victims of the 9/11 attacks to sue the Saudi government. The recent actions of the Saudi government have effectively deflected American attention toward Qatar, whose sympathy with Islamists it finds threatening, despite the fact that their presence has not led the Qatari government to Islamize life inside the state.

Islamism and a Changing Qatar

Despite the lack of formal Islamist organization inside Qatar, there is a sense that conservative Islam is on the rise in the country—in part as a reaction against the increasing Westernization in the state, especially as the number of expatriates increases in preparation for the World Cup in 2022. Competing visions appear to exist even among the Qatari leadership about the future direction of the country. As one scholar put it, "Salafization of the public sphere is driven by two forces driving the opposite direction: (1) Shaykha Moza and her modernist drive and (b) Salafis who aim to slow down the modernist drive. We see polarization of the two sides especially with the anti-expat movement."[169] Complaints about the lack of local culture and religion in Qatar are widespread, with many nationals feeling that "society is developing too quickly."[170] Notably, though, Shaykha Moza in particular has become far less visible since her son Shaykh Tamim came to power in 2013. The Qatari nationals' dilemma is described as follows: "We are caught between two worlds. Qatar will have development, a good life and income, but we can't build it on our own because we lack the number of people. So, like it or not, we have to rely on expatriates. Elements in society will be upset."[171] While there is no organized Islamist backlash, and indeed only an elected apolitical municipal council, discussions in *majālis*, calls to the aforementioned radio call-in program, and editorial columns reflect this attitude.[172]

It is remarkable that Qatar, a Wahhabi country, is as socially permissive as it is. In the late 1990s, laws concerning the availability of alcohol were relaxed, allowing its sale and consumption in five-star hotels, managed by the state-owned Qatar National Hotels Company.[173] Qatar, under Shaykh Hamad, also came to house Christian churches, with Shaykh Qaradawi instrumental in promoting interfaith dialogue. As one interviewee explained, "Qatar is not like Dubai or Aden—this was a Wahhabi shaykhdom. What Hamad did is remarkable. [Shaykh] Tamim and [Shaykh] Hamad are not committed to religious ideology."[174] Further, the highly public and influential stance of Shaykh Hamad's wife Shaykha Moza as "First Lady" of Qatar was unprecedented in the Gulf, yet sparked internal debate about her advocacy of Western policies. One analyst of the Gulf contended that "she is disliked by Qataris, is seen as moving the country toward the US. Qataris think she's selling the country."[175] Other al-Thani women have taken on public roles in government, with Shaykh Hamad and Shaykha Moza's daughter Shaykha Ahmad al-Mahmoud becoming the first female minister in the GCC following her appointment as minister of education in 2003.[176] As mentioned above, when a group of clerics addressed a petition to the Shaykh Hamad in June 1998, complaining about the granting of female suffrage, the government's response was unequivocal. Shaykh ʿAbd al-Rahman al- Nuʿaimi, leader of the movement, was jailed, and women's voting rights were not revoked, demonstrating the regime's willingness to fight the Islamist backlash on certain large-scale issues, especially those in which the ruling family seems to have a personal stake.[177]

Criticism from Qatari nationals about social policies is likely to persist, as they become an increasingly smaller minority in the country, making it more difficult for the government to balance its preferences with those of the much larger expatriate population. Fortunately, such social backlash has very seldom turned extremist or violent. In 2005, a suicide car bomb, rigged by an Egyptian expatriate, destroyed the Doha Players theater, killing one British citizen and injuring fifteen.[178] Previous attacks included a shooting in 2001 of two military contractors, perpetrated by Qatari ʿAbdullah Mubarak Tashal al-Hajiri, and an attempt by an unnamed attacker to ram the gate of American base al-Udeid in 2002, signaling disapproval of Qatar's close ties with the United States.[179] Some claim, as cited in a *The Telegraph*, that members of the ruling family support extremism, with former Interior Minister Shaykh ʿAbdullah bin Khalid al-Thani allegedly having granted shelter to 9/11 mastermind Khalid Shaykh Muhammad, who worked for the Qatari government in the 1990s.[180]

Former government employees, including Salim Hassan Khalifa Rashid al-Kuwari of the Ministry of Interior, were also accused of funneling money to jihadist organizations between 2013 and 2014.[181] ʿAbd al-Rahman al-Nuʿaimi, a founder of Eid Mohammad Al-Thani Charitable Association, is also accused of sending money to jihadists in Iraq and Syria.[182] Meanwhile, Khalifa Muhammad Turki al-Subaʿi, imprisoned for six months for his help in funding Khalid Shaykh Muhammad, appears to have been permitted to continue fundraising after his release.[183] Even in wealthy Qatar, then, extremism has found limited support—an outcome that rentier state theory would not predict—and has been a challenge to a Qatari government that hopes to appear sympathetic to Islam to maintain religious legitimacy and popular support.

Just as Qatar balances foreign interests against each other to maintain relative peace, it does the same in weighing the interests of locals and expatriates in the domestic sphere. The Qatari leadership is particularly careful about appearing supportive of Islam, while also giving weight to the opinions of famed Arab nationalist and advisor to Shaykh Tamim, ʿAzmi Bishara. As Mohammed al-Mukhtar al-Shangiti puts it, Qatar's policies are "more realpolitik and balancing than promoting a specific group. The Awqaf Ministry is in the hands of the Salafis and part of society has this tendency. You find a big presence of Brotherhood in some institutions like Al Jazeera, but not just the Brotherhood, Islamists in general. The Qatari ministry of culture is dominated by Arab nationalists."[184] It is difficult to determine what is meant by "Brotherhood presence" or what constitutes a supporter in a state lacking a Brotherhood organization. Nonetheless, the regime balances gains for one group against the other in social issues. While pork is allowed at the Qatar Distribution Company, alcohol is banned in the Pearl. While Qatar Foundation's branch campuses educate in English, Qatar University is run in Arabic. This balancing also takes place at the level of the ruling family as well, as it contains liberal strands that many consider too Western, along with conservative, traditionally minded elements.[185] It is still uncertain, however, whether such balancing will continue to satisfy a national population facing an increasing expatriate presence. What is even less certain, however, is whether Qatar will manage to continue balancing its foreign interests in a way that is satisfying for its GCC neighbors, especially for an Emirati government that considers any sympathy toward Islamism a fundamental political threat.

THE EMIRATI IKHWAN AFTER THE CRACKDOWN

Emirati Politics: Stability above All

By and large, the Emirati political scene resembles that of Qatar more closely than that of Kuwait. As Michael Herb summarizes, "When the politics of Kuwait are raucous, freewheeling, and at least partially democratic, the politics of the UAE are subdued, largely hidden, and not at all democratic."[186] Because politics remains top-down, even at the local level, it is difficult to determine the level of Islamist sentiment in the country unless sympathetic individuals have links to ruling families or hold ministerial positions. The state's only elected federal body, the Federal National Council (FNC), is chosen by a small fraction of the Emirati population and remains "a purely advisory body and more of a civilized 'talking shop' than anything else."[187] Nonetheless, it, like Qatar's CMC, is considered to hold a large number of tribal figures and, as such, has often favored conservative policies of the type traditionally supported by the Ikhwan. In 2014, for example, the FNC called for legislation to ban women from working late at night in shisha cafes and has advocated for the addition of a mandatory breastfeeding clause in a child's rights law.[188] One member also famously called for a federal law banning revealing clothing in 2012.[189] Even in its elected body, then, the UAE has experienced backlash challenging the socially liberal vision of the leading emirates.

At the local level, plans to expand the participatory nature of emirate-level councils have been rejected, largely due to fears that they would promote Islamist influence. In February 2007, a proposal for an elected Dubai-based District Council was denied in favor of an appointed council, after its announcement in April 2003 was met with considerable fanfare.[190] Mohammed al-Gergawi from the Executive Office of Dubai ruler, Vice President Shaykh Mohammed bin Rashid al-Maktoum, explained, as recounted through an American diplomatic cable, "[T]he decision was taken mainly to ensure that 'extremists' and other disruptive elements were not given a platform. He added that, in his opinion, UAE society was not mature enough to deal with the inherent instability of an electoral free-for-all, even at the local/district level."[191] The ruler of Sharjah, Shaykh Sultan bin Mohammed al-Qasimi, expressed similar concerns in a meeting in 2004 with American officials in Abu Dhabi, stating that "holding elections now could result in the election of members of radical Islamist organizations like the Muslim Brotherhood."[192] Fears of independent Islamist political actors, then, have stunted the growth of participatory government in the UAE, despite the fact that they have never formed a cohesive UAE-wide political bloc with a unified agenda.

For leaders of the UAE, political stability remains of utmost importance. In Minister of FNC Affairs and Minister of State for Foreign Affairs Anwar Gargash's words, " 'stability is what built this country,' and is, and will remain, a top priority for the UAEG [UAE Government]."[193] In a divided environment, the primary means of retaining a placid political environment has been through enhancing central government control. The leading emirates have guided such policies to marginalize independent political figures, especially Islamists.

Government Control of the Religious Sector

The UAE, similar to the other countries under study, has attempted to contain the possible emergence of an independent religious sector.[194] While it lacks institutionalized state ulama, Emirati ruling families "have been solicitous of their relations with the ulama," by granting them privileged government positions."[195] Despite efforts at modernization and liberalization, Emirati rulers also try to appear supportive of Islam. Christopher Davidson explains, "[I]f they can at least be seen to openly promote Islam then they will be held in high esteem. Since the first oil booms the simplest way to carry out such promotion has been to build mosques and pay the salaries of all ulema or preachers."[196] As one Emirati academic put it, "The sovereign created a church for himself, created an Islamic establishment."[197]

Aiding Emirati rulers' ability to control the religious sector is the fact that, as in Kuwait and Qatar, most imams are expatriates and therefore risk deportation if their sermons are met with government disapproval. In addition, 95 percent of Sunni mosques in the UAE are state-owned, while the remainder (excluding Shiʿi mosques) receive government subsidies.[198] Furthermore, as Davidson points out, "[a]lmost all clerics are government employees, and these are quite closely monitored. Most have to carry photo identification cards, and their sermons usually have to be chosen from an official list of approved topics, drawn up by the relevant government body each week."[199] Granting an additional incentive to imams to remain loyal to the regime is the government's provision of substantial salaries, thus bringing religious leaders into the rentier bargain.[200]

Government-approved sermons, printed in local newspapers, often cover social topics and only touch on the political arena peripherally or through inference.[201] One researcher and longtime resident of the UAE explained, "The UAE government controls all of the mosques. Friday sermons are centrally prepared. There is no free speech in mosques."[202] Such government influence in the religious sphere dates back to the beginning of the union. One historian of the UAE and longtime resident of Abu Dhabi related a story of the shutdown of a mosque in the 1970s because it was patronized by many Yemenis who expressed anti-Western views.[203] Since that time, "[t]he government has removed some clerics for re-education purposes after they used their Friday sermons inappropriately."[204] Then Minister of Justice and Islamic Affairs Mohammed al-Dhaheri, in a September 2004 interview, explained the necessity of providing guidance to imams because "experience has shown that many of the people who applied to the Awqaf department for the posts of Imams in the mosques were far below the required standards."[205] Al-Dhaheri also highlighted the need for greater oversight of mosques, recognizing that some sermons are not aligned with the ministry's preapproved topics and that the government has removed imams for incorrect or inappropriate use of their Friday sermons.[206]

A 2006 cable from the American embassy in Abu Dhabi confirms that sermons are meant to discourage what the government considers extremist behavior, in particular after the 9/11 attacks, yet they have also diminished the ability of any independent strand of Islam to develop.[207] As Malcolm C. Peck explains, "There are proponents of a reinvigorated assertion of Islamic values. But generally, in the UAE, Islam serves more to support the political system than to threaten governmental stability or survival."[208] The only mosques with messages differing slightly from those appointed by the government are small and largely insignificant. One interviewee recounted, "Some imams are Egyptians. Abu Hail on the Sharjah-Dubai border has mosques with a Brotherhood feel. These mosques are not as infiltrated by the government because they are not a threat and are not seen as such."[209] It is difficult to determine the degree to which such mosques are linked to the Brotherhood on an organizational level or simply represent a conservative strand of Islam; it is therefore uncertain whether they are politically relevant, particularly for Emiratis, rather than for expatriates.

Due to central government controls, it is ethnicity or nationality, rather than ideology, that distinguishes most imams in the UAE.[210] The only means by which major mosques could become centers for political discussion is through private conversation and debate after sermons, yet fears of government informers infiltrating mosques limit even these conversations.[211] Ultimately, as one US Department of State report describes it, "[t]he [UAE] government controls virtually all Sunni mosques and places general restrictions on freedom of assembly and association, including for religious purposes."[212] Using the pretext of rooting out extremism, the government has succeeded in limiting freedom of the religious sector.

In one departure from a government policy of promoting so-called "moderate" Islam, Egyptian Islamic scholar ʿUmar ʿAbd al-Kafi, director of the Qurʾanic Studies Center associated with Dubai International Holy Qurʾan Award, has been allowed to retain a prominent public role inside the UAE. In addition to his official role, al-Kafi has hosted a number of radio and television programs and helps to organize and judge heavily publicized government-sponsored Qurʾanic recitation contests. He is considered to be "a link between the Egyptian Salafis and Muslim Brotherhood,"[213] and is useful as such, appealing to the conservative population of Emirati nationals. Notably, al-Kafi's sermons tend to highlight social and cultural issues like whether Muslims should greet Christians on Christian holidays.[214] He thus engages with debates about maintaining the Emirati and Islamic nature of the state without being prescriptive in political matters. By allowing a voice to such a figure, Emirati rulers enhance their own religious legitimacy while also helping to control the religious narrative, similar to the Qatari government's approach, yet pursued on a much more limited scale.

The government also augments its religious credentials by sponsoring a variety of Islamic events, charities, and scholarship, activities that super-rentier governments are uniquely able to finance.[215] Qurʾanic recitation competitions, mentioned above, have become particularly popular. The most famous is an annual contest, in which prisoners are released from Dubai jails if they can recite the entire Qurʾan.[216] The federal government also quite visibly donates a great deal of money for the hosting of religious conferences and events. In 2004, Dubai hosted a symposium on the Prophet's Way of Daʿwa and Guidance with several hundred people, including the Grand Imam of al-Azhar.[217] During Ramadan 2008, Shaykh Khalifa invited thirty religious leaders to Abu Dhabi to "expose the UAE to the latest learned debate on Islam."[218] The office of Shaykh Mohammed bin Zayed al-Nahyan, Crown Prince of Abu Dhabi and Deputy Supreme Commander of the UAE Armed Forces, "also sponsored lectures during Ramadan, including esteemed Saudi scholars and a number of non-Muslim lecturers and dignitaries. Delivered in Arabic and English, they were held in the crown prince's majlis twice a week."[219] The Dubai International Holy Qurʾan Award Committee is another government-sponsored initiative and aims to create a collection of books to be dubbed the Sheikh Khalifa bin Zayed al-Nahyan Mushaf.[220]

Even more conspicuously, Emirati rulers have gone to great expense to construct impressive mosques. The most famous is Abu Dhabi's Sheikh Zayed Mosque, the third largest in the world, which was completed in 2007 at a cost of over $540 million.[221] In Dubai, mosques are increasingly less visible, reflecting that emirate's largely expatriate population.[222] Nonetheless, the Dubai government has made considerable efforts to promote Islamic banking in its financial markets, perhaps in an attempt to maintain the support of its conservative national population while also retaining the secular façade that appeals to a growing number of Western expatriates and tourists.[223] Most recently, as a means of bolstering the state as the arbiter of correct religious practice, the UAE announced the creation of a federal fatwa council to "counter controversial and hardline fatwas that are spread on the internet by unauthorised sources."[224] Although such a body is an important means of delegitimizing extremist fatwas, it also highlights the central government's position of determining proper Islamic practice for a population that may disagree with its interpretation.

Complicating centralized government co-optation of the religious sphere is the variation in schools of Islamic jurisprudence in different emirates of the UAE. While Abu Dhabi and Dubai officially recognize the Maliki School (also dominant in Kuwait), adherents to the Hanbali School (predominant in Qatar and Saudi Arabia) are found elsewhere, and Fujairah follows the Shafiʿi School.[225] Divisions between Malikis and Hanbalis reflect rifts among tribal confederations in the emirates, making them more difficult to overcome.[226] The government, by imposing its own vision of so-called moderate, and largely apolitical, Islam, tries to override such differences. The pragmatic Emirati rulers thus endeavor to promote Islam that is not politically threatening. As one anthropologist of the Gulf put it, "In the UAE it is alright to be religious, but to organize yourself as a political party has not been done in the UAE before."[227] Nonetheless, a variety of religious outlooks have emerged, ranging from the more moderate to the extreme.

The UAE has experienced limited violent Islamist reaction, in large measure due to its liberal social policies. In April 1981, a bomb planted in Dubai's Hyatt Regency Hotel killed two people and was meant to protest the hotel's policy of serving liquor to Emiratis wearing national dress, a taboo in Gulf countries.[228] In February 1999, authorities found two bombs at shopping centers frequented by Western expatriates.[229] The September 11, 2001 attacks (9/11) raised international suspicions about the UAE's commitment to countering extremism, as two hijackers were Emirati nationals, one from Ras al-Khaimah and one from Fujairah, and much funding for the attack had been wired through Dubai banks.[230] In late 2002, Saudi citizen ʿAbd al-Rahim al-Nashiri, who planned attacks on the *USS Cole, USS The Sullivans*, and the French oil tanker *MV Limburg*, was also arrested in Abu Dhabi. At the time of his arrest, al-Nashiri was planning attacks on "vital economic targets" inside the UAE.[231]

A June 2008 report from the British government's Joint Terrorism Analysis Centre warned of planned terrorist attacks inside the UAE, leading the British Foreign and Commonwealth Office to increase the terror threat warning to the highest possible level for the country.[232] Most recently, in December 2014, an Emirati woman, accused of planting a homemade bomb at the home of an American doctor's house, stabbed to death a female American teacher in a mall bathroom in Abu Dhabi.[233] The US Embassy in Abu Dhabi had released a statement in October 2014, alerting Americans about an Internet posting that "encouraged attacks against teachers at American and other international schools."[234] Clearly, tension with the West exists within the UAE and has spurred limited extremist action, unexpected according to rentier state theory.

Despite the lack of terrorist activity in the UAE, because known terrorists have come from the country and because many claim the UAE has been used as a base for terror financing, it has been accused of "turning a blind eye to terror organizations within its country."[235] In recent years, the Emirati government has used the threat of extremism to justify its crackdown on peaceful Islamist groups like Jamʿiat al-Islah wa-l-Tawjih al-Ijtimaʿi (Islah). As noted in a US diplomatic cable, "[I]n their diplomatic activities, Sheikh Mohammed bin Zayed [Abu Dhabi Crown Prince] and his brothers Hamdan [the Abu Dhabi Ruler's representative in Dhafra Region and head of Emirates Red Crescent] and Hazza [National Security Adviser] rarely fail to tell high-level USG [US government] interlocutors about the threat to stability posed by the 'Muslim Brotherhood,' their generic term for extremists."[236] The conflation of Brotherhood figures with violent Islamists has proven dangerous, as it has granted the Emirati government a security excuse for eliminating nonviolent Islamists for purely political reasons.

The Extent of the Emirati Brotherhood's Popular Support

The UAE government's crackdown on Islah and extreme rhetoric about the Muslim Brotherhood are puzzling, considering that the Emirati Brotherhood never seemed to pose a major political threat, and certainly not the existential threat the government portrays it to be. Examination of its internal documents reveals that Islah held few political aspirations beyond enhancing the role of Islam in Emirati society, adjusting government spending, and, more recently, enhancing popular participation in government, not overthrowing it. Perhaps most worrying to the government is the difficulty in determining how much popular support Islah held among nationals. A report submitted to a meeting of the international Muslim Brotherhood in Medina in 2008, cited in an article in Emirati-owned *Gulf News* yet not independently corroborated, indicated that the Brotherhood held considerable appeal among the UAE's expatriate community.[237] It claimed that the Emirati Brotherhood had 1,700 expatriate members, including 300 initiates (younger members being taught about the group), 300 novices (who have already pledged allegiance to the supreme guide), 150 associates, 500 regular associates, and 350 working members (who can vote and run for office in the Egyptian organization).[238] As far as Emirati members, estimates of Brotherhood membership vary widely, ranging from 400[239] to 20,000.[240]

Shaykh Mohammed bin Zayed, in a 2004 US Department of State diplomatic cable, estimated that the UAE contained up to 700 Brotherhood members and claimed the State Security Directorate had identified 50–60 Emirati Brotherhood members in the military alone.[241] He also explained efforts to co-opt Islamists in the military: "when the Armed Forces discovered Muslim Brotherhood sympathizers within their ranks, they were arrested and given a form of reverse brainwashing. All but one of the forty military personnel detained were subsequently released, convinced that they had been led astray."[242] Shaykh Mohammed also estimated that some 50 to 80 percent of the 60,000 UAE armed forces "would respond to the call of 'some holy man in Mekkah,' " going on to say that he would be " 'stoned' by his own citizens if he pushed some subjects too openly."[243] Shaykh Mohammed's fears, which do not seem based in fact, undermine a main premise of rentier state theory: hydrocarbon wealth cannot buy off political competitors, particularly ideological ones. Further, Islah's primary mode of expression has been social, yet the Abu Dhabi government has considered it a political threat, demonstrating the ability of the Brotherhood to function in both spheres, particularly in super-rentiers that do not allow institutionalized means of political participation.

Inspired by Shaykh Mohammed bin Zayed's extreme distrust of the Muslim Brotherhood, the government of Abu Dhabi has advocated the toughest stance of any emirate toward Islamists. Dubai's government, on the other hand, has focused primarily on " 'tracking' individuals known to be sympathetic to the Islamist agenda."[244] In an effort to dissuade Dubai citizens from Islamism, Shaykh Mohammed bin Rashid al-Maktoum, until the 2012 crackdown, met with members "to explain to them the error of their ways, and to tell them that if they are looking for a job, or land, or any other assistance, they should not hesitate to ask. Apparently, this approach (direct appeal from the ruler) is often effective, especially for younger devotees. Those who are resistant to change, however, are locked up, sometimes repeatedly, for months at a time in hopes that this will dissuade them from acting on their Islamist tendencies."[245] Abu Dhabi, meanwhile, prefers a security approach and has always been cautious about the

Muslim Brotherhood, having denied the organization formal permission to operate in the emirate decades earlier.

While determining the number of Islah members in the UAE is difficult, perhaps more challenging is defining what it means to be a member of Islah in the UAE today. Even before the most recent crackdown, the majority of those who supported the organization would admit to it only behind closed doors, and mainly in an informal capacity, much like in Qatar. Due in part to the imposition of restrictions beginning in the 1990s, "most Islamists and Islamic activists in the UAE do not operate within structured groups, but as individuals connected through networks based on a Muslim identity."[246] In terms of group activities in which Islamists participate openly, charities and *ḥalaqāt* have been most prominent.[247] The government has found means of infiltrating *ḥalaqāt*, of which there were said to be over six hundred in one emirate alone in 2008.[248] Such meetings "enable the ruler to place circles of religious study in places of potential gatherings that would otherwise be independently run; thus, they operate as massive apparatuses of control."[249]

Government crackdowns have certainly influenced the means in which Brotherhood organizations operate. Wanda Krause explains, "[E]xisting Islamist groups are not necessarily growing in number because they risk state interference by seeking recruits to join the group. Thus, while a lot of activity is halted in the UAE under great pressure, much simply goes further underground and thus is much harder to observe and detect. In effect, networking is becoming the dominant mode of action among those wanting to effect change and make a difference."[250] The Brotherhood's move toward secrecy in turn has made the Emirati government more suspicious, as it assumes that the organization has gone underground to conceal a nefarious plot for government takeover.

The central government, having used the 2011 petition movement and the Arab Spring as a pretext for ramping up security, has strengthened its control throughout the country. In the words of one interviewee, "The Muslim Brotherhood was no real security threat, but the way the security system is built here is to always be on alert . . . . The petition was a trigger to be used."[251] For its part, Islah, now formally disbanded and designated a terrorist group since November 2014, insists that it is "an independent, patriotic group that has received no funds from abroad . . . [and] is loyal to the Emirati government."[252] The organization continues, primarily from abroad, especially from the United Kingdom and Turkey.

The London-based Emirates Centre for Human Rights (ECHR) and International Campaign for Freedom in the UAE (ICFUAE) have been particularly outspoken in their criticism of the government's crackdown. Islah also uses its website to demand the release of its detained members and has called for the prosecution of government officials whom it believes to have tortured Islah detainees to obtain false confessions from them about the group's militant nature.[253] Jam'iat al-Irshad wa-l-Tawjih al-Ijtima'i (Irshad) in Ajman, under the supervision of the Ministry of Labor and Social Affairs, has been renamed Ajman Association of Social and Cultural Development to "keep pace with the vision and goals of the future assembly and responsibilities of active participation in development."[254] It also changed its logo to reflect its new mission, which adheres to provisions of Federal Law 2 of 2008 on associations and public interest groups, described in chapter 3.[255] Now that Islah is organizationally defunct and membership to it has been criminalized, it is extremely difficult to determine the degree to which the organization's ideology remains influential inside the UAE.

The government's crackdown on Islah may indicate that the organization and Brotherhood ideology more broadly held more popular support than was previously believed. In fact, "Abu Dhabi's crown prince provides a good insight into the strategy, having been recorded in a 2006 US diplomatic cable referencing a meeting with US diplomats as stating that 'if there were an election [in the UAE] tomorrow, the Muslim Brotherhood would take over.' "[256] The administration, especially Shaykh Mohammed bin Zayed, clearly considers Islah to be an existential political threat and has couched his government's crackdown on the group as a security matter, urging citizens turn against the Brotherhood and making them more willing to accept increased central government control to counter the so-called Muslim Brotherhood threat. Reflecting this policy, in January 2014, the UAE jailed thirty, including twenty Egyptians and ten Emiratis, over supposed links to the Muslim Brotherhood; the judge also reportedly "ordered the closure of 'all branches of the Brotherhood in the country the group had been running' and the seizure of 'all funds and properties' related to it."[257]

What remains puzzling is the question of whether the crackdown on Islah was necessary, especially if Emiratis are as satisfied as the government claims they are. As one Emirati political scientist put it, "Trust is high, and confidence in the government is high."[258] The Brotherhood's push for more representative government should not have been considered a threat to the government if it truly held control of the population as it claims to do. In the words of one secular Emirati activist,

> The Muslim Brotherhood had an influence on the social level in the UAE for quite a long time, even though the Emirati rulers are popular—because they have been historically good to the people, so there was no threat to the people. There was no need to make the Brotherhood an enemy. I, as a liberal, have more radical views on the government than those Islamists, yet I am not facing the same challenges. The Brotherhood is popular and the only group in the region that could challenge the rulers . . . . The Islamists had the ground to establish themselves, share some views more than liberals because they had legitimacy through the street . . . . During the Arab Spring, nations were jumping forward, and governments stepped back, so the government began to bribe people with wages and infrastructure improvements, etc. Bribes will put off demands for some time, are only a temporary extinguisher.[259]

Despite seeming an extreme and illogical reaction, the crackdown has become a source of pride for many Emiratis, who boast of their country's security services' ability to "eradicate the Muslim Brotherhood all at once," something they claim Saudi Arabia and Kuwait could not accomplish due to the organization's prevalence in those countries.[260] Try as it might, the Emirati government can never fully eradicate the Brotherhood's ideology, however; as one Gulf correspondent put it, "Islah was a viable and very prominent opposition."[261] Further, simply because it is organizationally defunct does not mean that its ideology is unappealing or uninfluential, as illustrated by the Qatari case. As Emirati rulers endeavor to promote secular nationalism under their own control, they will continue to come into conflict with any organization that promotes traditional Islamic values. As Shaykh Mohammed bin Zayed put it in his discussion of Islamist influence over educational curricula in the UAE, "We are having a (culture) war with the 'Muslim Brotherhood' in this country."[262] The Emirati stance, then, differs greatly from that taken by Qatar, positing that confrontation between the state and conservative Islam or those who represent it is inevitable, as they have fundamentally different political and social goals.

Those inside the UAE who remain sympathetic to the Brotherhood "are very careful and keep it quiet."[263] In terms of policy output, there is little evidence of Brotherhood influence outside of the Ministry of Education in the 1970s and 1980s. Still, the government remains "very nervous," having seen the appeal of the Brotherhood and the ability of its members to influence government ministries in the past, and it has used the existence of Islah as an excuse to further centralize security and surveillance within the country.[264] In fact, a 2011 report by *The New York Times* revealed that Shaykh Mohammed bin Zayed put together an eight-hundred-member mercenary force, which was meant to "conduct special operations missions inside and outside the country, defend oil pipelines and skyscrapers from terrorist attacks and put down internal revolts."[265] Such action suggests that the Emirati government remains vigilant about any possible threats to its authority. Perhaps the government's vigilance with regard to avoiding political contestation is clearest when we examine the degree to which it has mitigated Brotherhood influence in the education sector in recent years.

Brotherhood Influence in Education Today

Education has been reformed considerably since the 1970s, when Brotherhood members held significant institutionalized influence in that sector. The central government has exercised increasing control over public education, in terms of hiring and curriculum development, to prevent an outside ideology from taking hold there as in the 1970s and 1980s, promoting state-based nationalism instead. As Davidson puts it, "Despite massively improved access and a large number of schools and universities being established, educational curricula have usually been tightly monitored or even shaped to support directly the state or the ruling family in question."[266]

The central government considers its efforts to modernize education critical to fighting Islamist influence. Shaykh Mohammed bin Zayed estimated in 2007 that it would take twenty-five to fifty years to root out extremism from the education system, claiming that, in the western part of Abu Dhabi emirate alone, the government shut 80 percent of 262 "talebani [Talibani] Quran schools."[267] In an effort to root out Islamist influence of any type, the government has strictly overseen hiring decisions: "teachers deemed extremists have been quietly dismissed or given non-teaching positions."[268]

The highest-profile incident involving reassignment of allegedly Islamist-linked educators took place in September 2007, when eighty-three Emirati teachers, who represented 10–15 percent of the citizen teaching population, were dismissed, allegedly due to their Islamist leanings.[269] The teachers protested in front of the Ministry of Education, demanding that their official complaints be reviewed by President Shaykh Khalifa bin Zayed and Prime Minister Shaykh Mohammed bin Rashid.[270] The teachers also contended that their spouses working in the ministry had been refused promotions, while their children were penalized with the denial of scholarships.[271] Meanwhile, "[t]he UAE Government's view on the dismissals is that the teachers represented a creeping Islamist threat to the UAE's traditionally tolerant approach to Islam."[272] Most of these eighty-three Emirati teachers were affiliated with Islah or the Emirates People's Rights Organization (EPRO) and considered themselves to be "human rights activists and political reformists with Islamist leanings."[273]

One of the dismissed teachers, Ahmad Rashid al-Nuaʿimi, posited that the government used the teachers' Islamist leanings as an excuse to root out debate about political reform of the type supported by the EPRO and other Islamist movements, blaming the State Security Directorate rather than the Ministry of Education for his dismissal.[274] The Education Minister at this time, Hanif Hassan ʿAli, conceded that reforms in the Emirati education sector are "designed to bring Islamic studies (which are mandatory for all Emirati and Muslim students) in accordance with UAE traditions, rather than imported ones."[275] Although dozens of Islamist-leaning teachers held a sit-in outside Dubai's Education Ministry, the decision was not reversed, and the ministry maintained that the shuffling of the teachers to other ministries was "in accordance with the requirements of the ministry's strategic plan."[276]

In terms of curricula reform, the number of courses in culture or religion has been limited, a measure that has provoked backlash from a large number of nationals.[277] Interestingly, Arabic and Islamic Studies courses were first revised in the overhaul of university-level curriculum, and inspectors visit classrooms to ensure that guidelines are being adhered to assiduously.[278] Further, "[t]eachers of Islam have had to be re-trained as part of the reforms instituted by the Education Ministry."[279] Reflecting local discussions about the need to promote Emirati heritage while maintaining international educational standards, the FNC recommended in 1998 that new curricula place, in the words of Andrzej Kapiszewski,

> more emphasis on themes related to the homeland as well as Arab heritage and culture. The Council called for the imposition of more controls over imported print and audio-visual materials, as some of them have a negative influence on society. It also recommended the establishment of a "higher council for culture, arts and literature" to be responsible for developing a federal strategy to preserve the nation's culture and heritage. One of the main duties of the council would be "to eliminate the influence of foreign satellite television channels and to confront alien cultures that contradict Islamic values."[280]

The request for such measures sounds strikingly similar to complaints by Islah about the introduction of foreign materials into Emirati education.[281] Even in the absence of an organized group, then, Islah's ideology is espoused.

Certainly, government educational "reforms are contentious; increasing reliance on Western instructors and the dilution of Arabic and Islamic studies allows the MB [Muslim Brotherhood] to play on widespread fears that such changes will threaten the Emirati identity and traditional values."[282] The fact the FNC voiced such a complaint also demonstrates the degree to which Islam has been de-emphasized in the Emirati public school system. Indeed, the UAE's public schools and universities "have seen some of the most sweeping aspects of the crackdown against Islamists."[283] Perhaps in an effort to strengthen the local character of Emirati education, in the face of concerns about Westernization of the education sector, a law passed in 1999 made the teaching of Arabic mandatory in all private schools—even those for non-Arab expatriate students.[284] In addition, the government has attempted to gradually replace expatriate Arab instructors with Emiratis; in 2002, ninety non-Emiratis were released from their positions or given non-teaching roles.[285]

As in Qatar, there has also been considerable popular backlash against the increasingly imported (and Western) policies implemented in the 1990s and still in place in higher education. The faculties of the national university, UAE University (UAEU), were modeled on the American system, with many professors American-educated and some lectures given in English.[286] In addition, as described by Malcolm C. Peck, "each student is required to take general courses in basic English as well as statistics, Arabic, Arabic society, and Islamic thought. Thus, at the university level, many Emiratis are significantly exposed to Western, particularly U.S., modes of research and intellectual discourse."[287] Also in an effort to promote Western education at UAEU, several Arab (including Emirati) deans and one Arab-American have been replaced by non-Arab Americans due to the government's theory that Americans would be better equipped to oversee reforms and conduct classes in English, and would be less likely to inject their own opinions about regional politics.[288] Furthermore, a number of high-profile and highly funded Western branch campuses has been established in the UAE, including Sorbonne University, New York University, and the Masdar Institute of Science and Technology, built in partnership with the Massachusetts Institute of Technology. There are forty branch campuses in total, with twenty-seven in Dubai alone.[289]

Although the Education Ministry still faces limited criticism from religious conservatives for its reforms, it has continued to implement such changes, while also ensuring that university student unions, especially at UAEU, do not become influenced by political Islam as they were in the 1970s. The Emirati government has thus made sweeping reforms in education to annul the residual influence from the period of Muslim Brotherhood control in that area. Nonetheless, the government still promotes the study of religion and has upheld gender segregation in public schools. In fact, the six core values of the Ministry of Education reflect the importance of religious values, as they are listed as "citizenship and responsibility; the principles and values of Islam; commitment and transparency; contribution and accountability; the right to education for all; and quality and innovation."[290] The government has thus sought to promote Islam, but solely of the type it deems nonthreatening and controllable. It also has tried to balance the interests of a growing expatriate population and a much smaller national population, which is complicated by the fact that each of the seven emirates boasts a distinct social environment and political culture. The government has also taken measures in the charity sector, another area once dominated by Islamists, to ensure that it is focused on state nationalist, rather than on Islamist ideology.

The Brotherhood in the Charity Sector

The agenda of the Muslim Brotherhood has traditionally included an emphasis on philanthropic work. As mentioned above, Islah's largest charity group in the UAE, the Committee for Relief and Outside Activities (established in 1987), became embroiled in conflict following charges that it had funded a terrorist organization in Egypt. To this day, skepticism remains about the political motives of Islamist (or even Islamic) charity endeavors. The aforementioned list of terrorist organizations published in November 2014 included charities like the Islamic Relief Organization in London as an affiliate of the Muslim Brotherhood, indicating the government's seriousness in taking control of the sector.[291] A study by Falah ʿAbdullah al-Mdaires reveals that groups like the Dubai Charity Association and the Charitable Society for the Memorization of the Qurʾan in Umm al-Quwain have been suspected of maintaining links with the Ikhwan.[292] Such mistrust about the use of Brotherhood-affiliated charities for political ends has led to greater government presence in the sector and has enabled the state to justify its increased presence therein.

At the federal level, the Cooperative Society Department at the Ministry of Social Affairs receives applications for charitable societies and refers them to the cabinet for a decision on whether such groups can form.[293] The other bodies capable of approving of a charitable association include Dubai's Islamic Affairs and Charitable Activities Department, the International Humanitarian City in Dubai, and the Community and Development Authority of Dubai.[294] The Islamic Affairs and Charitable Activities Department of the Government of Dubai, in its regulations, stipulates that a charitable society "may practice both religious and charitable activity."[295] In fact, it provides eight examples of the accepted activities of such societies: construction of mosques, schools, health care facilities; building of roads; collection and distribution of zakat; engaging in *daʿwa*; caring for those in need such as orphans and the elderly; preparing people for hajj and *umra*; performance of religious sacrifice; and gathering of people in charitable meetings.[296] All of these activities closely resemble those that Islah previously organized in the UAE yet have been subsumed under government authority in the UAE.

The central government also expressly prohibits charities from participating in political activities, supporting a political cause, or adopting political attitudes; fomenting sectarian, racial, or ideological divisions; taking part in any commercial business independently, aside from the investment of its endowments; trying to gain profits; or using funds in another way than is intended.[297] Further aiding state support, charitable and religious societies are required to provide the emirate-level government with detailed information about their organizational structures and activities both inside and outside of the UAE, in addition to their annual budget and the names of people invited to the UAE for events.[298] If it does not abide by the Islamic Affairs and Charitable Activities Department's standards, a society's license can be revoked.[299]

Federal and emirate-level governments, in particular the leading emirates of Abu Dhabi and Dubai, have proactively promoted charity efforts in recent years. By funneling charity money through government agencies, state largesse is re-emphasized. The Khalifa bin Zayed Al Nahyan Foundation, as described by Davidson, "donates to a wide range of causes, and the Emirates Foundation which is chaired by Sheikh Mohammed bin Zayed . . . has recently focused on distributing grants for nationals with special needs. In fact, giving money to the poor directly and thereby bypassing such state-sanctioned charities is difficult, and actually frowned upon."[300] Dubai's government similarly funds large charity organizations, namely the Mohammed bin Rashid Al Maktoum Foundation and the Mohammed bin Rashid Charitable and Humanitarian Establishment, which fund projects inside and outside the UAE.[301] The clearest example of government co-optation of the religious charity sector is the UAE Red Crescent Society, which "receives considerable financial and organizational support from the various ruling families and, predictably, serves as an umbrella organization for other smaller charities."[302] While Abu Dhabi's government dominates the Red Crescent Society, with Shaykh Hamdan al-Nahyan serving as its president, Shaykh Mohammed Humanitarian Charity Foundation in Dubai is a smaller complement, focused on the northern emirates.[303]

The government similarly grants funding to other UAE-based charities, thereby binding them to the state through financial ties.[304] Despite government controls, one of the most prominent charities in the UAE today, the Dar Al Ber Society, is a "Salafi foundation linked to Saudi Arabia," active in funding a number of education institutions within the UAE; it also circulates a magazine, broadcasts a radio show, and runs several retail businesses,[305] in addition to running a variety of charities abroad.[306] Islamism thus remains popular in the charity sector, though its expression is regulated through the UAE's legal framework.

Islamism and Emirati Society

While organized political opposition does not exist, on the social level, as one Emirati political scientist put it, "it's everywhere."[307] The advocacy of certain social policies undoubtedly informs political opinions and views about the proper role of governments in society; as such, support for certain social policies has translated into political complaint. The UAE, Dubai in particular, has made less of an effort than neighboring Kuwait and Qatar to maintain its traditional image and values, with alcohol in easy supply and with the promotion of Western tourism ubiquitous. The situation was described by Mohammed al-Roken to *The Washington Post* in 2006:

> The itinerant city Roken sees today is unrecognizable, not even Arab. All that remains of the neighborhood of his youth is the mosque. When he goes to a mall, he estimates that 99 percent of the patrons are foreigners, and he rarely hears Arabic. Despite religious prohibitions, drinking is unabashed, and he fears public wine-tasting parties are on the way. The beaches of his youth were either taken over by hotels and their occasionally topless sunbathers or frequented by Westerners whose dress he deems inappropriate. He grimaces at women jogging in the streets, sometimes with their dogs, considered unclean under Islamic law. The celebration of Islamic holidays and the country's national day on Dec. 2 pale before the more commercialized commemoration of Christmas.[308]

Al-Roken has been in prison since 2012, when he was sentenced on charges of attempting to overthrow the government. He described his situation prior to the arrest as "internal exile," as he has moved farther away from Dubai "[t]o maintain his identity as an Arab and Muslim."[309] This feeling is certainly evident among certain nationals in the UAE, particularly in Dubai. Such complaints are unique to the Gulf's super-rentiers and fuel support for Islamism.

There also exists a sense among the local population that the business-minded Emirati rulers "want to Westernize people here."[310] Despite the fact that the constitution affirms Islam as the official religion and sharia as a principal source of legislation,[311] doubts remain about the commitment of the ruling families, in particular those of the leading emirates, to such ideals. The leading emirates' policy on alcohol is particularly telling, as it is significantly laxer than that of neighboring countries, with some hotels in Abu Dhabi and Dubai serving alcohol during Ramadan and with bars remaining open before major holidays or during mourning periods.[312]

Limited steps have been taken to address complaints: Dubai introduced a series of new decency regulations in 2009, primarily concerning proper dress and public displays of affection, and in summer 2011 restrictions prohibited the display of alcohol in full view.[313] Nonetheless, one Emirati went so far as to say that "if it were up to the rulers of Abu Dhabi and Dubai, they wouldn't have Islam as part of our culture at all. In public they have to keep this persona, but they're chipping away at that slowly. They sponsor parties with alcohol. They're trying to get people to change how they view the line between what is acceptable and not."[314] Complaints about the ruling families of the increasingly wealthy leading emirates often concern their un-Islamic behavior and creeping Westernization. In such an environment, groups like the Ikhwan hold appeal as moral watchdogs, and monitoring social policies and public morality becomes the primary cause for Brotherhood movements, as in other super-rentiers.

The leading emirates' efforts at catering to their large expatriate populations have become more controversial in recent years and suggest a lack of cultural sensitivity. For example, Abu Dhabi's Emirates Palace Hotel displayed a forty-three-foot-tall Christmas tree adorned with diamonds and costing nearly $10 million in 2010.[315] Facing complaints, the hotel "was forced to admit that it had 'taken the holiday spirit a bit too far' and removed the tree."[316] Prostitution is also rather common in Dubai: "Although there are occasional crackdowns, usually preceding Ramadan, in practice the police rarely intervene and soliciting and kerb crawling is usually left unchecked."[317] Locals further bemoan the inappropriate dress of many expatriates and tourists. In 2012, a grassroots social media campaign emerged to promote modest dress, using the Twitter hashtag UAEDressCode; according to Davidson, "the campaign has seen large numbers of UAE nationals criticize the inaction of their government to enforce basic standards."[318] Dubai has taken Westernization the furthest in an effort to appeal to tourists who fuel a large portion of its economy. Remarkably, beginning in 2006, Dubai taxi drivers were fined if their cars had Arabic rather than English signs, and nowhere in that emirate, as of 2010, could nationals receive a university education in Arabic.[319]

As the imbalance between expatriates and nationals becomes more extreme, the two communities are becoming increasingly polarized. Outspoken former police chief and current Head of General Security for Dubai Dhahi Khalfan described the situation: "[I]f the Gulf governments do not take bold steps to check the inflow of foreign workforce, a day could come when locals would be marginalized in their own countries and become like Red Indians [*sic*] in the US."[320] Discussion about infringement of non-nationals has been more heated in the UAE than elsewhere in the Gulf largely because the central government is considered unresponsive to concerns of nationals, particularly because the leading emirates have boosted their tourism sectors to diversify away from hydrocarbon resources and particularly to attract Western, secular visitors. Having once been a key cause for Islah, the expatriate imbalance in the UAE "unites all ideologies. It's now difficult to find a majlis; there is little Arabic; there are more business opportunities.... The issue of national identity terrifies everyone."[321] Social policies that alienate the national population have spurred Islamist movements throughout the Gulf, as citizens fear the loss of their influence as increasingly Western policies are advocated. Political mobilization through the informal sector, then, becomes the primary means of expressing disapproval of social policies, which constitute principal grievances in the super-rentiers.

The Muslim Brotherhood in the UAE gained popular appeal primarily as a vehicle for complaint against increasing Westernization. In the words of an Emirati political scientist, "One-third of the population probably thinks this way, that the state could be more Islamic."[322] The Emirati government has understood the influence of Brotherhood organizations to be primarily political and thus threatening to their ruling system. In the face of such ideological competition, they hope that promoting secular nationalism and establishment Islam will harbor loyalty to the regime.

Having granted the Brotherhood government positions in the 1970s, the UAE has come to recognize the organization's political weight, though its members have only ever held limited institutionalized influence. The government has failed to co-opt opposition stemming from the Ikhwan in recent years, due to the appeal that its ideology holds for a population largely opposed to the state's increasing Westernization. The Emirati government has thus turned its attention to forcing the organization's closure by vilifying its ideology and by framing the Ikhwan as a political and security threat. Ironically, the more the government cracked down on the Brotherhood as a political bloc, the more politically involved it became in the UAE, until the most recent clampdown in 2012 largely halted its domestic activities; as in Kuwait, greater restriction on all political blocs led Islamists to focus on political reform ahead of traditional concerns about social policies.

In its recent crackdown on local Muslim Brotherhood affiliates, the Emirati government actually contributed to the Ikhwan's political influence, openly describing it as a serious threat to the existing order. This response has been distinct among the super-rentiers. While Kuwait has largely accommodated the Muslim Brotherhood, and while Qatar has backed an Islamist agenda to a limited extent, the UAE took an active, and more repressive, approach. In Jim Krane's words, "Radicals are drummed out. Islamists, even those with mild views who would be allowed on the air in Qatar and Kuwait, are frozen out of public debate . . . . 'We don't have radicalism,' [Nabil] al-Yousuf [from Dubai's Executive Office] says. 'It has been contained.'"[323] Having described the Brotherhood as a major security and political threat, the government was able to tout its victory over extremism after the crackdown, in an effort to advance nationalist feelings inside the country.

By inflating the Brotherhood's political importance, the Emirati government forced the dismantling of the organization and incited hatred toward it more generally. The crackdown also garnered negative international attention and threatened some regional relations. As conservative Islam continues to be a force within Emirati society, the government will likely need to take a different, more sustainable tack toward handling Islamist opposition.

CONCLUSIONS

Through our examination of the super-rentiers, we have demonstrated the degree to which and means in which they have become politically relevant actors—both domestically and abroad. Distinct from other Ikhwan movements in their lack of responsibilities to provide material benefits for followers, they have had to rely on their ideological message—something that has become increasingly appealing in the three states with the least balanced populations in terms of expatriates to nationals and facing considerable Western encroachment and pressure to diversify their economies through the development of a tourism sector. Rentier Islamism thus becomes a form of nationalism in such environments and is likely to remain so even after the losses experienced by the Ikhwan elsewhere during and after the Arab Spring. In the concluding chapter below, we elaborate upon the concept of rentier Islamism and how it is a critical addition to the existing literature on the Muslim Brotherhood and the Arabian Peninsula.

8

Rentier Islamism

EXPLAINING IKHWAN POLITICS IN THE SUPER-RENTIERS

MODELS OF MUSLIM BROTHERHOOD POLITICAL ACTIVITY IN THE GULF

In the preceding analysis, we have demonstrated that Muslim Brotherhood organizations in super-rentiers operate through their successful integration into, and in some places domination of, the social and educational spheres. As their influence expanded through grassroots social outreach and their members' privileged positions in government ministries in the 1960s and 1970s, the Brotherhood attracted a considerable following and came to inspire a limited degree of political mobilization. In such an environment where the Brotherhood stirs political commitment, in Lisa Anderson's words, "[g]rievances came to be cast not in terms of material demands but in the idiom of moral responsibility and ideological commitment."[1]

Ideology motivates members of super-rentier states to join Muslim Brotherhood affiliates, as such groups provide spiritual welfare through their informal networks and educational activities. Notably, most members of these groups come from the educated elite, a class that one would not expect to join political blocs out of a feeling of disenfranchisement. Economic motivations in super-rentier states, as expected, hold limited appeal in spurring political action where ideology remains influential. In this conclusion, we examine the degree to which our findings, through three diverse country cases, highlight the need to update the theoretical framework concerning political Islam in the Arabian Peninsula by differentiating Brotherhood mobilization in that region through developing the concept of rentier Islamism.

THE EMERGENCE OF RENTIER ISLAMISM

Gulf rulers have, using their vast hydrocarbon resources, "sought to make Islamic institutions into agencies of the state," with government-sponsored religious scholars particularly important in, as F. Gregory Gause III puts it, "the states' legitimation strategies, providing religious sanction to the political order."[2] Despite government control over major institutions, independent imams and Islamist movements remain influential. Because Islamist groups exist outside the realm of formal politics or civil society, many scholars believe that the Gulf lacks any political actors whatsoever, relegating these Islamist actors to the social sphere.[3] Such informal organizations, however, hold ideological appeal and thus become important social and political groups. As Gause explains, "Organized social movements have never been absent from the political life of the Gulf. But through the 1980s, they operated largely on the fringes of the political system, and their influence was based to a great extent on personal, client relations with important members of the government and ruling families."[4] The question thus becomes not whether Islamism is politically relevant, but in what ways its influence is expressed in the prevailing political systems.[5]

That the Muslim Brotherhood in the Gulf does not resemble its affiliates elsewhere in the region should be unsurprising. In fact, there is no one form of Islamism even within states like the super-rentiers that feature striking economic, political, and social similarities. Certainly, as Salwa Ismail points out, "the fortunes of Islamism as a political movement are conditioned by the structures of opportunities, and by political configurations and contingent identities."[6] The grassroots, primarily informal, and gradual approach to politics taken by Muslim Brotherhood affiliates is sharply contrasted with the largely top-down governments under which they operate in the Gulf, yet their informal arrangement in states like Qatar and the UAE also aligns with the more personalized systems of government in the region.

The Muslim Brotherhood, as an organization whose ideology dictates that Islam should be part of every aspect of life, exists in super-rentiers in both the social and political realms, using the social to gain access to the political due to the political opportunity structures of such states. The movement in all three countries began with the goal of Islamizing society in the face of foreign, especially Western, encroachment. Since their establishment, these groups have altered their priorities to varying degrees. The Kuwaiti Brotherhood has come to privilege electoral success and political influence more broadly by promoting a wide-ranging reform agenda over the initial social agenda that it pushed in the 1980s. The Qatari Brotherhood, on the other hand, has favored the ideological and social elements of its platform over pursuing structural or institutionalized power. Even what appears to be social power in the Qatari case is hardly politically neutral, particularly in a super-rentier that allows few outlets for institutionalized political participation. Finally, the Emirati Brotherhood, before the most recent crackdown began in 2012, operated in a space between the purely political, inhabited by the Kuwaiti Brotherhood, and the amorphous, represented by the Qatari Ikhwan. While some of its members advocated for social reforms, Jamʿiat al-Islah al-Ijtimaʿi (Islah) came to voice concerns about political freedoms more broadly, thereby leading to restrictions from the regime. The government thus made it unlikely for the Emirati Brotherhood to evolve to the state of its Kuwaiti counterpart, which has developed a clearly defined political platform accompanying a broader social vision.

THE ALLURE OF ISLAMISM IN THE GULF

While wealthy super-rentier governments are able to deliver resources and services to their citizens, they tend not to offer a compelling ideological justification for their rule beyond the use of symbols appealing to religion or shared heritage.[7] Islam, on the other hand, provides a common and indigenous language for political ideas and thus has become the central ideological pillar for independent movements in such states.[8] Due to its ideology's broad-ranging appeal among majority Sunni populations, Brotherhood members have managed, in Jill Crystal's estimation, to "recruit differentially along lines of class, gender, and age. But they are able to cast themselves as universal."[9] Furthermore, a political ideology based in Islamic principles remains attractive in environments wherein governments have at their disposal large sums of money. In such settings, John Waterbury points out, "[t]he lack of articulation between the state and civil society has provided an opening for Islamic movements to attack governments, not on issues of the use of tax revenues, but on issues of corruption and moral turpitude in the governments' disposal of rents."[10]

Brotherhood affiliates in the Gulf also benefit from their ability to gather in seemingly apolitical areas, namely mosques and schools, some of the social spaces in which free debate takes place in the Gulf. Due to the fact that super-rentier monarchs wish to appeal to national populations that are, on the whole, conservative and religious, they tend to avoid cracking down on Islamist movements for fear that it harms their legitimacy as Muslim rulers, and they even granted members of the Brotherhood critical posts in educational and judicial sectors in their first decades. Indeed, as Gause points out, "[b]ecause Islam is part and parcel of the legitimation strategies of these regimes, they must support, and be seen to support, Islamic institutions."[11] As such, it is difficult for Gulf monarchies to dismantle Islamist blocs without losing a degree of their credibility as Muslim rulers. The very fact that super-rentier governments spend a considerable amount of oil rent on Islamic causes highlights the degree to which religion is a primary part of their legitimation strategy and of rentier politics more broadly.

Grassroots social outreach programs undoubtedly aid Brotherhood members in spreading their ideology and garnering support. Although they are not needed on the material level in the Arabian Peninsula (aside from Iraqi-occupied Kuwait), such programs have become popular in their provision of ideological guidance and social activities in societies that are often criticized for lacking indigenous intellectual or cultural vibrancy. They also link the Brotherhood to political life: "by engaging in hands-on activist work in popular neighbourhoods, they [Islamists] have learned the informal language of politics spoken by the people."[12] Muslim Brotherhood-affiliated charitable and social organizations that appear to be divorced from political life prevail in a gradual and "quiet encroachment" toward political capital rather than confrontational or overtly political approach.[13]

The political environments of the super-rentiers of Qatar and the United Arab Emirates (UAE), with few institutionalized political outlets, make the informal social sphere the most plausible arena for independent political activity. This sector, in the past managed by tribes, has a long history in the Gulf. Since independence, super-rentier governments have taken on most material responsibilities that previously lay with tribes whose authority predated their own.[14] In such environments in which tribal affiliations remain strong, Muslim Brotherhood organizations are traditionally thought to have difficulty garnering support, as tribal ties obviate the need for the social network provided by the organization. Importantly, however, "[t]he strength of tribal social structures does not preclude citizen demands for a role in politics."[15] In fact, tribes retain a great deal of political capital, perhaps most clearly seen in Kuwait through the (technically illegal) institution of tribal primary elections, in which tribes determine which parliamentary candidates they will back as a bloc. As much as the state has co-opted tribes' functions in terms of service provision, it has not removed their social and political relevance, similar to the state's experience with attempts to co-opt the Islamic sector. The Kuwaiti case presents something of an outlier, as the Brotherhood there can compete in institutionalized political life. Nonetheless, it began its activities in the informal social sphere and used social support, as well as positions in government bureaucracy, to promote and develop its coherent domestic political agenda.

As expatriate populations increase, political Islam is likely to remain a powerful political force against increasing modernization, accompanied often with secularization and Westernization. Super-rentier governments endeavor to balance their desires to modernize and to accommodate their largely nonnational and non-Muslim populations with the need to address grievances of national populations that remain, for the most part, socially conservative. A division between the rulers of the super-rentiers and their citizens thus often emerges. In Kuwait, the only super-rentier with an active parliament, the legislature appears to be in tune with the population to a large extent, preserving the socially conservative environment favored by its national population. Nonetheless, divisions between the executive and legislature have become visible. Most notably, in 2005, Amir Shaykh Jaber decreed the right of women to vote even after it was vetoed in parliament, thereby enforcing a move toward liberalism onto a population that had effectively rejected it. Electoral politics in the Gulf thus seems to favor the election of illiberal legislatures, of which more liberal ruling families sometimes disapprove. According to Michael Herb, "All of this prompts further skepticism about parliaments, and gives grounds to wonder if there is a serious disconnect between democracy and liberalism in the Gulf: Modestly democratic parliaments generate a good deal of illiberal policy."[16]

Though it lacks a parliament, the same dynamic exists, to a limited extent, in the UAE. Often vocal campaigns inside the Federal National Council (FNC) for the implementation of conservative social policies are a source of embarrassment for rulers, who hope to project an image of a modern and largely secular society. Considering these dynamics, it is perhaps unsurprising that Qatar has not instituted its elected Advisory Council, with its Central Municipal Council (CMC) often voicing similarly conservative views as those expressed in the FNC. Still, the government overrode Islamist complaints, articulated in a petition in 1998, about the granting of female suffrage for its municipal council. Islamist contestation, then, is quelled in certain instances when it fails to align with major points of regime policy.

By and large, in the Gulf context, as throughout the Middle East, we can expect, as Herb highlights, "[p]arliaments [to] reflect the illiberal views of the Islamists elected to them."[17] We can also presume that society more generally reflects such views. Because Brotherhood members disassociate their opinions about democratic political reform from their views on social policy, this pattern of illiberal policies arriving through democratic processes is likely to remain. The fact that Brotherhood influence is felt even in states without elected legislatures also demonstrates the degree to which religious ideology influences political belief in the super-rentiers.

The extent to which the political influence of Brotherhood affiliates in the super-rentiers is institutionalized depends on the degree to which the systems wherein they operate are also formalized, as this shapes political opportunity structures. The Qatari Muslim Brotherhood, for example, is the least overtly politically active of the three under study because its system allows the least institutionalized space for formal political participation. Though the means in which they exercise political pressure differ, the way in which Brotherhood affiliates in the super-rentiers gather political capital is the same, as illustrated in the preceding chapters and reviewed below.

KUWAIT: MUSLIM BROTHERHOOD AS PARLIAMENTARY OPPOSITION

The Kuwaiti Muslim Brotherhood undoubtedly boasts the most clearly developed political platform of all Brotherhood affiliates in the super-rentier states, as it is the only one that participates in electoral politics. It is also the only branch of the Brotherhood in the super-rentiers that was forced to take on the responsibility of service provision during the Iraqi occupation. This era represented a turning point in the development of the Kuwaiti Brotherhood, as it gained considerable popularity after showing itself capable of providing services to a population lacking a functioning government. Following the Iraqi occupation, the Kuwaiti Brotherhood also voiced its support for the restoration of parliamentary life and created a political bloc (*ḥizb*) distinct from its larger social movement (*ḥaraka*). The fact that the Kuwaiti Brotherhood divided itself into social and political blocs demonstrates the leadership's awareness of the different demands on each branch in a state with parliamentary elections, though both share a common ideology. As summarized by Shadi Hamid, "Where one is governed by more explicit religious concerns as well as an overwhelming concern with self-preservation, the other is driven more by political imperatives."[18]

While the Kuwaiti Muslim Brotherhood before the Iraqi invasion focused on ensuring the Islamization of society and the implementation of sharia through Islah, the Islamic Constitutional Movement (ICM) has garnered popular support through its more flexible and increasingly pro-democracy agenda. The ICM has become outspoken, increasingly since the Arab Spring, in its criticism of the regime and of the government system more broadly, pushing for the passage of a political parties law, the creation of a constitutional monarchy, and the advancement of an independent judiciary, often allying with secular liberal groups to advance these aims. By forming coalitions with other opposition blocs, the Kuwaiti Brotherhood has become increasingly politically relevant and has continued to emphasize the need for reform above social Islamization. The ICM also retains "political cover" in working with such forces, "making it harder for regimes to portray Islamists as extremists or terrorists."[19]

Notwithstanding the Brotherhood's popularity,[20] the most elected seats it has ever won in parliament was six out of fifty seats in 2006. The Brotherhood has never contested a plurality of seats, preferring to form coalitions with other blocs that grant it a degree of political protection.[21] By tempering its demands for laws to Islamize society and for the implementation of sharia, the ICM has come to hold a more powerful political position as a leading opposition bloc. Its political capital, though, is not expressed solely through its representation in parliament, demonstrating the limited ability of government institutions in the Gulf to reflect popular opinion.

Regardless of government structure, Islam retains substantial social capital in Kuwait. Tawfic E. Farah explains, "Islam prevails in all aspects of social, economic, and political life in Kuwait and has always done so. Islam imposes communal obligations on the faithful in this world. Politics is a function of religion."[22] Today, effectively controlling four seats in parliament after ending its nearly four-year boycott, the Brotherhood remains a major social and political force through Islah, demonstrating the degree to which the informal sector influences institutionalized politics and the extent to which it relies on gradualism working *through* the system rather than confrontation with it to gain political capital. The ICM also continues working alongside both secular liberal and Salafi movements for enhanced parliamentary powers and an independent judiciary, issues not traditionally so central to Brotherhood party agendas.[23]

QATAR: THE MUSLIM BROTHERHOOD AS SILENT PARTNER?

Muslim Brotherhood affiliates are largely not discussed in states lacking parliamentary elections, since they have fundamentally different roles in such political environments. These organizations are, however, by their very nature, multidimensional, as they aim to influence all parts of a Muslim's life in their pursuit of *tawḥīd*: "[e]lections are just one facet—albeit the one most visible to outside observers—of what they do."[24] Importantly, an ideological commitment and spiritual obligation are involved in joining the Brotherhood. This component is in fact what makes the Brotherhood so adaptable to various political systems. The Qatari Brotherhood recognized the power of the organization's philosophy over its formal structure when it willingly dissolved itself in 1999. Even in the absence of an organizational structure, the ideology has remained and has retained political and social relevance inside Qatar.

In the Qatari system, though not democratic, mechanisms exist through which citizens, of whom there are only a small number, can voice their concerns to the government, which makes decisions based on the opinions of very few people. As an advisor to Amir Shaykh Tamim explained, "Free discussion in the majlis gets to the amir, and he has to take this into consideration."[25] A great deal of debate within Qatari *majālis* deals with religious life and commitment inside the country, something that is reflected in the leadership's broader policy decisions. Recent decisions to restrict the sale of alcohol, to remove statues considered religiously offensive, and to publicize a campaign for proper dress all indicate grassroots support for, as well as government backing of, conservative Islam. Whether it is specifically of the Brotherhood strand is less clear. Similarly, the government's support of foreign Islamist movements of varying political strands reflects its desire to carve a place for Qatari foreign policy independent of other states in the region, or alternatively to support an ideology that resonates with segments of the local population.

Certainly, as noted by Ismail, "[a] number of studies assume implicitly that religiosity feeds into political engagement."[26] If religiosity is meant to serve as a predictor of political involvement, we should expect many more Qataris, and Gulf nationals generally, to become politically active—yet not necessarily in the ways that we may anticipate. There are no legislative elections to take part in; there are no political parties to support; there are no political campaigns to be run. Politics is displaced into the social sphere, and, in this environment, religion becomes the central ideological pillar for political and social opinions. The ruling al-Thani family appears to understand the overarching significance of Islam in Qatar and therefore provides a number of political concessions to religiously conservative members of its national population through social policies and foreign policies, neither of which threaten the government's central authority or regime security.

THE UAE: THE MUSLIM BROTHERHOOD AS ENEMY WITHIN

The crackdown on Emirati affiliates of the Muslim Brotherhood that began in the 1990s and was completed in 2012 reflects the regime's understanding of the organization as primarily a political threat, something that rentier state theory would not predict. In fact, recent Emirati government actions are in many respects reminiscent of earlier repression of the organization in Egypt in the early 2000s after it had proven its strength as a political competitor. The Emirati regime's emphasis on maintaining national security as an excuse for limiting civil liberties and civil society is particularly familiar.[27] Writing by journalist Max Rodenbeck on Egypt in 2000 aptly reflects the present-day Emirati condition: "More stifling still is the government's paternalist claim to monopolize the middle ground of public discourse. What this means in practice is that while the state bureaucracy tries to consolidate a single national voice that it can present on television, at international conferences, and the like, dissonant voices are constantly pushed to the margins."[28] The Emirati government, much like Egypt's Hosni Mubarak regime, has appealed to the international audience by playing up its commitment to social liberalism, to fighting extremism, to promoting so-called moderate Islam, and to protecting free speech, while contrasting its vision with the desires of Brotherhood supporters whom it describes as threatening national security.

When the state attempts to serve as the primary arbiter of ideological inspiration, backlash often emerges from marginalized political and social forces. The fact that the UAE is divided into seven different and unequal emirates makes relative deprivation a relevant political factor, increasing the likelihood of an opposition build-up and leading to more severe government action. Recent crackdowns on free expression targeted both liberal and Islamist critics of its policies, thereby uniting them against the government—a dynamic observed during periods of the suspension of parliamentary life in Kuwait. In the words of Hamid, "The shared experience of repression . . . encourages opposition groups to focus on what they have in common. After all, they have a shared enemy—the regime. So they agree to prioritize the fight for basic freedoms and democracy. Ideological divisions are put to the side."[29]

The fact that the Emirati government has endeavored to conflate the previously distinct Islamist and secular liberal reform movements has had the opposite effect to what was intended, as the two have cooperated increasingly in the face of the regime's crackdown. This cooperation complicates, rather than justifies, the Emirati government's actions. Hamid explains, "It was easier for them [autocratic rulers] to portray Islamists as a threat when they spoke of imposing Islamic law and keeping women locked up at home. It became more difficult when they spent much of the 2000s talking about human rights and political freedoms."[30] In situations in which their freedom to operate as political blocs is threatened, Brotherhood organizations tend to stress the need for democratic, rather than Islamic reform, in part to garner broader-based support and international sympathy for protection, in something of an exclusion-moderation dynamic.[31]

In contrast to the Kuwaiti and Qatari systems, in which political life is greatly influenced by conservative understandings of Islam, in the Emirati system, the more liberal ruling families of Abu Dhabi and Dubai have taken the reins. Although the leading emirates are central in policymaking, some of the ruling families of the other emirates have closer ties to the Brotherhood, complicating the government's unity on this issue and leading to a backlash from segments of the national population in certain emirates. Over time, "[t]he more regimes seek to present themselves as legitimate on newer lines and sponsor socioeconomic change, the more they lose credibility with the traditionalist elements of society and expose themselves to charges that they are un-Islamic."[32] As the distance grows greater between the beliefs of the Emirati government and those of nationals, Brotherhood complaint may again become politically vocal or, more likely, the crackdown will become more severe in the name of national security. While the Emirati government claims to have defeated the threat of political Islam inside its borders, it has in fact merely driven the movement further underground. As the Qatari experience demonstrates, the Muslim Brotherhood's ideology does not disappear in the absence of a formal organization; rentier Islamists are adaptable enough to effect policy change even without a defined structure.

RENTIER ISLAMISM AS POLITICAL CONTESTATION

Due to strict laws concerning civil society in Qatar and the UAE, Muslim Brotherhood affiliates tend to be relegated to the social realm, while members of the Ikhwan can run for parliament in Kuwait. Islamists adapt their activities within the systems in which they operate. In none of the super-rentiers can Brotherhood ideology be bought off through government disbursements. Brotherhood organizations in the region were first established outside of institutionalized political systems as social, educational, and charitable associations. By creating ideological links at the grassroots, they have amassed long-term popular support that can be sustained even without institutionalized political roles.[33] Importantly, the Brotherhood's social organizations, emphasizing the unity, or *tawḥīd*, inherent in Islamism, link the grassroots to political debates. Janine A. Clark affirms that "[w]ithin the Islamist worldview is an understanding of Islam as a comprehensive system encompassing all things material, spiritual, social, individual, political, and personal."[34] Super-rentier Brotherhood affiliates establish their potential for political leadership by demonstrating their appeal in this sector. Existing literature fails to describe the importance of political opportunity structures for Muslim Brotherhood groups in the Arabian Peninsula.

Because of the lack of institutionalized political space and the overarching relevance of Islam, the social and the political are strongly linked in the super-rentiers. Debates about culture and social values are highly politicized—especially in the Gulf, where governments spend significant amounts to promote indigenous culture as a means of boosting national identity. Nonstate *daʿwa* activities are thus inherently political, as they compete with the state-supported institutions.[35] Brotherhood-run organizations inform their members' views about a government's duty toward its citizens as well as how political discourse should evolve. They therefore enter the political sphere peripherally: "[r]ather than directly confronting the state or participating in formal politics, Islamic NGOs are engaged in social struggle at the level of cultural discourse and values. It is not that Islamic NGOs necessarily seek to convert those who use

NGO services to the Islamist cause; the political nature of Islamic NGO activities instead lies at the symbolic and discursive level."[36] These symbols, which influence daily life, constitute a critical part of political debate.[37] In fact, Dale Eickelman and James Piscatori contend that symbols lie at the heart of Muslim politics, defining the very phrase as "the competition and contest over both interpretation of symbols and control of the institutions, both formal and informal, that produce and sustain them."[38] The fact that Brotherhood organizations take on such debates distinguishes them from purely political parties. Far from functioning solely to advance political aims, Brotherhood affiliates endorse social organizations, schools, charities, and businesses, particularly when political opportunity structures allow them few alternatives.[39] The structure of the Muslim Brotherhood in itself provides far more than merely a political affiliation. While rentier state theory is correct in describing Islamist complaint as "cultural or ideological,"[40] it fails to take into account the links between the political and cultural/social in states with under-institutionalized political systems. Certainly, in states that allow for limited political participation, politics is often displaced to the social sphere.

Beyond the strictly political, Brotherhood ideology specifies that the organization should serve as "a training site for the pure, a synthesis between a political actor and a moral instructor."[41] Rather than scheming to gain power, then, the organization endeavors to transform the individual and to function as "a mirror of what the *umma* in general should be."[42] Each member is obliged to follow certain moral standards upon joining the Brotherhood, and becomes part of an *usra*, or family, which holds weekly meetings to read Islamic texts as well as discuss personal life and religion.[43] Faith is therefore the backbone of the Muslim Brotherhood and is what will likely continue to fuel its growth. According to Hamid,

> Islamist groups historically privileged self-preservation over political contestation. Their electoral success is dependent on the success of their charity, educational, and preaching activities, rather than the other way around. Since Islamist groups are largely blocked from the national broadcast and print media, the avenues for disseminating their message to voters are limited. Islamists compensate for this by attracting new supporters—and votes—through their grassroots outreach deep within local communities.[44]

Brotherhood affiliates in the super-rentiers exercise political influence primarily due to their ideological appeal and spread through the informal sector. In Kuwait, the Brotherhood influences political outcomes in a straightforward way through its participation in electoral politics and through its grassroots outreach, particularly in the youth and education sector, which helps influence new generations of voters. In Qatar, the Brotherhood maintains social influence, which is communicated to the political leadership largely through the informal sector of the majlis. The Emirati Brotherhood, though outlawed today, operated in the social sphere primarily yet also came to join forces with other political opposition movements, at least to a limited extent, in the efforts to expand popular participation in government.

WHITHER RENTIER ISLAMISM?

Rentier Islamism is a domestic political arrangement in which Muslim Brotherhood affiliates exercise political capital through informal and gradual means, despite (or perhaps due to) the presence of hydrocarbon wealth. In the super-rentiers of the Gulf perhaps more than anywhere else in the world, ideological affinity is powerful, and social capital translates into political influence. The presence of oil rents does not mitigate Islamist complaints, nor does it make such voices politically irrelevant. In fact, the availability of capital grants rulers of super-rentiers more opportunities to co-opt the religious sphere and to attempt to impose their own ideologies gradually. Emirati rulers are particularly attuned to the political influence held by their domestic Brotherhood movements and even consider the Ikhwan an existential threat not just domestically, but regionally as well. Kuwait and Qatar, on the other hand, have granted the Ikhwan more freedom, reflecting those leaders' beliefs that co-optation and containment are more effective than crackdown. Perhaps due to the precarious nature of the UAE's unequal union of emirates, the state has been more concerned about the emergence of ideological politics. States that seem similar from the outside, then, have very different considerations when formulating policy toward the Muslim Brotherhood.

Rulers in the Gulf enjoyed a brief détente concerning the position of the Muslim Brotherhood between November 2014 and June 2017. Ultimately, however, Emirati and Saudi fears, and perhaps their recognition of the political potency of rentier Islamism, have led to a second major clash over Qatari policy toward Islamists, alongside a coalition of Bahrain and Egypt. During the period of détente, Saudi Arabia notably hosted the International Union for Muslim Scholars, headed by Shaykh Yusuf al-Qaradawi and dubbed a terrorist organization by the UAE, for the Islamic Conference convened in February 2015 by King Salman.[45] Earlier that month, Saudi Foreign Minister Saud bin Faysal even stated that his government has "no problem with the Muslim Brotherhood."[46]

Less than two years later, however, in June 2017, the Saudi and Emirati leaderships severed diplomatic ties with Qatar for the second time in three years, cutting land, air, and sea links between them, again over Qatar's support for the Brotherhood. The coalition of Bahraini, Egyptian, Saudi, and Emirati leaders has determined Islamist activity of any type too dangerous to be allowed to exist—not because they consider it linked to terrorism, which follows a completely different strand of literature, but because of its ability to raise serious questions about legitimacy and morality of rulers, even when these rulers provide materially for their citizens. The likely impact of such a policy will be to drive Brotherhood activity further underground, as these movements, especially those in the super-rentiers, enjoy structural flexibility that have allowed them to sustain themselves even in periods of political containment. While these rulers have rightly recognized the power of Islamist groups to inspire political and social mobilization, they have underestimated their ability to survive even in a climate of political crackdown and limited institutionalized political participation.

With the Muslim Brotherhood unlikely to disappear from the political or social scene, as it can maintain its position in the social sphere, a strategy of co-optation or cooperation is more sustainable than one of crackdown. Because they gain appeal primarily through an ideology unaffected by the presence of wealth, Islamist organizations, in particular the Muslim Brotherhood, will not become any less influential in the Gulf in the coming years, despite campaigns against them. Rather, they will take on different forms, depending on the political freedom afforded them. Further, because Ikhwan groups in the super-rentiers do not need to provide goods and services, as they do in poorer states like Egypt and Jordan, they have more freedom in terms of structural appearance.

Rentier Islamists will continue to hold sway primarily through the informal sector. The means through which such Islamists gain support is not threatened by changes to the Ikhwan's strength elsewhere in the Middle East due to the power of their ideological message. Furthermore, as long as the state continues to politicize Islam, which seems likely as a legitimation strategy, political Islam will remain relevant. The super-rentiers of the Gulf have never been, nor are they likely to become, purely secular states, and so Islam will remain a political force. When it comes to political Islam in the super-rentiers of the Gulf, ideas matter; people matter; and faith prevails. To think that the political weight of faith is contingent on the presence of hydrocarbon wealth is misplaced cynicism and grossly simplifies politics in super-rentiers. As Hootan Shambayati points out, "The rentier nature of the state changes the nature of challenges it faces," rather than destroying them completely.[47] Due to their strength in the economic and political spheres, then, rentier governments, logically, face primary opposition to their rule in the cultural and religious spheres. At the same time, the presence of vast amounts of wealth and the implementation of restrictions on political life have led Brotherhood affiliates in super-rentiers to use the informal sector as a means of enhancing their political capital—a key characteristic of rentier Islamism.

NOTES

CHAPTER 1

1. We use Salwa Ismail's definition of political Islam, a term here used synonymously with "Islamism" as the use of Islamic symbols in political discourse, as well as "re-Islamisation, the process whereby various domains of social life are invested with signs and symbols associated with Islamic cultural traditions." Salwa Ismail, *Rethinking Islamist Politics: Culture, the State and Islamism* (London: I. B. Tauris, 2006), 2.

2. We consider an Islamist one who "mobilise[s] and agitate[s] in the political sphere while deploying signs and symbols from Islamic traditions." Ismail, *Rethinking Islamist Politics*, 2.

3. Hussein Mahdavy, "The Patterns and Problems of Economic Development in Rentier States: The Case of Iran," in *Studies in the Economic History of the Middle East*, ed. M. A. Cook (Oxford: Oxford University Press, 1970), 428–467.

4. Hazem Beblawi, "The Rentier State in the Arab World," in *The Rentier State: Nation, State and Integration in the Arab World*, ed. Hazem Beblawi and Giacomo Luciani (London: Croom Helm, 1987), 53.

5. For a definitional description of the Muslim Brotherhood, see chapter 2.

6. We introduce the term "super-rentier" to describe Kuwait, Qatar, and the UAE, as the states with the highest per capita income, lowest proportion of nationals to expatriates, and greatest overall "rentier" package as a consequence of these dynamics.

7. Giacomo Luciani, "Allocation vs. Production States: A Theoretical Framework," in *The Arab State*, ed. Giacomo Luciani (Berkeley: University of California Press, 1990), 75.

8. Hootan Shambayati, "The Rentier State, Interest Groups, and the Paradox of Autonomy: State and Business in Turkey and Iran," *Comparative Politics* 26, no. 3 (1994): 308.

9. Stéphane Lacroix, *Awakening Islam: Religious Dissent in Contemporary Saudi Arabia* (Cambridge, MA: Harvard University Press, 2011), 17.

10. Ulama are Muslim religious authorities or scholars.

11. Lacroix, *Awakening Islam*, 263.

12. Ibid., 265–266.

13. We use the phrase "political capital" to refer to nongovernmental actors' ability to influence government policymaking, which is aided by (though not conditional upon) their capacity to gain popular support among the citizenry.

14. Gwenn Okruhlik, "Making Conversation Permissible," in *Islamic Activism: A Social Movement Theory Approach*, ed. Quintan Wiktorowicz (Bloomington: Indiana University Press, 2004), 255.

15. Ibid., 265.

16. Ibid.

17. Ibid.

18. Ibid., 263.

19. Wahhabi Islam is a strand of orthodox and highly textualist Islam that originated in and prevails in Saudi Arabia, similar to Salafism yet following the teachings of Muhammad ibn ʿAbd al-Wahhab.

20. Eric Rouleau, "Trouble in the Kingdom," *Foreign Affairs* 81, no. 4 (2002): 79.

21. Ibid.

22. Interview with long-time resident of Qatar, Doha, Qatar, December 6, 2013.

23. *Awqāf* is the plural form of *waqf*, which in the religious context is a voluntary endowment collected from among Muslims to be used for charitable or religious purposes. A ministry of *awqāf* oversees the collection of and possible uses for such funds.

24. Imams are those who lead prayers and give sermons in mosques.

25. Herbert P. Kitschelt, "Political Opportunity Structures and Political Protest: Anti-Nuclear Movements in Four Democracies," *British Journal of Political Science* 16, no. 1 (1986): 59.

26. Sidney Tarrow, *Power in Movement: Social Movements, Collective Action and Politics* (Cambridge: Cambridge University Press, 1994), 77.

27. Ian Black, "Qatar-Gulf Deal Forces Expulsion of Muslim Brotherhood Leaders," *The Guardian*, September 16, 2014, http://www.theguardian.com/world/2014/sep/16/qatar-orders-expulsion-exiled-egyptian-muslim-brotherhood-leaders.

28. "Gulf Ambassadors Pulled from Qatar over 'Interference,'" BBC News, March 5, 2014, http://www.bbc.co.uk/news/world-middle-east-26447914.

29. Tamara Qiblawi, Mohammed Tawfeeq, Elizabeth Roberts, and Hamdi Alkhshali, "Qatar Rift: Saudi, UAE, Bahrain, Egypt Cut Diplomatic Ties," CNN News, June 5, 2017, http://edition.cnn.com/2017/06/05/middleeast/saudi-bahrain-egypt-uae-qatar-terror/index.html.

30. We define civil society as "the constellation of associational forms that occupy the terrain between individuals and the state. It is viewed as a mechanism of collective empowerment that enhances the ability of citizens to protect their interests and rights from arbitrary or capricious state power." Quintan Wiktorowicz, "Civil Society as Social Control: State Power in Jordan," *Comparative Politics* 33, no. 1 (2000): 43.

31. Universities visited included the American University in Dubai, the American University of Kuwait, Georgetown University School of Foreign Service in Qatar, Kuwait University, Qatar Faculty of Islamic Studies, Qatar University, and UAE University (UAEU).

32. In Kuwait, think tanks visited included the Center for Strategic and Future Studies at Kuwait University, the Gulf Center for Development Policies, and the Kuwait Center for

Strategic Studies. In Qatar, the author visited the Al Jazeera Center for Studies, the Arab Center for Research and Policy Studies, the Brookings Doha Center, the Center for International and Regional Studies at the Georgetown School of Foreign Service in Qatar, the Qatar Foundation, the RAND-Qatar Policy Institute, the Royal United Services Institute (RUSI) Qatar, and the Social and Economic Survey Research Institute. In the UAE, think tanks visited included the Al Mezmaah Studies and Research Center, the Emirates Policy Center, the Institute for Near East and Gulf Military Analysis (INEGMA), and the Sheikh Saud bin Saqr Al Qasimi Foundation.

33. Michael Herb, "A Nation of Bureaucrats: Political Participation and Economic Diversification in Kuwait and the United Arab Emirates," *International Journal of Middle East Studies* 41, no. 3 (2009): 376.

34. Ibid., 383.

35. Ibid., 382.

36. Michael Herb, *The Wages of Oil: Parliaments and Economic Development in Kuwait and the UAE* (Ithaca, NY: Cornell University Press, 2014), 2.

37. "Gross National Income Per Capita 2013, Atlas Method and PPP," *World Development Indicators Database*, The World Bank, March 12, 2015, http://databank.worldbank.org/data/download/GNIPC.pdf.

38. Ibid.

39. Martin Baldwin-Edwards, "Labour Immigration and Labour Markets in the GCC Countries: National Patterns and Trends," research paper, LSE Kuwait Programme on Development, Governance and Globalisation in the Gulf States, no. 15, March 2011,10, http://eprints.lse.ac.uk/55239/1/Baldwin-Edwards_2011.pdf.

40. Ibid., 9.

41. Zohrul Bari, "Islamic Revival in the Gulf: An Overview," *International Studies* 31, no. 49 (1994): 51.

42. Lori Plotkin Boghardt, "The Muslim Brotherhood in the Gulf: Prospects for Agitation," The Washington Institute, June 10, 2013, http://www.washingtoninstitute.org/policy-analysis/view/the-muslim-brotherhood-in-the-gulf-prospects-for-agitation.

43. F. Gregory Gause III, *Political Opposition in the Gulf Monarchies* (San Domenico di Fiesole, IT: European University Institute, 2000), 23.

44. See Plotkin Boghardt, "The Muslim Brotherhood in the Gulf"; and N. Janardhan, "Islamists Stay Clear of Terrorism in Oman," The Jamestown Foundation, March 9, 2006, http://www.jamestown.org/single/?no_cache=1&tx_ttnews[tt_news]=698#.VETiieflf-Z.

45. See Daniel L. Byman and Jerrold D. Green, *Political Violence and Stability in the States of the Northern Persian Gulf* (Santa Monica, CA: RAND Corporation, 1999); Thomas Hegghammer, *Jihad in Saudi Arabia: Violence and Pan-Islamism since 1979* (Cambridge, MA: Cambridge University Press, 2010); Bruce Riedel and Bilal Y. Saab, "Al Qaeda's Third Front: Saudi Arabia," *The Washington Quarterly* 31, no. 2 (2008): 33–46; Sarah N. Stern, ed., *Saudi Arabia and the Global Islamic Terrorist Network: America and the West's Fatal Embrace* (New York: Palgrave Macmillan, 2011).

46. See Madawi al-Rasheed, Muted Modernists: The Struggle over Divine Politics in Saudi Arabia (London: Hurst, 2015); Mansoor Jassem Alshamsi, *Islam and Political Reform in Saudi Arabia: The Quest for Change and Reform* (London: Routledge, 2010); R. Hrair Dekmejian, "The Rise of Political Islamism in Saudi Arabia," *Middle East Journal* 48, no. 4 (1994): 627–643; Mamoun Fandy, *Saudi Arabia and the Politics of Dissent* (New York: Palgrave MacMillan, 1999); Lacroix, *Awakening Islam*; William Ochsenwald, "Saudi Arabia and the Islamic Revival,"

International Journal of Middle East Studies 13, no. 3 (1981): 271–286; Okruhlik, "Making Conversation Permissible"; Rouleau, "Trouble in the Kingdom."

47. Here we define liberal as who one aspires to political values of "psychological security and personal independence for all, legal impartiality within a single system of laws applied equally to all, the human diversity fostered by liberty, and collective self-rule through elected government and uncensored discussion." Stephen Holmes, *Passions and Constraint: On the Theory of Liberal Democracy* (Chicago: The University of Chicago Press, 1995), 16.

48. "UAE Coup Plot Trial Begins in Abu Dhabi," Al Jazeera, March 4, 2013, http://www.aljazeera.com/news/middleeast/2013/03/201334725468 66175.html.

49. We define the political as "of, relating to, or concerned with the making as distinguished from the administration of governmental policy." *Merriam-Webster Dictionary Online*, 2014, s.v. "political," http://www.merriam-webster.com/dictionary/political.

50. Kitschelt, "Political Opportunity Structures and Political Protest," 58.

CHAPTER 2

1. Gwenn Okruhlik, "Rentier Wealth, Unruly Law, and the Rise of the Opposition," *Comparative Politics* 31, no. 3 (1999): 296.

2. Mahdavy, "The Patterns and Problems of Economic Development in Rentier States," 428.

3. Ibid., 467.

4. Ibid., 443.

5. Ibid., 437.

6. Beblawi, "The Rentier State in the Arab World," 51–52.

7. Ibid., 62.

8. Ibid., 53–54.

9. Luciani, "Allocation vs. Production States," 73.

10. Ibid., 75.

11. Ibid.

12. Ibid., 78.

13. Ibid., 76.

14. Giacomo Luciani, "The Oil Rent, The Fiscal Crisis of the State and Democratization," in *Democracy Without Democrats?: Renewal of Politics in the Muslim World*, ed. Ghassam Salamé (London: I. B. Tauris, 1994), 144.

15. Shambayati, "The Rentier State, Interest Groups, and the Paradox of Autonomy," 308.

16. Ibid., 329.

17. Michael Ross, *The Oil Curse* (Princeton, NJ: Princeton University Press, 2012), 69.

18. Ibid.

19. Kiren Aziz Chaudhry, *The Price of Wealth: Economies and Institutions in the Middle East* (Ithaca, NY: Cornell University Press, 1997), 314.

20. Ibid., 306.

21. Michael Herb, "Taxation and Representation," *Studies in Comparative International Development* 38, no. 3 (2003): 3–31.

22. Ibid., 26.

23. Ibid.

24. Ibid., 26–27.

25. Ibid., 26.

26. Michael Ross, "Does Oil Hinder Democracy?," *World Politics* 53, no. 3 (2001): 347.

27. Ibid.

28. Okruhlik, "Rentier Wealth, Unruly Law, and the Rise of the Opposition," 296.

29. Ibid., 308.

30. Ibid., 297.

31. Steffen Hertog, *Princes, Brokers, and Bureaucrats: Oil and the State in Saudi Arabia* (Ithaca, NY: Cornell University Press, 2011), 18–20.

32. Ibid., 20.

33. Ibid., 4.

34. Ibid., 5.

35. Ibid., 251.

36. Ibid., 273.

37. Mohammed Ayoob, *The Many Faces of Political Islam: Religion and Politics in the Muslim World* (Ann Arbor: University of Michigan Press, 2008), 15.

38. Ismail, *Rethinking Islamist Politics*, 2.

39. John L. Esposito, introduction to *Islam and Development: Religion and Sociopolitical Change*, ed. John L. Esposito (Syracuse, NY: Syracuse University Press, 1980), ix.

40. John Obert Voll, *Islam: Continuity and Change in the Modern World* (Boulder, CO: Westview Press, 1982), 4.

41. Olivier Roy, *The Failure of Political Islam* (London: I. B. Tauris, 1996), 40.

42. Ibid., 40–41.

43. Ibid., 14.

44. Ayoob, *The Many Faces of Political Islam*, 13–14.

45. Roy, *The Failure of Political Islam*, 39.

46. Quintan Wiktorowicz, *Islamic Activism: A Social Movement Theory Approach* (Bloomington: Indiana University Press, 2004), 3.

47. Ibid., 6.

48. Ibid.

49. Frauke Heard-Bey, "The Tribal Society of the UAE and Its Traditional Economy," in *United Arab Emirates: A New Perspective*, ed. Ibrahim al-Abed (London: Trident Press, 2001), 101.

50. Frauke Heard-Bey, "The United Arab Emirates: Statehood and Nation-Building in a Traditional Society," *The Middle East Journal* 59, no. 3 (2005): 357–375.

51. Wiktorowicz, *Islamic Activism*, 7.

52. François Burgat, *Face to Face with Political Islam* (London: I. B. Tauris, 2003), 21.

53. Nazih Ayubi, *Political Islam: Religion and Politics in the Arab World* (London: Routledge, 1991), 176.

54. Ibid.

55. Ibid., 177.

56. Janine A. Clark, "Patronage, Prestige, and Power: The Islamic Center Charity Society's Political Role within the Muslim Brotherhood," in *Islamist Politics in the Middle East: Movements and Change*, ed. Samer S. Shehata (London: Routledge, 2012), 69.

57. Ibid., 70.

58. Wiktorowicz, *Islamic Activism*, 8.

59. Ibid., 9.

60. Ibid., 12.

61. Carrie Rosefky Wickham, *Mobilizing Islam: Religion, Activism, and Political Change in Egypt* (New York: Columbia University Press, 2002), 7–8.

62. John Obert Voll, foreword to *The Society of Muslim Brothers*, by Richard P. Mitchell (Oxford: Oxford University Press, 1993), xiii.

63. Wickham, 174–175.

64. J. A. Clark, "Patronage, Prestige, and Power," 70.

65. Kitschelt, "Political Opportunity Structures and Political Protest," 58.

66. Ayoob, *The Many Faces of Political Islam*, 33.

67. F. Gregory Gause III, *Oil Monarchies: Domestic and Security Challenges in the Arab Gulf States* (New York: Council on Foreign Relations Press, 1994), 14.

68. Wiktorowicz, *Islamic Activism*, 18.

69. Ayubi, *Political Islam*, 29.

70. Vickie Langohr, "An Exit from Arab Autocracy," *Journal of Democracy* 13, no. 3 (2002): 120.

71. Ismail, *Rethinking Islamist Politics*, 170.

72. Ibid., 176.

73. Ibid.

74. Ibid.

75. Ghassan Salamé, "Islam and the West," *Foreign Policy* 90 (Spring 1993): 23.

76. Ayubi, *Political Islam*, 123.

77. Ayoob, *The Many Faces of Political Islam*, 17.

78. Ibid., 18.

79. Salafis are orthodox Sunni Muslims who advocate a return to the practices of early Islam, as described in the Qur'an and Sunna and as practiced by the *salaf*, or pious ancestors.

80. Guilain Denoeux, "The Forgotten Swamp: Navigating Political Islam," *Middle East Policy* 9, no. 2 (2002): 69.

81. See then Muslim Brotherhood General Guide Hasan al-Hudaybi's Du'at la Qudat [Preachers not judges], released in 1969 internally and publicly in 1977. Available in Arabic at http://okhowah.com/file/5/attach201603315496446015328.pdf.

82. Michael C. Hudson, "Islam and Political Development," in *Islam and Development: Religion and Sociopolitical Change*, ed. John L. Esposito (Syracuse, NY: Syracuse University Press, 1980), 20.

83. Ibid.

84. Roy, *The Failure of Political Islam*, 52.

85. David Commins, "Hasan al-Banna," in *Pioneers of Islamic Revival*, ed. Ali Rahnema (London: Zed Books, 1994), 130.

86. Robert S. Leiken and Steven Brooke, "The Moderate Muslim Brotherhood," *Foreign Affairs* 86, no. 2 (2007): 108.

87. Ibid.

88. Voll, *Islam*, 176.

89. L. Carl Brown, *Religion and State: The Muslim Approach to Politics* (New York: Columbia University Press, 2000), 147.

90. Shadi Hamid, *Temptations of Power* (Oxford: Oxford University Press, 2014), 9.

91. John L. Esposito and James P. Piscatori, "Democratization and Islam," *Middle East Journal* 45, no. 3 (1991): 429.

92. *Tarbīa* is usually used in reference to educating or raising children in accordance with Islam.

93. Hasan al-Banna, quoted in L. C. Brown, *Religion and State*, 146.

94. Hasan al-Banna, quoted in Voll, *Islam*, 175–176.

95. L. C. Brown, *Religion and State*, 146.

96. Ibid., 147.

97. Richard P. Mitchell, *The Society of the Muslim Brothers* (Oxford: Oxford University Press, 1969), 246.

98. Ayubi, *Political Islam*, 130.

99. Mitchell, *The Society of the Muslim Brothers*, 103.

100. Leiken and Brooke, "The Moderate Muslim Brotherhood," 110.

101. Commins, "Hasan al-Banna," 136–137.

102. Ayoob, *The Many Faces of Political Islam*, 29.

103. Voll, *Islam*, 176.

104. Ibid.

105. Ayubi, *Political Islam*, 145.

106. ʿUmar al-Tilmisani, quoted in Ayoob, *The Many Faces of Political Islam*, 80.

107. Leiken and Brooke, "The Moderate Muslim Brotherhood," 107.

108. Ibid., 108.

109. Samer S. Shehata, introduction to *Islamist Politics in the Middle East: Movements and Change*, ed. Samer S. Shehata (London: Routledge, 2012), 7.

110. Ayoob, *The Many Faces of Political Islam*, 154.

111. Leiken and Brooke, "The Moderate Muslim Brotherhood," 111.

112. Ibid., 115.

113. Roy, *The Failure of Political Islam*, 75.

114. David D. Kirkpatrick, "Army Ousts Egypt's President; Morsi Is Taken into Military Custody," *The New York Times*, July 3, 2013, http://www.nytimes.com/2013/07/04/world/middleeast/egypt.html?_r=0.

115. Ahmed El Amraoui, "Tunisia's Ennahda 'Faced Defeat' in Elections," Al Jazeera, October 28, 2014, http://www.aljazeera.com/news/africa/2014/10/tunisia-ennahda-says-secular-rivals-ahead-20141027141737474289.html.

116. John L. Esposito, "Political Islam and Gulf Security," in *Political Islam: Revolution, Radicalism, or Reform?*, ed. John L. Esposito (Boulder, CO: Lynne Rienner Publishers, 1997), 71.

117. Ibid., 68.

118. Ibid., 60.

119. Ibid., 58.

120. Sami Zubaida, *Islam, the People and the State: Political Ideas and Movements in the Middle East* (London: I. B. Tauris, 2001), xix.

121. Esposito, "Political Islam and Gulf Security," 71.

122. Ayubi, *Political Islam*, 118.

123. Burgat, *Face to Face with Political Islam*, 173.

124. A *dīwāniyya* (plural *dīwāniyyāt*) is an informal meeting, which has long been a part of Kuwaiti political life. Such gatherings, hosted by members of the ruling family, politicians, and private individuals, are most often convened in homes and cover topics ranging from social life to religious ideology to politics.

125. The *majlis* (plural *majālis*), similar to Kuwait's *dīwāniyya*, is a crucial element of civil society. Such meetings are hosted by rulers, as well as by private citizens in Qatar and the UAE.

126. A. Ann Fyfe, "Wealth and Power: Political and Economic Change in the United Arab Emirates" (PhD diss., Durham University, 1989), 14.

127. Ibid.

128. Gause, *Oil Monarchies*, 11.

129. Ibid.

130. Ibid., 25.

CHAPTER 3

1. Mehran Kamrava, *The Modern Middle East: A Political History since the First World War*, 2nd ed. (Berkeley: University of California Press, 2011), 315.

2. Ibid.

3. Ibid., 314.

4. They include al-Nahyan of Abu Dhabi, al-Nuʿaimi of Ajman, al-Maktoum of Dubai, al-Sharqi of Fujairah, al-Qasimi of Ras al-Khaimah and Sharjah, and al-Muʿalla of Umm al-Quwain.

5. Jacqueline S. Ismael, *Kuwait: Dependency and Class in a Rentier State* (Gainesville: University Press of Florida, 1993), 23.

6. Ibid., 27.

7. Ibid.

8. Mary Ann Tétreault, *Stories of Democracy: Politics and Society in Contemporary Kuwait* (New York: Columbia University Press, 2000), 34.

9. Helen Mary Rizzo, *Islam, Democracy, and the Status of Women: The Case of Kuwait* (New York: Routledge, 2005), 11.

10. Peter Mansfield, *Kuwait: Vanguard of the Gulf* (London: Hutchinson, 1990), 18.

11. Jill Crystal, *Kuwait: The Transformation of an Oil State* (Boulder, CO: Westview Press, 1992), 10.

12. Ibid., 8.

13. Ibid., 12.

14. Ibid., 12–13.

15. Jill Crystal, *Oil and Politics in the Gulf: Rulers and Merchants in Kuwait and Qatar* (Cambridge: Cambridge University Press, 1990), 38–39.

16. Crystal, *Kuwait*, 18.

17. Ibid., 72.

18. Ibid., 59.

19. Ibid., 23.

20. Crystal, *Oil and Politics*, 81.

21. Mansfield, *Kuwait*, 49.

22. Ibid., 54.

23. Ibid.

24. Abdo I. Baaklini, Guilain Denoeux, and Robert Springborg, *Legislative Politics in the Arab World: The Resurgence of Democratic Institutions* (Boulder, CO: Lynne Rienner Publishers, 1999), 175.

25. Ismael, *Kuwait*, 82.

26. Doron Shultziner and Mary Ann Tétreault, "Representation and Democratic Progress in Kuwait," *Representation* 48, no. 3 (2012): 281.

27. Ismael, *Kuwait*, 83.

28. Article 107, Constitution of the State of Kuwait, Diwan of His Highness the Prime Minister, 1962, https://www.pm.gov.kw/kuwait-constitution.aspx.

29. In practice, this has not always happened, as in 1976 and 1986.

30. Tétreault, *Stories of Democracy*, 146.

31. Shultziner and Tétreault, "Representation and Democratic Progress in Kuwait," 286–287.

32. Ismael, *Kuwait*, 82.

33. Tétreault, *Stories of Democracy*, 146.

34. Shultziner and Tétreault, "Representation and Democratic Progress in Kuwait," 286–287.

35. Ibid., 281.

36. Tétreault, *Stories of Democracy*, 186.

37. Crystal, *Kuwait*, 72.

38. David Roberts, "Kuwait," in *Power and Politics in the Persian Gulf Monarchies*, ed. Christopher M. Davidson (London: Hurst and Company, 2011), 92.

39. Nathan J. Brown, "Pushing toward Party Politics?: Kuwait's Islamic Constitutional Movement," *Carnegie Papers* 79, January 2007, 4, http://carnegieendowment.org/files/cp79_brown_kuwait_final.pdf.

40. Article 43, Constitution of the State of Kuwait.

41. Neil Hicks and Ghanim al-Najjar, "The Utility of Tradition: Civil Society in Kuwait," in *Civil Society in the Middle East*, ed. Augustus Richard Norton (Leiden: E. J. Brill, 1995), 1:195.

42. Mary Ann Tétreault, "A State of Two Minds: State Cultures, Women, and Politics in Kuwait," *International Journal of Middle East Studies* 33, no. 2 (2001): 205.

43. Hicks and Al-Najjar, "The Utility of Tradition," 187–188.

44. Mary Ann Tétreault, "Civil Society in Kuwait: Protected Spaces and Women's Rights," *Middle East Journal* 47, no. 2 (1993): 276.

45. Mary Ann Tétreault and Mohammed al-Ghanim, "The Day after 'Victory': Kuwait's 2009 Election and the Contentious Present," *Middle East Report Online*, July 8, 2009, http://www.merip.org/mero/mero070809.

46. Anh Nga Longva, "Neither Autocracy nor Democracy but Ethnocracy: Citizens, Expatriates and the Socio-Political System in Kuwait," in *Monarchies and Nations: Globalisation and Identity in the Arab States of the Gulf*, ed. Paul Dresch and James Piscatori (London: I. B. Tauris, 2013), 120.

47. Tétreault, "Civil Society in Kuwait," 276.

48. Pete W. Moore, "What Makes Successful Business Lobbies?: Business Associations and the Rentier State in Jordan and Kuwait," *Comparative Politics* 33, no. 2 (2001): 143.

49. Rizzo, *Islam, Democracy, and the Status of Women*, 16–17.

50. Ibid., 17.

51. Hicks and Al-Najjar, "The Utility of Tradition," 190.

52. Paul Salem, "Kuwait: Politics in a Participatory Emirate," *Carnegie Papers* 3, July 2007, 10, http://carnegieendowment.org/files/cmec3_salem_kuwait_final.pdf.," 10.

53. Ibid., 10–11.

54. Ibid.

55. Marc Lynch, *The Arab Uprising: The Unfinished Revolutions of the New Middle East* (New York: PublicAffairs, 2012), 130.

56. P. Salem, "Kuwait," 11.

57. F. Gregory Gause III, "Kings for All Seasons: How the Middle East's Monarchies Survived the Arab Spring," Brookings Doha Center Analysis Paper, no. 8, September 2013, 19, http://www.brookings.edu/~/media/research/files/papers/2013/09/24%20resilience%20arab%20monarchies%20gause/resilience%20arab%20monarchies_english.pdf.

58. *The 'Iron Fist Policy': Criminalization of Peaceful Dissent in Kuwait*, Amnesty International, 2015, 5, https://www.amnesty.org/download/Documents/MDE1729872015ENGLISH.PDF.

59. "Kuwait: Telecom Law Violates Free Speech," Human Rights Watch, August 20, 2014, https://www.hrw.org/news/2014/08/20/kuwait-telecom-law-violates-free-speech; "Kuwait: Cybercrime Law a Blow to Free Speech," Human Rights Watch, July 22, 2015, https://www.hrw.org/news/2015/07/22/kuwait-cybercrime-law-blow-free-speech.

60. Hicks and Al-Najjar, "The Utility of Tradition," 188.

61. Nicolas Gavrielides, "Tribal Democracy: The Anatomy of Parliamentary Elections in Kuwait," in *Elections in the Middle East: Implications of Recent Trends*, ed. Linda L. Layne (Boulder, CO: Westview Press, 1987), 194.

62. Allen J. Fromherz, *Qatar: A Modern History* (London: I. B. Tauris, 2012), 53.

63. Ibid., 54.

64. Ibid., 55.

65. Ibid.

66. Ibid., 67.

67. Crystal, *Oil and Politics*, 5.

68. Ibid., 11.

69. Ibid., 9.

70. Ibid., 13.

71. Ibid., 168.

72. Rosemarie Said Zahlan, *The Creation of Qatar* (London: Routledge, 1979), 104.

73. Ibid.

74. David Commins, *The Gulf States: A Modern History* (London: I. B. Tauris, 2012), 213.

75. Mehran Kamrava, "Royal Factionalism and Political Liberalization in Qatar," *Middle East Journal* 63, no. 3 (2009): 413.

76. Crystal, *Oil and Politics*, 157.

77. Commins, *The Gulf States*, 213.

78. Crystal, *Oil and Politics*, 156–157.

79. Jill Crystal, "Coalitions in Oil Monarchies: Kuwait and Qatar," *Comparative Politics* 21, no. 4 (1989): 440.

80. Elisheva Rosman-Stollman, "Qatar: Liberalization as Foreign Policy," in *Political Liberalization in the Persian Gulf*, ed. Joshua Teitelbaum (London: Hurst and Company, 2009), 192.

81. Shaykh Hamad, quoted in Rosman-Stollman, "Qatar," 192.

82. Ahmed Abdelkareem Saif, "Deconstructing before Building: Perspectives on Democracy in Qatar," in *Reform in the Middle East Oil Monarchies*, ed. Anoushiravan Ehteshami and Steven Wright (Reading, UK: Ithaca Press, 2008), 110.

83. Article 1, Constitution of Qatar, Government of Qatar, 2003, http://portal.www.gov.qa/wps/wcm/connect/5a5512804665e3afa54fb5fd2b4ab27a/Constitution+of+Qatar+EN.pdf?MOD=AJPERES.

84. Rosemarie Said Zahlan, *The Making of the Modern Gulf States: Kuwait, Bahrain, the United Arab Emirates and Oman* (Reading, UK: Ithaca Press, 1998), 89.

85. Fromherz, *Qatar*, 130.

86. Kamrava, "Royal Factionalism and Political Liberalization," 414.

87. Commins, *The Gulf States*, 213.

88. Louay Bahry, "Elections in Qatar: A Window of Democracy Opens in the Gulf," *Middle East Policy* 6, no. 4 (1999): 120.

89. Fromherz, *Qatar*, 137.

90. Kamrava, "Royal Factionalism and Political Liberalization," 417.

91. Ibid., 418.

92. Ibid.

93. Saif, "Deconstructing before Building," 110–111.

94. Ibid.

95. Shabina S. Khatri, "Legislative Elections Postponed until at Least 2019," *Doha News*, June 17, 2016, https://dohanews.co/legislative-elections-in-qatar-postponed-until-at-least-2019/.

96. Bahry, "Elections in Qatar," 122–123.

97. Kamrava, "Royal Factionalism and Political Liberalization," 416.

98. Jill Crystal, "Political Reform in Qatar," in *Political Change in the Arab Gulf States: Stuck in Transition*, ed. Mary Ann Tétreault, Gwenn Okruhlik, and Andrzej Kapiszewski (Boulder, CO: Lynne Rienner Publishers, 2011), 122.

99. "2013 Survey of Civil Society Organizations in Qatar: Report of Findings," Social and Economic Survey Research Institute (SESRI), commissioned by the National Human Rights Committee, June 2013, 9, http://www.nhrc-qa.org/wp-content/uploads/2014/01/2013_Report-NHRC-_Final-_English-with-intro-from-NHRC-.pdf.

100. Crystal, "Political Reform in Qatar," 122.

101. Ibid., 121–122.

102. Commins, *The Gulf States*, 284.

103. Article 116, Law No. 14 of the Year 2004: The Labour Law, International Labour Organization, February 2010, http://www.ilo.org/wcmsp5/groups/public/---ed_protect/---protrav/---ilo_aids/documents/legaldocument/wcms_125871.pdf.

104. Article 119.1, Law No. 14 of the Year 2004.

105. Crystal, "Political Reform in Qatar," 130.

106. Bahry, "Elections in Qatar," 120.

107. Saif, "Deconstructing before Building," 112.

108. Fromherz, *Qatar*, 23.

109. Anealla Safdar and Ben Flanagan, "Royal Family Member Put in Charge at Al Jazeera," *The National*, September 22, 2011, http://www.thenational.ae/news/world/middle-east/royal-family-member-put-in-charge-at-al-jazeera.

110. "Dar al-Watan" [in Arabic], Al-Watan, April 2015, http://www.al-watan.com/watan.aspx?d=20150416&page=%D8%AF%D8%A7%D8%B1_%D8%A7%D9%84%D9%88%D8%B7%D9%86/%D9%85%D8%B9%D9%84%D9%88%D9%85%D8%A7%D8%AA.

111. "H. E. Shaikh Thani ibn Abdullah al-Thani, Chairman of the Board," Dar al-Sharq, April 2015, http://daralsharq.net/ar/node/36?language=en.

112. Article 53, Draft Media Law, quoted in "Qatar: Revise Draft Media Law to Allow Criticism of Rulers," Human Rights Watch, October 30, 2012, http://www.hrw.org/news/2012/10/30/qatar-revise-draft-media-law-allow-criticism-rulers.

113. "Qatari Draft Media Law Criticized by Rights Group," Reuters, October 30, 2012, http://www.reuters.com/article/2012/10/30/us-media-qatar-idUSBRE89T17620121030.

114. "Qatar: Revise Draft Media Law."

115. "Qatar: New Cybercrimes Law Endangers Freedom of Expression," Amnesty International, September 18, 2014, https://www.amnesty.org/en/latest/news/2014/09/qatar-new-cybercrimes-law-endangers-freedom-expression/.

116. "Qatar: Independent News Website Blocked," Human Rights Watch, December 7, 2016, https://www.hrw.org/news/2016/12/07/qatar-independent-news-website-blocked.

117. Shadi Hamid, "There Aren't Protests in Qatar—So Why Did the Emir Just Announce Elections?," *The Atlantic*, November 1, 2011, http://www.theatlantic.com/international/archive/2011/11/there-arent-protests-in-qatar-so-why-did-the-emir-just-announce-elections/247661/.

118. Kevin Fenelon, quoted in Christoper M. Davidson, *The United Arab Emirates: A Study in Survival* (Boulder, CO: Lynne Rienner Publishers, 2005), 14–15.

119. Christopher M. Davidson, "Arab Nationalism and British Opposition in Dubai, 1920–1966," *Middle Eastern Studies* 43, no. 6 (2007): 880.

120. Malcolm C. Peck, "Formation and Evolution of the Federation and Its Institutions," in *Perspectives on the United Arab Emirates*, ed. Edmund A. Ghareeb and Ibrahim al-Abed (London: Trident Press, 1999), 124.

121. Davidson, *The United Arab Emirates*, 44–45.

122. Frauke Heard-Bey, "The United Arab Emirates: A Quarter Century of Federation," in *Middle East Dilemma: The Politics and Economics of Arab Integration*, ed. Michael C. Hudson (London: I. B. Tauris, 1999), 136.

123. Peck, "Formation and Evolution," 129–130.

124. Heard-Bey, "A Quarter Century of Federation," 135.

125. William A. Rugh, "The United Arab Emirates: What Are the Sources of Its Stability?," *Middle East Policy* 5, no. 3 (1997): 21.

126. Heard-Bey, "A Quarter Century of Federation," 135.

127. W. A. Rugh, "The United Arab Emirates," 18.

128. Peck, "Formation and Evolution," 151–152.

129. Frauke Heard-Bey, *From Trucial States to United Arab Emirates: A Society in Transition* (London: Longman, 1982), 376.

130. Davidson, *The United Arab Emirates*, 204.

131. Article 51, United Arab Emirates Constitution, Federal National Council, 2010 Edition, http://www.uaecabinet.ae/English/UAEGovernment/Pages/ConstitutionOfUAE.aspx.

132. W. A. Rugh, "The United Arab Emirates," 19.

133. Heard-Bey, *From Trucial States to United Arab Emirates*, 376.

134. Article 54, quoted in Heard-Bey, *From Trucial States to United Arab Emirates*, 374.

135. Peck, "Formation and Evolution," 130.

136. Article 49, United Arab Emirates Constitution.

137. We hereafter refer to Abu Dhabi and Dubai with the term leading emirates, as they are undoubtedly the country's most influential economic and political players and, as such, set much of statewide policy.

138. Ali Mohammad Khalifa, *The United Arab Emirates: Unity in Fragmentation* (Boulder, CO: Westview Press, 1979), 92.

139. Peck, "Formation and Evolution," 130.

140. Ibid., 130–131.

141. Davidson, *The United Arab Emirates*, 190.

142. W. A. Rugh, "The United Arab Emirates," 19.

143. Fyfe, "Wealth and Power," 47.

144. Khalifa, *The United Arab Emirates*, 48.

145. Peck, "Formation and Evolution," 131.

146. "UAE's Electoral Base for FNC Polls Gets 66% Wider," *Khaleej Times*, July 6, 2015, http://www.khaleejtimes.com/nation/government/uae-s-electoral-base-for-fnc-polls-gets-66-wider.

147. Yasin Kakande, "Umm al Qaiwain Forms Last of UAE's Executive Councils," *The National*, July 12, 2011, http://www.thenational.ae/news/uae-news/umm-al-qaiwain-forms-last-of-uaes-executive-councils.

148. Heard-Bey, "The United Arab Emirates," 369.

149. Article 23, United Arab Emirates Constitution.

150. Heard-Bey, *From Trucial States to United Arab Emirates*, 398.

151. Heard-Bey, "The United Arab Emirates," 363.

152. Ibid.

153. Ibid., 359.

154. Ibid., 360.

155. Khalifa, *The United Arab Emirates*, 94–95.

156. Federal Law no. 2 of 2008 Concerning Associations and Domestic Institutions of Public Interest, quoted in *"There Is No Freedom Here": Silencing Dissent in the United Arab Emirates (UAE)*, Amnesty International, November 2014, 55–56, https://www.amnestyusa.org/files/mde_2501822014.pdf

157. Davidson, *The United Arab Emirates*, 270.

158. Articles 19 and 20, Federal Law No. 2 of 2008.

159. Christopher M. Davidson, *Dubai: The Vulnerability of Success* (Oxford: Oxford University Press, 2009), 211.

160. Michael C. Hudson, "The Incremental Approach to Political Reform in the Gulf," in *The Arabian Gulf: Between Conservatism and Change*, ed. Emirates Center for Strategic Studies and Research (Abu Dhabi: Emirates Center for Strategic Studies and Research, 2009), 57.

161. Mouza Ghubash, "Social Development in the United Arab Emirates," in *Perspectives on the United Arab Emirates*, ed. Edmund Ghareeb and Ibrahim al-Abed (London: Trident Press, 1997), 285.

162. "NGO Directory of UAE," arab.org, 2017, https://arab.org/countries/uae/.

163. Article 180, Chapter 2, Crimes Against the Internal Security of the State, UAE Penal Code, amended 2005, https://www.scribd.com/doc/122309224/182/Article-182.

164. Michael Herb, "Kuwait and the United Arab Emirates," in *Politics and Society in the Contemporary Middle East*, ed. Michele Penner Angrist (Boulder, CO: Lynne Rienner Publishers, 2010), 361.

165. Davidson, *The United Arab Emirates*, 279–280.

166. Ibid.

167. Ibid., 280.

168. Christopher M. Davidson, "The United Arab Emirates," in *Power and Politics in the Persian Gulf Monarchies*, ed. Christopher M. Davidson (London: Hurst and Company, 2011), 27.

169. Ibid.

170. Chris Arsenault, "Striking Dubai Workers Face Mass Deportation," Al Jazeera, May 23, 2013, http://www.aljazeera.com/indepth/features/2013/05/201352375248751541.html.

171. Ramola Talwar Badam, "Striking Labourers Back to Work on Dubai Construction Site," *The National*, March 11, 2015, https://www.thenational.ae/uae/government/striking-labourers-back-to-work-on-dubai-construction-site-1.54234.

172. W. A. Rugh, "The United Arab Emirates," 20.

173. Mansour al-Nogaidan, "Al-Ikhwan al-Muslimun fi al-Imirat: Al-Tamaddad wa-l-Inhisar" [The Muslim Brotherhood in the Emirates: Expansion and decline], in *Al-Ikhwan al-Muslimun wa-l Salafiyyun fi al-Khalij* [The Muslim Brotherhood in the Gulf], ed. Al-Mesbar Studies and Research Center (Dubai, UAE: Al-Mesbar Studies and Research Center, 2012), 65.

174. Christopher M. Davidson, *Abu Dhabi: Oil and Beyond* (Oxford: Oxford University Press, 2011), 158.

175. Ibid.

176. Federal Press and Publications Law, quoted in Christopher M. Davidson, *After the Sheikhs: The Coming Collapse of the Gulf Monarchies* (Oxford: Oxford University Press, 2013), 148.

177. *'There Is No Freedom Here,'* 55–56.

178. "UAE: Terrorism Law Threatens Lives, Liberty," Human Rights Watch, December 3, 2014, https://www.hrw.org/news/2014/12/03/uae-terrorism-law-threatens-lives-liberty.

179. Herb, "Kuwait and the United Arab Emirates," 361.

180. Davidson, *Dubai*, 214.

181. Ibid.

182. Ibid.

183. Ibid.

184. Davidson, *Abu Dhabi*, 160.

185. Interview with Emirati human rights activist, Sharjah, UAE, March 26, 2014.

186. Article 2, Constitution of the State of Kuwait; Article 1, Constitution of Qatar; Article 7, United Arab Emirates Constitution.

187. Shafeeq Ghabra, "Balancing State and Society: The Islamic Movement in Kuwait," *Middle East Policy* 5, no. 2 (1997): 59.

188. Crystal, "Coalitions in Oil Monarchies," 430.

189. Davidson, "The United Arab Emirates," 28.

CHAPTER 4

1. The Qatari Muslim Brotherhood was founded in 1975, and the Emirati branch in 1974, while the Kuwaiti branch was established in 1951.

2. Interview with current ICM MP, Kuwait City, Kuwait, November 24, 2013.

3. *Daʿwa*, literally translated to "call" or "invitation," refers to preaching or proselytizing the Islamic religion.

4. Interview with current ICM MP.

5. Ibid.

6. Ibid.

7. Ibid.

8. Ibid.

9. Tawfic E. Farah, "Political Culture and Development in a Rentier State: The Case of Kuwait," *Journal of Asian and African Studies* 24, nos. 1–2 (1989): 108.

10. Crystal, *Kuwait*, 69.

11. Farah, "Political Culture and Development in a Rentier State," 108.

12. Ali Fahed Al-Zumai, "The Intellectual and Historical Development of the Islamic Movement in Kuwait 1950–1981" (PhD diss., University of Exeter, 1988), 23.

13. Carine Lahoud-Tatar, *Islam et Politique au Koweït* [Islam and politics in Kuwait] (Paris: Presses Universitaires de France, 2011), 50.

14. Al-Zumai, "The Intellectual and Historical Development," 28.

15. Lahoud-Tatar, *Islam et Politique au Koweït*, 50–51.

16. Ibid., 51–52.

17. Ibid.

18. Al-Zumai, "The Intellectual and Historical Development," 70.

19. Ibid.

20. Lahoud-Tatar, *Islam et Politique au Koweït*, 52.

21. Al-Zumai, "The Intellectual and Historical Development," 70–71.

22. Ibid., 71.

23. Ibid.

24. Lahoud-Tatar, *Islam et Politique au Koweït*, 52.

25. Al-Zumai, "The Intellectual and Historical Development," 69.

26. Lahoud-Tatar, *Islam et Politique au Koweït*, 52.

27. Hajj, literally pilgrimage, refers to an annual religious pilgrimage to Mecca that every adult Muslim is obliged to perform once as one of the five pillars of Islam.

28. Al-Zumai, "The Intellectual and Historical Development," 70.

29. Ibid., 73.

30. ʿAbdullah al-ʿAli al-Mutawa, quoted in Sami Awadh, "Islamic Political Groups in Kuwait: Roots and Influence" (PhD diss., University of Portsmouth, 1999), 162.

31. Al-Zumai, "The Intellectual and Historical Development," 72.

32. Ibid., 73.

33. Ibid.

34. Interview with Tareq al-Suwaidan, Kuwait City, Kuwait, November 14, 2013.

35. Al-Zumai, "The Intellectual and Historical Development," 73.

36. Mustafa Muhammad al-Tahan, *ʿAbdullah al-ʿAli al-Mutawa wa-Qadayya al-Muslimin fi al-ʿAlam* [ʿAbdullah al-ʿAli al-Mutawa and the issues of Muslims in the world] (Kuwait: Mustafa Muhammad al-Tahan, 2010), 68.

37. Falah ʿAbdullah al-Mdaires, *Jamaʿat al-Ikhwan al-Muslimin fi al-Kuwait* [The Muslim Brotherhood group in Kuwait] (Kuwait: Huquq al-Taba' wa-l-Nashar Mahfuza, 1994), 15. Al-Mdaires, a Kuwaiti political scientist, has been distinguished by his suspicion toward Islamists groups of all strands inside the country. His account is used in balance with those of Islamist sympathizers, namely al-Zumai and al-Tahan, and more neutral writers like Sami Nassir al-Khalidi. Importantly, these sources do not differ greatly in terms of historical background.

38. "Al-Qanun al-Asasi li Jamʿiat al-Irshad al-Islami" [The basic law of the Islamic Guidance Association], quoted in al-Zumai, "The Intellectual and Historical Development," 74.

39. Sami Nasir al-Khalidi, *Al-Ahzab al-Islamiyya fi al-Kuwait: Al-Shiʿa, al-Ikhwan, al-Salaf* [The Islamic parties in Kuwait: The Shias, the Brotherhood, the Salafis] (Kuwait: Dar al-Nabaʿ li-l-Nashar wa-l-Tawziʿ, 1999), 163.
40. Al-Mdaires, *Jamaʿat al-Ikhwan al-Muslimin*, 15.
41. Al-Tahan, *ʿAbdullah al-ʿAli al-Mutawa*, 68.
42. Ibid.
43. Awadh, "Islamic Political Groups in Kuwait," 163–164.
44. Al-Khalidi, *Al-Ahzab al-Islamiyya fi al-Kuwait*, 163.
45. Al-Tahan, *ʿAbdullah al-ʿAli al-Mutawa*, 68.
46. Al-Khalidi, *Al-Ahzab al-Islamiyya fi al-Kuwait*, 163.
47. Al-Zumai, "The Intellectual and Historical Development," 79–80.
48. Ibid., 80.
49. Al-Khalidi, *Al-Ahzab al-Islamiyya fi al-Kuwait*, 166.
50. Al-Zumai, "The Intellectual and Historical Development," 80–81.
51. Ibid., 81.
52. Al-Tahan, *ʿAbdullah al-ʿAli al-Mutawa*, 71.
53. Zakat, the third of the five pillars of Islam, is an obligatory annual payment, or tax, given toward charity.
54. Al-Zumai, "The Intellectual and Historical Development," 79.
55. Ibid., 82.
56. Ibid.
57. Al-Mdaires, *Jamaʿat al-Ikhwan al-Muslimin*, 19.
58. Ibid.
59. Al-Zumai, "The Intellectual and Historical Development," 84–85.
60. Ibid., 85.
61. Ibid., 86–87.
62. Al-Khalidi, *Al-Ahzab al-Islamiyya fi al-Kuwait*, 165.
63. Al-Tahan, *ʿAbdullah al-ʿAli al-Mutawa*, 69.
64. Ibid.
65. Al-Mdaires, *Jamaʿat al-Ikhwan al-Muslimin*, 17.
66. Ibid.
67. Ibid., 19.
68. Al-Zumai, "The Intellectual and Historical Development," 90–91.
69. Ibid., 91.
70. Ibid., 92.
71. Ibid.
72. Al-Mdaires, *Jamaʿat al-Ikhwan al-Muslimin*, 20.
73. Al-Zumai, "The Intellectual and Historical Development," 92.
74. Ibid., 94.
75. Ibid., 95.
76. Awadh, "Islamic Political Groups in Kuwait," 166–168.
77. Al-Zumai, "The Intellectual and Historical Development," 97.
78. Four Brotherhood members won seats, and narrowly so.
79. Awadh,"Islamic Political Groups in Kuwait," 169.

80. Al-Tahan, *'Abdullah al-'Ali al-Mutawa*, 72.

81. Al-Zumai, "The Intellectual and Historical Development," 95.

82. Al-Khalidi, *Al-Ahzab al-Islamiyya fi al-Kuwait*, 162; Al-Mdaires, *Jama'at al-Ikhwan al-Muslimin*, 20–21.

83. Al-Zumai, "The Intellectual and Historical Development," 95.

84. Ibid., 97.

85. Law No. 24 for the Year 1962 Concerning Clubs and Public Welfare Societies, in *Records of Kuwait 1961–1965: 1965*, ed. Anita L. P. Burdett (Cambridge: Cambridge Archive Editions, 1997), 513–520.

86. Ibid., 514.

87. Al-Zumai, "The Intellectual and Historical Development," 179.

88. Ibid., 181.

89. Ibid., 182.

90. Al-Tahan, *'Abdullah al-'Ali al-Mutawa*, 74–75.

91. Al-Zumai, "The Intellectual and Historical Development," 183.

92. Ibid.

93. Ibid.

94. Al-Khalidi, *Al-Ahzab al-Islamiyya fi al-Kuwait*, 168.

95. Ibid.

96. N. J. Brown, "Pushing Toward Party Politics?," 6.

97. Interview with Tareq al-Suwaidan.

98. Al-Tahan, *'Abdullah al-'Ali al-Mutawa*, 82.

99. Al-Mdaires, *Jama'at al-Ikhwan al-Muslimin*, 22.

100. Awadh, "Islamic Political Groups in Kuwait," 191.

101. Al-Mdaires, *Jama'at al-Ikhwan al-Muslimin*, 22.

102. Ibid.

103. "BBC Monitor Report of 3 May 1966: Kuwait Premier Accuses 'Newcomers' of 'Harmful Activities' against National Unity," in *Records of Kuwait 1966–1971: 1966*, ed. Anita L. P. Burdett (Cambridge: Cambridge Archive Editions, 2003), 170–172; "Counter Subversion Committee: Working Group on the Persian Gulf (Including Kuwait)," Meeting Record, August 12, 1965, in *Records of Kuwait 1961–1965: 1965*, ed. Anita L. P. Burdett (Cambridge: Cambridge Archive Editions, 1997), 323–329.

104. Al-Mdaires, *Jama'at al-Ikhwan al-Muslimin*, 22.

105. Al-Khalidi, *Al-Ahzab al-Islamiyya fi al-Kuwait*, 173.

106. Ibid.

107. Awadh, "Islamic Political Groups in Kuwait," 181.

108. Al-Khalidi, *Al-Ahzab al-Islamiyya fi al-Kuwait*, 173.

109. Ibid.

110. Commins, *The Gulf States*, 236.

111. Al-Khalidi, *Al-Ahzab al-Islamiyya fi al-Kuwait*, 169.

112. Al-Mdaires, *Jama'at al-Ikhwan al-Muslimin*, 27.

113. Awadh, "Islamic Political Groups in Kuwait," 173–174.

114. Ibid., 175.

115. Ibid., 173.

116. Al-Zumai, "The Intellectual and Historical Development," 184.

117. Awadh, "Islamic Political Groups in Kuwait," 174.

118. Al-Zumai, "The Intellectual and Historical Development," 184.

119. Ibid., 186–187.

120. Ibid., 186.

121. Ibid., 176.

122. Ibid., 174.

123. Ibid.

124. Ibid., 186–187.

125. Ibid., 187.

126. Al-Khalidi, *Al-Ahzab al-Islamiyya fi al-Kuwait*, 171.

127. Al-Zumai, "The Intellectual and Historical Development," 188–189.

128. Ibid., 190.

129. Umrah is known as the "lesser pilgrimage" to Mecca. Unlike hajj, it can be performed at any time during the year and is not compulsory.

130. Al-Zumai, "The Intellectual and Historical Development," 191.

131. Ibid., 193.

132. Mustafa ʿAshur, "Tajribat al-Ikhwan al-Muslimin fi Qatar" [The experience of the Muslim Brotherhood in Qatar], in *Al-Ikhwan al-Muslimun wa-l-Salafiyyun fi al-Khalij* [The Muslim Brotherhood and Salafis in the Gulf], ed. Al-Mesbar Studies and Research Center (Dubai, UAE: Al-Mesbar Studies and Research Center, 2011), 191.

133. Ibid., 191–192.

134. Ibid., 192.

135. Ibid., 193.

136. Ibid., 194.

137. Ibid.

138. Ibid., 191.

139. ʿAbdullah al-Nafisi, "Al-Hala al-Islamia fi Qatar," [The Islamic situation in Qatar], *IslamToday*, March 12, 2007, http://www.islamtoday.net/bohooth/artshow-19-8828.htm.

140. Ibid.

141. Zuhair Ahmed Nafi, *Economic and Social Development in Qatar* (London: Frances Pinter Publishers, 1983), 96.

142. Ibid.

143. Ibid.

144. Matthew Gray, *Qatar: Politics and the Challenges of Development* (Boulder, CO: Lynne Rienner Publishers, 2013), 134.

145. David Roberts, "Qatar and the Muslim Brotherhood: Pragmatism or Preference?," *Middle East Policy* 21, no. 3 (2014): 85–86.

146. Ibid.

147. Abdulla Juma Kobaisi, "The Development of Education in Qatar, 1950–1966 with an Analysis of Some Educational Problems" (PhD diss., Durham University, 1979), 122–123.

148. Ibid., 122.

149. Roberts, "Pragmatism or Preference?," 86.

150. Kobaisi, "The Development of Education in Qatar," 123.

151. Ibid.

152. Ibid., 124.

153. Ibid.

154. Ibid., 125.

155. Ibid.

156. Roberts, "Qatar and the Brotherhood," 24.

157. Circular issued by Shaykh Khalifa al-Thani, quoted in Kobaisi, "The Development of Education in Qatar," 125.

158. Kobaisi, "The Development of Education in Qatar," 126.

159. Roberts, "Pragmatism or Preference?," 86

160. Kobaisi, "The Development of Education in Qatar," 126.

161. Roberts, "Pragmatism or Preference?," 86.

162. Ibid.

163. Ibid.

164. Ibid., 86–87.

165. Roberts, "Qatar and the Brotherhood," 24.

166. Ibid.

167. Ibid.

168. Ibid., 86–87.

169. Ibid., 87.

170. Ibid.

171. Ibid.

172. Ibid.

173. A *ḥalaqa* (plural *ḥalaqāt*) is a meeting, or study circle, about Islamic theology.

174. Al-Nafisi, "Al-Hala al-Islamiyya fi Qatar."

175. Roberts, "Pragmatism or Preference?," 89.

176. Ibid., 88.

177. Kobaisi, "The Development of Education in Qatar," 128.

178. Gray, *Qatar*, 33–34.

179. Ibid.

180. Crystal, *Oil and Politics*, 141.

181. Commins, *The Gulf States*, 151.

182. Crystal, *Oil and Politics*, 127.

183. Commins, *The Gulf States*, 188.

184. Fromherz, *Qatar*, 145.

185. Commins, *The Gulf States*, 188.

186. Crystal, *Oil and Politics*, 153.

187. Commins, *The Gulf States*, 188–189

188. Fromherz, *Qatar*, 146.

189. Ibid.

190. Ibid.

191. Louay Bahry, "Elections in Qatar: A Window of Democracy Opens in the Gulf," *Middle East Policy* 6, no. 4 (1999): 119.

192. Crystal, *Oil and Politics*, 139.

193. ʿAbdul Ghaffar Hussain, quoted in ʿAmr al-Turabi and Tarek al-Mubarak, "Qatar's Introspective Islamists," *Asharq al-Awsat*, June 18, 2013, https://english.aawsat.com/turabi-mubarak/features/qatars-introspective-islamists.

194. Mohamed al-Thani, *The Arab Spring and the Gulf States: Time to Embrace Change* (London: Profile Books, 2012), xiv–xv.

195. Ragaei El Mallakh, *Qatar: Development of an Oil Economy* (London: Croom Helm, 1979), 113.

196. Ibid.

197. Muhammad T. Sadik and William P. Snavely, *Bahrain, Qatar, and the United Arab Emirates: Colonial Past, Present Problems, and Future Prospects* (Lexington, MA: Lexington Books, 1972), 78.

198. Ibid., 79.

199. Al-Nafisi, "Al-Hala al-Islamiyya fi Qatar."

200. Ibid.

201. The *khuṭba* (plural *khuṭub*), literally "speech," is the formal sermon preached on Fridays, as well as on holidays of ʿ*Īd al-Fiṭr* and ʿ *Īd al-Aḍḥā*.

202. ʿAshur, "Tajribat al-Ikhwan al-Muslimin fi Qatar," 193.

203. Ibid., 191–192.

204. Ibid., 195.

205. Interview with Jassim Sultan, Doha, Qatar, November 4, 2013.

206. Al-Nafisi, "Al-Hala al-Islamiyya fi Qatar."

207. Interview with Jassim Sultan.

208. ʿAbdulaziz al-Mahmoud, "Al-Ikhwan al-Muslimun fi Qatar . . . Man hum?" [The Muslim Brotherhood in Qatar . . . who are they?], *Al-Arab*, August 1, 2012, http://www.alarab.qa/story/166996/%D8%A7%D9%84%D8%A5%D8%AE%D9%88%D8%A7%D9%86-%D8%A7%D9%84%D9%85%D8%B3%D9%84%D9%85%D9%88%D9%86-%D9%81%D9%8A-%D9%82%D8%B7%D8%B1-%D9%85%D9%86-%D9%87%D9%85.

209. Interview with Michael Stephens, Doha, Qatar, November 1, 2013.

210. Ibid.

211. Interview with Qatari majlis convener, Doha, Qatar, October 22, 2013.

212. ʿAshur, "Tajribat al-Ikhwan al-Muslimin fi Qatar," 196.

213. Interview with Dubai-based news editor, Dubai, UAE, February 12, 2014.

214. Sultan Sooud al-Qassemi, "The Brothers and the Gulf," *Foreign Policy*, December 14, 2012, http://www.foreignpolicy.com/articles/2012/12/14/Muslim_Brotherhood_Gulf_UAE_Qassemi.

215. Andrea B. Rugh, *The Political Culture of Leadership in the United Arab Emirates* (New York: Palgrave Macmillan, 2007), 4.

216. Davidson, *After the Sheikhs*, 131.

217. Okruhlik, "Rentier Wealth, Unruly Law, and the Rise of the Opposition," 297.

218. Davidson, *After the Sheikhs*, 132–133.

219. Ibid.

220. Ibid., 116.

221. For theoretical groundings in the deliberate underdevelopment of the periphery by the core, see literature on dependency theory, in particular Charles Lemert, "Wallerstein and the Uncertain Worlds," in *Uncertain Worlds: World-Systems Analysis in Changing Times*, ed.

Immanuel Wallerstein, Carlos Aguirre Rojas, and Charles Lemert (Boulder, CO: Paradigm Publishers, 2012), 151–193; Immanuel Wallerstein, *World-Systems Analysis: An Introduction* (Durham, NC: Duke University Press, 2004).

222. Davidson, *After the Sheikhs*, 132.

223. Interview with researcher based in Ras al-Khaimah, Ras al-Khaimah, UAE, March 3, 2014.

224. Interview with Dubai-based Gulf correspondent, Dubai, UAE, March 6, 2014.

225. Sean Foley, "What Wealth Cannot Buy: UAE Security at the Turn of the Twenty-First Century," in *Crises in the Contemporary Persian Gulf*, ed. Barry Rubin (London: Frank Cass, 2002), 36.

226. Sarah Mishkin, "UAE Acts to Bridge Northern Divide," *Financial Times*, June 22, 2011, http://www.ft.com/cms/s/0/b80064ba-9cef-11e0-8678-00144feabdc0.html#axzz3TJrgNtCk.

227. Interview with Dubai-based Gulf correspondent.

228. ʿAnwar Ahmad, "Abu Dhabi Population Doubles in Eight Years," *The National*, November 4, 2014, http://www.thenational.ae/uae/government/abu-dhabi-population-doubles-in-eight-years.

229. Ibid.

230. "United Arab Emirates: Statistical Appendix," International Monetary Fund Country Report 09/120, April 2009, 5, https://www.imf.org/external/pubs/ft/scr/2009/cr09120.pdf.

231. "About UAE," Abu Dhabi Chamber, 2015, https://www.abudhabichamber.ae/English/AboutUs/Pages/About-UAE-Country.aspx.

232. "Ajman Population Crosses the 262,000 Mark," *Emirates 24/7*, August 16, 2011, http://www.emirates247.com/news/ajman-population-crosses-the-262-000-mark-2011-08-16-1.413624.

233. "Annual Economic Report Ajman 2013," Department of Economic Development-Ajman, 2013, http://www.ajmanded.ae/Portal/userfiles/2013%20ADED%20Annual%20Report%20EN.pdf.

234. "United Arab Emirates: Statistical Appendix."

235. "About UAE."

236. Vivian Nereim, "Population of Dubai Rises 5 Per Cent to 2.1 Million, *The National*, February 13, 2013, http://www.thenational.ae/news/uae-news/population-of-dubai-rises-5-per-cent-to-2-1-million.

237. Tom Arnold, "Dubai Economy Expanded at Fastest Rate in Six Years in 2013," *The National*, June 18, 2014, http://www.thenational.ae/business/industry-insights/economics/dubai-economy-expanded-at-fastest-rate-in-six-years-in-2013.

238. "United Arab Emirates: Statistical Appendix."

239. "About UAE."

240. Sarah al-Deberky, "Fujairah Population up by 5.5 Per Cent," *Khaleej Times*, April 8, 2014, http://www.khaleejtimes.com/nation/inside.asp?xfile=/data/community/2014/April/community_April7.xml&section=community.

241. "Market Pulse: Fujairah," HVS Consulting, March 2014, http://rss.hsyndicate.com/file/152005343.pdf.

242. "United Arab Emirates: Statistical Appendix."

243. "About UAE."

244. Oxford Business Group, *The Report: Ras al-Khaimah 2013* (2014), 13, https://www.oxfordbusinessgroup.com/uae-ras-al-khaimah-2013.

245. "RAK's GDP at Dh30.9b in 2013: Report," *Gulf News*, October 9, 2014, http://gulfnews.com/business/economy/rak-s-gdp-at-dh30-9b-in-2013-report-1.1396508.

246. "United Arab Emirates: Statistical Appendix."

247. "About UAE."

248. FDI Intelligence, "Sharjah: Combining Cultural Heritage with Business Competitiveness," *FDI Supplement*, April/May 2013, 3.

249. Ibid.

250. "United Arab Emirates: Statistical Appendix."

251. FDI Intelligence, "Sharjah," 3.

252. Rezan Oueiti, "Businesses in Umm Al Quwain Struggle to Survive," *The National*, August 4, 2014, https://www.thenational.ae/business/travel-and-tourism/businesses-in-uaq-struggle-to-survive-1.652834.

253. "Haqa'iq wa-Arqam" [Facts and figures], Government of Umm al-Quwain, 2015, https://www.uaq.ae/ar/umm-al-quwain/about-umm-al-quwain/facts-and-figures.html.

254. "United Arab Emirates: Statistical Appendix."

255. "Saba' Imarat" (Seven Emirates), His Highness Sheikh Mohammed bin Rashid Al Maktoum, www.sheikhmohammed.com/vgn-ext-templating/v/index.jsp?vgnextoid=7dbb4c8631cb4110VgnVCM100000b0140a0aRCRD.

256. Layachi and Haireche, quoted in Mark Tessler, "The Origins of Popular Support for Islamist Movements: A Political Economy Analysis," in *Islam, Democracy, and the State in North Africa*, ed. John P. Entelis (Bloomington: Indiana University Press, 1997), 109.

257. Tessler, "The Origins of Popular Support for Islamist Movements," 99.

258. R. Hrair Dekmejian, "Islamic Revival: Catalysts, Categories, and Consequences," in *The Politics of Islamic Revivalism: Diversity and Unity*, ed. Shireen T. Hunter (Bloomington: Indiana University Press, 1988), 8.

259. Lori Plotkin Boghardt, "The Muslim Brotherhood on Trial in the UAE," The Washington Institute, April 12, 2013, http://www.washingtoninstitute.org/policy-analysis/view/the-muslim-brotherhood-on-trial-in-the-uae.

260. Interview with Emirati academic, Dubai, UAE, March 18, 2014.

261. Neil Halligan, "Citizens Rank UAE High on Quality of Life Survey," *Arabian Business*, July 20, 2014, http://www.arabianbusiness.com/citizens-rank-uae-high-on-quality-of-life-survey-558474.html.

262. Herb, "Kuwait and the United Arab Emirates," 352.

263. J. E. Peterson, *The Arab Gulf States: Steps Toward Political Participation* (New York: Praeger, 1988), 100.

264. Ibid.

265. Davidson, *After the Sheikhs*, 254.

266. Interview with researcher based in Ras al-Khaimah.

267. 'Abdullah al-Rashid, "Al-Ikhwan al-Muslimun fi al-Imarat . . . Judhur al-Fikr wa-l-Tanzim" [The Muslim Brotherhood in the Emirates . . . the roots of thought and organization], *al-Majalla*, February 10, 2013, http://www.majalla.com/arb/2013/02/article55242417/%D8%A7%D9%84%D8%A5%D8%AE%D9%88%D8%A7%D9%86-%D8%A7%D9%84%D9%85%D8%B3%D9%84%D9%85%D9%88%D9%86-%D9%81%D9%8A-%D8%A7%D9%84%D8%A5%D9%85%D8%A7%D8%B1%D8%A7%D8%AA-%D8%AC%D8%B0%D9%88%D8%B1-%D8%A7%D9%84%D9%81.

268. Davidson, *Dubai*, 256.

269. Ibid.

270. Ibid., 260.

271. Interview with researcher based in Ras al-Khaimah.

272. Ibid.

273. Davidson, *After the Sheikhs*, 185.

274. Interview with Emirati sociologist, Dubai, UAE, March 30, 2014.

275. "UAE: Authorities Enhance Surveillance of Critics," Human Rights Watch, January 12, 2017, https://www.hrw.org/news/2017/01/12/uae-authorities-enhance-surveillance-critics.

276. Interview with Dubai-based news editor.

277. Al-Nogaidan, "Al-Ikhwan al-Muslimun fi al-Imarat," 60.

278. Mohammed al-Roken, quoted in "Al-Ikhwan al-Muslimun fi al-Imirat . . . Al-Qisat al-Kamila" [The Muslim Brotherhood in the Emirates . . . the whole story], *Al-Sharq al-Awsat*, February 1, 2013, http://classic.aawsat.com/details.asp?article=715512&issueno=12484&section=4#.VGtRRofBZKp.

279. Ibid.

280. Ibid.

281. Ibid.

282. Ibid.

283. Al-Nogaidan, "Al-Ikhwan al-Muslimun fi al-Imarat," 60.

284. Ibid.

285. Interview with Emirati economist, Dubai, UAE, April 19, 2014.

286. "Al-Ikhwan al-Muslimun fi al-Amirat . . . Al-Hasim fi Muwajihat Atma' al-Jama'a" [The Muslim Brotherhood in the Emirates . . . decisiveness in the face of the group's ambitions], *Bawabat al-Harakat al-Islamiyya*, July 9, 2014, http://www.islamist-movements.com/2980. *Bawabat al-Harakat al-Islamiyya* is an Arabic language online publication run by Cairo-based researcher of Islamist movements, 'Abdul Rahim 'Ali.

287. Ibid.

288. Ibid.

289. Ibid.

290. Al-Turabi and al-Mubarak, "Qatar's Introspective Islamists."

291. Interview with Emirati political scientist, Dubai, UAE, February 10, 2014.

292. Said Nasser al-Teniji, "The UAE's Descent into Oppression," *The Guardian*, October 2, 2012, http://www.guardian.co.uk/commentisfree/2012/oct/02/uae-descent-oppression?INTCMP=SRCH.

293. Al-Nogaidan, "Al-Ikhwan al-Muslimun fi al-Imarat," 60–61.

294. Ibid., 61.

295. Interview with Emirati political scientist, Dubai.

296. Al-Nogaidan, "Al-Ikhwan al-Muslimun fi al-Imarat," 61.

297. Ibid.

298. Ibid.

299. Ibid.

300. Wanda Krause, *Women in Civil Society: The State, Islamism, and Networks in the UAE* (New York: Palgrave Macmillan, 2008), 98.

301. Al-Qassemi, "The Brothers and the Gulf."

302. Krause, *Women in Civil Society*, 98.

303. Interview with Emirati political scientist.

304. Interview with Dubai-based news editor.

305. Davidson, "Arab Nationalism and British Opposition in Dubai," 882.

306. Davidson, *The United Arab Emirates*, 81.

307. Davidson, "Arab Nationalism and British Opposition in Dubai," 885.

308. Neil Partrick, "Nationalism in the Gulf States," Kuwait Programme on Development, Governance and Globalisation in the Gulf States, no. 5, October 2009, 17, http://eprints.lse.ac.uk/55257/1/Patrick_2009.pdf.

309. Interview with Emirati political scientist.

CHAPTER 5

1. Interview with Shafeeq Ghabra, Kuwait City, Kuwait, November 21, 2013.

2. Al-Zumai, "The Intellectual and Historical Development," 201.

3. Ibid., 202.

4. Baaklini, Denoeux, and Springborg, *Legislative Politics in the Arab World*, 181.

5. Al-Zumai, "The Intellectual and Historical Development," 162–163.

6. Shafeeq Ghabra, "Voluntary Associations in Kuwait: The Foundations of a New System?," *Middle East Journal* 45, no. 2 (1991): 205.

7. Ibid.

8. Ibid.

9. Al-Mdaires, *Jamaʿat al-Ikhwan al-Muslimin*, 30–31.

10. Ghabra, "Voluntary Associations," 206.

11. Al-Mdaires, *Jamaʿat al-Ikhwan al-Muslimin*, 31.

12. In the Kuwaiti context, cooperative societies are essentially modern commercial complexes accounting for about 70 percent of total retail trade in the country. They also have a social function, spending 25 percent of their annual profits on social services for the local community, often organizing pilgrimage trips, equipping schools and hospitals, and providing social and recreational activities for local residents. "Kuwait Today," Al-Diwan Al-Amiri State of Kuwait, 2017, http://www.da.gov.kw/eng/aboutkuwait/Kuwaittoday.php.

13. Ghabra, "Voluntary Associations," 208.

14. Awadh, "Islamic Political Groups in Kuwait," 178.

15. Ghabra, "Balancing State and Society," 60.

16. Kristian Coates Ulrichsen, *Insecure Gulf: The End of Certainty and the Transition to the Post-Oil Era* (London: Hurst and Company, 2011), 98.

17. Awadh, "Islamic Political Groups in Kuwait," 178.

18. Ibid.

19. Al-Mdaires, *Jamaʿat al-Ikhwan al-Muslimin*, 32.

20. Al-Tahan, *ʿAbdullah al-ʿAli al-Mutawa*, 139.

21. Awadh, "Islamic Political Groups in Kuwait," 178.

22. Al-Zumai, "The Intellectual and Historical Development," 200.

23. Joseph Kostiner, "Kuwait and Bahrain," in *The Politics of Islamic Revivalism: Diversity and Unity*, ed. Shireen Hunter (Bloomington: Indiana University Press, 1988), 126.

24. Al-Khalidi, *Al-Ahzab al-Islamiyya fi al-Kuwait*, 171.

25. Awadh, "Islamic Political Groups in Kuwait," 178.

26. Al-Zumai, "The Intellectual and Historical Development," 200.

27. Ghabra, "Balancing State and Society," 59.

28. Al-Mdaires, *Jamaʿat al-Ikhwan al-Muslimin*, 32–34.

29. Ibid., 34.

30. Ibid., 35.

31. Ibid.

32. Ibid., 35–36.

33. Ibid., 36.

34. Al-Khalidi, *Al-Ahzab al-Islamiyya fi al-Kuwait*, 172.

35. Interview with Shafeeq Ghabra.

36. Commins, *The Gulf States*, 236.

37. Anh Nga Longva, "Nationalism in Pre-Modern Guise: The Discourse on Hadhar and Badu in Kuwait," *Middle East Studies* 38, no. 2 (2006): 176.

38. N. J. Brown, "Pushing toward Party Politics?," 14.

39. Mary Ann Tétreault, "Political Activism in Kuwait: Reform in Fits and Starts," in *Taking to the Streets: The Transformation of Arab Activism*, ed. Lina Khatib and Ellen Lust (Baltimore, MD: Johns Hopkins University Press, 2014), 281.

40. Al-Zumai, "The Intellectual and Historical Development," 197.

41. Ibid.

42. Ibid., 191–192.

43. Ibid.

44. Ibid., 192.

45. *Fiqh*, the Arabic word for "deep understanding," is Islamic jurisprudence.

46. Al-Tahan, *ʿAbdullah al-ʿAli al-Mutawa*, 76–78.

47. Ibid., 79–80.

48. Ibid., 81–84.

49. Al-Zumai, 195.

50. Ibid., 196.

51. Ibid.

52. Ibid.

53. Ibid.

54. Al-Khalidi, *Al-Ahzab al-Islamiyya fi al-Kuwait*, 175.

55. Ibid.

56. Ibid.

57. Jassim Muhalhal al-Yasin, quoted in al-Khalidi, *Al-Ahzab al-Islamiyya fi al-Kuwait*, 177.

58. Al-Zumai, "The Intellectual and Historical Development," 192.

59. Fred Lawson, "Class and State in Kuwait," *MERIP Reports* 132 (May 1985): 20.

60. Baaklini, Denoeux, and Springborg, *Legislative Politics in the Arab World*, 182.

61. Ibid.

62. Ibid.

63. Ibid.

64. Ibid.

65. Tétreault, *Stories of Democracy*, 110.

66. Carrie Rosefsky Wickham, *The Muslim Brotherhood: Evolution of an Islamist Movement* (Princeton, NJ: Princeton University Press, 2013), 200.

67. Nathan J. Brown, *When Victory Is Not an Option: Islamist Movements in Arab Politics* (Ithaca, NY: Cornell University Press, 2012), 238.

68. Crystal, *Kuwait*, 112.

69. Al-Khalidi, *Al-Ahzab al-Islamiyya fi al-Kuwait*, 176.

70. Ibid.

71. Crystal, *Kuwait*, 108.

72. Ibid., 112–113.

73. Ibid., 113.

74. Ibid.

75. Ibid.

76. Lori Plotkin Boghardt, *Kuwait amid War, Peace and Revolution: 1979–1991 and New Challenges* (London: St. Antony's College and Palgrave Macmillan, 2007), 70.

77. Ibid., 100.

78. Ibid.

79. Crystal, *Kuwait*, 114.

80. Ibid., 172.

81. Mansfield, *Kuwait*, 108.

82. Al-Tahan, *'Abdullah al-'Ali al-Mutawa*, 93.

83. Awadh, "Islamic Political Groups in Kuwait," 186.

84. Crystal, *Kuwait*, 112.

85. Kostiner, "Kuwait and Bahrain," 126.

86. Baaklini, Denoeux, and Springborg, *Legislative Politics in the Arab World*, 183.

87. Crystal, *Kuwait*, 112.

88. Plotkin Boghardt, *Kuwait amid War, Peace and Revolution*, 100.

89. Baaklini, Denoeux, and Springborg, *Legislative Politics in the Arab World*, 183.

90. Ibid., 184.

91. Crystal, *Kuwait*, 114.

92. Jill Crystal and Abdullah al-Shayeji, "The Pro-Democratic Agenda in Kuwait: Structures and Context," in *Political Liberalization and Democratization in the Arab World*, ed. Rex Brynen, Bahgat Korany, and Paul Noble (Boulder, CO: Lynne Rienner Publishers, 1998), 2:105.

93. Mansfield, *Kuwait*, 115.

94. Awadh, "Islamic Political Groups in Kuwait," 187.

95. Ghabra, "Voluntary Associations," 212.

96. Ibid.

97. Al-Tahan, *'Abdullah al-'Ali al-Mutawa*, 139.

98. Crystal and al-Shayeji, "The Pro-Democratic Agenda in Kuwait," 105.

99. Awadh, "Islamic Political Groups in Kuwait," 193–194.

100. Ibid.

101. Crystal and al-Shayeji, "The Pro-Democratic Agenda in Kuwait," 105.

102. Baaklini, Denoeux, and Springborg, *Legislative Politics in the Arab World*, 186.

103. Mansfield, *Kuwait*, 116–117.

104. Awadh, "Islamic Political Groups in Kuwait," 194.

105. Ibid.

106. Al-Mdaires, *Jamaʿat al-Ikhwan al-Muslimin*, 40.

107. Plotkin Boghardt, *Kuwait amid War, Peace and Revolution*, 143.

108. Tétreault, *Stories of Democracy*, 73.

109. Baaklini, Denoeux, and Springborg, *Legislative Politics in the Arab World*, 187.

110. Al-Tahan, *ʿAbdullah al-ʿAli al-Mutawa*, 94–95.

111. ʿAbdullah al-Nafisi, quoted in al-Khalidi, *Al-Ahzab al-Islamiyya fi al-Kuwait*, 180.

112. Kostiner, "Kuwait and Bahrain," 126.

113. Ibid.

114. Awadh, "Islamic Political Groups in Kuwait," 192.

115. Ibid.

116. Ibid., 193.

117. Al-Mdaires, *Jamaʿat al-Ikhwan al-Muslimin*, 22.

118. Awadh, "Islamic Political Groups in Kuwait," 194–195.

119. Ibid.

120. Crystal, *Oil and Politics*, 174.

121. Ibid.

122. Ibid., 175.

123. Ibid.

124. Al-Khalidi, *Al-Ahzab al-Islamiyya fi al-Kuwait*, 181.

125. Al-Mdaires, *Jamaʿat al-Ikhwan al-Muslimin*, 40–41.

126. Ibid.

127. Al-Tahan, *ʿAbdullah al-ʿAli al-Mutawa*, 106.

128. Falah Abdullah al-Mdaires, *Islamic Extremism in Kuwait: From the Muslim Brotherhood to Al-Qaeda and Other Islamist Political Groups* (London: Routledge, 2010), 40–41.

129. Ibid., 106.

130. Ibid.

131. "The Gulf Crisis, Day by Day: A Daily Newsletter from Solidarity International for Kuwait," 5th ed., Solidarity International for Kuwait, January 19, 1991, http://freekuwait.org.kw/search.php?page=086603_January-19,-1991&search=solidarity&mode=9.

132. Al-Tahan, *ʿAbdullah al-ʿAli al-Mutawa*, 107.

133. Interview with Tareq al-Suwaidan.

134. Ghabra, "Voluntary Associations," 213.

135. Awadh, "Islamic Political Groups in Kuwait," 196.

136. Ibid.

137. Ibid., 195–196.

138. Ibid., 196.

139. Crystal and al-Shayeji, "The Pro-Democratic Agenda in Kuwait," 105–106.

140. Ismael, *Kuwait*, 172–173.

141. Ibid., 173.

142. Ibid., 172.

143. Crystal, *Oil and Politics*, 176.

144. Crystal, *Kuwait*, 173.

145. Ismael, *Kuwait*, 176.
146. Al-Tahan, *ʿAbdullah al-ʿAli al-Mutawa*, 108–109.
147. Crystal, *Oil and Politics*, 178.
148. Ibid.
149. Ismael, *Kuwait*, 179.
150. Crystal, *Oil and Politics*, 178.
151. Ibid.
152. Ibid., 176.
153. Zubaida, *Islam, the People and the State*, xix.
154. N. J. Brown, "Pushing Toward Party Politics?," 6.
155. Al-Khalidi, *Al-Ahzab al-Islamiyya fi al-Kuwait*, 182.
156. Ibid.
157. Awadh, "Islamic Political Groups in Kuwait," 197.
158. Ibid.
159. Al-Khalidi, *Al-Ahzab al-Islamiyya fi al-Kuwait*, 182.
160. Awadh, "Islamic Political Groups in Kuwait," 197–198.
161. Ibid.
162. Ibid., 198.
163. Ibid.
164. Al-Khalidi, *Al-Ahzab al-Islamiyya fi al-Kuwait*, 183.
165. Awadh, "Islamic Political Groups in Kuwait," 199.
166. ʿAbbasi Madani, quoted in al-Khalidi, *Al-Ahzab al-Islamiyya fi al-Kuwait*, 183.
167. Awadh, "Islamic Political Groups in Kuwait," 199.
168. Ibid.
169. Al-Khalidi, *Al-Ahzab al-Islamiyya fi al-Kuwait*, 183.
170. Ibid., 183–184.
171. Awadh, "Islamic Political Groups in Kuwait," 202.
172. Ibid.
173. Al-Tahan, *ʿAbdullah al-ʿAli al-Mutawa*, 104.
174. Awadh, "Islamic Political Groups in Kuwait," 202.
175. Al-Khalidi, *Al-Ahzab al-Islamiyya fi al-Kuwait*, 184.
176. Ibid., 203–204.
177. A fatwa is a judgment on a matter of Islamic law handed down by a religious leader.
178. Awadh, "Islamic Political Groups in Kuwait," 205.
179. The *umma*, literally "nation," describes the entire Muslim community.
180. Awadh, "Islamic Political Groups in Kuwait," 205–206.
181. Al-Khalidi, *Al-Ahzab al-Islamiyya fi al-Kuwait*, 185.
182. Awadh, "Islamic Political Groups in Kuwait," 206–207.
183. Ibid.
184. Al-Khalidi, *Al-Ahzab al-Islamiyya fi al-Kuwait*, 185.
185. Awadh, "Islamic Political Groups in Kuwait," 208–209.
186. Al-Mdaires, *Jamaʿat al-Ikhwan al-Muslimin*, 43.
187. Al-Tahan, *ʿAbdullah al-ʿAli al-Mutawa*, 110–111.
188. N. J. Brown, *When Victory Is Not an Option*, 110.
189. Founding Statement of the ICM, quoted in al-Mdaires, *Jamaʿat al-Ikhwan al-Muslimin*, 39.

190. N. J. Brown, *When Victory Is Not an Option*, 109.
191. Al-Tahan, *'Abdullah al-'Ali al-Mutawa*, 123.
192. Interview with former ICM MP, Kuwait City, Kuwait, November 21, 2013.
193. Interview with current ICM MP.
194. Interview with former ICM MP.
195. Al-Khalidi, *Al-Ahzab al-Islamiyya fi al-Kuwait*, 189.
196. Awadh, "Islamic Political Groups in Kuwait," 210.
197. Ibid.
198. Tareq al-Suwaidan, quoted in Awadh, "Islamic Political Groups in Kuwait," 210.
199. Awadh, "Islamic Political Groups in Kuwait," 210.
200. Ibid., 211.
201. Rosefky Wickham, *The Muslim Brotherhood*, 221.
202. Awadh, "Islamic Political Groups in Kuwait," 212.
203. Crystal and al-Shayeji, "The Pro-Democratic Agenda in Kuwait," 107.
204. Ibid.
205. Interview with former ICM MP.
206. Crystal, *Kuwait*, 175.
207. Crystal, *Oil and Politics*, 180.
208. Awadh, "Islamic Political Groups in Kuwait," 212–213.
209. Ibid., 213.
210. Uzi Rabi, "The Kuwaiti Royal Family in the Postliberation Period: Reinstitutionalizing the 'First among Equals' System in Kuwait," in *Middle East Monarchies: The Challenge of Modernity*, ed. Joseph Kostiner (Boulder, CO: Lynne Rienner Publishers, 2000), 160.
211. Baaklini, Denoeux, and Springborg, *Legislative Politics in the Arab World*, 192.
212. Ghabra, "Balancing State and Society," 64.
213. Awadh, "Islamic Political Groups in Kuwait," 213.
214. Ghabra, "Balancing State and Society," 66.
215. Ibid.
216. Wickham, *The Muslim Brotherhood*, 221.
217. Ghabra, "Balancing State and Society," 65.
218. Ibid., 66.
219. Ibid.
220. Wickham, *The Muslim Brotherhood*, 221.
221. Ghabra, "Balancing State and Society," 66.
222. N. J. Brown, "Pushing Toward Party Politics?," 8.
223. Ghabra, "Balancing State and Society," 66.
224. N. J. Brown, "Pushing Toward Party Politics?," 8.
225. N. J. Brown, *When Victory Is Not an Option*, 110.
226. Awadh, "Islamic Political Groups in Kuwait," 216.
227. Ibid., 215–216.
228. N. J. Brown, *When Victory Is Not an Option*, 110.
229. N. J. Brown, "Pushing Toward Party Politics?," 13.
230. Tétreault, *Stories of Democracy*, 206.
231. Ibid.
232. Ghabra, "Balancing State and Society," 67.

233. Tétreault, *Stories of Democracy*, 206.
234. Ghabra, "Balancing State and Society," 67.
235. Rabi, "The Kuwaiti Royal Family in the Postliberation Period," 163.
236. Tétreault, "A State of Two Minds," 215.
237. Ibid.
238. Al-Mahmoud, "Al-Ikhwan al-Muslimun fi Qatar."
239. ʿAshur, "Tajribat al-Ikhwan al-Muslimin fi Qatar," 192.
240. Ibid.
241. Ibid.
242. Al-Turabi and al-Mubarak, "Qatar's Introspective Islamists."
243. Al-Mahmoud, "Al-Ikhwan al-Muslimun fi Qatar."
244. Al-Nafisi, "Al-Hala al-Islamiyya fi Qatar."
245. Ibid.
246. This publication can be found in Arabic, "Hawla Asasiyyat al-Mashruaʿ al-Islami l-Nahdat al-Umma: Qiraʿat fi fikr al-Imam al-Shahid Hasan al-Banna," Dakahlia Ikhwan, 2013, http://www.dakahliaikhwan.com/viewarticle.php?id=19446.
247. Al-Turabi and al-Mubarak, "Qatar's Introspective Islamists."
248. Ibid.
249. Ibid.
250. Al-Nafisi, "Al-Hala al-Islamiyya fi Qatar."
251. Ibid.
252. ʿAshur, "Tajribat al-Ikhwan al-Muslimin fi Qatar," 197.
253. Al-Nafisi, "Al-Hala al-Islamiyya fi Qatar."
254. Al-Turabi and al-Mubarak, "Qatar's Introspective Islamists."
255. Marc Lynch, "Muslim Brotherhood Debates," *Abu Aardvark* (blog), February 28, 2007, http://abuaardvark.typepad.com/abuaardvark/2007/02/muslim_brotherh.html.
256. ʿAshur, "Tajribat al-Ikhwan al-Muslimin fi Qatar," 188.
257. Ibid., 190.
258. Interview with Jassim Sultan.
259. Interview with Michael Stephens.
260. Ibid.
261. "The Advent of Terrorism in Qatar," *Forbes*, March 25, 2005, https://www.forbes.com/2005/03/25/cz_0325oxan_qatarattack.html.
262. Ibid.
263. Ibid.
264. Ibid.
265. Interview with Jassim Sultan.
266. Muhammad Habib, quoted in Al-Turabi and al-Mubarak, "Qatar's Introspective Islamists."
267. Al-Turabi and al-Mubarak, "Qatar's Introspective Islamists."
268. ʿAshur, "Tajribat al-Ikhwan al-Muslimin fi Qatar," 197.
269. Ibid., 198.
270. Al-Nafisi, "Al-Hala al-Islamiyya fi Qatar."
271. ʿAshur, "Tajribat al-Ikhwan al-Muslimin fi Qatar," 198.
272. Interview with Jassim Sultan.
273. Ibid.

274. Ibid.

275. Interview with Qatari majlis convener.

276. Al-Turabi and al-Mubarak.

277. Interview with Jassim Sultan.

278. Ibid.

279. Interview with Qatari academic, Doha, Qatar, November 5, 2013.

280. Interview with former resident of Qatar and current researcher of the Gulf, Skype, November 7, 2013.

281. ʿAshur, "Tajribat al-Ikhwan al-Muslimin fi Qatar," 188.

282. Interview with Jassim Sultan.

283. Interview with Qatari political commentator, Doha, Qatar, October 28, 2013.

284. Al-Nafisi, "Al-Hala al-Islamiyya fi Qatar," 198.

285. Ibid.

286. Ibid.

287. Interview with Michael Stephens.

288. Interview with Qatari political commentator.

289. Interview with Qatari educator, Doha, Qatar, October 24, 2013.

290. Al-Turabi and al-Mubarak.

291. Interview with Jassim Sultan.

292. Jassim Sultan, "Gulf Perspectives on the Muslim Brotherhood" (lecture, Brookings Doha Center, Doha, Qatar, October 9, 2013).

293. For the full Arabic text, see "Nas ʿArida 1991 wa-Asmaʿ al-Muwaqiʿyyin ʿaliha" [Text of the 1991 petition and names of signatories of it], dr-alkuwari.net, December 21, 1991, http://dr-alkuwari.net/node/151.html.

294. Crystal, "Political Reform in Qatar," 120.

295. Commins, *The Gulf States*, 282.

296. 1992 petition, quoted in Youssef M. Ibrahim, "54 Qatar Citizens Petition Emir for Free Elections," *The New York Times*, May 12, 1992, http://www.nytimes.com/1992/05/13/world/54-qatar-citizens-petition-emir-for-free-elections.html.

297. Commins, *The Gulf States*, 283.

298. Sean Foley, *The Arab Gulf States: Beyond Oil and Islam* (Boulder, CO: Lynne Rienner Publishers, 2010), 108.

299. Ibid.

300. Commins, *The Gulf States*, 283.

301. Kamrava, "Royal Factionalism and Political Liberalization," 415.

302. Rosman-Stollman, "Qatar," 191.

303. Bahry, "Elections in Qatar," 126.

304. Rosman-Stollman, "Qatar," 199.

305. Crystal, "Political Reform in Qatar," 122.

306. "Qatar," Freedom House, Countries at the Crossroads, 2004, https://freedomhouse.org/report/countries-crossroads/2004/qatar#.VRmZxkbndKo.

307. ʿAisha al-Muhannadi, quoted in Jaber al-Harmi, "Qataris Criticize Royal Funds," Associated Press, June 19, 1999, http://www.apnewsarchive.com/1999/Qataris-Criticize-Royal-Funds/id-2c814d2de83d9708694248284bbff17e.

308. Naomi Sakr, "Dynamics of GCC Press-Government Relations in the 1990s," in *Good Governance in the Middle East Oil Monarchies*, ed. Tom Pierre Najem and Martin Hetherington (London: Routledge, 2003), 107–108.

309. Ibid.

310. Bahry, "Elections in Qatar," 118.

311. Gray, *Qatar*, 56.

312. Crystal, *Oil and Politics*, 148.

313. I. William Zartman, "Opposition as Support of the State," in *Beyond Coercion: The Durability of the Arab State*, ed. Adeed I. Dawisha and I. William Zartman (London: Croom Helm, 1988), 62.

314. Fromherz, *Qatar*, 156.

315. Bernard Haykel, "Qatar and Islamism," NOREF Norwegian Peacebuilding Resource Centre, Policy Brief, February 2013, 2, https://noref.no/Publications/Regions/The-Gulf/Qatar-and-Islamism.

316. Bettina Graf and Jakob Skovogaard-Petersen, introduction to *Global Mufti: The Phenomenon of Yusuf al-Qaradawi*, ed. Bettina Graf and Jakob Skovogaard-Petersen (New York: Columbia University Press, 2009), 2.

317. Ibid., 2–3.

318. Ibid., 3.

319. Ibid.

320. Ibid.

321. Ibid.

322. Ana Belén Soage, "Yusuf Al-Qaradawi: The Muslim Brothers' Favorite Ideological Guide," in *The Muslim Brotherhood: The Organization and Policies of a Global Islamist Movement*, ed. Barry Rubin (New York: Palgrave Macmillan, 2010), 20.

323. Graf and Skovogaard-Petersen, introduction to *Global Mufti*, 5.

324. Ibid., 3.

325. Haykel, "Qatar and Islamism," 2.

326. Ibid.

327. Hicham Mourad, "Revising Qatari Policy on Egypt," *Ahram Online*, October 13, 2013, http://english.ahram.org.eg/NewsContentP/4/83822/Opinion/Revising-Qatari-policy-on-Egypt.aspx.

328. Lynch, *The Arab Uprising*, 209.

329. Bettina Graf, "Sheikh Yusuf Al-Qaradawi in Cyberspace," *Die Welt des Islams* 47, nos. 3–4 (2007): 405–406.

330. Birol Baskan and Steven Wright, "Seeds of Change: Comparing State-Religion Relations in Qatar and Saudi Arabia," *Arab Studies Quarterly* 33, no. 2 (2011): 100.

331. Ibid.

332. "Qaradawi Viewed Locally as a Moderate Scholar," WikiLeaks, Embassy of the United States Doha, July 12, 2005, https://www.wikileaks.org/plusd/cables/05DOHA1268_a.html.

333. Louay Bahry, "The New Arab Media Phenomenon: Qatar's Al Jazeera," *Middle East Policy* 8, no. 2 (2001): 93.

334. Ehab Galal, "Yūsuf al-Qaraḍāwī and the New Islamic TV," in *Global Mufti: The Phenomenon of Yusuf al-Qaradawi*, ed. Bettina Graf and Jakob Skovogaard-Petersen (New York: Columbia University Press, 2009), 157.

335. Amena Bakr, "Qaradawi's U-Turn: I Love the UAE, Saudi Arabia," Al Arabiya, April 20, 2014, http://english.alarabiya.net/en/News/2014/04/20/Qaradawi-s-U-Turn-I-love-Saudi-Arabia-UAE-.html.

336. Graf, "Sheikh Yusuf Al-Qaradawi in Cyberspace," 406–407.

337. Ibid., 416.

338. Ibid., 418–419.

339. Interview with Qatari majlis convener.

340. Roberts, "Pragmatism or Preference?," 89–90.

341. Ibid., 90.

342. Ibid.

343. Davidson, *After the Sheikhs*, 194.

344. Al-Nogaidan, "Al-Ikhwan al-Muslimun fi al-Imarat," 63.

345. Ibid.

346. Ibid.

347. Marta Saldaña, "Rentierism and Political Culture in the United Arab Emirates: The Case of UAEU Students" (PhD diss., University of Exeter, 2014), 138.

348. Al-Nogaidan, "Al-Ikhwan al-Muslimun fi al-Imarat," 63.

349. Saldaña, "Rentierism and Political Culture in the United Arab Emirates," 138.

350. Partrick, "Nationalism in the Gulf States," 15.

351. Abu Dhabi had its own system of education, with state education beginning in 1960/1961, when the first three schools were opened in that emirate. Kevin G. Fenelon, *The United Arab Emirates: An Economic and Social Survey*, 2nd ed. (London: Longman, 1973), 100.

352. Ragaei El Mallakh, *The Economic Development of the United Arab Emirates* (London: Croom Helm, 1981), 64.

353. Fenelon, *The United Arab Emirates*, 99.

354. El Mallakh, *The Economic Development*, 67.

355. Malcolm C. Peck, *The United Arab Emirates: A Venture in Unity* (Boulder, CO: Westview Press, 1986), 76.

356. Ibid.

357. Fyfe, "Wealth and Power," 324.

358. *Al-Khaleej*, quoted in Fyfe, "Wealth and Power," 325.

359. Ibid.

360. Al-Nogaidan, "Al-Ikhwan al-Muslimun fi al-Imarat," 64–65.

361. Fyfe, "Wealth and Power," 325.

362. Al-Nogaidan, "Al-Ikhwan al-Muslimun fi al-Imarat," 64.

363. Andrzej Kapiszewski, *Nationals and Expatriates: Population and Labour Dilemmas of the Gulf Cooperation Council* (Reading, UK: Ithaca Press, 2001), 165.

364. Interview with Emirati political scientist, Abu Dhabi, UAE, February 24, 2014.

365. W. A. Rugh, "The United Arab Emirates," 17.

366. "The University between Hope and Social Impact," *al-Islah* 50, no. 49 (1982), in *The Roots of Conspiracy Against the UAE*, ed. ʿAli Salem Humaid (Dubai, UAE: Al Mezmaah Studies and Research Centre, 2013), 1:105–106.

367. Interview with Emirati political scientist, Abu Dhabi.

368. Fyfe, "Wealth and Power," 324.

369. Ibid.

370. Al-Nogaidan, "Al-Ikhwan al-Muslimun fi al-Imarat," 66.

371. Ibid.

372. Ibid.

373. Ibid., 67–68.

374. Fyfe, "Wealth and Power," 327.

375. Ibid.

376. Ibid.

377. "UAE Minimizing Influence of Islamic Extremists," WikiLeaks, Embassy of the United States Abu Dhabi, November 10, 2004, http://www.wikileaks.org/plusd/cables/04ABUDHABI4061_a.html.

378. Ibid.

379. Al-Nogaidan, "Al-Ikhwan al-Muslimun fi al-Imarat," 67.

380. Ibid., 67–68.

381. Ibid., 68.

382. Ibid., 68–69.

383. Ibid., 69.

384. Ibid., 62.

385. Fyfe, "Wealth and Power," 326.

386. Ibid.

387. Ibid.

388. Butti Sultan al-Muhairi, "The Islamisation of Laws in the UAE: The Use of the Penal Code," *Arab Law Quarterly* 11, no. 4 (1996): 354–355.

389. Ibid., 362.

390. Fyfe, "Wealth and Power," 325.

391. Ibid.

392. Ibid., 326.

393. *Hudūd* refers to the portion of sharia that concerns the most egregious crimes, "crimes against God," such as adultery, fornication, apostasy, consuming intoxicants, murder, and theft. Punishments for such crimes are physical and include amputation, flagellation, and beheading. The UAE Penal Code has upheld the *hudūd* punishment for apostasy, while Qatar has also, in Law 11 of 2004, incorporated such punishments. In practice, however, *hudūd* punishments have not been applied. "Laws Criminalizing Apostasy in Selected Jurisdictions," Law Library of Congress, May 2014, http://www.loc.gov/law/help/apostasy/apostasy.pdf.

394. W. A. Rugh, "The United Arab Emirates," 17.

395. Ibid.

396. Al-Nogaidan, "Al-Ikhwan al-Muslimun fi al-Imarat," 62.

397. Ibid., 63.

398. See "Readings into Some Curricula of Private Schools in the Emirates," *al-Islah* 57 (1982), in *The Roots of Conspiracy Against the UAE*, ed. ʿAli Salem Humaid (Dubai, UAE: Al Mezmaah Research and Studies Center, 2013), 2:180–188.

399. See "Our Children and the Lovely Pig," *al-Islah* 34, no. 49 (1982), in *The Roots of Conspiracy against the UAE*, ed. ʿAli Salem Humaid (Dubai, UAE: Al Mezmaah Studies and Research Center, 2013), 1:48.

400. See "We Are Waiting for Final Ban," *al-Islah* 7, no. 50 (1982), in *The Roots of Conspiracy Against the UAE*, ed. ʿAli Salem Humaid (Dubai, UAE: Al Mezmaah Studies and Research Center, 2013), 1:69.

401. See "Frugality and Extravagance," *al-Islah* 50, no. 51 (1982), in *The Roots of Conspiracy Against the UAE*, ed. ʿAli Salem Humaid (Dubai, UAE: Al Mezmaah Studies and Research Center, 2013), 1:98–99.

402. See Omar Abdul Rahman, "The Devil Kai and the English Language," *al-Islah* 26–27, no. 49 (1982), in *The Roots of Conspiracy Against the UAE*, ed. ʿAli Salem Humaid (Dubai, UAE: Al Mezmaah Studies and Research Center, 2013), 1:40.

403. Interview with Dubai-based Gulf correspondent.

404. Al-Nogaidan, "Al-Ikhwan al-Muslimun fi al-Imarat," 62.

405. Ibid., 65.

406. Ibid.

407. "UAE University Hosts Elections for First Student Council," *The National*, October 18, 2012, http://www.thenational.ae/news/uae-news/uae-university-hosts-elections-for-first-student-council.

408. Krause, *Women in Civil Society*, 99.

409. Interview with Emirati political scientist, Dubai.

410. Al-Qassemi, "The Brothers and the Gulf."

411. Ibid.

412. Pekka Hakala, "Opposition in the United Arab Emirates," Directorate-General for External Policies, Policy Department, European Parliament, November 15, 2012, 2, http://www.europarl.europa.eu/committees/en/studiesdownload.html?languageDocument=EN&file=78691.

413. Al-Nogaidan, "Al-Ikhwan al-Muslimun fi al-Imarat," 65–66.

414. ʿAbdullah ʿAbu al-Hadi, "Why Ban Islamic Magazines?," *al-Islah* 30, no. 50 (1982), in *The Roots of Conspiracy Against the UAE*, ed. ʿAli Salem Humaid (Dubai, UAE: Al Mezmaah Studies and Research Center, 2013), 2:172.

415. "The First General Conference of Emirates Students," *al-Islah* 32 (1982), in *The Roots of Conspiracy Against the UAE*, ed. ʿAli Salem Humaid (Dubai, UAE: Al Mezmaah Studies and Research Center, 2013), 2:58–61.

416. Krause, *Women in Civil Society*, 99.

417. "Al-Ikhwan al-Muslimun fi al-Imirat."

418. Interview with Emirati political scientist, Abu Dhabi.

419. Interview with Emirati International Relations scholar, Al Ain, UAE, February 17, 2014.

420. Al-Nogaidan, "Al-Ikhwan al-Muslimun fi al-Imarat," 77.

421. Saldaña, "Rentierism and Political Culture in the United Arab Emirates," 139.

422. Hakala, "Opposition in the United Arab Emirates," 2.

423. "Al-Ikhwan al-Muslimun fi al-Imirat."

424. Ibid.

425. Hakala, "Opposition in the United Arab Emirates," 2.

426. Al-Nogaidan, 61.

427. Ibid.

428. Interview with Emirati human rights activist.

429. Al-Nogaidan, "Al-Ikhwan al-Muslimun fi al-Imarat," 78.

430. Ibid.

431. Al-Nogaidan, "Al-Ikhwan al-Muslimun fi al-Imarat," 69.

432. Ibid.

433. Mohammed al-Roken, quoted in Yara Bayoumy, "UAE Islamist Group Had No Desire to Topple Government: Families," Reuters, July 3, 2013, http://www.reuters.com/article/2013/07/02/us-emirates-trial-islah-idUSBRE9610PT20130702.

434. Al-Nogaidan, "Al-Ikhwan al-Muslimun fi al-Imarat," 71.

435. Ibid., 72.

436. " 'There Is no Freedom Here,' " 46.

437. Ibid.

438. Ibid.

CHAPTER 6

1. John Kifner, "Islamic Traditionalists Sweep Liberals in Kuwaiti Election," *The New York Times*, July 7, 2003, http://www.nytimes.com/2003/07/07/world/islamic-traditionalists-sweep-liberals-in-kuwaiti-election.html.

2. N. J. Brown, *When Victory Is Not an Option*, 111.

3. Wickham, *The Muslim Brotherhood*, 225.

4. Ibid., 228.

5. Ibid., 223.

6. Interview with current ICM MP.

7. Ghanim al-Najjar, "The Challenges Facing Kuwaiti Democracy," *Middle East Journal* 54, no. 2 (2000): 245.

8. N. J. Brown, "Pushing Toward Party Politics?," 13.

9. Ibid.

10. Ibid.

11. Margot Badran, "Gender, Islam, and the State: Kuwaiti Women in Struggle, Pre-Invasion to Postliberation," in *Islam, Gender, and Social Change*, ed. Yvonne Yazbeck Haddad and John L. Esposito (Oxford: Oxford University Press, 1998), 192.

12. Alessandra L. González, *Islamic Feminism in Kuwait: The Politics and Paradoxes* (New York: Palgrave Macmillan, 2013), 52–53.

13. Haya al-Mughni, *Women in Kuwait: The Politics of Gender* (London: Saqi Books, 1993), 120.

14. N. J. Brown, *When Victory Is Not an Option*, 111–112.

15. Ibid.

16. P. Salem, "Kuwait," 5.

17. Kjetil Selvik, "Elite Rivalry in a Semi-Democracy: The Kuwaiti Press Scene," *Middle Eastern Studies* 47, no. 3 (2011): 483.

18. Ibid., 483–484.

19. P. Salem, "Kuwait," 5.

20. Al-Tahan, *'Abdullah al-'Ali al-Mutawa*, 125.

21. Ibid., 124.

22. N. J. Brown, "Pushing Toward Party Politics?," 9.

23. Mary Ann Tétreault, "Kuwait's Annus Mirabilis," *Middle East Report Online*, September 7, 2006, http://www.merip.org/mero/mero090706.

24. P. Salem, "Kuwait," 6.

25. Tétrealt, "Kuwait's Annus Mirabilis."

26. Ibid.

27. Nathan J. Brown, "Kuwait's 2008 Parliamentary Elections: A Setback for Democratic Islamism?," Carnegie Endowment for International Peace, May 2008, 3, http://carnegieendowment.org/files/brown_kuwait2.pdf.

28. Tétreault, "Kuwait's Annus Mirabilis."

29. Ibid.

30. N. J. Brown, "Kuwait's 2008 Parliamentary Elections," 3.

31. Ibid.

32. Kenneth Katzman, "Kuwait: Security, Reform, and U.S. Policy," *Congressional Research Service*, April 26, 2011, 3, http://www.fas.org/sgp/crs/mideast/RS21513.pdf.

33. Ibid.

34. Mary Ann Tétreault, "Bottom-Up Democratization in Kuwait," in *Political Change in the Arab Gulf States*, 88.

35. Tétreault, "Political Activism in Kuwait," 281.

36. Ibid., 282.

37. Tétreault, "Bottom-Up Democratization," 88.

38. Katzman, "Kuwait," 3.

39. N. J. Brown, "Kuwait's 2008 Parliamentary Elections," 8.

40. Ibid.

41. Tétreault, "Bottom-Up Democratization," 88.

42. N. J. Brown, "Kuwait's 2008 Parliamentary Elections," 9.

43. Ibid., 5.

44. N. J. Brown, *When Victory Is Not an Option*, 113.

45. Tétreault and al-Ghanim, "The Day after 'Victory.' "

46. Ibid.

47. Wickham, *The Muslim Brotherhood*, 229.

48. N. J. Brown, *When Victory Is Not an Option*, 113.

49. Tétreault and al-Ghanim, "The Day after 'Victory.' "

50. Sharmaake Sabrie and Pekka Hakala, "Kuwait's Political Crisis Deepens," European Parliament Directorate-General for External Policies, January 2013, 10, http://www.europarl.europa.eu/delegations/en/studiesdownload.html?languageDocument=EN&file=91150.

51. Tétreault, "Bottom-Up Democratization," 91.

52. Ibid.

53. Selvik, "Elite Rivalry in a Semi-Democracy," 479.

54. Shultziner and Tétreault, Representation and Democratic Progress in Kuwait," 287.

55. Katzman, "Kuwait," 5.

56. Ibid.

57. Ibid.

58. Shultziner and Tétreault, Representation and Democratic Progress in Kuwait," 288.

59. Ibid., 287.

60. Ibid., 289.

61. Sabrie and Hakala, "Kuwait's Political Crisis Deepens, 10.

62. Ibid., 11–12.

63. Kristin Smith Diwan, "Kuwait's Balancing Act," *Foreign Policy*, October 13, 2012, http://mideast.foreignpolicy.com/posts/2012/10/23/kuwait_s_balancing_act.

64. Sabrie and Hakala, "Kuwait's Political Crisis Deepens," 11.

65. Mary Ann Tétreault, "Looking for Revolution in Kuwait," *Middle East Report Online*, November 1, 2012, http://www.merip.org/mero/mero110112.

66. Sabrie and Hakala, "Kuwait's Political Crisis Deepens," 11.

67. "Kuwait Election: Opposition Hails Boycott as Turnout Falls," BBC News, December 2, 2012, http://www.bbc.co.uk/news/world-middle-east-20571958.

68. Ibid.

69. Sabrie and Hakala, "Kuwait's Political Crisis Deepens," 6.

70. Interview with former ICM MP.

71. Ibid.

72. Fromherz, *Qatar*, 310.

73. Kamrava, "Royal Factionalism and Political Liberalization," 412.

74. Ibid.

75. Ibid., 413.

76. Fromherz, *Qatar*, 29.

77. Ibid., 144.

78. Gray, *Qatar*, 61.

79. Davidson, *After the Sheikhs*, 184.

80. Crystal, "Political Reform in Qatar," 120.

81. Heba Fahmy, "CMC Calls on Qatar's Malls to Revive 'Family Day' Policy," *Doha News*, November 17, 2015, http://dohanews.co/cmc-calls-on-qatars-malls-to-revive-family-day-policy/.

82. Heba Fahmy, "CMC Calls for Expansion of Female Taxi Driver Service in Qatar," *Doha News*, December 29, 2015, https://dohanews.co/cmc-calls-expansion-female-taxi-driver-service-qatar/.

83. Heba Fahmy, "CMC: Women in Qatar Uncomfortable with Male Salespeople," *Doha News*, March 29, 2016, https://dohanews.co/cmc-women-in-qatar-uncomfortable-with-male-salespeople/.

84. Peter Kovessy, "Qatar Ministry Bans Men from Al Khor Park on Thursdays," *Doha News*, April 4, 2016, https://dohanews.co/qatar-ministry-bans-men-al-khor-park-thursdays/.

85. Interview with long-term resident of Qatar.

86. Interview with Justin Gengler, Doha, Qatar, October 23, 2013.

87. Qatari nationals number only 278,000 as of 2014; Jure Snoj, "Population of Qatar by Nationality," *BQ Doha*, December 7, 2014, http://gulfmigration.eu/qatar-estimates-of-foreign-nationals-residing-in-qatar-by-country-of-citizenship-selected-countries-2014/. This is compared to a population of 1.4 million Emiratis as of 2013—see Mahmoud Habboush, "Call to Naturalise Some Expats Stirs Anxiety in the UAE," Reuters, October 10, 2013, http://uk.reuters.com/article/2013/10/10/uk-emirates-citizenship-feature-idUKBRE99904J20131010—and 1.1 million Kuwaitis as of 2012; "Population of Kuwait," Kuwait Government Online, June 30, 2012, http://www.e.gov.kw/sites/kgoenglish/portal/Pages/Visitors/AboutKuwait/KuwaitAtaGlane_Population.aspx.

88. Interview with Justin Gengler.

89. Interview with Qatari majlis convener.

90. Hamid, "There Aren't Protests in Qatar."

91. Ibid.

92. Interview with Qatari majlis convener.

93. Ibid.

94. Interview with current advisor to the Amiri Diwan, Doha, Qatar, October 5, 2013.

95. Interview with long-term resident of Qatar.

96. "Citizens Want Kuwait-like Govt Bounty," *The Peninsula*, January 17, 2011, http://thepeninsulaqatar.com/news/qatar/139495/citizens-want-kuwait-like-govt-bounty.

97. Ibid.

98. Ibid.

99. Ibid.

100. Zamila Bunglawala, "Young, Educated and Dependent on the Public Sector: Meeting Graduates' Aspirations and Diversifying Employment in Qatar and the UAE," Brookings Doha Center, Analysis Paper no. 4, December 2011, 21, https://www.brookings.edu/wp-content/uploads/2016/06/1215_qatar_diversify_employment_bunglawala_english.pdf.

101. Regan Doherty, "Qatar Hikes State Salaries, Pensions," Reuters, September 7, 2011, http://www.reuters.com/article/2011/09/07/qatar-salaries-idAFL5E7K70KY20110907.

102. Fromherz, *Qatar*, 30.

103. Lina Khatib, "Qatar's Foreign Policy: The Limits of Pragmatism," *International Affairs* 89, no. 2 (2013): 430.

104. ʿAli Khalifa al-Kuwari, ed., *Al-Shaʿab Yurid al-Islah fi Qatar . . . Aidan* [The people want reform in Qatar . . . too] (Beirut: Al Maaref Forum, 2012).

105. ʿAli Khalifa al-Kuwari, *Qataris for Reform*, dr-alkuwari.net, 2011, 7, http://dr-alkuwari.net/sites/akak/files/qatarisforreform-translation.pdf.

106. Interview with Michael Stephens.

107. ʿAli Khalifa al-Kuwari, quoted in "Interview with Dr. Ali Khalifa Al Kuwari, Author of 'The People Want Reform . . . in Qatar, Too'—Statehood & Participation," Heinrich Böll Stiftung Middle East, March 3, 2014, http://lb.boell.org/en/2014/03/03/interview-dr-ali-khalifa-al-kuwari-author-people-want-reform-qatar-too-statehood.

108. Interview with Qatari majlis convener.

109. "Qatar Court Upholds Poet Mohammed al-Ajami's Sentence," BBC News, October 21, 2013, http://www.bbc.co.uk/news/world-middle-east-24612650.

110. Shabina S. Khatri and Omar Chatriwala, "Lawyer: Poet Pardoned by Emir Leaving Qatar," *Doha News*, March 22, 2016, http://dohanews.co/lawyer-poet-pardoned-emir-leaving-qatar/.

111. Interview with Qatari political commentator.

112. "Freedom in the World 2012—Qatar," Freedom House, July 24, 2012, http://www.refworld.org/cgi-bin/texis/vtx/rwmain?page=country&category=&publisher=&type=&coi=QAT&rid=4562d8cf2&docid=500fda332&skip=0.

113. Kristian Coates Ulrichsen, *Qatar and the Arab Spring* (London: Hurst and Company, 2014), 54–55.

114. Ibid., 55.

115. Adam Taylor, "Qatar Arrests Reporters Investigating Migrant Worker Conditions, Again," *The Washington Post*, May 18, 2015, http://www.washingtonpost.com/blogs/worldviews/wp/2015/05/18/qatar-arrests-reporters-investigating-migrant-worker-conditions-again/.

116. Although this institute is linked to government-funded Qatar University, SESRI is also a multiyear partnership with the Institute for Social Research at the University of Michigan and is transparent about its survey methodology and sources.

117. Justin Gengler, "Qatar's Ambivalent Democratization," *Foreign Policy*, November 1, 2011, http://mideast.foreignpolicy.com/posts/2011/11/01/qataris_lesson_in_revolution.

118. Ibid.

119. Ibid.

120. Lesley Walker, "Qatar Hotels Told Not to Sell Alcohol in Run-up to Eid Al Adha," *Doha News*, April 27, 2015, http://dohanews.co/qatar-hotels-told-not-to-sell-alcohol-in-run-up-to-eid-al-adha/.

121. Lesley Walker, "QDC Starts Charging Annual Fee to Buy Alcohol in Qatar," *Doha News*, November 29, 2016, https://dohanews.co/qdc-starts-charging-annual-fee-to-buy-alcohol-in-qatar/.

122. Shabina S. Khatri, "QDC Tells Customers to Stock Up before Qatar Raises Alcohol Tax," *Doha News*, March 23, 2017, https://dohanews.co/qdc-tells-customers-stock-qatar-raises-alcohol-tax/.

123. Shabina S. Khatri, "IMF: Qatar is Postponing New Taxes on Junk Food and Alcohol," *Doha News*, August 31, 2017, https://dohanews.co/imf-qatar-is-postponing-new-taxes-on-junk-food-and-alcohol/.

124. Interview with current advisor to the Amiri Diwan.

125. Justin Gengler, "The Political Costs of Qatar's Western Orientation," *Middle East Policy* 14, no. 4 (2012): 71.

126. Elizabeth Broomhall, "Twitter Users Blast Qatar Airways, Call for Boycott," *Arabian Business*, January 9, 2012, http://www.arabianbusiness.com/twitter-users-blast-qatar-airways-call-for-boycott-439307.html.

127. Ed Attwood, "Nationals Slam Qatar Airways over Poor Service," *Arabian Business*, July 20, 2011, http://www.arabianbusiness.com/nationals-slam-qatar-airways-over-poor-service-411509.html.

128. Interview with Qatari academic.

129. Susan Hack, "Qatar's Billion-Dollar Art Collection Causes Controversy," Bloomberg, October 2, 2014, http://www.bloomberg.com/news/articles/2014-10-02/qatar-s-billion-dollar-art-collection-causes-controversy.

130. Interview with former advisor to the Amiri Diwan, Doha, Qatar, December 4, 2013.

131. Umm ʿAbdullah, quoted in Lesley Walker, "Modest Dress Campaign Revived with New 'You Matter in Qatar' Slogan," *Doha News*, May 4, 2015, http://dohanews.co/modest-dress-campaign-revived-with-new-you-matter-in-qatar-slogan/.

132. Walker, "Modest Dress Campaign."

133. Interview with Justin Gengler.

134. Ibid.

135. Ibid.

136. Zohrul Bari, "Islamic Revival in the Gulf: An Overview," *International Studies* 31, no. 49 (1994): 52.

137. Interview with Michael Stephens.

138. "Qatari Premier Says the West Should Embrace 'Arab Spring' Islamists," Al Arabiya, December 1, 2011, http://english.alarabiya.net/articles/2011/12/01/180189.html.

139. Shaykh Hamad, quoted in Khatib, "Qatar's Foreign Policy," 424

140. Interview with Steven Wright, Doha, Qatar, September 23, 2013.

141. Interview with David Roberts, Doha, Qatar, September 23, 2013.

142. Interview with member of the, British Embassy Doha, April 22, 2014.

143. Rime Allaf, "Qatar's Influence Increases in the Middle East," *The Guardian*, December 15, 2011, http://www.theguardian.com/commentisfree/2011/dec/15/qatar-influence-middle-east.

144. "The Rise of Qatar: Pygmy with the Punch of a Giant," *The Economist*, November 5, 2011, http://www.economist.com/node/21536659.

145. Interview with Gerd Nonneman, Doha, Qatar, September 22, 2013.

146. As'ad AbuKhalil, "Change in Qatar?," *Al Akhbar English*, July 2, 2013, http://english.al-akhbar.com/node/16303.

147. Interview with Mehran Kamrava, Doha, Qatar, September 19, 2013.

148. Khatib, "Qatar's Foreign Policy," 422.

149. H. Mourad, "Revising Qatari Policy on Egypt."

150. Black, "Qatar-Gulf Deal Forces Expulsion of Muslim Brotherhood Leaders."

151. 'Abdul Latif al-Zayani, quoted in "GCC Backs Qatar in Row with Egypt over Libya," Al Arabiya English, February 19, 2015, http://english.alarabiya.net/en/News/middle-east/2015/02/19/GCC-backs-Qatar-in-row-with-Egypt-over-Libya.html.

152. Habib Toumi, "Qatar Denies Involvement in Libya's Internal Conflict," *Gulf News*, March 8, 2017, http://gulfnews.com/news/gulf/qatar/qatar-denies-involvement-in-libya-s-internal-conflict-1.1990279.

153. Interview with Gulf foreign policy analyst, Doha, Qatar, October 30, 2013.

154. Interview with Jassim Sultan.

155. Gray, *Qatar*, 210.

156. Interview with Gulf foreign policy analyst.

157. Interview with Qatari educator.

158. Davidson, *After the Sheikhs*, 226.

159. Ibid.

160. Khatib, "Qatar's Foreign Policy," 423.

161. "The Rise of Qatar."

162. Omar Ashour, "Libyan Islamists Unpacked: Rise, Transformation, and Future," Brookings Doha Center, Policy Briefing, May 2012, 4, https://www.brookings.edu/wp-content/uploads/2016/06/Omar-Ashour-Policy-Briefing-English.pdf.

163. Khatib, "Qatar's Foreign Policy," 424–425.

164. Ibid.

165. Ibid.

166. Jim Sciutto, "Qatar Knocks U.S.-Led Coalition on ISIS," CNN News, February 26, 2015, http://www.cnn.com/2015/02/25/politics/isis-syria-qatar-blasts-us-coalition/.

167. "Stricter Rules to Regulate Charities," *The Peninsula*, September 16, 2014, http://thepeninsulaqatar.com/news/qatar/300295/stricter-rules-to-regulate-charities.

168. "Egypt Returns $2 Billion to Qatar in Sign of Growing Tensions," Reuters, September 19, 2013, http://www.reuters.com/article/2013/09/19/us-egypt-qatar-deposits-idusbre98i0n020130919.

169. H. Mourad, "Revising Qatari Policy on Egypt."

170. Ibid.

171. "Egypt Returns $2 Billion to Qatar."

172. Ibid.

173. "Egypt Crisis: Al-Jazeera Journalists Arrested in Cairo," BBC News, December 30, 2013, http://www.bbc.co.uk/news/world-middle-east-25546389.

174. Andrew Hammond, "Arab Awakening: Qatar's Controversial Alliance with Arab Islamists," Open Democracy, April 25, 2013, http://www.opendemocracy.net/andrew-hammond/arab-awakening-qatar's-controversial-alliance-with-arab-islamists.

175. Muhammad al-Mukhtar al-Shangiti, quoted in Hammond, "Arab Awakening."

176. Tamim bin Hamad al-Thani, "Qatar's Message to Obama," *The New York Times*, February 24, 2015, http://www.nytimes.com/2015/02/24/opinion/qatars-message-to-obama.html?_r=0.

177. Ian Black, "Qatar Emir's Mother Speaks Out over Treatment of Muslims by the West," *The Guardian*, May 26, 2015, http://www.theguardian.com/world/2015/may/26/qatar-emirs-mother-speaks-out-over-treatment-of-muslims-by-west.

178. "Islamic Leaders Describe Qatar's Moderation," Embassy of the United States Doha, WikiLeaks, March 19, 2006, https://wikileaks.org/cable/2006/03/06DOHA418.html.

179. Qatari official, quoted in Foley, *The Arab Gulf States*, 139.

180. Rosman-Stollman, "Qatar," 205–206.

181. Khatib, "Qatar's Foreign Policy," 420.

182. Interview with foreign policy expert, Doha, Qatar, October 30, 2013.

183. Gray, *Qatar*, 167.

184. Marc Lynch, *Voices of the New Arab Public: Iraq, Al-Jazeera, and Middle East Politics Today* (New York: Columbia University Press, 2006), 80.

185. Gray, *Qatar*, 168.

186. Al Jazeera employee, quoted in Danna Harman, "Backstory: Qatar Reformed by a Modern Marriage," *Christian Science Monitor*, March 6, 2007, http://www.csmonitor.com/2007/0306/p20s01-wome.html.

187. Fromherz, *Qatar*, 23.

188. Ibid., 101.

189. Interview with member of Al Jazeera International Relations management, Doha, Qatar, October 30, 2013.

190. Fromherz, *Qatar*, 24.

191. Interviews with employees of Al Jazeera English, Doha, Qatar, No September 24, 2013 and October 30, 2013.

192. Sultan Sooud al-Qassemi, "Morsi's Win Is Al Jazeera's Loss," Al-Monitor, July 1, 2012, http://www.al-monitor.com/pulse/originals/2012/al-monitor/morsys-win-is-al-jazeeras-loss.html.

193. The Amiri Diwan is the office of the amir in Qatar.

194. Interview with former advisor to the Amiri Diwan.

195. "Al Jazeera Employees Complain of Editorial Bias with Egypt Coverage," *Doha News*, September 5, 2013, http://dohanews.co/al-jazeera-employees-complain-of-editorial-bias-with-2/.

196. Ibid.

197. Ibid.

198. Interviews with employees of Al Jazeera English.

199. Lynch, *Voices of the New Arab Public*, 36–37.

200. Interview with Jamal Abdullah, Doha, Qatar, October 23, 2013.

201. Dania Saadi, "Qatar Broadcaster Al Jazeera Cuts 500 Jobs," *The National*, March 27, 2016, http://www.thenational.ae/business/media/qatar-broadcaster-al-jazeera-cuts-500-jobs.

202. Galal, "Yūsuf al- Qaraḍāwī and the New Islamic TV," 157.

203. Ibid., 159.

204. Haykel, "Qatar and Islamism," 2.

205. Ibid.

206. Ibid.

207. Interview with Qatari majlis convener.

208. Interview with Michael Stephens.

209. Ulrichsen, *Qatar and the Arab Spring*, 101–102.

210. Haykel, "Qatar and Islamism," 2.

211. "Al-Ikhwan al-Muslimun fi al-Imirat."

212. Plotkin Boghardt, "The Muslim Brotherhood in the Gulf."

213. Ibid.

214. Saldaña, "Rentierism and Political Culture in the United Arab Emirates," 140.

215. Interview with Emirati political scientist, Dubai.

216. Ibid.

217. "Al-Ikhwan al-Muslimun fi al-Imirat."

218. Interview with Saudi columnist, Doha, Qatar, October 23, 2013.

219. Al-Nogaidan, "Al-Ikhwan al-Muslimun fi al-Imarat," 72.

220. Sultan Sooud al-Qassemi, "Will Egypt's New President Rebuild Ties with the UAE?," *Gulf News*, June 27, 2012, http://gulfnews.com/opinion/thinkers/will-egypt-s-new-president-rebuild-ties-with-the-uae-1.1040772.

221. Ola Salem, "Islah 'Does Not Represent UAE Interests,'" *The National*, October 5, 2012, http://www.thenational.ae/news/uae-news/islah-does-not-represent-uae-interests.

222. Interview with Emirati political scientist, Abu Dhabi.

223. Al-Nogaidan, "Al-Ikhwan al-Muslimun fi al-Imarat," 70.

224. Ibid., 73.

225. Davidson, *After the Sheikhs*, 194–195.

226. Al-Nogaidan, "Al-Ikhwan al-Muslimun fi al-Imarat," 74.

227. Ibid., 72.

228. Ibid., 70.

229. Herb, "Kuwait and the United Arab Emirates," 359.

230. "UAE Minimizing Influence of Islamic Extremists."

231. "Ministry of Education Dismissed Eighty Three Emirati Teachers," Embassy of the United States Abu Dhabi, WikiLeaks, December 22, 2008, https://cablegatesearch.wikileaks.org/cable.php?id=08ABUDHABI1440.

232. Ibid.

233. Ibid.

234. Ibid.

235. Ibid.

236. United Arab Emirates (UAE): Events of 2008, Human Rights Watch, http://www.hrw.org/world-report-2009/united-arab-emirates-uae.

237. Ibid.

238. "UAE Criticises US Human Rights Report," *The National*, March 10, 2014, http://www.thenational.ae/uae/government/uae-criticises-us-human-rights-report.

239. "UAE Blacklists 82 Groups as 'Terrorist,'" Al Arabiya, November 15, 2014, http://english.alarabiya.net/en/News/middle-east/2014/11/15/UAE-formally-blacklists-82-groups-as-terrorist-.html.

240. Joseph Braude, "The Muslim Brotherhood's More Frightening Offshoot," *The Atlantic*, July 15, 2013, http://www.theatlantic.com/international/archive/2013/07/the-muslim-brotherhoods-more-frightening-offshoot/277786/.

241. Ministry of Foreign Affairs, quoted in "UAE Criticises US Human Rights Report."

242. Davidson, *After the Sheikhs*, 220.

243. Christopher M. Davidson, "Fear and Loathing in the Emirates," *Sada*, September 18, 2012, http://carnegieendowment.org/sada/2012/09/18/fear-and-loathing-in-emirates/fdw2.

244. Ibid.

245. Interview with Emirati human rights activist.

246. Shaykh Khalifa bin Zayed al-Nahyan, quoted in Davidson, *Abu Dhabi*, 155.

247. Interview with Emirati political scientist, Abu Dhabi.

248. Interview with Gulf analyst, Dubai, UAE, February 19, 2014.

249. Jean-Pierre Filiu, quoted in Davidson, *After the Sheikhs*, 195.

250. *'There Is No Freedom Here,'* 6.

251. Interview with Emirati human rights activist.

252. Text of the petition can be found at: "Al-Imaratiyyun Yarfa'un Risala li-Hukkam al-Imarat Tutalib bi-Islah Kolli li-l-Nizam al-Barlamani" [Emiratis address message to the rulers of the UAE calling for holistic reform of the parliamentary system], ipetitions, March 3, 2011, http://www.ipetitions.com/petition/uaepetition71/.

253. Joint statement from civil society organizations, quoted in Davidson, "Fear and Loathing in the Emirates."

254. Abdulaziz Alhies, "Concerns in the Gulf," *Al-Ahram*, December 19, 2012, http://weekly.ahram.org.eg/Print/620.aspx.

255. Interview with Emirati human rights activist.

256. Ibid.

257. The five included human rights activist Ahmed Mansoor, economist Nasser bin Ghaith, and online activists Fahad Salim Dalk, Hassan 'Ali al-Khamis, and Ahmed 'Abdul Khaleq.

258. *'There Is No Freedom Here,'* 6

259. Opinion no. 64/2011 (United Arab Emirates), United Nations Working Group on Arbitrary Detention, Alkarama Foundation, September 13, 2011, http://en.alkarama.org/documents/WGAD64-2011_UAE_ALK2011-2768_AhmedMansoor_221211_EN_Onlineversion.pdf.

260. Davidson, *After the Sheikhs*, 225.

261. Rori Donaghy, "UAE Arrest Prominent Economist and Pro-Democracy Activist," *Middle East Eye*, August 19, 2015, http://www.middleeasteye.net/news/uae-arrest-prominent-economist-and-pro-democracy-activist-2147452605.

262. Nasser bin Ghaith, quoted in "Whispered Dissent in UAE: No Sheikh-up Here," *The Economist*, March 17, 2012, http://www.economist.com/node/21550288.

263. "UAE Jails Prominent Academic for 10 Years over Tweets," *The New Arab*, March 30, 2017, https://www.alaraby.co.uk/english/news/2017/3/30/uae-jails-prominent-academic-for-10-years-over-tweets.

264. "UAE: Leading Activist Ahmed Mansoor Arrested, Says State News," *Middle East Eye*, March 21, 2017, http://www.middleeasteye.net/news/uae-arrests-prominent-activist-incitement-state-news-398273178.

265. Davidson, *After the Sheikhs*, 223.

266. *'There Is No Freedom Here,'* 7.

267. Ibid.

268. "LSE Cancels Arab Spring Forum in UAE, Citing Local Curbs," Reuters, February 23, 2013, http://uk.reuters.com/article/2013/02/23/uk-uae-university-conference-idUKBRE91M0AI20130223.

269. "Turnout in UAE's Second Election Low at 28 Percent of Handpicked Voters," Al Arabiya, September 24, 2011, http://www.alarabiya.net/articles/2011/09/24/168394.html.

270. "The United Arab Emirates: Getting Twitchy about Democracy," *The Economist*, June 30, 2011, http://www.economist.com/node/18898137.

271. Davidson, *After the Sheikhs*, 224.

272. "UAE to Invest in Poorer Northern Emirates," Reuters, March 2, 2011, http://www.reuters.com/article/2011/03/02/oukwd-uk-emirates-utilities-idAFTRE72121720110302.

273. Ibid.

274. "Turnout in UAE's Second Election Low."

275. Interview with Dubai-based political scientist, Dubai, UAE, March 13, 2014.

276. Interview with Emirati political scientist, Abu Dhabi.

277. Interview with Emirati human rights activist.

278. The seven included Shaykh Mohammad ʿAbdul Razzaq al-Siddiq, Ahmed Ghaith al-Suwaidi, ʿAli Hussain al-Hammadi, Shaheen ʿAbdullah al-Hosani, Hussain Munif ʿAbdullah al-Jabri, Hassan Al-Jabri, and Ibrahim Hassan al-Marzouqi.

279. *'There Is No Freedom Here,'* 7.

280. Davidson, *After the Sheikhs*, 225.

281. Ibid.

282. *'There Is No Freedom Here,'* 7.

283. ʿAli Salem al-Tunaiji, quoted in *'There Is No Freedom Here,'* 7–8.

284. Ibid., 7–8.

285. "UAE Islamists Deny Forming Military Wing," *Ahram Online*, September 22, 2012, http://english.ahram.org.eg/News/53525.aspx.

286. Ibid.

287. Ibid.

288. Islah statement, quoted in "UAE Islamists Deny Forming Military Wing."

289. Davidson, *After the Sheikhs*, 225.

290. *'There Is No Freedom Here,'* 7.

291. Ibid., 8.

292. Ibid.

293. Ibid.

294. "Calls for UAE to Open Islamist Trial," *News24*, April 3, 2013, http://www.news24.com/World/News/Calls-for-UAE-to-open-Islamist-trial-20130403.

295. *'There Is No Freedom Here,'* 8.

296. Interview with Emirati human rights activist.

297. *'There Is No Freedom Here,'* 9.

298. "Whispered Dissent in the UAE."

299. Hudson, "The Incremental Approach to Political Reform," 57.

300. *'There Is No Freedom Here,'* 9.

301. Ibid.

302. Ibid., 28.

303. "LSE Cancels Arab Spring Forum in UAE."

304. *'There Is No Freedom Here,'* 10.

305. Ibid., 10.

306. Sarah Leah Whitson, quoted in "UAE: Terrorism Law Threatens Lives, Liberty," Human Rights Watch, December 4, 2014, http://www.hrw.org/news/2014/12/03/uae-terrorism-law-threatens-lives-liberty.

307. "UAE Blacklists 82 Groups as 'Terrorist.' "

308. Interview with Dubai-based news editor.

309. Interview with Emirati political scientist, Dubai.

310. Ibid.

311. Ingo Forstenlechner, Emilie Rutledge, and Rashed Salem al-Nuaimi, "The UAE, the 'Arab Spring' and Different Types of Dissent," *Middle East Policy* 19, no. 4 (2012): 55.

312. Interview with Emirati political scientist, Dubai.

313. Dhahi Khalfan, quoted in Abdullah al-Rashid, "The Brothers and the Emirates," *Majalla*, February 14, 2013, http://www.majalla.com/eng/2013/02/article55238281.

314. Shaykh ʿAbdullah bin Zayed al-Nahyan, quoted in Ian Black, "Emirati Nerves Rattled by Islamists' Rise," *The Guardian*, October 12, 2012, http://www.guardian.co.uk/world/on-the-middle-east/2012/oct/12/uae-muslimbrotherhood-egypt-arabspring.

315. "Strong Words in Private from MBZ at IDEZ—Bashes Iran, Qatar, Russia," WikiLeaks, February 25, 2009, https://wikileaks.org/plusd/cables/09ABUDHABI193_a.html.

316. Yusuf al-Qaradawi, quoted in "Qatar Distances Itself from Al-Qaradawi's Remarks against UAE," *Middle East Monitor*, February 1, 2014, https://www.middleeastmonitor.com/news/middle-east/9538-qatar-distances-itself-from-al-qaradawis-remarks-against-uae.

317. "UAE Summons Qatar Envoy over Qaradawi Remarks," Al Jazeera, February 2, 2014, http://www.aljazeera.com/news/middleeast/2014/02/uae-summons-qatar-envoy-over-qaradawi-remarks-20142215393855165.html.

318. "Al-Ikhwan al-Muslimun fi al-Imirat."

319. Shaykh Yusuf al-Qaradawi, quoted in Bakr.

320. David D. Kirkpatrick, "Qatar's Support of Islamists Alienates Allies Near and Far," *The New York Times*, September 7, 2014, http://www.nytimes.com/2014/09/08/world/middleeast/qatars-support-of-extremists-alienates-allies-near-and-far.html?_r=0.

321. Mahmoud Mourad, "Prominent Muslim Brotherhood Figures to Leave Qatar," Reuters, September 13, 2014, http://www.reuters.com/article/us-egypt-qatar-brotherhood-idUSKBN0H807R20140913.

322. Shabina S. Khatri, "UAE Pardons Qatari Doctor Jailed for Supporting Banned Islamist Group," *Doha News*, May 24, 2015, http://dohanews.co/uae-pardons-qatari-doctor-jailed-for-supporting-banned-islamist-group/.

323. Ibid.

324. "UAE's Electoral Base for FNC Polls Gets 66% Wider."

325. "UAE Advisory Body Elections See 35.29% Turnout: Official," Al Arabiya, October 3, 2015, https://english.alarabiya.net/en/News/middle-east/2015/10/03/Over-224-000-eligible-UAE-voters-cast-their-ballot-in-advisory-body.html.

326. Interview with Professor of Psychology, UAE University, Al Ain, UAE, February 17, 2014.

327. Interview with Emirati academic.

328. Interview with Emirati political scientist, Abu Dhabi.

329. Ola Salem, "94 Emiratis Charged with Compromising UAE Security," *The National*, January 28, 2013. http://www.thenational.ae/news/uae-news/politics/94-emiratis-charged-with-compromising-uae-security.

330. Interview with Gulf analyst.

331. Interview with founder of Al-Mezmaah Studies and Research Center, Dubai, UAE, March 4, 2014.

CHAPTER 7

1. Interview with Kuwaiti academic, Kuwait City, Kuwait, January 29, 2014.

2. Interview with Kuwaiti political scientist, Kuwait City, Kuwait, November 17, 2013.

3. See, for example, Elizabeth Dickinson, "Why Private Gulf Financing for Syria's Extremist Rebels Risks Igniting Sectarian Conflict at Home," Saban Center at the Brookings Institution, Analysis Paper no. 16, December 2013, https://www.brookings.edu/wp-content/uploads/2016/06/private-gulf-financing-syria-extremist-rebels-sectarian-conflict-dickinson.pdf.

4. Simeon Kerr, "Kuwait Clamps Down on Terror Financing," *Financial Times*, September 9, 2014, http://www.ft.com/cms/s/0/1cd94792-3812-11e4-b69d-00144feabdc0.html#axzz3ZGcZU800.

5. Interview with former ICM MP.

6. Awadh, "Islamic Political Groups in Kuwait," 215–216.

7. "ICM Vision, Mission and Objectives," *Islamic Constitutional Movement*, 3rd ed., January 2007, 3–4.

8. N. J. Brown, "Pushing Toward Party Politics?," 11.

9. Ibid.

10. Ibid.

11. Interview with Kuwaiti political scientist.

12. Ibid.

13. Interview with a member of the British Embassy Kuwait, Kuwait City, Kuwait, November 14, 2013.

14. N. J. Brown, "Kuwait's 2008 Parliamentary Elections," 9.

15. Interview with current ICM MP, Kuwait City, Kuwait, November 18, 2013.

16. N. J. Brown, "Pushing Toward Party Politics?," 7.

17. Ibid.

18. Ibid.

19. N. J. Brown, "Kuwait's 2008 Parliamentary Elections," 7.

20. N. J. Brown, "Pushing Toward Party Politics?," 17.

21. Interview with former ICM MP; interview with Tareq al-Suwaidan.

22. Interview with Kuwaiti political scientist, Kuwait City, Kuwait, November 14, 2013.

23. Isma'il al-Shatti, quoted in Ghabra, "Balancing State and Society," 69.

24. N. J. Brown, "Kuwait's 2008 Parliamentary Elections," 6.

25. Interview with current ICM MP.

26. Ibid.

27. Interview with Kuwaiti sociologist, Kuwait City, Kuwait, November 25, 2013.

28. Interview with current ICM MP.

29. Interview with Kuwaiti political commentator, Kuwait City, Kuwait, November 27, 2013.

30. N. J. Brown, "Pushing Toward Party Politics?," 15.

31. "Kuwait to Ban Muslim Brotherhood," *Middle East Monitor*, March 16, 2014, https://www.middleeastmonitor.com/news/middle-east/10329-kuwait-to-ban-muslim-brotherhood.

32. Courtney Trenwith, "MP Calls for Ban on Kuwait's Muslim Brotherhood," *Arabian Business*, July 13, 2014, http://www.arabianbusiness.com/mp-calls-for-ban-on-kuwait-s-muslim-brotherhood-557658.html.

33. Scott Williamson and Nathan J. Brown, "Kuwait's Muslim Brotherhood under Pressure," *Foreign Policy*, November 20, 2013, http://foreignpolicy.com/2013/11/20/kuwaits-muslim-brotherhood-under-pressure/?wp_login_redirect=0.

34. "Freed Kuwait Opposition Leader Vows Protests Will Continue," *Gulf News*, July 8, 2014, http://gulfnews.com/news/gulf/kuwait/freed-kuwait-opposition-leader-vows-protests-will-continue-1.1357223.

35. E. A. D., "Kuwait's Opposition: A Reawakening," *The Economist*, April 17, 2014, http://www.economist.com/blogs/pomegranate/2014/04/kuwaits-opposition.

36. Ibid.

37. Ibid.

38. Alastair Sloan, "A Renewed Kuwaiti Opposition Rises to Fight Corruption," *Middle East Monitor*, June 11, 2014, https://www.middleeastmonitor.com/articles/middle-east/12053-a-renewed-kuwaiti-opposition-rises-to-fight-corruption.

39. Joe Stork, quoted in "Kuwait: 5 Critics Stripped of Citizenship," Human Rights Watch, August 10, 2014, http://www.hrw.org/news/2014/08/10/kuwait-5-critics-stripped-citizenship.

40. "Kuwait: Government Critics Stripped of Citizenship," Human Rights Watch, October 19, 2014, https://www.hrw.org/news/2014/10/19/kuwait-government-critics-stripped-citizenship.

41. Former Salafi MP ʿAbdullah al-Barghash, two of his brothers, and his sister were arrested, along with Ahmad Jabir al-Shammari, owner of al-Yawm satellite television and *Al-ʾAlam al-Yawm* newspaper, which are said to have ties with the secular liberal Popular Bloc.

42. A. Saleh, "ICM Accuses Government of 'Using' Citizenship File," *Kuwait Times*, August 2, 2014, http://news.kuwaittimes.net/icm-accuses-government-using-citizenship-file/.

43. "UAE to Try Kuwaiti Ex-MP over Remarks on Abu Dhabi Crown Prince," *Middle East Eye*, March 9, 2015, http://www.middleeasteye.net/news/uae-try-kuwaiti-ex-mp-over-remarks-abu-dhabi-crown-prince-1546132555.

44. Ayesha al-Khoori, "Kuwaiti Politician Convicted of Insulting UAE Leader," *The National*, November 23, 2015, http://www.thenational.ae/uae/courts/kuwaiti-politician-convicted-of-insulting-uae-leader.

45. Hamid, *Temptations of Power*, 54–55.

46. "Al-Duwailah: ʿAla al-Quwwa al-Siyasiyya an Tafham Hassasiyyat al-Marhala Tatatalab al-Taʿali ʿan al-Khilafat al-Taqlidiyya" [Al-Duwailah: The political forces must understand that the sensitivity of the stage requires the transcendence of traditional differences], Al-Harakat al-Islamiyya al-Dusturiyya, January 11, 2015, http://www.icmkw.org/site/pages/topics/alduilx_-yl649-alqu649-alsiasi629-623n-tfx_m-623n-xhsasi629-almrxhl629-ttt_lb-altyali-yn-alxlafat-altqlidi629.php?p=60#.VTOHgxfndKo.

47. Dahlia Kholaif, "Kuwait's Opposition Movements Feel the Squeeze on Freedoms," *Middle East Eye*, March 30, 2015, http://www.middleeasteye.net/news/kuwaits-opposition-movements-feel-squeeze-freedoms-1703345061.

48. "Kuwait: Opposition Protest Broken Up," Human Rights Watch, March 29, 2015, http://www.hrw.org/news/2015/03/29/kuwait-opposition-protest-broken.

49. "Kuwait Sentences Opposition Politician Mussallam Al Barrak to Two Years in Jail for 'Insulting Ruler,'" Global Voices, February 22, 2015, http://globalvoicesonline.org/2015/02/22/kuwait-sentences-opposition-politician-mussallam-al-barrak-to-two-years-in-jail-for-insulting-ruler/.

50. Linah Alsaafin, "Kuwait Security Forces Violently Disperse Anti-Government Protest," *Middle East Eye*, March 23, 2015, http://www.middleeasteye.net/news/kuwaiti-security-forces-violently-disperse-anti-government-protest-1878869579.

51. "Freed Kuwait Opposition Leader Calls for Reconciliation," *The New Arab*, April 27, 2017, https://www.alaraby.co.uk/english/news/2017/4/25/freed-kuwait-opposition-leader-calls-for-reconciliation.

52. Ibid.

53. "New Law: Kuwaitis Who Insult Emir Can't Run for Office," *Al-Monitor*, June 22, 2016, http://www.al-monitor.com/pulse/afp/2016/06/kuwait-politics-opposition-reform-parties.html.

54. Hanan al-Saadoun, "Kuwait Set to Enforce DNA Testing on All," *Kuwait Times*, January 23, 2016, http://news.kuwaittimes.net/website/kuwait-to-enforce-dna-testing-law-on-citizens-expats-visitors-tests-wont-be-used-to-determine-genealogy-affect-freedoms/.

55. "Kuwait: Court Strikes Down Draconian DNA Law," *Human Rights Watch*, October 27, 2017, https://www.hrw.org/news/2017/10/17/kuwait-court-strikes-down-draconian-dna-law..

56. "Kuwait Opposition in Strong Election Showing, *Al-Monitor*, November 24, 2016, http://www.al-monitor.com/pulse/afp/2016/11/kuwait-vote.html.

57. Kristin Smith Diwan, "Kuwait's Snap Parliamentary Elections Bring Return of the Opposition," Arab Gulf States Institute in Washington, November 29, 2016, http://www.agsiw.org/kuwaits-snap-parliamentary-elections-bring-return-opposition/.

58. B. Izzak, "Opposition Again Fails to Agree on Speaker," *Kuwait Times*, December 7, 2016, http://news.kuwaittimes.net/website/opposition-fails-agree-speaker/.

59. "Kuwait Parliament Holds Marathon Grilling of PM, Minister," Kuwait News Agency, May 11, 2017, http://www.kuna.net.kw/ArticleDetails.aspx?id=2610426&language=en.

60. B. Izzak, "Amir Agrees to Reinstate Revoked Citizenships: MPs," *Kuwait Times*, June 3, 2017, http://news.kuwaittimes.net/website/amir-agrees-reinstate-revoked-citizenships-mps/.

61. B. Izzak, "Appeals Court Jails 67 over Storming Assembly in 2011," Kuwait Times, November 27, 2017, http://news.kuwaittimes.net/website/appeals-court-jails-67-storming-assembly-2011/.

62. B Izzak, "MPs Request to Meet Amir over Tough Jail Sentences," Kuwait Times, November 28, 2017, http://news.kuwaittimes.net/website/mps-request-meet-amir-tough-jail-sentences/.

63. Ibid.

64. Interview with Kuwaiti political commentator.

65. Interview with current ICM MP.

66. N. J. Brown, "Pushing Toward Party Politics?," 13.

67. Qatar is ranked thirty-first, while the UAE came twenty-fourth. "Corruption Perceptions Index," Transparency International, 2014, https://www.transparency.org/cpi2014/results/.

68. Interview with former Kuwaiti MP, Kuwait City, Kuwait, February 2, 2014.

69. Ahmed al-Baghdadi, quoted in Wickham, *The Muslim Brotherhood*, 230.

70. Kamal al-Manufi quoted in Abdulkarim al-Dekhayal, *Kuwait: Oil, State and Political Legitimation* (Reading, UK: Ithaca Press, 2000), 77.

71. Al-Dekhayal, *Kuwait*, 77.

72. Interview with Kuwaiti columnist, Kuwait City, Kuwait, November 17, 2013.

73. Michael C. Hudson, *Arab Politics: The Search for Legitimacy* (New Haven, CT: Yale University Press, 1977), 151.

74. Interview with Kuwait-based professor of political science, Kuwait City, Kuwait, November 10, 2013.

75. Interview with Kuwaiti historian, Kuwait City, Kuwait, November 24, 2013.

76. Khalid F. al-Mutawa, Twitter post, May 16 2015, https://twitter.com/KFAlMutawa/status/599552570147737600.

77. Article 5, Legislative Degree No.4 of 1987: Concerning Public Education, in Kuwait's Report on the Elimination of Discrimination Against Women in Education to the United Nations Educational, Scientific and Cultural Organization (UNESCO), http://www.unesco.org/education/edurights/media/docs/4d4e58c1783175a9f990a10d759b758277028 27f.pdf.

78. Wickham, *The Muslim Brotherhood*, 221.

79. Establishment of Private Universities Law no. 34 for 2000, Private Universities Council, Kuwaiti Ministry of Higher Education, July 11, 2000, http://iasas.global/wp-content/uploads/2016/02/Kuwait-Int-of-Student-Affairs-Services.pdf.

80. "Case against Gender Segregation Rejected," *Arab Times*, December 17, 2015, http://www.arabtimesonline.com/news/case-against-gender-segregation-rejected-part-of-domestic-workers-law-unconstitutional/.

81. "About Kuwait University," Kuwait University, 2015, ecmwlst1.ku.edu.kw:16210/ku/AboutUniversity/AboutKU/index.htm.

82. Interview with Kuwaiti economist, Kuwait City, Kuwait, February 4, 2014. Fahad al-Zumai.

83. Interview with Kuwaiti columnist.

84. Interview with Kuwaiti economist.

85. Interview with Kuwaiti columnist.

86. Interview with former president of NUKS, January 31, 2014.

87. Ibid.

88. Ibid.

89. Interview with Kuwaiti columnist.

90. Interview with Ministry of Information officer, Kuwait City, Kuwait, November 13, 2013.

91. Interview with Kuwaiti former MP.

92. Birol Baskan and Steven Wright, "Seeds of Change: Comparing State-Religion Relations in Qatar and Saudi Arabia," *Arab Studies Quarterly* 33, no. 2 (2011): 106.

93. The grand mufti is the highest religious authority in a Sunni country.

94. Baskan and Wright, "Seeds of Change," 99.

95. Kamrava, "Royal Factionalism and Political Liberalization," 409–410.

96. Baskan and Wright, "Seeds of Change," 108.

97. Fromherz, *Qatar*, 150.

98. Baskan and Wright, "Seeds of Change," 100.

99. Ibid., 109.

100. Kamrava, "Royal Factionalism and Political Liberalization," 411.

101. Ibid.

102. Interview with Michael Stephens.

103. Ibid.

104. Kamrava, "Royal Factionalism and Political Liberalization," 408.

105. Ibid.

106. Ibid.

107. Mahi Khalaf, "The State of Qatar," in *From Charity to Social Change: Trends in Arab Philanthropy*, ed. Barbara Lethem Ibrahim and Dina H. Sherif (Cairo: The American University in Cairo Press, 2008), 156.

108. "Annual Omnibus Survey: A Survey of Life in Qatar, Executive Summary Report," Social and Economic Research Institute (SESRI), November 2012, 16, http://sesri.qu.edu.qa/sites/default/files/Eng/ExecutiveReports/2012/OmniBus2012.pdf.

109. Ibid., 15.

110. Interview with Jassim Sultan.

111. Khatib, "Qatar's Foreign Policy," 426.

112. Zoltan Pall, "Kuwaiti Salafism and Its Growing Influence in the Levant," Carnegie Endowment for International Peace, May 2014, 12, http://carnegieendowment.org/files/kuwaiti_salafists.pdf.

113. "Stricter Rules to Regulate Charities."

114. Muna Shikaki, "U.S. Targets Alleged Qatari Militant Backers," Al Arabiya, August 5, 2015, http://english.alarabiya.net/en/News/middle-east/2015/08/05/U-S-targets-alleged-Qatari-financiers-of-Al-Nusra-and-Al-Qaeda.html.

115. John Duke Anthony, *Arab States of the Lower Gulf: People, Politics, Petroleum* (Washington, DC: Middle East Institute, 1975), 81–82.

116. Ibid., 82.

117. Ibid.

118. Victoria Scott, "Selling Books in Qatar to Become Easier, Minister Vows," *Doha News*, December 15, 2013, http://dohanews.co/selling-books-in-qatar-to-become-easier-minister-vows/.

119. Interview with Shadi Hamid, Doha, Qatar, November 5, 2013.

120. Interview with Gulf analyst, Doha, Qatar, November 6, 2013.

121. Interview with Shadi Hamid.

122. Interview with Michael Stephens.

123. Ibid.

124. Interview with Qatari academic.

125. Interview with Qatari columnist.

126. Interview with Michael Stephens.

127. Interview with Qatari educator.

128. *Tafsīr*, or "explanation," is Qur'anic exegisis.

129. Interview with Qatari columnist.

130. Rosman-Stollman, "Qatar," 206.

131. Jassim Sultan, quoted in Andrew Hammond, "Arab Awakening: Qatar's Controversial Alliance with Arab Islamists," openDemocracy, April 25, 2013, http://www.opendemocracy.net/andrew-hammond/arab-awakening-qatar's-controversial-alliance-with-arab-islamists.

132. Interview with former advisor to the Amiri Diwan.

133. Al-Nafisi, "Al-Hala al-Islamiyya fi Qatar."

134. Ibid.

135. "Qatar Education Study 2012: Curriculum Report," Social and Economic Survey Research Institute (SESRI), May 2014, 7, sesri.qu.edu.qa/web/.../Qatar_Education_Study_Curriculum_Report_12.01.pdf.

136. Maha Ellili-Cherif and Michael Romanowski, "Education for a New Era: Stakeholders' Perception of Qatari Education Reform," *International Journal of Education Policy and Leadership* 8, no. 6 (2013): 1–2.

137. Ibid., 2.

138. Interview with Gerd Nonneman.

139. Ibid.

140. Interview with education policy analyst in Qatar, Doha, Qatar, September 24, 2013.

141. "Qatar Education Study 2012," 7.

142. Alisa Rubin, "Higher Education Reform in the Arab World: The Model of Qatar," Middle East Institute, July 31, 2012, http://www.mei.edu/content/higher-education-reform-arab-world-model-qatar.

143. Ellili-Cherif and Romanowski, "Education for a New Era," 13.

144. Ibid.

145. Interview with former advisor to the Amiri Diwan.

146. Shabina S. Khatri, "Nepalese Teacher Accused of Insulting Islam Released from Qatar Jail," *Doha News*, May 12, 2013, http://dohanews.co/nepalese-teacher-accused-of-insulting-islam-released/.

147. Ibid.

148. Interview with David Roberts.

149. Ibid.

150. Interview with Justin Gengler.

151. *Al-Sharq*, quoted in Gengler, "The Political Costs of Qatar's Western Orientation," 71.

152. Interview with current advisor to the Amiri Diwan.

153. Quintan Wiktorowicz and Suha Taji Farouki, "Islamic NGOs and Muslim Politics: A Case from Jordan," *Third World Quarterly* 21, no. 4 (2000): 688.

154. Nour Youssef, "Al Jazeera Film Critical of Egyptian Army Strains Egypt-Qatar Ties Further," *The New York Times*, November 28, 2016, https://www.nytimes.com/2016/11/28/world/middleeast/al-jazeera-egypt-qatar.html?_r=0.

155. "Church Bombing Inflames Already Strained Egypt-Qatar Relations," *The New Arab*, December 15, 2016, https://www.alaraby.co.uk/english/news/2016/12/15/church-bombing-inflames-already-strained-egypt-qatar-relations.

156. Associated Press, "Qatar State News Agency 'Hacked with Fake Positive Story about Israel and Iran,'" *The Telegraph*, May 24, 2017, http://www.telegraph.co.uk/news/2017/05/24/qatar-state-news-agency-hacked-fake-positive-story-israel-iran/.

157. Shabina S. Khatri, "Hackers Take Aim at Qatar by Publishing Fake News on QNA," *Doha News*, May 24, 2017, https://dohanews.co/hackers-take-aim-at-qatar-by-publishing-fake-news-on-qna/.

158. Simeon Kerr, "Saudi Arabia, UAE, Bahrain and Egypt Cut Ties with Qatar," *Financial Times*, June 5, 2017, https://www.ft.com/content/dc24473c-499e-11e7-a3f4-c742b9791d43.

159. Ibid.

160. "Qatar Crisis: UAE Threatens Sympathisers with Prison," BBC News, June 7, 2017, http://www.bbc.co.uk/news/world-middle-east-40192730.

161. Kerr, "Saudi Arabia, UAE, Bahrain and Egypt Cut Ties with Qatar."

162. "Arab Powers List 59 Individuals as Qatar-linked Terrorism Supporters," Al Arabiya, June 9, 2017, https://english.alarabiya.net/en/News/gulf/2017/06/09/Arab-countries-release-list-of-terrorist-financiers-supported-by-Qatar.html.

163. Shabina S. Khatri, "'We Are Not Ready to Surrender,' Qatar FM Says," *Doha News*, June 9, 2017, https://dohanews.co/we-are-not-ready-to-surrender-qatar-fm-says/.

164. Peter Baker, "White House Weighs Terrorist Designation for Muslim Brotherhood," *The New York Times*, February 7, 2017, https://www.nytimes.com/2017/02/07/world/middleeast/muslim-brotherhood-terrorism-trump.html.

165. Patrick Wintour, "Hamas Presents New Charter Accepting a Palestine Based on 1967 Borders," *The Guardian*, May 1, 2017, https://www.theguardian.com/world/2017/may/01/hamas-new-charter-palestine-israel-1967-borders.

166. Shabina S. Khatri, "Saudis Demand That Qatar Change the Name of Its State Mosque," *Doha News*, May 29, 2017, https://dohanews.co/saudis-demand-that-qatar-change-the-name-of-its-state-mosque/.

167. Mohammed al-Sulaimi, "'We Don't, Won't and Didn't Support the Muslim Brotherhood,' Qatar FM Tells Arab News," *Arab News*, May 17, 2017, http://www.arabnews.com/node/1100781/middle-east.

168. "Mohammed bin Salman, Trump Discuss Bin Laden's Ties to the Muslim Brotherhood," Al-Arabiya, March 16, 2017, https://english.alarabiya.net/en/features/2017/03/16/Mohammed-bin-Salman-Trump-discuss-Osama-bin-Laden-s-ties-to-Muslim-Brotherhood.html.

169. Interview with Qatar-based Gulf analyst, Doha, Qatar, September 18, 2013.

170. Interview with Steven Wright.

171. Interview with Qatari academic.

172. Interview with Qatari political commentator.

173. Gray, *Qatar*, 178–179.

174. Interview with current advisor to the Amiri Diwan.

175. Interview with former Qatar resident and current researcher of the Gulf.

176. Louay Bahry and Phebe Marr, "Qatari Women: A New Generation of Leaders?," *Middle East Policy* 12, no. 2 (2005): 110.

177. Rosman-Stollman, "Qatar," 199.

178. "The Advent of Terrorism in Qatar."

179. Anthony H. Cordesman and Khalid R. al-Rodhan, "The Gulf Military Forces in an Era of Asymmetric War: Qatar," Center for Strategic and International Studies, June 28, 2006, 158, http://csis.org/files/media/csis/pubs/060728_gulf_qatar.pdf.

180. Robert Mendick, "Al-Qaeda Terror Financier Worked for Qatari Government," *The Telegraph*, October 12, 2014, http://www.telegraph.co.uk/news/11156327/Al-Qaeda-terror-financier-worked-for-Qatari-government.html.

181. Ibid.

182. Ibid.

183. Ibid.

184. Al-Shangiti, quoted in Hammond, "Arab Awakening."

185. Hammond, "Arab Awakening."

186. Herb, "Kuwait and the United Arab Emirates," 348.

187. Davidson, *The United Arab Emirates*, 194.

188. Ola Salem, "FNC Passes Mandatory Breastfeeding Clause for Child Rights Law," *The National*, January 21, 2014, http://www.thenational.ae/uae/government/fnc-passes-mandatory-breastfeeding-clause-for-child-rights-law.

189. Ola Salem, "Call for Federal Dress-Code Law in the UAE," *The National*, June 12, 2012, http://www.thenational.ae/news/uae-news/call-for-federal-dress-code-law-in-the-uae.

190. "Local Views on Prospects for UAE Democratization, Embassy of the United States Abu Dhabi, Wikileaks, September 16, 2004, http://cables.mrkva.eu/cable.php?id=20666."

191. Ibid.

192. Ibid.

193. Anwar Gargash, quoted in "FNC Elections: 'Political Participation, Not Democracy,'" Embassy of the United States Abu Dhabi, WikiLeaks, June 27, 2006, http://wikileaks.wikimee.org/cable/2006/06/06ABUDHABI2655.html.

194. Peck, *The United Arab Emirates*, 126.

195. Ibid.

196. Davidson, *Abu Dhabi*, 135.

197. Interview with Emirati economist.

198. Davidson, *The United Arab Emirates*, 275.

199. Davidson, *After the Sheikhs*, 74.

200. Ibid.

201. Interview with researcher based in Ras al-Khaimah.

202. Ibid.

203. Interview with historian of the UAE, Abu Dhabi, UAE, April 7, 2014.

204. "UAE Minimizing Influence of Islamic Extremists."

205. Mohammed al-Dhaheri, quoted in Davidson, *The United Arab Emirates*, 275.

206. "UAE Minimizing Influence of Islamic Extremists."

207. Davidson, *After the Sheikhs*, 74.

208. Peck, *The United Arab Emirates*, 61.

209. Interview with historian of the Middle East, Dubai, UAE, March 2, 2014.

210. Ibid.

211. Interview with Emirati student, Dubai, UAE, March 17, 2014.

212. "United Arab Emirates: International Religious Freedom Report 2008," US Department of State, September 19, 2008, http://2001-2009.state.gov/g/drl/rls/irf/2008/108495.htm.

213. Interview with historian of the Middle East.

214. Andrew Hammond, *Pop Culture Arab World!: Media, Arts, and Lifestyle* (Santa Barbara, CA: ABC-CLIO, 2004), 226.

215. Partrick, "Nationalism in the Gulf States," 15–16.

216. Davidson, *Dubai*, 174.

217. Ibid.

218. Shaykh Khalifa bin Zayed al-Nahyan, quoted in Davidson, *Abu Dhabi*, 136.

219. Davidson, *Abu Dhabi*, 136.

220. Davidson, *After the Sheikhs*, 75.

221. Davidson, *Abu Dhabi*, 135.

222. Davidson, *Dubai*, 198.

223. Davidson, "The United Arab Emirates," 231.

224. Haneen Dajani, "UAE's Fatwa Council 'Will Help Fight Extreme Religious Teachings,'" *The National*, June 5, 2017, https://www.thenational.ae/uae/uae-s-new-fatwa-council-will-help-fight-extreme-religious-teachings-1.18475.

225. Peck, *The United Arab Emirates*, 60.

226. Ibid.

227. Interview with anthropologist of the Gulf, Abu Dhabi, UAE April 7, 2014.

228. Al-Nogaidan, "Al-Ikhwan al-Muslimun fi al-Imarat," 61.

229. Neil Quilliam, "The States of the Gulf Co-operation Council," in *Good Governance in the Middle East Oil Monarchies*, ed. Tom Pierre Najem and Martin Hetherington (London: Routledge, 2003), 54.

230. Davidson, "The United Arab Emirates," 10–11.

231. Davidson, *Abu Dhabi*, 148.

232. Ibid.

233. Nicola Goulding and Jason Hanna, "UAE Woman Arrested in U.S. Teacher's Mall Restroom Stabbing," CNN News, December 5, 2014, http://edition.cnn.com/2014/12/04/world/meast/uae-us-mall-killing/.

234. "Security Message for U.S. Citizens 8: Teachers at International Schools," U.S. Citizens Services, Embassy of the United States Abu Dhabi, October 29, 2014, https://www.osac.gov/pages/ContentReportDetails.aspx?cid=16516.

235. Davidson, "The United Arab Emirates," 10–11.

236. "UAE Minimizing Influence of Islamic Extremists."

237. Sami Salama, "Rise and Fall of Muslim Brotherhood in UAE," *Gulf News*, April 13, 2013, http://gulfnews.com/news/region/egypt/rise-and-fall-of-muslim-brotherhood-in-uae-1.1170002.

238. Ibid.

239. Interview with Dubai-based Gulf correspondent.

240. Plotkin Boghardt, "The Muslim Brotherhood on Trial."

241. "UAE Minimizing Influence of Islamic Extremists."

242. Ibid.

243. "U/S Burns' January 22 Meeting with Abu Dhabi Crown Prince and UAE Foreign Minister," United States Embassy Abu Dhabi, WikiLeaks, January 24, 2007. https://wikileaks.org/plusd/cables/07ABUDHABI97_a.html.

244. "UAE Minimizing Influence of Islamic Extremists."

245. Ibid.

246. Krause, *Women in Civil Society*, 104.

247. Ibid.

248. Ibid., 105.

249. Ibid.

250. Ibid., 104.

251. Interview with Emirati sociologist.

252. "UAE Islamists Deny Forming Military Wing."

253. "Nashitun Yutalibun Shuyukh al-Dawla al-Ahrar bi-l-Tadakhkhul li-Waqf Hamaqat Jihaz al-Aman bi-Haq Ahali al-Muʿtaqalin" [Activists demand the shaykhs of the free state to intervene to stop the follies of the security apparatus against the detainees' families], Jamʿiat al-Islah wa-l-Tawjih al-Ijtimaʿi, April 4, 2013, http://www.aleslaah.net/site/showthred.php?id=4493.

254. " 'Al-Irshad wa-l-Tawjih' Tughayyir Masamaha ila 'Jamʿiat Ajman li-l-Tanmia al-Ijtimaʿiyya wa-l-Thaqafiyya' " ['Guidance and Counseling' changes its name to 'Ajman Association for Social and Cultural Development'], *al-Ittihad*, February 28, 2014, http://www.alittihad.ae/details.php?id=18234&y=2014.

255. Ibid.

256. Davidson, *After the Sheikhs*, 14.

257. "UAE Jails 30 over 'Muslim Brotherhood Ties,'" BBC News, January 21, 2014, http://www.bbc.co.uk/news/world-middle-east-25824395.

258. Interview with Emirati political scientist, Dubai.

259. Interview with Emirati human rights activist.

260. Interview with founder of Al-Mezmaah Studies and Research Center.

261. Interview with Dubai-based Gulf correspondent.

262. Shaykh Mohammed bin Zayed, quoted in "UAE Minimizing Influence of Islamic Extremists."

263. Interview with Dubai-based Gulf correspondent.

264. Interview with analyst of the UAE, Dubai, March 10, 2014.

265. Mark Mazzetti and Emily B. Hager, "Secret Desert Force Set Up by Blackwater's Founder," *The New York Times*, May 14, 2011, http://www.nytimes.com/2011/05/15/world/middleeast/15prince.html.

266. Davidson, *After the Sheikhs*, 196–197.

267. "U/S Burns' January 22 Meeting."

268. "UAE Minimizing Influence of Islamic Extremists."

269. "Ministry of Education Dismissed Eighty Three Emirati Teachers."

270. Ibid.

271. Ibid.

272. Ibid.

273. Ibid.

274. Ibid.

275. Ibid.

276. Muhammad bin Hendi, quoted in Claire Ferris-Lay, "Islamic Teachers Strike over Removal," *Arabian Business*, June 16, 2008, http://www.arabianbusiness.com/islamic-teachers-strike-over-removal-48176.html.

277. "UAE Minimizing Influence of Islamic Extremists."

278. Ibid.

279. Ibid.

280. Kapiszewski, *Nationals and Expatriates*, 165–166.

281. See, for example, "Readings into Some Curricula of Private Schools in the Emirates," 180–188.

282. Forstenlechner, Rutledge, and al-Nuaimi, "The UAE, the 'Arab Spring' and Different Types of Dissent," 55.

283. "UAE Minimizing Influence of Islamic Extremists."

284. Kapiszewski, *Nationals and Expatriates*, 166.

285. "UAE Minimizing Influence of Islamic Extremists."

286. Peck, *The United Arab Emirates*, 76.

287. Ibid.

288. "UAE Minimizing Influence of Islamic Extremists."

289. Melanie Swan, "International Branch Campuses' Key Role in the UAE," *The National*, September 18, 2013, http://www.thenational.ae/uae/education/international-branch-campuses-key-role-in-the-uae.

290. "Vision and Mission and Values of MoE," United Arab Emirates Ministry of Education, https://www.moe.gov.ae/En/AboutTheMinistry/Pages/VisionMission.aspx.

291. "UAE Publishes List of Terrorist Organisations," *Gulf News*, November 15, 2014, http://gulfnews.com/news/uae/government/uae-publishes-list-of-terrorist-organisations-1.1412895.

292. Falah ʿAbdullah al-Mdaires, "Darasa hawla al-Harakat wa-l-Jamaʿat al-Siyasiyya fi al Bahrain (1938–2001): Al-Juz' 12: Jamʿiat al-Islah Tutalab bi-Iʿadat al-Nazar fi al-Qawanin allati Sadarat fi Zul Taʿtil al-Dustur" [Study on the movements and political groups in Bahrain: Part 12: Islah association calls for a restoration of the laws passed under the suspended constitution], Gulf Centre for Development Policies, 2011, https://www.gulfpolicies.com/index.php?option=com_content&view=article&id=676:-1938-2001-12-&catid=147:2011-04-09-07-47-31.

293. "Charity and Humanitarian Work," government.ae, 2015, http://beta.government.ae/en/information-and-services/charity-and-humanitarian-work.

294. Ibid.

295. Section 1, Article 3, no. 2, Rules for Licenses of Religious and Charitable Societies and Organization of their Activities in the Emirate of Dubai, Islamic Affairs and Charitable Activities Department, Government of Dubai, 2006, http://www.iacad.gov.ae/admin/storage/other/htmlDocs/Rules%20of%20Religious.pdf.

296. Ibid.

297. Section 1, Article 4, Rules for Licenses of Religious and Charitable Societies.

298. Section 2, Article 37, Rules for Licenses of Religious and Charitable Societies.

299. Article 41, Rules for Licenses of Religious and Charitable Societies.

300. Davidson, *Abu Dhabi*, 129.

301. Davidson, "The United Arab Emirates," 230.

302. Davidson, *The United Arab Emirates*, 276.

303. Ibid.

304. Ibid.

305. Noorhaidi Hasan, "Saudi Expansion, the Salafi Campaign and Arabised Islam in Indonesia," in *Kingdom without Borders: Saudi Political, Religious and Media Frontiers*, ed. Madawi al-Rasheed (London: Hurst and Company, 2008), 275.

306. "Dar Al Ber Builds More Than 200 Mosques Abroad," *The National*, April 26, 2017, http://www.thenational.ae/uae/dar-al-ber-builds-more-than-200-mosques-abroad.

307. Interview with Emirati political scientist, Abu Dhabi.

308. Mohammed al-Roken, quoted in Anthony Shadid, "The Towering Dream of Dubai," *The Washington Post*, April 30, 2006, http://www.washingtonpost.com/wp-dyn/content/article/2006/04/29/AR2006042901457.html.

309. Ibid.

310. Interview with Emirati academic.

311. Article 7, United Arab Emirates Constitution.

312. Davidson, *After the Sheikhs*, 157.

313. Ibid., 162.

314. Interview with Emirati academic.

315. Davidson, *After the Sheikhs*, 159.

316. Ibid.

317. Ibid., 160.

318. Ibid., 161.

319. Davidson, *Dubai*, 202.

320. Dhahi Khalfan, quoted in Davidson, *After the Sheikhs*, 161–162.

321. Interview with Dubai-based news editor.

322. Interview with Emirati political scientist, Dubai.

323. Jim Krane, *Dubai: The Story of the World's Fastest City* (London: Atlantic Books, 2009), 277–278.

CHAPTER 8

1. Lisa Anderson, "Fulfilling Prophecies: State Policy and Islamist Radicalism," in *Political Islam: Revolution, Radicalism, or Reform?*, ed. John L. Esposito (Boulder, CO: Lynne Rienner Publishers, 1997), 21.

2. Gause, *Oil Monarchies*, 14.

3. Ibid., 80.

4. Ibid.

5. Esposito and Piscatori, "Democratization and Islam," 429.

6. Ismail, *Rethinking Islamist Politics*, 176.

7. Jill Crystal, "Civil Society in the Arabian Gulf," in *Civil Society in the Middle East*, ed. Augustus R. Norton (New York: E.J. Brill, 1996), 2:273.

8. Ibid., 2:275.

9. Ibid.

10. John Waterbury, "From Social Contracts to Extraction Contracts," in *Islam, Democracy, and the State in North Africa*, ed. John P. Entelis (Bloomington, IN: Indiana University Press, 1997), 152.

11. Gause, *Political Opposition*, 16.

12. Ismail, *Rethinking Islamist Politics*, 176.

13. Asef Bayat, "Un-Civil Society: The Politics of the 'Informal People,'" *Third World Quarterly* 18, no. 1 (1997): 67.

14. Gause, *Oil Monarchies*, 11.

15. Ibid., 85.

16. Michael Herb, "Emirs and Parliaments in the Gulf," *Journal of Democracy* 13, no. 4 (2002): 42.

17. Ibid., 47.

18. Hamid, *Temptations of Power*, 83.

19. Ibid., 51.

20. There is no publicly available official membership list, though some one hundred people are in leadership positions, suggesting a broad following. Furthermore, regardless of official membership, nonmembers often vote for the ICM due to its involvement in broader political coalitions.

21. Hamid, *Temptations of Power*, 51.

22. Tawfic E. Farah, "Politics and Religion in Kuwait: Two Myths Examined," in *Islamic Resurgence in the Arab World*, ed. Ali E. Hillal Dessouki (New York: Praeger, 1982), 176.

23. E. A. D., "Kuwait's Opposition."

24. Hamid, *Temptations of Power*, 14.

25. Interview with current advisor to the Amiri Diwan.

26. Ismail, *Rethinking Islamist Politics*, 19.

27. Max Rodenbeck, "Witch Hunt in Egypt," *New York Review of Books*, November 16, 2000, http://www.nybooks.com/articles/archives/2000/nov/16/witch-hunt-in-egypt/.

28. Ibid.

29. Hamid, *Temptations of Power*, 54–55.

30. Ibid., 136.

31. Ibid., 117. See also Courtney Freer, "Exclusion-Moderation in the Gulf Context: Tracing the Development of Pragmatic Islamism in Kuwait," *Middle Eastern Studies*, August 2017.

32. Peterson, *The Arab Gulf States*, 11.

33. Larry Diamond, "Why Are There No Arab Democracies?," *Journal of Democracy* 21, no. 1 (2010): 100–101.

34. J. A. Clark, "Patronage, Prestige, and Power," 70.

35. Charles Hirschkind, "What Is Political Islam?," in *Political Islam: A Critical Reader*, ed. Frédéric Volpi (London: Routledge, 1997), 14.

36. Wiktorowicz and Farouki, "Islamic NGOs and Muslim Politics," 686.

37. Ibid., 688.

38. Dale F. Eickelman and James Piscatori, *Muslim Politics* (Princeton, NJ: Princeton University Press, 1996), 5.

39. Hamid, *Temptations of Power*, 11–12.

40. Luciani, "Allocation vs. Production States," 78.

41. Roy, *The Failure of Political Islam*, 68.

42. Ibid., 70.

43. Hamid, *Temptations of Power*, 14.

44. Ibid., 116–117.

45. "Saudi King Hosts Muslim Scholars Close to Brotherhood," *Middle East Monitor*, February 24, 2015, https://www.middleeastmonitor.com/news/middle-east/17159-saudi-king-hosts-muslim-scholars-close-to-brotherhood.

46. Saud bin Faysal, quoted in Mary Atkins, "Saudi Arabia Has 'No Problem' with Muslim Brotherhood: Foreign Minister," *Middle East Eye*, February 11, 2015, http://www.middleeasteye.net/news/saudi-foreign-minister-no-problem-muslim-brotherhood-230201904.

47. Shambayati, "The Rentier State, Interest Groups, and the Paradox of Autonomy," 308.

REFERENCES

ʿAbdul Rahman, Omar. "The Devil Kai and the English Language." *Al-Islah*, no. 49 (1982). In *The Roots of Conspiracy Against the UAE*, edited by ʿAli Salem Humaid, 1:39–40. Dubai, UAE: Al Mezmaah Studies and Research Center, 2013.

ʿAbu al-Hadi, ʿAbdullah. "Why Ban Islamic Magazines?" *Al-Islah* 30, no. 50 (1982). In *The Roots of Conspiracy Against the UAE*, edited by ʿAli Salem Humaid, 2:172–173. Dubai, UAE: Al Mezmaah Studies and Research Center, 2013.

Abu Dhabi Chamber. "About UAE." 2015. https://www.abudhabichamber.ae/English/AboutUs/Pages/About-UAE-Country.aspx.

AbuKhalil, Asʿad. "Change in Qatar?" *Al-Akhbar*, July 2, 2013. http://english.al-akhbar.com/node/16303.

Ahmad, Anwar. "Abu Dhabi Population Doubles in Eight Years." *The National*, November 4, 2014. http://www.thenational.ae/uae/government/abu-dhabi-population-doubles-in-eight-years.

Ahram Online. "UAE Islamists Deny Forming Military Wing." September 22, 2012. http://english.ahram.org.eg/News/53525.aspx.

Al Arabiya English. "GCC Backs Qatar in Row with Egypt over Libya." February 19, 2015. http://english.alarabiya.net/en/News/middle-east/2015/02/19/GCC-backs-Qatar-in-row-with-Egypt-over-Libya.html.

Al Arabiya News. "Qatari Premier Says the West Should Embrace 'Arab Spring' Islamists." December 1, 2011. http://english.alarabiya.net/articles/2011/12/01/180189.html.

Al-Deberky, Salah. "Fujairah Population up by 5.5 Per Cent." *Khaleej Times*, April 8, 2014. http://www.khaleejtimes.com/nation/inside.asp?xfile=/data/community/2014/April/community_April7.xml&section=community.

Al-Dekhayal, Abdulkarim. *Kuwait: Oil, State and Political Legitimation*. Reading, UK: Ithaca Press, 2000.

Al-Diwan Al-Amiri State of Kuwait. "Kuwait Today." 2017. http://www.da.gov.kw/eng/aboutkuwait/Kuwaittoday.php.

Al-Ghazali, ʿAbd al-Hamid. "Hawla Asasiyyat al-Mashruaʿ al-Islami l-Nahdat al-Umma: Qiraʿat fi fikr al-Imam al-Shahid Hasan al-Banna" [On the basics of the Islamic plan for the renaissance of the Umma: Readings in the thought of the martyr Hassan al-Banna]. Dakahlia Ikhwan, 2013. http://www.dakahliaikhwan.com/viewarticle.php?id=19446.

Al-Harakat al-Islamiyya al-Dusturiyya. "Al-Duwailah: ʿAla al-Quwwa al-Siyasiyya an Tafham Hassasiyyat al-Marhala Tatatallab al-Taʿali ʿan al-Khilafat al-Taqlidiyya" [Al-Duwailah: The political forces must understand that the sensitivity of the stage requires the transcendence of traditional differences]. January 11, 2015. http://www.icmkw.org/site/pages/topics/alduilx_-yl649-alqu649-alsiasi629-623n-tfx_m-623n-xhsasi629-almrxhl629-ttt_lb-altyali-yn-alxlafat-altqlidi629.php?p=60#.VTOHgxfndKo.

Al-Harmi, Jaber. "Qataris Criticize Royal Funds." Associated Press, June 19, 1999. http://www.apnewsarchive.com/1999/Qataris-Criticize-Royal-Funds/id-2c814d2de83d9708694248284bbff17e.

Alhies, Abdulaziz. "Concerns in the Gulf." *Al-Ahram Weekly*, December 19, 2012.
http://weekly.ahram.org.eg/Print/620.aspx.

Al-Ittihad. "'Al-Irshad wa-l-Tawjih' Tughayyir Masamaha ila 'Jamʿiat Ajman li-l-Tanmia al-Ijtimaʿiyya wa-l-Thaqafiyya'" ['Guidance and Counseling' changes its name to 'Ajman Association for Social and Cultural Development']. February 28, 2014. http://www.alittihad.ae/details.php?id=18234&y=2014.

Al-Khalidi, Sami Nasir. *Al-Ahzab al-Islamiyya fi al-Kuwait: Al-Shiʿa, al-Ikhwan, al-Salaf* [The Islamic parties in Kuwait: The Shias, the Brotherhood, the Salafis]. Kuwait: Dar al-Nabaʿ li-l-Nashar wa-l-Tawziʿ, 1999.

Al-Khoori, Ayesha. "Kuwaiti Politician Convicted of Insulting UAE Leader." *The National*, November 23, 2015. http://www.thenational.ae/uae/courts/kuwaiti-politician-convicted-of-insulting-uae-leader.

Al-Kuwari, Ali Khalifa, ed. *Al-Shaʿab Yurid al-Islah fi Qatar . . . Aidan* [The people want reform in Qatar . . . too]. Beirut: Al Maaref Forum, 2012.

Al-Kuwari, Ali Khalifa. *Qataris for Reform*. Blog of Ali Khalifa al-Kuwair, dr-alkuwari.net. 2011. http://dr-alkuwari.net/sites/akak/files/qatarisforreform-translation.pdf.

Allaf, Rime. "Qatar's Influence Increases in the Middle East." *The Guardian*, December 15, 2011. http://www.theguardian.com/commentisfree/2011/dec/15/qatar-influence-middle-east.

Al-Mahmoud, ʿAbdulaziz. "Al-Ikhwan al-Muslimun fi Qatar . . . Man hum?" [The Muslim Brotherhood in Qatar . . . who are they?]. *Al-Arab*, August 1, 2012. http://www.alarab.qa/story/166996/%D8%A7%D9%84%D8%A5%D8%AE%D9%88%D8%A7%D9%86-%D8%A7%D9%84%D9%85%D8%B3%D9%84%D9%85%D9%88%D9%86-%D9%81%D9%8A-%D9%82%D8%B7%D8%B1-%D9%85%D9%86-%D9%87%D9%85.

Al-Mdaires, Falah ʿAbdullah. "Darasa hawla al-Harakat wa-l Jamaʿat al-Siyasiyya fi al Bahrain (1938–2001): Al-Juz' 12: Jamʿiat al-Islah Tutalab bi-Iʿadat al-Nazar fi al-Qawanin allati Sadarat fi Zul Taʿtil al-Dustur" [Study on the movements and political groups in Bahrain: Part 12: Islah association calls for a restoration of the laws passed under the suspended constitution]. Gulf Center for Development Policies. 2011. https://www.gulfpolicies.com/index.php?option=com_content&view=article&id=676:-1938-2001-12-&catid=147:2011-04-09-07-47-31.

Al-Mdaires, Falah Abdullah. *Islamic Extremism in Kuwait: From the Muslim Brotherhood to Al-Qaeda and Other Islamist Groups*. London: Routledge, 2010.

Al-Mdaires, Falah Abdullah. *Jamaʿat al-Ikhwan al-Muslimin fi al-Kuwait* [The Brotherhood group in Kuwait]. Kuwait: Huquq al-Taba' wa-l-Nashar Mahfuza, 1994.

Al-Mesbar Studies and Research Center, ed. *Al-Ikhwan al-Muslimun wa-l Salafiyyun fi al-Khalij* [The Muslim Brotherhood and the Salafis in the Gulf]. Dubai, UAE: Al-Mesbar Studies and Research Center, 2012.

Al-Monitor. "Kuwait Opposition in Strong Election Showing." November 24, 2016. http://www.al-monitor.com/pulse/afp/2016/11/kuwait-vote.html.

Al-Mughni, Haya. *Women in Kuwait: The Politics of Gender*. London: Saqi Books, 1993.

Al-Muhairi, Butti Sultan. "The Islamisation of Laws in the UAE: The Use of the Penal Code." *Arab Law Quarterly* 11, no. 4 (1996): 350–371.

Al-Mutawa, Khaled F. Twitter post. May 16, 2015.
https://twitter.com/KFAlMutawa/status/599552570147737600.

Al-Nafisi, ʿAbdullah. "Al-Hala al-Islamiyya fi Qatar" [The Islamic situation in Qatar]. *IslamToday*, March 12, 2007. http://www.islamtoday.net/bohooth/artshow-19-8828.htm.

Al-Najjar, Ghanim. "The Challenges Facing Kuwaiti Democracy." *Middle East Journal* 54, no. 2 (2000): 242–258.

Al-Nogaidan, Mansour. "Al-Ikhwan al-Muslimun fi al-Imarat: Al-Tamaddad wa-l-Inhisar" [The Muslim Brotherhood in the Emirates: Expansion and decline]. In *Al-Ikhwan al-Muslimun fi al Khalij* [The Muslim Brotherhood in the Gulf], edited by Al-Mesbar Studies and Research Center, 55–105. Dubai, UAE: Al-Mesbar Studies and Research Center, 2012. Al-Qassemi, Sultan Sooud. "Morsi's Win Is Al Jazeera's Loss." Al-Monitor, July 1, 2012. http://www.al-monitor.com/pulse/originals/2012/al-monitor/morsys-win-is-al-jazeeras-loss.html.

Al-Qassemi, Sultan Sooud. "The Brothers and the Gulf." *Foreign Policy*, December 14, 2012. http://www.foreignpolicy.com/articles/2012/12/14/Muslim_Brotherhood_Gulf_UAE_Qassemi.

Al-Qassemi, Sultan Sooud. "Will Egypt's New President Rebuild Ties with the UAE?" *Gulf News*, June 27, 2012. http://gulfnews.com/opinion/thinkers/will-egypt-s-new-president-rebuild-ties-with-the-uae-1.1040772.

Al-Rashid, ʿAbdullah. "Al-Ikhwan al-Muslimun fi al-Imarat . . . Judhur al-Fikr wa-l-Tanzim" [The Muslim Brotherhood in the Emirates . . . the roots of thought and organization]. *Al-Majalla*, February 10, 2013. http://www.majalla.com/arb/2013/02/article55242417/%D8%A7%D9%84%D8%A5%D8%AE%D9%88%D8%A7%D9%86-%D8%A7%D9%84%D9%85%D8%B3%D9%84%D9%85%D9%88%D9%86-%D9%81%D9%8A-%D8%A7%D9%84%D8%A5%D9%85%D8%A7%D8%B1%D8%A7%D8%AA-%D8%AC%D8%B0%D9%88%D8%B1-%D8%A7%D9%84%D9%81.

Al-Rashid, Abdullah. "Article on History of Establishment of Muslim Brotherhood Movement in UAE." *Duhur*, February 14, 2013. http://www.duhur.com/article-on-history-of-establishment-of-muslim-brotherhood-movement-in-uae/.

Al-Rashid, Abdullah. "The Brothers and the Emirates." *Majalla*, February 14, 2013. http://www.majalla.com/eng/2013/02/article55238281.

Al-Saadoun, Hanan. "Kuwait Set to Enforce DNA Testing on All." *Kuwait Times*, January 23, 2016. http://news.kuwaittimes.net/website/kuwait-to-enforce-dna-testing-law-on-citizens-expats-visitors-tests-wont-be-used-to-determine-genealogy-affect-freedoms/.

Alsaafin, Linah. "Kuwait Security Forces Violently Disperse Anti-Government Protest." *Middle East Eye*, March 23, 2015. http://www.middleeasteye.net/news/kuwaiti-security-forces-violently-disperse-anti-government-protest-1878869579.

Alshamsi, Mansoor Jassem. *Islam and Political Reform in Saudi Arabia: The Quest for Change and Reform*. London: Routledge, 2010.

Al-Sharq al-Awsat. "Al-Ikhwan al-Muslimun fi al-Imarat . . . Al-Qisat al-Kamila" [The Muslim Brotherhood in the Emirates . . . the whole story]. February 1, 2013. http://classic.aawsat.com/details.asp?article=715512&issueno=12484&section=4#.VGtRRofBZKp.

Al-Sulaimi, Mohammed. "'We Don't, Won't and Didn't Support the Muslim Brotherhood,' Qatar FM Tells Arab News." *Arab News*, May 17, 2017. http://www.arabnews.com/node/1100781/middle-east.

Al-Tahan, Mustafa Muhammad. *'Abdullah al-'Ali al-Mutawa wa-Qadayya al-Muslimin fi al-'Alam* ['Abdullah al-'Ali al-Mutawa and the issues of Muslims in the world]. Kuwait: Mustafa Muhammad al-Tahan, 2010.

Al-Teniji, Said Nasser. "The UAE's Descent into Oppression." *The Guardian*, October 2, 2012. http://www.guardian.co.uk/commentisfree/2012/oct/02/uae-descent-oppression?INTCMP=SRCH.

Al-Thani, Mohamed. *The Arab Spring and the Gulf States: Time to Embrace Change*. London: Profile Books, 2012.

Al-Thani, Tamim bin Hamad. "Qatar's Message to Obama." *The New York Times*, February 24, 2015. http://www.nytimes.com/2015/02/24/opinion/qatars-message-to-obama.html?_r=0.

Al-Turabi, Amr, and Tarek al-Mubarak. "Qatar's Introspective Islamists." *Asharq al-Awsat*, June 18, 2013. https://english.aawsat.com/turabi-mubarak/features/qatars-introspective-islamists.

Al-Watan. "Dar al-Watan." April 2015. http://www.al-watan.com/watan.aspx?d=20150416&page=%D8%AF%D8%A7%D8%B1_%D8%A7%D9%84%D9%88%D8%B7%D9%86/%D9%85%D8%B9%D9%84%D9%88%D9%85%D8%A7%D8%AA.

Al-Zumai, Ali Fahed. "The Intellectual and Historical Development of the Islamic Movement in Kuwait 1950–1981." PhD diss., University of Exeter, 1988.

Amnesty International. *The 'Iron Fist Policy': Criminalization of Peaceful Dissent in Kuwait*. 2015. https://www.amnesty.org/download/Documents/MDE1729872015ENGLISH.PDF.

Amnesty International. "Qatar: New Cybercrimes Law Endangers Freedom of Expression." September 18, 2014. https://www.amnesty.org/en/latest/news/2014/09/qatar-new-cybercrimes-law-endangers-freedom-expression/.

Amnesty International. *'There Is No Freedom Here': Silencing Dissent in the United Arab Emirates (UAE)*. November 2014. https://www.amnestyusa.org/files/mde_250182014.pdf.

Anderson, Lisa. "Fulfilling Prophecies: State Policy and Islamist Radicalism." In *Political Islam: Revolution, Radicalism, or Reform?*, edited by John L. Esposito, 17–31. Boulder, CO: Lynne Rienner Publishers, 1997.

Anthony, John Duke. *Arab States of the Lower Gulf: People, Politics, Petroleum*. Washington, DC: Middle East Institute, 1975.

Al Arabiya. "Arab Powers List 59 Individuals as Qatar-linked Terrorism Supporters." June 9, 2017. https://english.alarabiya.net/en/News/gulf/2017/06/09/Arab-countries-release-list-of-terrorist-financiers-supported-by-Qatar.html.

Al Arabiya. "Turnout in UAE's Second Election Low at 28 Percent of Handpicked Voters." September 24, 2011. http://www.alarabiya.net/articles/2011/09/24/168394.html.

Al Arabiya. "UAE Advisory Body Elections See 35.29% Turnout: Official." October 3, 2015. https://english.alarabiya.net/en/News/middle-east/2015/10/03/Over-224-000-eligible-UAE-voters-cast-their-ballot-in-advisory-body.html.

Al Arabiya. "UAE Blacklists 82 Groups as 'Terrorist.'" November 15, 2014. http://english.alarabiya.net/en/News/middle-east/2014/11/15/UAE-formally-blacklists-82-groups-as-terrorist-.html.

Al Jazeera. "UAE Coup Plot Trial Begins in Abu Dhabi." March 4, 2013. http://www.aljazeera.com/news/middleeast/2013/03/201334725466866175.html.

Al Jazeera. "UAE Summons Qatar Envoy over Qaradawi Remarks." February 2, 2014. http://www.aljazeera.com/news/middleeast/2014/02/uae-summons-qatar-envoy-over-qaradawi-remarks-20142215393855165.html.

Al Monitor. "New Law: Kuwaitis Who Insult Emir Can't Run for Office." June 22, 2016. http://www.al-monitor.com/pulse/afp/2016/06/kuwait-politics-opposition-reform-parties.html.

Al-Rasheed, Madawi. *Muted Modernists: The Struggle over Divine Politics in Saudi Arabia*. London: Hurst, 2015.

Arnold, Tom. "Dubai Economy Expanded at Fastest Rate in Six Years in 2013." *The National*, June 18, 2014. http://www.thenational.ae/business/industry-insights/economics/dubai-economy-expanded-at-fastest-rate-in-six-years-in-2013.

Arsenault, Chris. "Striking Dubai Workers Face Mass Deportation." Al Jazeera, May 23, 2013. http://www.aljazeera.com/indepth/features/2013/05/201352375248751541.html.

Article 116, Law No. 14 of the Year 2004: The Labour Law, International Labour Organization, February 2010. http://www.ilo.org/wcmsp5/groups/public/---ed_protect/---protrav/---ilo_aids/documents/legaldocument/wcms_125871.pdf.

Ashour, Omar. "Libyan Islamists Unpacked: Rise, Transformation, and Future." Brookings Doha Center Policy Briefing, May 2012. https://www.brookings.edu/wp-content/uploads/2016/06/Omar-Ashour-Policy-Briefing-English.pdf.

ʿAshur, Mustafa. "Tajribat al-Ikhwan al-Muslimin fi Qatar" [The experience of the Muslim Brotherhood in Qatar]. In *Al-Ikhwan al-Muslimun wa-l-Salafiyyun fi al-Khalij* [The Muslim Brotherhood and Salafis in the Gulf], edited by Al-Mesbar Studies and Research Center, 187–204. Dubai, UAE: Al-Mesbar Studies and Research Center, 2011.

Associated Press. "Qatar State News Agency 'Hacked with Fake Positive Story about Israel and Iran.'" *The Telegraph*, May 24, 2017. http://www.telegraph.co.uk/news/2017/05/24/qatar-state-news-agency-hacked-fake-positive-story-israel-iran/.

Atkins, Mary. "Saudi Arabia Has 'No Problem' with Muslim Brotherhood: Foreign Minister." *Middle East Eye*, February 11, 2015. http://www.middleeasteye.net/news/saudi-foreign-minister-no-problem-muslim-brotherhood-230201904.

Attwood, Ed. "Nationals Slam Qatar Airways over Poor Service." *Arabian Business*, July 20, 2011. http://www.arabianbusiness.com/nationals-slam-qatar-airways-over-poor-service-411509.html.

Awadh, Sami. "Islamic Political Groups in Kuwait: Roots and Influence." PhD diss., University of Portsmouth, 1999.

Ayoob, Mohammed. *The Many Faces of Political Islam: Religion and Politics in the Muslim World*. Ann Arbor: University of Michigan Press, 2008.

Ayubi, Nazih. *Political Islam: Religion and Politics in the Arab World*. London: Routledge, 1991.

Baaklini, Abdo I., Guilain Denoeux, and Robert Springborg. *Legislative Politics in the Arab World: The Resurgence of Democratic Institutions*. Boulder, CO: Lynne Rienner Publishers, 1999.

Badam, Ramola Talwar Badam. "Striking Labourers Back to Work on Dubai Construction Site." *The National*, March 11, 2015. https://www.thenational.ae/uae/government/striking-labourers-back-to-work-on-dubai-construction-site-1.54234.

Badran, Margot. "Gender, Islam, and the State: Kuwaiti Women in Struggle, Pre-Invasion to Postliberation." In *Islam, Gender, and Social Change*, edited by Yvonne Yazbeck Haddad and John L. Esposito, 190–208. Oxford: Oxford University Press, 1998.

Bahry, Louay. "Elections in Qatar: A Window of Democracy Opens in the Gulf." *Middle East Policy* 6, no. 4 (1999): 118–127.

Bahry, Louay. "The New Arab Media Phenomenon: Qatar's Al Jazeera." *Middle East Policy* 8, no. 2 (2001): 88–99.

Bahry, Louay, and Phebe Marr. "Qatari Women: A New Generation of Leaders?" *Middle East Policy* 12, no. 2 (2005): 104–119.

Baker, Peter. "White House Weighs Terrorist Designation for Muslim Brotherhood." *The New York Times*, February 7, 2017. https://www.nytimes.com/2017/02/07/world/middleeast/muslim-brotherhood-terrorism-trump.html.

Bakr, Amena. "Qaradawi's U-Turn: I Love the UAE, Saudi Arabia." Al Arabiya, April 20, 2014. http://english.alarabiya.net/en/News/2014/04/20/Qaradawi-s-U-Turn-I-love-Saudi-Arabia-UAE-.html.

Bakr, Amena. "Qatar's Embattled Brotherhood Exiles See Hope in New Saudi King." Reuters, February 5, 2015. http://uk.reuters.com/article/2015/02/05/uk-egypt-qatar-brotherhood-idUKKBN0L913320150205.

Baldwin-Edwards, Martin. "Labour Immigration and Labour Markets in the GCC Countries: National Patterns and Trends." Research paper, Kuwait Programme on Development, Governance and Globalisation in the Gulf States, no. 15, March 2011. http://www2.lse.ac.uk/government/research/resgroups/kuwait/documents/Baldwin-Edwards,%20Martin.pdf.

Bari, Zohrul. "Islamic Revival in the Gulf: An Overview." *International Studies* 31, no. 49 (1994): 49–67.

Baskan, Birol, and Steven Wright. "Seeds of Change: Comparing State-Religion Relations in Qatar and Saudi Arabia." *Arab Studies Quarterly* 33, no. 2 (2011): 96–111.

Bawabat al-Harakat al-Islamia. "Al-Ikhwan al-Muslimun fi al-Imarat . . . Al-Hasim fi Muwajihat Atma' al-Jama'a" [The Muslim Brotherhood in the Emirates. . . decisiveness in the face of the group's ambitions]. July 9, 2014. http://www.islamist-movements.com/2980.

Bayat, Asef. "Un-Civil Society: The Politics of the 'Informal People.'" *Third World Quarterly* 18, no. 1 (1997): 53–72.

Bayoumy, Yara. "UAE Islamist Group Had No Desire to Topple Government: Families." Reuters, July 3, 2013. http://www.reuters.com/article/2013/07/02/us-emirates-trial-islah-idUSBRE9610PT20130702.

"BBC Monitor Report of 3 May 1966: Kuwait Premier Accuses 'Newcomers' of 'Harmful Activities' against National Unity." In *Records of Kuwait 1966–1971: 1966*, edited by Anita L. P. Burdett, 170–172. Cambridge, UK: Cambridge Archive Editions, 2003.

BBC News. "Egypt Crisis: Al-Jazeera Journalists Arrested in Cairo." December 30, 2013. http://www.bbc.co.uk/news/world-middle-east-25546389.

BBC News. "Gulf Ambassadors Pulled from Qatar over 'Interference.'" March 5, 2014. http://www.bbc.co.uk/news/world-middle-east-26447914.

BBC News. "Kuwait Election: Opposition Hails Boycott as Turnout Falls." December 2, 2012. http://www.bbc.co.uk/news/world-middle-east-20571958.

BBC News. "Qatar Court Upholds Poet Mohammed al-Ajami's Sentence." October 21, 2013. http://www.bbc.co.uk/news/world-middle-east-24612650.

BBC News. "Qatar Crisis: UAE Threatens Sympathisers with Prison." June 7, 2017. http://www.bbc.co.uk/news/world-middle-east-40192730.

BBC News. "UAE Jails 30 over 'Muslim Brotherhood Ties.'" January 21, 2014. http://www.bbc.co.uk/news/world-middle-east-25824395.

Beblawi, Hazem. "The Rentier State in the Arab World." In *The Rentier State: Nation, State and Integration in the Arab World*, edited by Hazem Beblawi and Giacomo Luciani, 49–62. London: Croom Helm, 1987.

Belén Soage, Ana. "Yusuf Al-Qaradawi: The Muslim Brothers' Favorite Ideological Guide." In *The Muslim Brotherhood: The Organization and Policies of a Global Islamist Movement*, edited by Barry Rubin, 19–37. New York: Palgrave Macmillan, 2010.

Black, Ian. "Emirati Nerves Rattled by Islamists' Rise." *The Guardian*, October 12, 2012. http://www.guardian.co.uk/world/on-the-middle-east/2012/oct/12/uae-muslimbrotherhood-egypt-arabspring.

Black, Ian. "Qatar Emir's Mother Speaks Out over Treatment of Muslims by the West." *The Guardian*, May 26, 2015. http://www.theguardian.com/world/2015/may/26/qatar-emirs-mother-speaks-out-over-treatment-of-muslims-by-west.

Black, Ian. "Qatar-Gulf Deal Forces Expulsion of Muslim Brotherhood Leaders." *The Guardian*, September 16, 2014. http://www.theguardian.com/world/2014/sep/16/qatar-orders-expulsion-exiled-egyptian-muslim-brotherhood-leaders.

Braude, Joseph. "The Muslim Brotherhood's More Frightening Offshoot." *The Atlantic*, July 15, 2013. http://www.theatlantic.com/international/archive/2013/07/the-muslim-brotherhoods-more-frightening-offshoot/277786/.

Broomhall, Elizabeth. "Twitter Users Blast Qatar Airways, Call for Boycott." *Arabian Business*, January 9, 2012. http://www.arabianbusiness.com/twitter-users-blast-qatar-airways-call-for-boycott-439307.html.

Brown, L. Carl. *Religion and State: The Muslim Approach to Politics*. New York: Columbia University Press, 2000.

Brown, Nathan J. "Kuwait's 2008 Parliamentary Elections: A Setback for Democratic Islamism?" Carnegie Endowment for International Peace, May 2008. http://carnegieendowment.org/files/brown_kuwait2.pdf.

Brown, Nathan J. "Pushing Toward Party Politics?: Kuwait's Islamic Constitutional Movement." *Carnegie Papers* 79, January 2007. http://carnegieendowment.org/files/cp79_brown_kuwait_final.pdf.

Brown, Nathan J. *When Victory Is Not An Option: Islamist Movements in Arab Politics*. Ithaca, NY: Cornell University Press, 2012.

Bunglawala, Zamila. "Young, Educated and Dependent on the Public Sector: Meeting Graduates' Aspirations and Diversifying Employment in Qatar and the UAE." Brookings Doha Center Analysis Paper, no. 4, December 2011. https://www.brookings.edu/wp-content/uploads/2016/06/1215_qatar_diversify_employment_bunglawala_english.pdf.

Burgat, François. *Face to Face with Political Islam*. London: I. B. Tauris, 2003.

Byman, Daniel L., and Jerrold D. Green. *Political Violence and Stability in the States of the Northern Persian Gulf*. Santa Monica, CA: RAND Corporation, 1999.

"Case against Gender Segregation Rejected," *Arab Times*, December 17, 2015, http://www.arabtimesonline.com/news/case-against-gender-segregation-rejected-part-of-domestic-workers-law-unconstitutional/.

Chaudhry, Kiren Aziz. *The Price of Wealth: Economies and Institutions in the Middle East*. Ithaca, NY: Cornell University Press, 1997.

Clark, Janine A. "Patronage, Prestige, and Power: The Islamic Center Charity Society's Political Role within the Muslim Brotherhood." In *Islamist Politics in the Middle East: Movements and Change*, edited by Samer S. Shehata, 68–87. London: Routledge, 2012.

Commins, David. "Hasan al-Banna." In *Pioneers of Islamic Revival*, edited by Ali Rahnema, 125–153. London: Zed Books, 1994.

Commins, David. *The Gulf States: A Modern History*. London: I. B. Tauris, 2012.

Constitution of Qatar. Government of Qatar, 2003. http://portal.www.gov.qa/wps/wcm/connect/5a5512804665e3afa54fb5fd2b4ab27a/Constitution+of+Qatar+EN.pdf?MOD=AJPERES.

Constitution of the State of Kuwait. Diwan of His Highness the Prime Minister, 1962. https://www.pm.gov.kw/kuwait-constitution.aspx.

Cordesman, Anthony H., and Khalid R. al-Rodhan. "The Gulf Military Forces in an Era of Asymmetric War: Qatar." Center for Strategic and International Studies. June 28, 2006. http://csis.org/files/media/csis/pubs/060728_gulf_qatar.pdf.

"Corruption Perceptions Index." Transparency International. 2014. https://www.transparency.org/cpi2014/results/.

"Counter Subversion Committee: Working Group on the Persian Gulf (Including Kuwait)." Meeting Record, August 12, 1965. In *Records of Kuwait 1961–1965: 1965*, edited by Anita L.P. Burdett, 323–329. Cambridge, UK: Cambridge Archive Editions, 1997.

Crimes against the Internal Security of the State. UAE Penal Code, amended 2005. https://www.scribd.com/doc/122309224/182/Article-182.

Crystal, Jill. "Civil Society in the Arabian Gulf." In *Civil Society in the Middle East*, edited by Augustus R. Norton, 2:259–286. New York: E. J. Brill, 1996.

Crystal, Jill. "Coalitions in Oil Monarchies: Kuwait and Qatar." *Comparative Politics* 21, no. 4 (1989): 427–443.

Crystal, Jill. *Kuwait: The Transformation of an Oil State*. Boulder, CO: Westview Press, 1992.

Crystal, Jill. *Oil and Politics in the Gulf: Rulers and Merchants in Kuwait and Qatar*. Cambridge: Cambridge University Press, 1990.

Crystal, Jill. "Political Reform in Qatar." In *Political Change in the Arab Gulf States: Stuck in Transition*, edited by Mary Ann Tétreault, Gwenn Okrulik, and Andrzej Kapiszewski, 119–135. Boulder, CO: Lynne Rienner Publishers, 2011.

Crystal, Jill, and Abdullah al-Shayji. "The Pro-Democratic Agenda in Kuwait: Structures and Context." In *Political Liberalization and Democratization in the Arab World*, edited by Baghat Korany, Paul Noble, and Rex Brynen, 2:101–125. Boulder, CO: Lynne Rienner Publishers, 1998.

D., E. A. "Kuwait's Opposition: A Reawakening." *The Economist*, April 17, 2014. http://www.economist.com/blogs/pomegranate/2014/04/kuwaits-opposition.

Dajani, Haneen. "UAE's Fatwa Council 'Will Help Fight Extreme Religious Teachings'." *The National*, June 5, 2017. https://www.thenational.ae/uae/uae-s-new-fatwa-council-will-help-fight-extreme-religious-teachings-1.18475

Dar al-Sharq. "H. E. Shaikh Thani ibn Abdullah al-Thani, Chairman of the Board." April 2015. http://daralsharq.net/ar/node/36?language=en.

Davidson, Christopher M. *Abu Dhabi: Oil and Beyond*. Oxford: Oxford University Press, 2011.

Davidson, Christopher M. *After the Sheikhs: The Coming Collapse of the Gulf Monarchies*. Oxford: Oxford University Press, 2013.

Davidson, Christopher M. "Arab Nationalism and British Opposition in Dubai, 1920–1966." *Middle Eastern Studies* 43, no. 6 (2007): 879–892.

Davidson, Christopher M. *Dubai: The Vulnerability of Success*. Oxford: Oxford University Press, 2009.

Davidson, Christopher M. "Fear and Loathing in the Emirates." *Sada*, September 18, 2012. http://carnegieendowment.org/sada/2012/09/18/fear-and-loathing-in-emirates/fdw2.

Davidson, Christopher M. "The United Arab Emirates." In *Power and Politics in the Persian Gulf Monarchies*, edited by Christopher M. Davidson, 7–30. London: Hurst and Company, 2011.

Davidson, Christopher M. *The United Arab Emirates: A Study in Survival*. Boulder, CO: Lynne Rienner Publishers, 2005.

Dekmejian, R. Hrair. "Islamic Revival: Catalysts, Categories, and Consequences." In *The Politics of Islamic Revivalism: Diversity and Unity*, edited by Shireen T. Hunter, 3–22. Bloomington: Indiana University Press, 1988.

Dekmejian, R. Hrair "The Rise of Political Islamism in Saudi Arabia." *Middle East Journal* 48, no. 4 (1994): 627–643.

Denoeux, Guilain. "The Forgotten Swamp: Navigating Political Islam." *Middle East Policy* 9, no. 2 (2002): 56–81.

Department of Economic Development-Ajman. "Annual Economic Report Ajman 2013." 2013. http://www.ajmanded.ae/Portal/userfiles/2013%20ADED%20Annual%20Report%20EN.pdf.

Diamond, Larry. "Why Are There No Arab Democracies?" *Journal of Democracy* 21, no. 1 (2010): 93–104.

Dickinson, Elizabeth. "Why Private Gulf Financing for Syria's Extremist Rebels Risks Igniting Sectarian Conflict at Home." Saban Center at the Brookings Institution, Analysis Paper, no. 16, December 2013. https://www.brookings.edu/wp-content/uploads/2016/06/private-gulf-financing-syria-extremist-rebels-sectarian-conflict-dickinson.pdf.

Doha News. "Al Jazeera Employees Complain of Editorial Bias with Egypt Coverage." September 5, 2013. http://dohanews.co/al-jazeera-employees-complain-of-editorial-bias-with-2/.

Doherty, Regan. "Qatar Hikes State Salaries, Pensions." Reuters, September 7, 2011. http://www.reuters.com/article/2011/09/07/qatar-salaries-idAFL5E7K70KY20110907.

Donaghy, Rori. "UAE Arrest Prominent Economist and Pro-Democracy Activist." *Middle East Eye*, August 19, 2015. http://www.middleeasteye.net/news/uae-arrest-prominent-economist-and-pro-democracy-activist-2147452605.

Dr-alkuwari.net. "Nas ʿArida 1991 wa-Asmaʾ al-Muwaqiʿyyin ʿaliha" [Text of the 1991 petition and names of signatories of it]. December 21, 1991. http://dr-alkuwari.net/node/151.html.

The Economist. "The Rise of Qatar: Pygmy with the Punch of a Giant." November 5, 2011. http://www.economist.com/node/21536659.

The Economist. "The United Arab Emirates: Getting Twitchy about Democracy." June 30, 2011. http://www.economist.com/node/18898137.

The Economist. "Whispered Dissent in UAE: No Sheikh-up Here." March 17, 2012. http://www.economist.com/node/21550288.

Eickelman, Dale F., and James P. Piscatori. *Muslim Politics*. Princeton, NJ: Princeton University Press, 1996.

Ekstein, Harry. "Case Study and Theory in Political Science." In *Handbook of Political Science*, edited by Fred I. Greenstein and Nelson W. Polsby, 7:79–138. Reading, UK: Addison-Wesley, 1975.

El Amraoui, Ahmed. "Tunisia's Ennahda 'Faced Defeat' in Elections." Al Jazeera, October 28, 2014. http://www.aljazeera.com/news/africa/2014/10/tunisia-ennahda-says-secular-rivals-ahead-20141027141737474289.html.

El Baltaji, Dana. "Qatar Bankrolls Muslim Brothers as U.A.E. Jails Them." Bloomberg, December 11, 2012. http://www.bloomberg.com/news/articles/2012-12-10/qatar-bankrolls-ascendant-muslim-brothers-as-u-a-e-jails-them.

El Ghobasy, Mona. "The Metamorphosis of the Egyptian Muslim Brothers." *International Journal of Middle East Studies* 37, no. 3 (2005): 373–395.

Ellili-Cherif, Maha, and Michael Romanowski. "Education for a New Era: Stakeholders' Perception of Qatari Education Reform." *International Journal of Education Policy and Leadership* 8, no. 6 (2013): 1–17.

El Mallakh, Ragaei. *Qatar: Development of an Oil Economy*. London: Croom Helm, 1979.

El Mallakh, Ragaei. *The Economic Development of the United Arab Emirates*. London: Croom Helm, 1981.

Embassy of the United States Abu Dhabi. "FNC Elections: 'Political Participation, Not Democracy.'" WikiLeaks. June 27, 2006. http://wikileaks.wikimee.org/cable/2006/06/06ABUDHABI2655.html.

Embassy of the United States Abu Dhabi. "Local Views on Prospects for UAE Democratization." WikiLeaks. September 16, 2004. http://cables.mrkva.eu/cable.php?id=20666.

Embassy of the United States Abu Dhabi. "Ministry of Education Dismissed Eighty Three Emirati Teachers." WikiLeaks. December 22, 2008. https://cablegatesearch.wikileaks.org/cable.php?id=08ABUDHABI1440.

Embassy of the United States Abu Dhabi. "UAE Minimizing Influence of Islamic Extremists." WikiLeaks. November 10, 2004. http://www.wikileaks.org/plusd/cables/04ABUDHABI4061_a.html.

Embassy of the United States Doha. "Islamic Leaders Describe Qatar's Moderation." WikiLeaks. March 19, 2006. https://wikileaks.org/cable/2006/03/06DOHA418.html.

Embassy of the United States Doha. "Qaradawi Viewed Locally as a Moderate Scholar." WikiLeaks. July 12, 2005. https://www.wikileaks.org/plusd/cables/05DOHA1268_a.html.

Emirates 24/7. "Ajman Population Crosses the 262,000 Mark." August 16, 2011. http://www.emirates247.com/news/ajman-population-crosses-the-262-000-mark-2011-08-16-1.413624.

Esposito, John L. Introduction to *Islam and Development: Religion and Sociopolitical Change*, edited by John L. Esposito, ix–xix. Syracuse, NY: Syracuse University Press, 1980.

Esposito, John L. "Political Islam and Gulf Security." In *Political Islam: Revolution, Radicalism, or Reform?*, edited by John L. Esposito, 53–74. Boulder, CO: Lynne Rienner Publishers, 1997.

Esposito, John L., and James P. Piscatori. "Democratization and Islam." *Middle East Journal* 45, no. 3 (1991): 427–440.

Establishment of Private Universities Law no. 34 for 2000. Private Universities Council. Kuwaiti Ministry of Higher Education. July 11, 2000. http://iasas.global/wp-content/uploads/2016/02/Kuwait-Int-of-Student-Affairs-Services.pdf.

Fahmy, Heba. "CMC Calls for Expansion of Female Taxi Driver Service in Qatar." *Doha News*, December 29, 2015. https://dohanews.co/cmc-calls-expansion-female-taxi-driver-service-qatar/.

Fahmy, Heba. "CMC Calls on Qatar's Malls to Revive 'Family Day' Policy." *Doha News*, November 17, 2015. http://dohanews.co/cmc-calls-on-qatars-malls-to-revive-family-day-policy/.

Fahmy, Heba. "CMC: Women in Qatar Uncomfortable with Male Salespeople." *Doha News*, March 29, 2016. https://dohanews.co/cmc-women-in-qatar-uncomfortable-with-male-salespeople/.

Fandy, Mamoun. *Saudi Arabia and the Politics of Dissent*. New York: Palgrave Macmillan, 1999.

Farah, Tawfic E. "Political Culture and Development in a Rentier State: The Case of Kuwait." *Journal of Asian and African Studies* 24, nos. 1–2 (1989): 106–113.

Farah, Tawfic E. "Politics and Religion in Kuwait: Two Myths Examined." In *Islamic Resurgence in the Arab World*, edited by Ali E. Hillal Dessouki, 170–178. New York: Praeger, 1982.

Faramazi, Scheherezade. "Kuwait's Muslim Brotherhood." *Jadaliyya*, April 18, 2012. http://www.jadaliyya.com/pages/index/5116/kuwaits-muslim-brotherhood.

FDI Intelligence. "Sharjah: Combining Cultural Heritage with Business Competitiveness." *FDI Supplement* April / May 2013.

Fenelon, Kevin G. *The United Arab Emirates: An Economic and Social Survey*. 2nd ed. London: Longman, 1973.

Ferris-Lay, Claire. "Islamic Teachers Strike over Removal." *Arabian Business*, June 16, 2008. http://www.arabianbusiness.com/islamic-teachers-strike-over-removal-48176.html.

Foley, Sean. *The Arab Gulf States: Beyond Oil and Islam*. Boulder, CO: Lynne Rienner Publishers, 2010.

Foley, Sean. "The UAE: Political Issues and Security Dilemmas." *Middle East Review of International Affairs* 3, no. 1 (1999): 25–45.

Foley, Sean. "What Wealth Cannot Buy: UAE Security at the Turn of the Twenty-First Century." In *Crises in the Contemporary Persian Gulf*, edited by Barry Rubin, 33–74. London: Frank Cass, 2002.

Forbes. "The Advent of Terrorism in Qatar." March 25, 2005. https://www.forbes.com/2005/03/25/cz_0325oxan_qatarattack.html.

Forstenlechner, Ingo, Emilie Rutledge, and Rashed Salem Al-Nuaimi. "The UAE, the 'Arab Spring' and Different Types of Dissent." *Middle East Policy Council* 19, no. 4 (2012): 54–67.

Freedom House. "Freedom in the World 2012-Qatar." July 24, 2012. http://www.refworld.org/cgi-bin/texis/vtx/rwmain?page=country&category=&publisher=&type=&coi=QAT&rid=4562d8cf2&docid=500fda332&skip=0.

Freedom House. "Qatar." Countries at the Crossroads. 2004. https://freedomhouse.org/report/countries-crossroads/2004/qatar#.VRmZxkbndKo.

Freer, Courtney. "Exclusion-Moderation in the Gulf Context: Tracing the Development of Pragmatic Islamism in Kuwait." *Middle Eastern Studies*, August 2017.

Fromherz, Allen J. *Qatar: A Modern History*. London: I. B. Tauris, 2012.

"Frugality and Extravagance." *Al-Islah* 50, no. 51 (1982). In *The Roots of Conspiracy Against the UAE*, edited by ʿAli Salem Humaid, 1:98–99. Dubai, UAE: Al Mezmaah Studies and Research Center, 2013.

Fyfe, A. Ann. "Wealth and Power: Political and Economic Change in the United Arab Emirates." PhD diss., Durham University, 1989.

Galal, Ehab. "Yūsuf al-Qaraḍāwī and the New Islamic TV." In *Global Mufti: The Phenomenon of Yusuf al-Qaradawi*, edited by Bettina Graf and Jakob Skovogaard-Petersen, 149–180. New York: Columbia University Press, 2009.

Gause, F. Gregory III. "Kings for All Seasons: How the Middle East's Monarchies Survived the Arab Spring." Brookings Doha Center Analysis Paper, no. 8, September 2013. http://www.brookings.edu/~/media/research/files/papers/2013/09/24%20resilience%20arab%20monarchies%20gause/resilience%20arab%20monarchies_english.pdf.

Gause, F. Gregory III. *Oil Monarchies: Domestic and Security Challenges in the Arab Gulf States*. New York: Council on Foreign Relations Press, 1994.

Gause, F. Gregory III. *Political Opposition in the Gulf Monarchies*. San Domenico di Fiesole, IT: European University Institute, 2000.

Gavrielides, Nicolas. "Tribal Democracy: The Anatomy of Parliamentary Elections in Kuwait." In *Elections in the Middle East: Implications of Recent Trends*, edited by Linda L. Layne, 153–183. Boulder, CO: Westview Press, 1987.

Gengler, Justin. "Qatar's Ambivalent Democratization." *Foreign Policy*, November 1, 2011. http://mideast.foreignpolicy.com/posts/2011/11/01/qataris_lesson_in_revolution.

Gengler, Justin. "The Political Costs of Qatar's Western Orientation." *Middle East Policy* 19, no. 4 (2012): 68–76.

Ghabra, Shafeeq. "Balancing State and Society: The Islamic Movement in Kuwait." *Middle East Policy* 5, no. 2 (1997): 58–72.

Ghabra, Shafeeq. "Kuwait and the Dynamics of Socio-Economic Change." *The Middle East Journal* 51, no. 3 (1997): 358–372.

Ghabra, Shafeeq. "Voluntary Associations in Kuwait: The Foundations of a New System?" *Middle East Journal* 45, no. 2 (1991): 199–215.

Ghubash, Mouza. "Social Development in the United Arab Emirates." In *Perspectives on the United Arab Emirates*, edited by Edmund Ghareeb and Ibrahim al-Abed, 273–289. London: Trident Press, 1997.

Global Voices. "Kuwait Sentences Opposition Politician Mussallam Al Barrak to Two Years in Jail for 'Insulting Ruler.'" February 22, 2015. http://globalvoicesonline.org/2015/02/22/kuwait-sentences-opposition-politician-mussallam-al-barrak-to-two-years-in-jail-for-insulting-ruler/.

González, Alessandra L. *Islamic Feminism in Kuwait: The Politics and Paradoxes*. New York: Palgrave Macmillan, 2013.

Goulding, Nicola, and Jason Hanna. "UAE Woman Arrested in U.S. Teacher's Mall Restroom Stabbing." CNN News, December 5, 2014. http://edition.cnn.com/2014/12/04/world/meast/uae-us-mall-killing/.

Government.ae. "Charity and Humanitarian Work." 2015. http://beta.government.ae/en/information-and-services/charity-and-humanitarian-work.

Government of Umm al-Quwain. "Haqaʾiq wa-Arqam" [Facts and figures]. 2015. https://www.uaq.ae/ar/umm-al-quwain/about-umm-al-quwain/facts-and-figures.html.

Graf, Bettina. "Sheikh Yusuf Al-Qaradawi in Cyberspace." *Die Welt des Islams* 47, nos. 3–4 (2007): 403–421.

Graf, Bettina, and Jakob Skovogaard-Petersen. Introduction to *Global Mufti: The Phenomenon of Yusuf al-Qaradawi*, edited by Bettina Graf and Jakob Skovogaard-Petersen, 1–15. New York: Columbia University Press, 2009.

Gray, Matthew. *Qatar: Politics and the Challenges of Development*. Boulder, CO: Lynne Rienner Publishers, 2013.

Gulf News. "Freed Kuwait Opposition Leader Vows Protests Will Continue." July 8, 2014. http://gulfnews.com/news/gulf/kuwait/freed-kuwait-opposition-leader-vows-protests-will-continue-1.1357223.

Gulf News. "RAK's GDP at Db30.9b in 2013: Report." October 9, 2014. http://gulfnews.com/business/economy/rak-s-gdp-at-dh30-9b-in-2013-report-1.1396508.

Gulf News. "UAE Publishes List of Terrorist Organisations." November 15, 2014. http://gulfnews.com/news/uae/government/uae-publishes-list-of-terrorist-organisations-1.1412895.

Hack, Susan. "Qatar's Billion-Dollar Art Collection Causes Controversy." Bloomberg, October 2, 2014. http://www.bloomberg.com/news/articles/2014-10-02/qatar-s-billion-dollar-art-collection-causes-controversy.

Habboush, Mahmoud. "Call to Naturalise Some Expats Stirs Anxiety in the UAE." Reuters, October 10, 2013. http://uk.reuters.com/article/2013/10/10/uk-emirates-citizenship-feature-idUKBRE99904J20131010.

Hakala, Pekka. "Opposition in the United Arab Emirates." European Parliament Directorate-General for External Policies. November 15, 2012. http://www.europarl.europa.eu/committees/en/studiesdownload.html?languageDocument=EN&file=78691.

Halligan, Neil. "Citizens Rank UAE High on Quality of Life Survey." *Arabian Business*, July 20, 2014. http://www.arabianbusiness.com/citizens-rank-uae-high-on-quality-of-life-survey-558474.html.

Hamid, Shadi. *Temptations of Power*. Oxford: Oxford University Press, 2014.

Hamid, Shadi. "There Aren't Protests in Qatar—So Why Did the Emir Just Announce Elections?" *The Atlantic*, November 1, 2011. http://www.theatlantic.com/international/archive/2011/11/there-arent-protests-in-qatar-so-why-did-the-emir-just-announce-elections/247661/.

Hammond, Andrew. "Arab Awakening: Qatar's Controversial Alliance with Arab Islamists." OpenDemocracy. April 25, 2013. http://www.opendemocracy.net/andrew-hammond/arab-awakening-qatar'scontroversial-alliance-with-arab-islamists.

Hammond, Andrew.*Pop Culture Arab World!: Media, Arts, and Lifestyle*. Santa Barbara: ABC-CLIO, 2004.

Hanieh, Adam. *Lineages of Revolt: Issues of Contemporary Capitalism in the Middle East*. Chicago, IL: Haymarket Books, 2013.

Harman, Danna. "Backstory: Qatar Reformed by a Modern Marriage." *Christian Science Monitor*, March 6, 2007. http://www.csmonitor.com/2007/0306/p20s01-wome.html.

Hasan, Noorhaidi. "Saudi Expansion, the Salafi Campaign and Arabised Islam in Indonesia." In *Kingdom without Borders: Saudi Political, Religious and Media Frontiers*, edited by Madawi al-Rasheed, 263–281. London: Hurst and Company, 2008.

Haykel, Bernard. "Qatar and Islamism." NOREF Norwegian Peacebuilding Resource Center Policy Brief, February 2013. https://noref.no/Publications/Regions/The-Gulf/Qatar-and-Islamism.

Heard-Bey, Frauke. *From Trucial States to United Arab Emirates: A Society in Transition.* London: Longman, 1982.

Heard-Bey, Frauke. "The Tribal Society of the UAE and Its Traditional Economy." In *United Arab Emirates: A New Perspective*, edited by Ibrahim al-Abed and Peter Hellyer, 98–116. London: Trident Press, 2001.

Heard-Bey, Frauke. "The United Arab Emirates: A Quarter Century of Federation." In *Middle East Dilemma: The Politics and Economics of Arab Integration*, edited by Michael C. Hudson, 128–149. London: I. B. Tauris, 1999.

Heard-Bey, Frauke. "The United Arab Emirates: Statehood and Nation-Building in a Traditional Society." *The Middle East Journal* 59, no. 3 (2005): 357–375.

Hegghammer, Thomas. *Jihad in Saudi Arabia: Violence and Pan-Islamism since 1979*. Cambridge, UK: Cambridge University Press, 2010.

Heinrich Böll Stiftung Middle East. "Interview with Dr. Ali Khalifa Al Kuwari, Author of 'The People Want Reform . . . in Qatar, Too'—Statehood & Participation." March 3, 2014. http://lb.boell.org/en/2014/03/03/interview-dr-ali-khalifa-al-kuwari-author-people-want-reform-qatar-too-statehood.

Herb, Michael. "A Nation of Bureaucrats: Political Participation and Economic Diversification in Kuwait and the United Arab Emirates." *International Journal of Middle East Studies* 41, no. 3 (2009): 375–395.

Herb, Michael. "Emirs and Parliaments in the Gulf." *Journal of Democracy* 13, no. 4 (2002): 41–47.

Herb, Michael. "Kuwait and the United Arab Emirates." In *Politics and Society in the Contemporary Middle East*, edited by Michele Penner Angrist, 335–365. Boulder, CO: Lynne Rienner Publishers, 2010.

Herb, Michael. "Taxation and Representation." *Studies in Comparative International Development* 38, no. 3 (2003): 3–31.

Herb, Michael. *The Wages of Oil: Parliaments and Economic Development in Kuwait and the UAE*. Ithaca, NY: Cornell University Press, 2014.

Hertog, Steffen. *Princes, Brokers, and Bureaucrats: Oil and the State in Saudi Arabia*. Ithaca, NY: Cornell University Press, 2011.

Hicks, Neil, and Ghanim al-Najjar. "The Utility of Tradition: Civil Society in Kuwait." In *Civil Society in the Middle East*, edited by Augustus R. Norton, 1:186–213. Leiden: E. J. Brill, 1995.

Hirschkind, Charles. "What Is Political Islam?" In *Political Islam: A Critical Reader*, edited by Frédéric Volpi, 13–15. London: Routledge, 1997.

His Highness Sheikh Mohammed bin Rashid Al Maktoum. "Sabaʿ Imarat" (Seven Emirates). 2015. www.sheikhmohammed.com/vgn-ext-templating/v/index.jsp?vgnextoid=7dbb4c8631cb4110VgnVCM1000000b0140a0aRCRD.

Holmes, Stephen. *Passions and Constraint: On the Theory of Liberal Democracy*. Chicago: The University of Chicago Press, 1995.

Hudson, Michael C. *Arab Politics: The Search for Legitimacy*. New Haven, CT: Yale University Press, 1977.

Hudson, Michael C. "The Incremental Approach to Political Reform in the Gulf." In *The Arabian Gulf: Between Conservatism and Change*, edited by The Emirates Center for Strategic Studies and Research, 45–62. Abu Dhabi, UAE: The Emirates Center for Strategic Studies and Research, 2009.

Hudson, Michael C. "Islam and Political Development." In *Islam and Development: Religion and Sociopolitical Change*, edited by John L. Esposito, 1–24. Syracuse, NY: Syracuse University Press, 1980.

Humaid, ʿAli Salem. *The Roots of Conspiracy Against the UAE*. Vols. 1 and 2. Dubai, UAE: Al Mezmaah Studies and Research Center, 2013.

Human Rights Watch. "Kuwait: 5 Critics Stripped of Citizenship." August 10, 2014. http://www.hrw.org/news/2014/08/10/kuwait-5-critics-stripped-citizenship.

Human Rights Watch. "Kuwait: Cybercrime Law a Blow to Free Speech." July 22, 2015. https://www.hrw.org/news/2015/07/22/kuwait-cybercrime-law-blow-free-speech.

Human Rights Watch. "Kuwait: Government Critics Stripped of Citizenship." October 19, 2014. https://www.hrw.org/news/2014/10/19/kuwait-government-critics-stripped-citizenship.

Human Rights Watch. "Kuwait: Opposition Protest Broken Up." March 29, 2015. http://www.hrw.org/news/2015/03/29/kuwait-opposition-protest-broken.

Human Rights Watch. "Kuwait: Telecom Law Violates Free Speech." August 20, 2014. https://www.hrw.org/news/2014/08/20/kuwait-telecom-law-violates-free-speech.

Human Rights Watch. "Qatar: Revise Draft Media Law to Allow Criticism of Rulers." October 30, 2012. http://www.hrw.org/news/2012/10/30/qatar-revise-draft-media-law-allow-criticism-rulers.

Human Rights Watch. "UAE: Authorities Enhance Surveillance of Critics." January 12, 2017. https://www.hrw.org/news/2017/01/12/uae-authorities-enhance-surveillance-critics.

Human Rights Watch. "UAE: Terrorism Law Threatens Lives, Liberty." December 3, 2014. https://www.hrw.org/news/2014/12/03/uae-terrorism-law-threatens-lives-liberty.

Human Rights Watch. "United Arab Emirates (UAE): Events of 2008." http://www.hrw.org/world-report-2009/united-arab-emirates-uae.

Huntington, Samuel P. "The Clash of Civilizations?" *Foreign Affairs* 72, no. 3 (1992): 22–49.

HVS Consulting. "Market Pulse: Fujairah." March 2014. http://rss.hsyndicate.com/file/152005343.pdf.

Ibrahim, Youssef M. "54 Qatar Citizens Petition Emir for Free Elections." *New York Times*, May 12, 1992. http://www.nytimes.com/1992/05/13/world/54-qatar-citizens-petition-emir-for-free-elections.html.

"ICM Vision, Mission and Objectives." *Islamic Constitutional Movement*, 3rd ed. January 2007.

International Monetary Fund. "United Arab Emirates: Statistical Appendix." International Monetary Fund Country Report 09/120, April 2009. https://www.imf.org/external/pubs/ft/scr/2009/cr09120.pdf.

Ipetitions. "Al-Imaratiyyun Yarfaʿun Risala li-Hukkam al-Imarat Tutalib bi-Islah Kolli li-l-Nizam al-Barlamani" [Emiratis address message to the rulers of the UAE calling for total reform to a parliamentary system]. March 3, 2011. http://www.ipetitions.com/petition/uaepetition71/.

Ismael, Jacqueline S. *Kuwait: Dependency and Class in a Rentier State*. Gainesville: University Press of Florida, 1993.

Ismail, Salwa. *Rethinking Islamist Politics: Culture, the State and Islamism*. London: I. B. Tauris, 2006.

Izzak, B. "Amir Agrees to Reinstate Revoked Citizenships: MPs." *Kuwait Times*, June 3, 2017. http://news.kuwaittimes.net/website/amir-agrees-reinstate-revoked-citizenships-mps/.

Izzak, B. "MPs Request to Meet Amir over Tough Jail Sentences." *Kuwait Times*, November 28, 2017. http://news.kuwaittimes.net/website/mps-request-meet-amir-tough-jail-sentences/.

Izzak, B. "Appeals Court Jails 67 over Storming Assembly in 2011." *Kuwait Times*, November 27, 2017. http://news.kuwaittimes.net/website/appeals-court-jails-67-storming-assembly-2011/.

Izzak, B. "Opposition Again Fails to Agree on Speaker." *Kuwait Times*, December 7, 2016. http://news.kuwaittimes.net/website/opposition-fails-agree-speaker/.

Jamʿiat al-Islah wa-l-Tawjih al-Ijtimaʿi. "Nashitun Yutalibun Shuyukh al-Dawla al-Ahrar bi-l-Tadakhkhul li-Waqf Hamaqat Jihaz al-Aman bi-Haq Ahali al-Muʿtaqalin" [Activists demand the shaykhs of the free state to intervene to stop the follies of the security apparatus against the detainees' families]. April 4, 2013. http://www.aleslaah.net/site/showthred.php?id=4493.

Janardhan, N. "Islamists Stay Clear of Terrorism in Oman." The Jamestown Foundation. March 9, 2006. http://www.jamestown.org/single/?no_cache=1&tx_ttnews[tt_news]=698#.VETiieflf-Z.

Kakande, Yasin. "Umm al Qaiwain Forms Last of UAE's Executive Councils." *The National*, July 12, 2011. http://www.thenational.ae/news/uae-news/umm-al-qaiwain-forms-last-of-uaes-executive-councils.

Kamrava, Mehran. "Mediation and Qatari Foreign Policy." *Middle East Journal* 65, no. 4 (2011): 539–556.

Kamrava, Mehran. *Qatar: Small State, Big Politics*. Ithaca, NY: Cornell University Press, 2013.

Kamrava, Mehran. "Royal Factionalism and Political Liberalization in Qatar." *Middle East Journal* 63, no. 3 (2009): 401–420.

Kamrava, Mehran. *The Modern Middle East: A Political History since the First World War*. 2nd ed. Berkeley: University of California Press, 2011.

Kapiszewski, Andrzej. *Nationals and Expatriates: Population and Labour Dilemmas of the Gulf Cooperation Council*. Reading, UK: Ithaca Press, 2001.

Katzman, Kenneth. "Kuwait: Security, Reform, and U.S. Policy." *Congressional Research Service*, April 26, 2011. http://www.fas.org/sgp/crs/mideast/RS21513.pdf.

Kerr, Simeon. "Kuwait Clamps Down on Terror Financing." *Financial Times*, September 9, 2014. http://www.ft.com/cms/s/0/1cd94792-3812-11e4-b69d-00144feabdc0.html#axzz3ZGcZU800.

Kerr, Simeon. "Saudi Arabia, UAE, Bahrain and Egypt Cut Ties with Qatar." *Financial Times*, June 5, 2017. https://www.ft.com/content/dc24473c-499e-11e7-a3f4-c742b9791d43.

Khalaf, Mahi. "The State of Qatar." In *From Charity to Social Change: Trends in Arab Philanthropy*, edited by Barbara Lethen Ibrahim and Dina H. Sherif, 150–164. Cairo: The American University in Cairo Press, 2008.

Khaleej Times. "UAE's Electoral Base for FNC Polls Gets 66% Wider." July 6, 2015. http://www.khaleejtimes.com/nation/government/uae-s-electoral-base-for-fnc-polls-gets-66-wider.

Khalifa, Ali Mohammad. *The United Arab Emirates: Unity in Fragmentation*. Boulder, CO: Westview Press, 1979.

Khatib, Lina. "Qatar's Foreign Policy: The Limits of Pragmatism." *International Affairs* 89, no. 2 (2013): 417–431.

Khatri, Shabina S. "IMF: Qatar is Postponing New Taxes on Junk Food and Alcohol." *Doha News*, August 31, 2017. https://dohanews.co/imf-qatar-is-postponing-new-taxes-on-junk-food-and-alcohol/.

Khatri, Shabina S. "Legislative Elections Postponed until at Least 2019." *Doha News*, June 17, 2016. https://dohanews.co/legislative-elections-in-qatar-postponed-until-at-least-2019/.

Khatri, Shabina S. "Nepalese Teacher Accused of Insulting Islam Released from Qatar Jail." *Doha News*, May 12, 2013. http://dohanews.co/nepalese-teacher-accused-of-insulting-islam-released/.

Khatri, Shabina S. "QDC Tells Customers to Stock Up before Qatar Raises Alcohol Tax." *Doha News*, March 23, 2017. https://dohanews.co/qdc-tells-customers-stock-qatar-raises-alcohol-tax/.

Khatri, Shabina S. "Saudis Demand That Qatar Change the Name of Its State Mosque." *Doha News*, May 29, 2017. https://dohanews.co/saudis-demand-that-qatar-change-the-name-of-its-state-mosque/.

Khatri, Shabina S. "UAE Pardons Qatari Doctor Jailed for Supporting Banned Islamist Group." *Doha News*, May 24, 2015. http://dohanews.co/uae-pardons-qatari-doctor-jailed-for-supporting-banned-islamist-group/.

Khatri, Shabina S. "'We Are Not Ready to Surrender,' Qatar FM Says." *Doha News*, June 9, 2017. https://dohanews.co/we-are-not-ready-to-surrender-qatar-fm-says/.

Khatri, Shabina S., and Omar Chatriwala, "Lawyer: Poet Pardoned by Emir Leaving Qatar." *Doha News*, March 22, 2016. http://dohanews.co/lawyer-poet-pardoned-emir-leaving-qatar/.

Kholaif, Dahlia. "Kuwait's Opposition Movements Feel the Squeeze on Freedoms." *Middle East Eye*, March 30, 2015. http://www.middleeasteye.net/news/kuwaits-opposition-movements-feel-squeeze-freedoms-1703345061.

Kholaif, Dahlia. "The GCC Survive Qatar-Saudi Rivalry?" Al Jazeera, March 18, 2014. http://www.aljazeera.com/indepth/features/2014/03/will-gcc-survive-qatar-saudi-rivalry-201431864034267256.html.

Kifner, John. "Islamic Traditionalists Sweep Liberals in Kuwaiti Election." *New York Times*, July 7, 2003. http://www.nytimes.com/2003/07/07/world/islamic-traditionalists-sweep-liberals-in-kuwaiti-election.html.

Kirkpatrick, David D. "Army Ousts Egypt's President; Morsi Is Taken into Military Custody." *The New York Times*, July 3, 2013. http://www.nytimes.com/2013/07/04/world/middleeast/egypt.html?_r=0.

Kirkpatrick, David D. "Qatar's Support of Islamists Alienates Allies Near and Far." *New York Times*, September 7, 2014. http://www.nytimes.com/2014/09/08/world/middleeast/qatars-support-of-extremists-alienates-allies-near-and-far.html?_r=0.

Kitschelt, Herbert P. "Political Opportunity Structures and Political Protest: Anti-Nuclear Movements in Four Democracies." *British Journal of Political Science* 16, no. 1 (1986): 57–85.

Kobaisi, Abdulla Juma. "The Development of Education in Qatar, 1950–1966 with an Analysis of Some Educational Problems." PhD diss., Durham University, 1979.

Kostiner, Joseph. "Kuwait and Bahrain." In *The Politics of Islamic Revivalism: Diversity and Unity*, edited by Shireen Hunter, 116–129. Bloomington: Indiana University Press, 1988.

Kovessy, Peter. "Qatar Ministry Bans Men from Al Khor Park on Thursdays. *Doha News*, April 4, 2016. https://dohanews.co/qatar-ministry-bans-men-al-khor-park-thursdays/.

Krane, Jim. *Dubai: The Story of the World's Fastest City*. London: Atlantic Books, 2009.

Krause, Wanda. *Women in Civil Society: The State, Islamism, and Networks in the UAE*. New York: Palgrave Macmillan, 2008.

Kuwait Government Online. "Population of Kuwait." June 30, 2012. http://www.e.gov.kw/sites/kgoenglish/portal/Pages/Visitors/AboutKuwait/KuwaitAtaGlane_Population.aspx.

Kuwait University. "About Kuwait University." 2015. ecmwlst1.ku.edu.kw:16210/ku/AboutUniversity/AboutKU/index.htm.

Kuwait News Agency. "Kuwait Parliament Holds Marathon Grilling of PM, Minister." May 11, 2017. http://www.kuna.net.kw/ArticleDetails.aspx?id=2610426&language=en.

Lacroix, Stéphane. *Awakening Islam: Religious Dissent in Contemporary Saudi Arabia*. Cambridge, MA: Harvard University Press, 2011.

Lahoud-Tatar, Carine. *Islam et Politique au Koweït* [Islam and politics in Kuwait]. Paris: Presses Universitaires de France, 2011.

Langohr, Vickie. "An Exit from Arab Autocracy." *Journal of Democracy* 13, no. 3 (2002): 116–122.

Law Library of Congress. "Laws Criminalizing Apostasy in Selected Jurisdictions." May 2014. http://www.loc.gov/law/help/apostasy/apostasy.pdf.

Law No. 24 for the Year 1962 Concerning Clubs and Public Welfare Societies. In *Records of Kuwait 1961–1965: 1965*, edited by Anita L. P. Burdett, 513–520. Cambridge, UK: Cambridge Archive Editions, 1997.

Lawson, Fred. "Class and State in Kuwait." *MERIP Reports* 132 (May 1985): 16–21, 32.

Leiken, Robert S., and Steven Brooke. "The Moderate Muslim Brotherhood." *Foreign Affairs* 86, no. 2 (2007): 107–121.

Lemert, Charles. "Wallerstein and the Uncertain Worlds." In *Uncertain Worlds: World-Systems Analysis in Changing Times*, edited by Immanuel Wallerstein, Carlos Aguirre Rojas, and Charles Lemert, 151–193. Boulder, CO: Paradigm Publishers, 2012.

Longva, Anh Nga. "Nationalism in Pre-Modern Guise: The Discourse on Hadhar and Badu in Kuwait." *International Journal of Middle East Studies* 38, no. 2 (2006): 171–187.

Longva, Anh Nga. "Neither Autocracy nor Democracy but Ethnocracy: Citizens, Expatriates and the Socio-Political System in Kuwait." In *Monarchies and Nations: Globalisation and Identity in the Arab States of the Gulf*, edited by Paul Dresch and James P. Piscatori, 114–135. London: I. B. Tauris, 2013.

Luciani, Giacomo. "Allocation vs. Production States: A Theoretical Framework." In *The Arab State*, edited by Giacomo Luciani, 65–84. Berkeley, CA: University of California Press, 1990.

Luciani, Giacomo. "The Oil Rent, The Fiscal Crisis of the State and Democratization." In *Democracy without Democrats?: Renewal of Politics in the Muslim World*, edited by Ghassam Salamé, 130–155. London: I.B. Tauris, 1994.

Lynch, Marc. *The Arab Uprising: The Unfinished Revolutions of the New Middle East*. New York: PublicAffairs, 2012.

Lynch, Marc. "Muslim Brotherhood Debates." *Abu Aardvark* (blog). February 28, 2007. http://abuaardvark.typepad.com/abuaardvark/2007/02/muslim_brotherh.html.

Lynch, Marc. *Voices of the New Arab Public: Iraq, Al-Jazeera, and Middle East Politics Today*. New York: Columbia University Press, 2006.

Mahdavy, Hussein. "The Patterns and Problems of Economic Development in Rentier States: The Case of Iran." In *Studies in the Economic History of the Middle East*, edited by M. A. Cook, 428–467. Oxford: Oxford University Press, 1970.

Mansfield, Peter. *Kuwait: Vanguard of the Gulf*. London: Hutchinson, 1990.

Mazzetti, Mark, and Emily B. Hager. "Secret Desert Force Set Up by Blackwater's Founder." *The New York Times*, May 14, 2011. http://www.nytimes.com/2011/05/15/world/middleeast/15prince.html.

Melikian, Levon H. "Gulf Reactions to Western Cultural Pressures." In *The Arab Gulf and the West*, edited by Brian R. Pridham, 203–218. London: Croom Helm, 1985.

Mendick, Robert. "Al-Qaeda Terror Financier Worked for Qatari Government." *The Telegraph*, October 12, 2014. http://www.telegraph.co.uk/news/11156327/Al-Qaeda-terror-financier-worked-for-Qatari-government.html.

Middle East Eye. "UAE: Leading Activist Ahmed Mansoor Arrested, Says State News." March 21, 2017. http://www.middleeasteye.net/news/uae-arrests-prominent-activist-incitement-state-news-398273178.

Middle East Eye. "UAE to Try Kuwaiti Ex-MP over Remarks on Abu Dhabi Crown Prince." March 9, 2015. http://www.middleeasteye.net/news/uae-try-kuwaiti-ex-mp-over-remarks-abu- dhabi-crown-prince-1546132555.

Middle East Monitor. "Kuwait to Ban Muslim Brotherhood." March 16, 2014. https://www.middleeastmonitor.com/news/middle-east/10329-kuwait-to-ban-muslim-brotherhood.

Middle East Monitor. "Qatar Distances Itself from Al-Qaradawi's Remarks against UAE." February 1, 2014. https://www.middleeastmonitor.com/news/middle-east/9538-qatar-distances-itself-from-al-qaradawis-remarks-against-uae.

Middle East Monitor. "Saudi King Hosts Muslim Scholars Close to Brotherhood." February 24, 2015. https://www.middleeastmonitor.com/news/middle-east/17159-saudi-king-hosts-muslim-scholars-close-to-brotherhood.

Miles, Hugh. "Al-Jazeera." *Foreign Policy*, July/August 2006, 20–24.

Mishkin, Sarah. "UAE Acts to Bridge Northern Divide." *Financial Times*, June 22, 2011. http://www.ft.com/cms/s/0/b80064ba-9cef-11e0-8678-00144feabdc0.html#axzz3TJrgNtCk.

Mitchell, Richard P. *The Society of the Muslim Brothers*. Oxford: Oxford University Press, 1969.

"Mohammed bin Salman, Trump Discuss Bin Laden's Ties to the Muslim Brotherhood." Al-Arabiya, March 16, 2017. https://english.alarabiya.net/en/features/2017/03/16/Mohammed-bin-Salman-Trump-discuss-Osama-bin-Laden-s-ties-to-Muslim-Brotherhood.html

Moore, Pete W. "What Makes Successful Business Lobbies?: Business Associations and the Rentier State in Jordan and Kuwait." *Comparative Politics* 33, no. 2 (2001): 127–147.

Mourad, Hicham. "Revising Qatari Policy on Egypt." *Ahram Online*, October 13, 2013. http://english.ahram.org.eg/NewsContentP/4/83822/Opinion/Revising-Qatari-policy-on-Egypt.aspx.

Mourad, Mahmoud. "Prominent Muslim Brotherhood Figures to Leave Qatar." Reuters, September 13, 2014. http://www.reuters.com/article/us-egypt-qatar-brotherhood-idUSKBN0H807R20140913.

Nafi, Zuhair Ahmed. *Economic and Social Development in Qatar*. London: Frances Pinter Publishers, 1983.

The National. "Dar Al Ber Builds More Than 200 Mosques Abroad." April 26, 2017, http://www.thenational.ae/uae/dar-al-ber-builds-more-than-200-mosques-abroad.

The National. "UAE Criticises US Human Rights Report." March 10, 2014. http://www.thenational.ae/uae/government/uae-criticises-us-human-rights-report.

The National. "UAE University Hosts Elections for First Student Council." October 18, 2012. http://www.thenational.ae/news/uae-news/uae-university-hosts-elections-for-first-student-council.

National Human Rights Committee (NHRC). "2013 Survey of Civil Society Organizations in Qatar: Report of Findings." Social and Economic Survey Research Institute (SESRI). June 2013. http://www.nhrc-qa.org/wp-content/uploads/2014/01/2013_Report-NHRC-_Final-_English-with-intro-from-NHRC-.pdf.

Nereim, Vivian. "Population of Dubai Rises 5 Per Cent to 2.1 Million." *The National*, February 13, 2013. http://www.thenational.ae/news/uae-news/population-of-dubai-rises-5-per-cent-to-2-1-million.

The New Arab. "Church Bombing Inflames Already Strained Egypt-Qatar Relations." December 15, 2016. https://www.alaraby.co.uk/english/news/2016/12/15/church-bombing-inflames-already-strained-egypt-qatar-relations.

The New Arab. "Freed Kuwait Opposition Leader Calls for Reconciliation." April 27, 2017. https://www.alaraby.co.uk/english/news/2017/4/25/freed-kuwait-opposition-leader-calls-for-reconciliation.

The New Arab. "UAE Jails Prominent Academic for 10 Years over Tweets." March 30, 2017. https://www.alaraby.co.uk/english/news/2017/3/30/uae-jails-prominent-academic-for-10-years-over-tweets.

News24. "Calls for UAE to Open Islamist Trial." April 3, 2013. http://www.news24.com/World/News/Calls-for-UAE-to-open-Islamist-trial-20130403.

Niblock, Tim, ed. *Social and Economic Development in the Arab Gulf*. London: Croom Helm, 1980.

Ochsenwald, William. "Saudi Arabia and the Islamic Revival." *International Journal of Middle East Studies* 13, no. 3 (1981): 271–286.

Okruhlik, Gwenn. "Making Conversation Permissible." In *Islamic Activism: A Social Movement Theory Approach*, edited by Quintan Wiktorowicz, 250–268. Bloomington: Indiana University Press, 2004.

Okruhlik, Gwenn. "Networks of Dissent: Islamism and Reform in Saudi Arabia." *Current History* 101, no. 541: 22–28.

Okruhlik, Gwenn. "Rentier Wealth, Unruly Law, and the Rise of the Opposition." *Comparative Politics* 31, no. 3 (1999): 295–315.

Opinion no. 64/2011 (United Arab Emirates). United Nations Working Group on Arbitrary Detention, Alkarama Foundation, September 13, 2011. http://en.alkarama.org/documents/WGAD64-2011_UAE_ALK2011-2768_AhmedMansoor_221211_EN_Onlineversion.pdf.

Oueiti, Rezan. "Businesses in Umm Al Quwain Struggle to Survive." *The National*, August 4, 2014. ttps://www.thenational.ae/business/travel-and-tourism/businesses-in-uaq-struggle-to-survive-1.652834.

"Our Children and the Lovely Pig." *Al-Islah* 34, no. 49 (1982).

In *The Roots of Conspiracy against the UAE*, edited by ʿAli Salem Humaid, 1:48. Dubai, UAE: Al Mezmaah Studies and Research Center, 2013.

Oxford Business Group. *The Report: Ras al-Khaimah 2013*. 2014. https://www.oxfordbusinessgroup.com/uae-ras-al-khaimah-2013.

Pall, Zoltan. "Kuwaiti Salafism and Its Growing Influence in the Levant." Carnegie Endowment for International Peace, May 2014. http://carnegieendowment.org/files/kuwaiti_salafists.pdf.

Partrick, Neil. "Nationalism in the Gulf States." Kuwait Programme on Development, Governance and Globalisation in the Gulf States, no. 5, October 2009. http://eprints.lse.ac.uk/55257/1/Patrick_2009.pdf.

Peck, Malcolm C. "Formation and Evolution of the Federation and Its Institutions." In *Perspectives on the United Arab Emirates*, edited by Edmund A. Ghareeb and Ibrahim al-Abed, 145–160. London: Trident Press, 1999.

Peck, Malcolm C. *The United Arab Emirates: A Venture in Unity*. Boulder, CO: Westview Press, 1986.

The Peninsula. "Citizens Want Kuwait-like Govt Bounty." January 17, 2011. http://thepeninsulaqatar.com/news/qatar/139495/citizens-want-kuwait-like-govt-bounty.

The Peninsula. "Stricter Rules to Regulate Charities." September 16, 2014. http://thepeninsulaqatar.com/news/qatar/300295/stricter-rules-to-regulate-charities.

Peterson, J. E. *The Arab Gulf States: Steps Toward Political Participation*. New York: Praeger, 1988.

Plotkin Boghardt, Lori. *Kuwait amid War, Peace and Revolution: 1979–1991 and New Challenges*. London: St. Antony's College and Palgrave Macmillan, 2007.

Plotkin Boghardt, Lori. "The Muslim Brotherhood in the Gulf: Prospects for Agitation." The Washington Institute. June 10, 2013. http://www.washingtoninstitute.org/policy-analysis/view/the-muslim-brotherhood-in-the-gulf-prospects-for-agitation.

Plotkin Boghardt, Lori. "The Muslim Brotherhood on Trial in the UAE." The Washington Institute. April 12, 2013. http://www.washingtoninstitute.org/policy-analysis/view/the-muslim-brotherhood-on-trial-in-the-uae.

Qiblawi, Tamara, Mohammed Tawfeeq, Elizabeth Roberts, and Hamdi Alkhshali. "Qatar Rift: Saudi, UAE, Bahrain, Egypt Cut Diplomatic Ties." CNN News, June 5, 2017. http://edition.cnn.com/2017/06/05/middleeast/saudi-bahrain-egypt-uae-qatar-terror/index.html.

Quilliam, Neil. "The States of the Gulf Co-operation Council." In *Good Governance in the Middle East Oil Monarchies*, edited by Tom Pierre Najem and Martin Hetherington, 29–59. London: Routledge, 2003.

Rabi, Uzi. "The Kuwaiti Royal Family in the Postliberation Period: Reinstitutionalizing the 'First among Equals' System in Kuwait." In *Middle East Monarchies: The Challenge of Modernity*, edited by Joseph Kostiner, 151–165. Boulder, CO: Lynne Rienner Publishers, 2000.

"Readings into Some Curricula of Private Schools in the Emirates." *Al-Islah* 57 (1982). In *The Roots of Conspiracy against the UAE*, edited by ʿAli Salem Humaid, 2:180–188. Dubai, UAE: Al Mezmaah Research and Studies Center, 2013.

Reuters. "Egypt Returns $2 Billion to Qatar in Sign of Growing Tensions." September 19, 2013. http://www.reuters.com/article/2013/09/19/us-egypt-qatar-deposits-idusbre98i0n020130919.

Reuters. "LSE Cancels Arab Spring Forum in UAE, Citing Local Curbs." February 23, 2013. http://uk.reuters.com/article/2013/02/23/uk-uae-university-conference-idUKBRE91M0AI20130223.

Reuters. "Qatari Draft Media Law Criticized by Rights Group." October 30, 2012. http://www.reuters.com/article/2012/10/30/us-media-qatar-idUSBRE89T17620121030.

Reuters. "UAE to Invest in Poorer Northern Emirates." March 2, 2011. http://www.reuters.com/article/2011/03/02/oukwd-uk-emirates-utilities-idAFTRE72121720110302.

Riedel, Bruce, and Bilal Y. Saab. "Al Qaeda's Third Front: Saudi Arabia." *The Washington Quarterly* 31, no. 2 (2008): 33–46.

Rizzo, Helen Mary. *Islam, Democracy, and the Status of Women: The Case of Kuwait*. London: Routledge, 2005.

Roberts, David. "Kuwait." In *Power and Politics in the Persian Gulf Monarchies*, edited by Christopher M. Davidson, 89–111. London: Hurst and Company, 2011.

Roberts, David. "Qatar and the Brotherhood." *Survival: Global Politics and Strategy* 56, no. 4 (2014): 23–32.

Roberts, David. "Qatar and the Muslim Brotherhood: Pragmatism or Preference?" *Middle East Policy* 21, no. 3 (2014): 84–94.

Rodenbeck, Max. "Witch Hunt in Egypt." *New York Review of Books*, November 16, 2000. http://www.nybooks.com/articles/archives/2000/nov/16/witch-hunt-in-egypt/.

Rosman-Stollman, Elisheva. "Qatar: Liberalization as Foreign Policy." In *Political Liberalization in the Persian Gulf*, edited by Joshua Teitelbaum, 187–209. London: Hurst and Company, 2009.

Ross, Michael. "Does Oil Hinder Democracy?" *World Politics* 53, no. 3 (2001): 325–361.

Ross, Michael. *The Oil Curse*. Princeton, NJ: Princeton University Press, 2012.

Rouleau, Eric. "Trouble in the Kingdom." *Foreign Affairs* 81, no. 4 (2002): 75–89.

Roy, Olivier. *The Failure of Political Islam*. London: I. B. Tauris, 1996.

Rubin, Alisa. "Higher Education Reform in the Arab World: The Model of Qatar." Middle East Institute. July 31, 2012. http://www.mei.edu/content/higher-education-reform-arab-world-model-qatar.

Rugh, Andrea B. *The Political Culture of Leadership in the United Arab Emirates*. New York: Palgrave Macmillan, 2007.

Rugh, William A. "The United Arab Emirates: What Are the Sources of Its Stability?" *Middle East Policy* 5, no. 3 (1997): 14–24.

Rules for Licenses of Religious and Charitable Societies and Organization of their Activities in the Emirate of Dubai. Islamic Affairs and Charitable Activities Department, Government of Dubai, 2006. http://www.iacad.gov.ae/admin/storage/other/htmlDocs/Rules%20of%20Religious.pdf.

Saadi, Dania. "Qatar Broadcaster Al Jazeera Cuts 500 Jobs." *The National*, March 27, 2016. http://www.thenational.ae/business/media/qatar-broadcaster-al-jazeera-cuts-500-jobs.

Sabrie, Sharmaake, and Pekka Hakala. "Kuwait's Political Crisis Deepens." European Parliament, Directorate-General for External Policies, January 2013. http://www.europarl.europa.eu/delegations/en/studiesdownload.html?languageDocument=EN&file=91150.

Sadik, Muhammad T., and William P. Snavely. *Bahrain, Qatar, and the United Arab Emirates: Colonial Past, Present Problems, and Future Prospects*. Lexington, MA: Lexington Books, 1972.

Safdar, Anealla, and Ben Flanagan. "Royal Family Member Put in Charge at Al Jazeera." *The National*, September 22, 2011. http://www.thenational.ae/news/world/middle-east/royal-family-member-put-in-charge-at-al-jazeera.

Said Zahlan, Rosemarie. *The Creation of Qatar*. London: Routledge, 1979.

Said Zahlan, Rosemarie. *The Making of the Modern Gulf States: Kuwait, Bahrain, Qatar, the United Arab Emirates and Oman*. Reading, UK: Ithaca Press, 1998.

Said Zahlan, Rosemarie. *Origins of the United Arab Emirates*. London: Macmillan, 1978.

Saif, Ahmed Abdelkareem. "Deconstructing before Building: Perspectives on Democracy in Qatar." In *Reform in the Middle East Oil Monarchies*, edited by Anoushiravan Ehteshami and Steven Wright, 103–128. Reading, UK: Ithaca Press, 2008.

Sakr, Naomi. "Dynamics of GCC Press-Government Relations in the 1990s." In *Good Governance in the Middle East Oil Monarchies*, edited by Tom Pierre Najem and Martin Hetherington, 102–118. London: Routledge, 2003.

Salama, Sami. "Rise and Fall of Muslim Brotherhood in UAE." *Gulf News*, April 13, 2013. http://gulfnews.com/news/region/egypt/rise-and-fall-of-muslim-brotherhood-in-uae-1.1170002.

Salamé, Ghassan. "Islam and the West." *Foreign Policy* 90 (1993): 22–37.

Saldaña, Marta. "Rentierism and Political Culture in the United Arab Emirates: The Case of UAEU Students." PhD diss., University of Exeter, 2014.

Saleh, A. "ICM Accuses Government of 'Using' Citizenship File." *Kuwait Times*, August 2, 2014. http://news.kuwaittimes.net/icm-accuses-government-using-citizenship-file/.

Salem, Ola. "94 Emiratis Charged with Compromising UAE Security." *The National*, January 28, 2013. http://www.thenational.ae/news/uae-news/politics/94-emiratis-charged-with-compromising-uae-security.

Salem, Ola. "Call for Federal Dress-Code Law in the UAE." *The National*, June 12, 2012. http://www.thenational.ae/news/uae-news/call-for-federal-dress-code-law-in-the-uae.

Salem, Ola. "FNC Passes Mandatory Breastfeeding Clause for Child Rights Law." *The National*, January 21, 2014. http://www.thenational.ae/uae/government/fnc-passes-mandatory-breastfeeding-clause-for-child-rights-law.

Salem, Ola. "Islah 'Does Not Represent UAE Interests.'" *The National*, October 5, 2012. http://www.thenational.ae/news/uae-news/islah-does-not-represent-uae-interests.

Salem, Paul. "Kuwait: Politics in a Participatory Emirate." *Carnegie Papers* 3, July 2007. http://carnegieendowment.org/2007/07/16/kuwait-politics-in-participatory-emirate/yoc.

Sciutto, Jim. "Qatar Knocks U.S.-led Coalition on ISIS." CNN News, February 26, 2015. http://www.cnn.com/2015/02/25/politics/isis-syria-qatar-blasts-us-coalition/.

Scott, Victoria. "Selling Books in Qatar to Become Easier, Minister Vows." *Doha News*, December 15, 2013. http://dohanews.co/selling-books-in-qatar-to-become-easier-minister-vows/.

Selvik, Kjetil. "Elite Rivalry in a Semi-Democracy: The Kuwaiti Press Scene." *Middle Eastern Studies* 47, no. 3 (2011): 477–496.

Shadid, Anthony. "The Towering Dream of Dubai." *The Washington Post*, April 30, 2006. http://www.washingtonpost.com/wp-dyn/content/article/2006/04/29/AR2006042901457.html.

Shambayati, Hootan. "The Rentier State, Interest Groups, and the Paradox of Autonomy: State and Business in Turkey and Iran." *Comparative Politics* 26, no. 3 (1994): 307–331.

Shehata, Samer S. Introduction to *Islamist Politics in the Middle East: Movements and Change*, edited by Samer S. Shehata, 1–20. London: Routledge, 2012.

Shikaki, Muna. "U.S. Targets Alleged Qatari Militant Backers." Al Arabiya, August 5, 2015. http://english.alarabiya.net/en/News/middle-east/2015/08/05/U-S-targets-alleged-Qatari-financiers-of-Al-Nusra-and-Al-Qaeda.html.

Shultziner, Doron, and Mary Ann Tétreault. "Representation and Democratic Progress in Kuwait." *Representation* 48, no. 3 (2012): 281–293.

Sloan, Alastair. "A Renewed Kuwaiti Opposition Rises to Fight Corruption." *Middle East Monitor*, June 11, 2014. https://www.middleeastmonitor.com/articles/middle-east/12053-a-renewed-kuwaiti-opposition-rises-to-fight-corruption.

Smith Diwan, Kristin. "Kuwait's Balancing Act." *Foreign Policy*, October 13, 2012. http://mideast.foreignpolicy.com/posts/2012/10/23/kuwait_s_balancing_act.

Smith Diwan, Kristin. "Kuwait's Snap Parliamentary Elections Bring Return of the Opposition." Arab Gulf States Institute in Washington, November 29, 2016. http://www.agsiw.org/kuwaits-snap-parliamentary-elections-bring-return-opposition/.

Social and Economic Research Institute (SESRI). "Annual Omnibus Survey: A Survey of Life in Qatar, Executive Summary Report." November 2012. http://sesri.qu.edu.qa/sites/default/files/Eng/ExecutiveReports/2012/OmniBus2012.pdf.

Social and Economic Survey Research Institute (SESRI). "Qatar Education Study 2012: Curriculum Report." May 2014. sesri.qu.edu.qa/web/.../Qatar_Education_Study_Curriculum_Report_12.01.pdf.

Solidarity International for Kuwait. "The Gulf Crisis, Day by Day: A Daily Newsletter from Solidarity International for Kuwait." 5th ed. January 19, 1991. http://freekuwait.org.kw/search.php?page=086603_January-19,-1991&search=solidarity&mode=9.

Snoj, Jure. "Population of Qatar by Nationality." *BQ Doha*, December 7, 2014. http://gulfmigration.eu/qatar-estimates-of-foreign-nationals-residing-in-qatar-by-country-of-citizenship-selected-countries-2014/.

Stern, Sarah N., ed. *Saudi Arabia and the Global Islamic Terrorist Network: America and the West's Fatal Embrace*. New York: Palgrave Macmillan, 2011.

Sultan, Jassim. "Gulf Perspectives on the Muslim Brotherhood." Lecture, Brookings Doha Center, Doha, Qatar, October 9, 2013.

Swan, Melanie. "International Branch Campuses' Key Role in the UAE." *The National*, September 18, 2013. http://www.thenational.ae/uae/education/international-branch-campuses-key-role-in-the-uae.

Tarrow, Sidney. *Power in Movement: Social Movements, Collective Action and Politics*. Cambridge, UK: Cambridge University Press, 1994.

Taylor, Adam. "Qatar Arrests Reporters Investigating Migrant Worker Conditions, Again." *The Washington Post*, May 18, 2015. http://www.washingtonpost.com/blogs/worldviews/wp/2015/05/18/qatar-arrests-reporters-investigating-migrant-worker-conditions-again/.

Tessler, Mark. "The Origins of Popular Support for Islamist Movements: A Political Economy Analysis." In *Islam, Democracy, and the State in North Africa*, edited by John P. Entelis, 93–126. Bloomington: Indiana University Press, 1997.

Tétreault, Mary Ann. "A State of Two Minds: State Cultures, Women, and Politics in Kuwait." *International Journal of Middle East Studies* 33, no. 2 (2001): 203–220.

Tétreault, Mary Ann. "Bottom-Up Democratization in Kuwait." In *Political Change in the Arab Gulf States: Stuck in Transition*, edited by Mary Ann Tétreault, Gwenn Okrulik, and Andrzej Kapiszewski, 73–98. Boulder, CO: Lynne Rienner Publishers, 2011.

Tétreault, Mary Ann. "Civil Society in Kuwait: Protected Spaces and Women's Rights." *Middle East Journal* 47, no. 2 (1993): 275–291.

Tétreault, Mary Ann. "Kuwait: Slouching toward Democracy?" In *Political Liberalization in the Persian Gulf*, edited by Joshua Teitelbaum, 107–131. London: Hurst and Company, 2009.

Tétreault, Mary Ann. "Kuwait's Annus Mirabilis." *Middle East Report Online*, September 7, 2006. http://www.merip.org/mero/mero090706.

Tétreault, Mary Ann. "Looking for Revolution in Kuwait." *Middle East Report Online*, November 1, 2012. http://www.merip.org/mero/mero110112.

Tétreault, Mary Ann. "Political Activism in Kuwait: Reform in Fits and Starts." In *Taking to the Streets: The Transformation of Arab Activism*, edited by Lina Khatib and Ellen Lust, 268–297. Baltimore, MD: Johns Hopkins University Press, 2014.

Tétreault, Mary Ann. *Stories of Democracy: Politics and Society in Contemporary Kuwait*. New York: Columbia University Press, 2000.

Tétreault, Mary Ann, and Mohammed al-Ghanim. "The Day after 'Victory': Kuwait's 2009 Election and the Contentious Present." *Middle East Report Online*, July 8, 2009. http://www.merip.org/mero/mero070809.

"The First General Conference of Emirates Students." *Al-Islah* 32 (1982). In *The Roots of Conspiracy Against the UAE*, edited by 'Ali Salem Humaid, 2:58–61. Dubai, UAE: Al Mezmaah Studies and Research Center, 2013.

"The University between Hope and Social Impact." *Al-Islah* 50, no. 49 (1982). In *The Roots of Conspiracy Against the UAE*, edited by 'Ali Salem Humaid, 1:105–106. Dubai, UAE: Al Mezmaah Studies and Research Center, 2013.

Toumi, Habib. "Qatar Denies Involvement in Libya's Internal Conflict." *Gulf News*, March 8, 2017. http://gulfnews.com/news/gulf/qatar/qatar-denies-involvement-in-libya-s-internal-conflict-1.1990279.

Trenwith, Courtney. "MP Calls for Ban on Kuwait's Muslim Brotherhood." *Arabian Business*, July 13, 2014. http://www.arabianbusiness.com/mp-calls-for-ban-on-kuwait-s-muslim-brotherhood-557658.html.

Ulrichsen, Kristian Coates. *Insecure Gulf: The End of Certainty and the Transition to the Post-Oil Era*. London: Hurst and Company, 2011.

Ulrichsen, Kristian Coates. *Qatar and the Arab Spring*. London: Hurst and Company, 2014.

United Arab Emirates Constitution. Federal National Council, 2010 Edition. http://www.uaecabinet.ae/English/UAEGovernment/Pages/ConstitutionOfUAE.aspx.

United Arab Emirates Ministry of Education. "Vision and Mission and Values of MoE." https://www.moe.gov.ae/En/AboutTheMinistry/Pages/VisionMission.aspx.

U.S. Citizens Services. "Security Message for U.S. Citizens 8: Teachers at International Schools." Embassy of the United States Abu Dhabi, October 29, 2014. https://www.osac.gov/pages/ContentReportDetails.aspx?cid=16516.

US Department of State. "United Arab Emirates: International Religious Freedom Report 2008." September 19, 2008. http://2001-2009.state.gov/g/drl/rls/irf/2008/108495.htm.

Voll, John Obert. Foreword to *The Society of Muslim Brothers*, by Richard P. Mitchell, vii–xxii. Oxford: Oxford University Press, 1993.

Voll, John Obert. *Islam: Continuity and Change in the Modern World*. Boulder, CO: Westview Press, 1982.

Wallerstein, Immanuel. *World-Systems Analysis: An Introduction*. Durham, NC: Duke University Press, 2004.

Walker, Lesley. "Modest Dress Campaign Revived with New 'You Matter in Qatar' Slogan." *Doha News*, May 4, 2015. http://dohanews.co/modest-dress-campaign-revived-with-new-you-matter-in-qatar-slogan/.

Walker, Lesley. "Qatar Hotels Told Not to Sell Alcohol in Run-up to Eid Al Adha." *Doha News*, April 27, 2015. http://dohanews.co/qatar-hotels-told-not-to-sell-alcohol-in-run-up-to-eid-al-adha/.

Walker, Lesley. "QDC Starts Charging Annual Fee to Buy Alcohol in Qatar." *Doha News*, November 29, 2016. https://dohanews.co/qdc-starts-charging-annual-fee-to-buy-alcohol-in-qatar/.

Waterbury, John. "From Social Contracts to Extraction Contracts." In *Islam, Democracy, and the State in North Africa*, edited by John P. Entelis, 141–176. Bloomington: Indiana University Press, 1997.

"We Are Waiting for Final Ban." *Al-Islah* 7, no. 50 (1982). In *The Roots of Conspiracy Against the UAE*, edited by ʿAli Salem Humaid, 1:69. Dubai, UAE: Al Mezmaah Studies and Research Center, 2013.

United States Embassy Abu Dhabi. "U/S Burns' January 22 Meeting with Abu Dhabi Crown Prince and UAE Foreign Minister." WikiLeaks. January 24, 2007. https://wikileaks.org/plusd/cables/07ABUDHABI97_a.html.

Wickham, Carrie. *Mobilizing Islam: Religion, Activism, and Political Change in Egypt*. New York: Columbia University Press, 2002.

Wickham, Carrie. *The Muslim Brotherhood: Evolution of an Islamist Movement*. Princeton, NJ: Princeton University Press, 2013.

WikiLeaks. "Strong Words in Private from MBZ at IDEZ—Bashes Iran, Qatar, Russia." February 25, 2009. https://wikileaks.org/plusd/cables/09ABUDHABI193_a.html.

Wiktorowicz, Quintan. "Civil Society as Social Control: State Power in Jordan." *Comparative Politics* 33, no. 1 (2000): 43–61.

Wiktorowicz, Quintan. *Islamic Activism: A Social Movement Theory Approach*. Bloomington: Indiana University Press, 2004.

Wiktorowicz, Quintan, and Suha Taji Farouki. "Islamic NGOs and Muslim Politics: A Case from Jordan." *Third World Quarterly* 21, no. 4 (2000): 685–699.

Williamson, Scott, and Nathan J. Brown. "Kuwait's Muslim Brotherhood under Pressure." *Foreign Policy*, November 20, 2013. http://foreignpolicy.com/2013/11/20/kuwaits-muslim-brotherhood-under-pressure/?wp_login_redirect=0.

Wintour, Patrick. "Hamas Presents New Charter Accepting a Palestine Based on 1967 Borders." *The Guardian*, May 1, 2017. https://www.theguardian.com/world/2017/may/01/hamas-new-charter-palestine-israel-1967-borders.

The World Bank. "Gross National Income per Capita 2013, Atlas Method and PPP." World Development Indicators Database. March 12, 2015. http://databank.worldbank.org/data/download/GNIPC.pdf.

Youssef, Nour. "Al Jazeera Film Critical of Egyptian Army Strains Egypt-Qatar Ties Further." *The New York Times*, November 28, 2016. https://www.nytimes.com/2016/11/28/world/middleeast/al-jazeera-egypt-qatar.html?_r=0.

Zartman, I. William. "Opposition as Support of the State." In *Beyond Coercion: The Durability of the Arab State*, edited by Adeed I. Dawisha and I. William Zartman, 61–87. London: Croom Helm, 1988.

Zubaida, Sami. *Islam, the People and the State: Political Ideas and Movements in the Middle East*. London: I. B. Tauris, 2001.

INDEX